EMPLOYMENT IN THE PUBLIC DOMAIN IN RECENT DECADES

GW00703367

Miceal Ross is a Senior Research Officer with
The Economic and Social Research Institute.
The Paper has been accepted for publication by
the Institute, which is not responsible for either
the content, or the views expressed therein.

EMPLOYMENT IN THE PUBLIC DOMAIN IN RECENT DECADES

MICEAL ROSS

DUBLIN, 1986

ISBN 0 7070 0079 3

Acknowledgements

This paper would not have been possible without the active collaboration of a vast number of people who gave unstinted help with numerous queries, letters and telephone calls. It is hoped that they will accept the commitment to meticulous accuracy in this study as their reward. Those deviations from this standard can be attributed to the author failing to identify the right person or to inform her of his interpretation of her information.

Special thanks has to be given to Fergus Glavey and his team at the Department of the Public Service — Sean Regan, Ann Doyle, Luke McBride and his successors, Robert Pye, Jerome Kelly and Maurice Merriman. Peter Kelly in the Department of Education and the group at the Higher Education Authority — Mary Kerr, Mary Armstrong and George Ryan — were also extremely supportive. Finally the Institute of Public Administration, which has done trojan work in this area and published an invaluable series of studies, made available its resources. This report benefited from the work on Local Government by Desmond Roche, on Health by Brendan Hensey and on Education by John Coolahan which Pat Hall provided. Donal Murphy made his files on health available.

The study was initiated about the same time as a major study by Dr Peter Humphreys into *Public Service Employment*. As far as possible this work and that of Humphreys have attempted to resolve data gaps using the same approach so that a consistent set of data are available to the public. Differences, which remain, can be attributed to the different focus of each report.

CONTENTS

LIST OF TABLES

LIST OF FIGURES

APPENDIX 1

APPENDIX 2

GENERAL SUMMARY

How many people are employed by the Government? How many are employed by the central Government compared with the local authorities? How many are employed in public enterprises? How much are they all paid? How much are they paid relative to each other, or relative to the private sector? Such questions interest people in general and economists and policy makers in particular. Nevertheless, Peter Heller and Alan Tait found it "remarkable how little information was readily accessible on these topics" when they published their international comparisons of *Government employment and pay* for the International Monetary Fund in 1983. This study answers the first two question for Ireland. The answers to the other questions are also being collated, but will be published separately.

These topics are interesting at the general level but are also important in more specialised ways as well. Only too often are assertions made that Government wages are too high or too low or that total Government employment is excessive. Such arguements have been more frequently heard over the last decade in the context of mounting concern over the level of Government spending in general, especially where the increased outlays have engendered crippling public deficits. To put such assertions in perspective it would be useful to be able to appeal to the experience of other countries but as Heller and Tait have noted "The statistics necessary to provide a cross-country comparative basis for such assertions have not been available".

One of the difficulties is that the institutional forms, which employment can take, have evolved differently in different societies and the legal bases of classification used in traditional national statistics can obscure the comparative position. For example, employment in both voluntary and health board hospitals in Ireland is funded by the State. If the legal basis of voluntary hospitals leads us to classify them as private then comparisons with other countries where the voluntary/public mix is different could be misleading. For this reason new conventions are developing internationally for common application in all countries. The criteria for determining whether a job is public or private are based on the nature of the function and the derivation of authority rather than

1

on the more usual criteria of legal standing or administrative conventions. General application of these new rules will facilitate greatly international comparisons. Part of the current study discusses these changes and evolves a general classificatory framework within which to slot the different types of public employment. Since different studies may call for different aggregations of the data the classification is designed to permit different combinations and, therefore, greater flexibility.

The study aims at being comprehensive. This poses two problems as the enumeration moves from the core staff towards the more peripheral jobs. First, there is the question of those whose work is not full time in the sense that a Department official is full time. Staff may be permanent but work less than the usual number of hours daily, for example, cleaners or canteen staff. Staff may only work part of the year, frequently on capital projects. How are these to be related to, e.g., secondary school teachers, whose teaching week may be 20 hours and whose annual number of working days is shorter than the Civil Service norm? What method of enumeration is to be used — numbers on a Census day, annual averages, etc., and how are we to cater for casual workers whose normal employment period does not include the Census date? What full-time equivalents are we to use in all these cases and is the concept meaningful?

The second difficulty relates to those who are peripheral in the sense that they have other employment. Heller and Tait ask "How should the use of consultants as a 'backdoor' form of employment be treated, such as in the defence sector of the United States?" The numerous Irish equivalents include not merely the growing army of consultants but also more traditional work, such as veterinarians in the bovine tuberculosis and brucellosis eradication schemes, doctors in the choice of doctor scheme and part-time architects engaged by local authorities. The yardstick for inclusion was whether the person concerned derived half their earned income from public sources though equally well the yardstick could have specified a level of salary as the cut-off point, given that private income would generally be unknown.

Apart from these professionals selling services to the Government, there is also the dwindling involvement of the voluntary sector, dwindling in the sense that inflation has severely damaged private sources of income. Voluntary bodies in health and education have often been funded on a capitation basis or per unit of service rendered. It was often left to the body itself to determine the level of staffing and/or the acceptable credentials for the staff. The absence of a departmental supervisory role in these instances usually meant that no records of employment were sought. Even today such information on some funded activities is sparse. This fact has given the tables in the final summary a somewhat ragged appearance due to the differing time spans over which time series on employment are available.

The longest records are those of the central Civil Service which extend back, at least in summary form, to the founding of the State. Some slight problems were found with this series due to redefinitions which occurred in 1952 and again in 1958. These were small compared with the uncertainty generated when the old Civil Service Census was replaced by the computerised Staff Information System in 1975. The problems caused by the transition are still not completely resolved and unfortunately occurred during a period of recruitment policy reversals, whose effects were, therefore, difficult to gauge. Given the importance of having an accurate time series considerable energy was expended in an attempt to correct the understatement. A valuable spin-off of this exercise was a series of estimates of recruitment and retirements for both the central Civil Service and the Department of Posts and Telegraphs. An attempt to extend this development and produce wastage functions[1] for the Civil Service has not yet yielded results of value to policy makers.

Delving beneath the figures for total employment a number of insights were obtained. The employment of women expanded as a proportion of the total up to the mid-seventies and then stabilised at about four women for each five men in the central Civil Service. It was four to twelve in the Department of Posts and Telegraphs. Women were more than twice as prone to leave than men so that few of them stayed more than a decade in the Service. This not only different-iated their age pyramid markedly from men but also meant that there were fewer women over 35 years of age to compete for promotion with the larger number of men. Such competition would only be relevant in grades which women did not already dominate, such as clerical assistant and clerical officer. These grades were lower than executive officer which marked the bottom rung of the career grades. Women who reached this level, or who entered it at, or above, appear to have been making greater impact on higher grades relative to their numbers at these more senior levels. Their lack of greater representation at the highest levels probably reflects their age profile but this could change now that marriage gratuities are becoming a thing of the past. One countervailing factor, however, has arisen as a consequence of the 1981 decision that only one vacancy in every three can be filled. A higher proportion of the departing staff, than of their replacements, are likely to be women. This decision is achieving its objective and overall staff numbers have been falling in recent years after the dramatic increases chalked up under the full employment programme.

The study also glanced briefly at the grade and departmental structures. In general there was a tendency for the higher paid grade groups to expand faster than the lower. Within the higher group, that of administrative and executive staff, it was difficult to present a clearcut picture due to the great multiplicity of

---

[1]Equations that predict the likely levels of departures for any given length of service.

grades but again it was the relatively senior — Principal Officers and Assistant Principal Officers — that made the greatest strides compared to higher or lower grades.

The change in emphasis in the growth of departments reflected the changing expressions of Government policy with the economic departments, industry and agriculture, expanding earlier than the social departments. More recently the accent has shifted somewhat to law and order. Any analysis of departmental shifts needs to cope with the dexterity by which departments fragment and reunite in different combinations of functions. For this reason the presentation preferred to deal with departmental groups.

While the higher grades were expanding opportunities in some of the more peripheral activities have contracted. There has been a marked fall in the number of part-time staff, partly due to trade union activity but mainly due to functions, such as cleaning, being contracted out. Contractors' staff are not recorded. Another group, that have become ever less numerous, are the so called industrial workers. Many of these were engaged by the agricultural and rural departments, e.g., forestry workers and workers on drainage schemes of the Office of Public Works. Much of their work was of a capital nature. In common with kindred staff engaged by the local authorities in road and housing construction, numbers have decreased. Part of this decline is due to the establishment of new State-sponsored bodies to which the workers are transferred, e.g., maintenance workers at airports, now with Aer Rianta or farm workers now with ACOT. However, there appears to be a growing trend to recruit more academic type staff and to cut back on skilled and unskilled workers in general. In certain working class areas of Dublin it is difficult for clients of public services to identify with these more middle class staff and a case could be made for making different criteria for recruitement for those who will service such districts.

For many, entry into the permanent defence forces involved a three year contract. New contracts and the renewal of old contracts are more in demand during periods of general job scarcity and much less favoured when the economy is booming. For this reason employment levels contain a counter-cyclical dimension. As with the police force the outbreak of communal violence in Northern Ireland caused an upsurge in recruitment but, unlike the former, the recruitment embargo has had greater force. Since such recruitment as is permitted is confined to combatant roles, the small numbers of women soldiers (all non-combatants) has had no opportunity to grow.

Numbers in An Garda Siochana remained roughly constant between 1950 and 1972. The first brief rise was halted by the postponement of recruitment competitions in 1975 while new regulations were being drafted. The police force differs from the army in the degree to which it has integrated women into its force and in the fact that it has not become more officer-intensive over the decades. Due to the excellent records kept of Gardai it was possible to present the series for inflows and outflows and so pick out years like 1972 and 1982 when additions to strength were particularly large.

This study draws on the work of Desmond Roche (1982) to sketch the evolution of local institutions over time. In the development of the Irish system many functions were taken over early on by the central Government which were to remain local in other systems, even in the UK, e.g., police. The first major step to bring order into the haphazard and piecemeal growth of local authorities was the Local Government Act of 1898. An act of 1926 began the process of regularising recruitment while the County Management Act of 1940 gave executive functions to a salaried manager. The Health Act of 1947 rationalised institutional structures and started the process of applying modern social thinking to the harsh Poor Law Relief which was inappropriate for Irish conditions even at its inception in 1831. At this stage records of local authority employment became available annually by institution but only lately by function. Much of the reform over the documented period related to health and culminated in the setting up of the regional health boards in 1971 and the formal agreements with the voluntary hospitals in 1973 which rearranged their public funding and established clearly their public nature. The splitting up of the local government and health functions, however, left some lacunae in the series which are still to be filled.

Since greater emphasis was placed on recording local authority employment by institutions, such as county councils or town commissioners, little is known about the areas of activity. It is clear that health employment rose steadily since the 1947 Act but less is known about local administration. Overall employment declined from over 62,000 in the early fifties to 44,000 in 1960 — a period which coincided with a general recession in Ireland's economic fortunes. Some of this decline was due to less work on the roads, and to the gradual abandonment of employment schemes including turf production. It seems to have hit skilled and unskilled workers severely since numbers of administrators, etc., grew continuously. Urban authorities also did better than their more rural opposite numbers though the reclassification of health employment even before 1971 made for complications in assessing the situation.

In the health area itself the Department of Health conducted an annual survey for a number of years but altered the method of compilation in 1982 with the result that numbers appeared to have fallen. This led to a comprehensive review of the recording procedures in the Spring of 1985 which should form a firm basis for any future census. The Institute of Public Administration, ubiquitous in the public areas, not only produced an excellent survey of health services in Hensey's (1979) book but also pioneered recording of health personnel in 1971. This was invaluable since voluntary hospitals were not clearly identified as public at that time and the Department of Health surveys had not yet been launched.

The health area witnessed the gradual absorption of voluntary agencies for the care of neglected children and of the mentally handicapped into the public area and the contracting of medical and pharmacy services between these professionals and the General Medical Services (Payments) Board. Time series on some of these employments are, therefore, fairly short run.

County Committees of Agriculture were an autonomous group of local authorities engaged in farm advisory work and rural development. On the professional side the Department of Agriculture kept first class records of employment which were published annually in its report. As so frequently happens in the case of professional services, especially those of an educational nature, the publishing of details of non-professional support staff has tended to be overlooked. Fortunately in this case the unpublished records existed for most years.

The final set of employment categories related to the wide and complex area of education. Coolahan's (1981) work for the IPA provided a superbly researched background. The area with the longest-standing State funding is primary or national education and indeed developments in this area preceded those in Britain by several decades. The few model schools of today are the only reminder of the comprehensive system of education then launched which also included agricultural training. The nucleus of the modern University system dates from 1908. Secondary education was private, much more poorly funded than the other two and largely in the hands of religious communities. Independence brought the incremental salary arrangement which is the basis of teacher payment to this day. Apart from a few isolated institutions techical (later vocational) education is the most recent arrival of the four. It has been entirely State-funded from the start.

The nineteenth century battles over control of education led certain religious-managed national schools to opt for payment of religious staff on a capitation basis — largely Christian Brothers' schools in the case of boys' education. This system has now vanished. Equally the existence of untrained teachers is virtually a thing of the past, as are the exceptionally large class sizes of 45 pupils or more. The number of schools has decreased over 30 per cent since 1950 although pupil numbers rose by over 25 per cent. In part this reflects the campaign to close one teacher and two teacher schools and introduce bus transport to larger centres. However, the statistics also indicate that many schools were "retired" and replaced with more modern buildings. Since 1950 the number of teachers has increased by 7,500 or almost 60 per cent. This was more than double what was required to keep pace with rising enrolments so that pupil-teacher ratios have fallen and attractive modern curricula taught. The rise in teacher numbers favoured women especially and they have come to account for 75 per cent of the total. A welcome innovation has been the expansion of special schools and special classes for the handicapped. Figures for inflows to and outflows from the teaching staff were formerly published together with numbers of those who completed training. Indications are that fewer teachers are resigning their posts in the current recession. This trend is aggravating the problems which the recruitment embargo has created for fresh lay graduates, which is only slightly mitigated by a fall in the number of religious. The recent decision to raise the school leaving age affords no comfort to unemployed primary teachers, now that almost all students transfer to second level at 12 years of age.

In the case of the former reformatories and industrial schools, now designated special schools[2] and residential homes, published employment data were unusually sparse until recently, an omission which has been again confounded by the decision to transfer residential homes to the Department of Health in 1983. This gap is probably due to the fact that most of these schools were funded on a capitation basis. Numbers of schools shrank over the recent past, in part reflecting the trend not to put children into their care. By 1970 the number of children had dwindled to 1,400 from 7,000 in 1943. By 1983 the figure was about 1,000. These schools cater for two types of children: delinquents and neglected children. The latter are catered for under the Health Acts and are the predominant group in residential homes. In fact delinquent children in these schools only numbered 320 in 1983. As the number of children declined the number of staff rose so that about half were not "care" staff. Even so, child/care staff ratios have declined very dramatically.

Secondary school numbers peaked about 1970 and schools became much larger. Three-quarters had less than 150 pupils in 1950. The same proportion had over 300 pupils in the early 1980s. The revolution was largely due to the upsurge in pupil numbers after the launching of the "free" scheme in 1967 and the tendency of pupils to transfer to second level at earlier ages as a consequence. Teacher numbers increased about 3.7 times over three decades and gradually women became more likely to be teaching the smaller classes.

To some extent a brake was put on the growth of secondary schools by the building of comprehensive, and later community, schools designed to bridge the chasm between secondary and vocational schooling and to upgrade the status of the latter. These schools are different in many respects. From an employment point of view men still hold about a sixth more full-time posts than women and numbers of religious are increasing. The latter phenomenon may be due to community schools being created by mergers of secondary and vocational schools.

Vocational schools are under the aegis of Vocational Education Committees

---

[2]A nomenclature also used for schools of the handicapped.

and comprise both second- and third-level courses. These schools have shown the most rapid growth in full-time staff, increasing over four times while part-time staff trebled in numbers since 1950. The fact that these schools operate at two levels, cater for full-time and day release students as well as adult education, makes it difficult to comment on changes especially since the practice of pub-lishing teaching hours was discontinued.

The major breakthrough at second level was the development of senior con-tinuation courses which hitherto had been absent by tacit agreement with the bishops. In fact, the *raison d'être* of vocational education, technical instruction, has diminished in importance by extending the "free" secondary scheme to vocational schools. This reflects, presumably, parental demand. Thus instead of the educational revolution injecting more technology into predominantly academic second-level instruction via the vocational and community schools, the latter has come to dominate in these schools themselves. Initially similar strictures could be applied to second-level courses offered at the regional tech-nical colleges, which date effectively from 1971, in that it was only when non-technical courses were being phased in in 1979 that technical students pre-dominated. In general technical courses can be expected to demand lower pupil-teacher ratios (PTR) so that to the extent that vocational courses offer such courses their PTRs should be lower on average. Data do not permit us to check this hypothesis readily.

In addition to these four main categories of second-level schools a number of specialist schools cater for special needs. Those funded by the Department of Education are the Church of Ireland preparatory college and some others financed under Section 109 of the 1930 Vocational Education Act. The former prepares Protestant students for teacher training, of the latter four teach home economics and one secretarial training (Alexandra). The nature of the payment method makes it difficult to determine the employment content. Two of these schools closed in 1984. The Department of Agriculture formerly funded a score of schools of agriculture, horticulture and rural home economics before respons-ibility was transferred to ACOT. Employment data have again proved difficult to obtain. The rural home economics colleges are now closed.

Apart from teachers, non-academic staff employed at first- and second-level include caretakers, secretarial assistants, child care assistants in special schools for the handicapped and bus drivers.[3] The first two categories were innovations ushered in under the full employment programme. Shortage of public funds has led to some reductions in their numbers. VEC schools, being fully State financed, have traditionally employed greater numbers of non-academic staff.

---

[3]Among the teaching staff provision was increasingly made for remedial and career guidance teachers.

Unfortunately, like all non-teaching posts publication of numbers has not been the practice.

At third level recent years have seen the development of a binary system, of which the traditional universities form one wing. Compared to the sitution in the other colleges, the State has only become the major source of funding for Trinity College relatively recently, probably some time in the 'fifties. In 1972 the Higher Education Authority took over the planning and financing of much third-level education. Its employment statistics have not been used as they only refer to HEA funded posts, i.e., excluding agricultural teachers, etc. Teaching inputs are difficult to measure as most colleges use part-time and fee-paid staff and not all of them convert these to full-time equivalents. This study provides details by college, including Maynooth, and shows the importance of non-academic support staff. It also shows the rise in popularity of the smaller TCD relative to UCD.

In teacher training it has been customary to document pupil levels but even a study, such as that of Burke and Nolan, (1982) has tended to ignore employment levels, be they teachers or others. Data have been made available from departmental files where possible. Even so, some of the numbers in Table 104 are only estimates. This is particularly true of non-academic staff and in some of the smaller colleges.

As already noted, VEC schools include the third-level regional technical colleges and technological colleges. Most of the latter are associated together in the Dublin Institute of Technology and include many of the oldest technical institutions in the State. Records of teachers have been accurately recorded over the years but publication of non-academic staff numbers has yet to occur even though sizeable numbers are involved. Although apprenticeship courses make it difficult to be precise, pupil-teacher ratios in these colleges of technology are quite low.

VEC colleges are not funded by the Higher Education Authority though four other colleges are, including the National Institutes of Higher Education. Employment information is collated by the HEA but is difficult to present accurately due to the latter's preference for establishment levels (i.e., including vacancies). Comparisons are also complicated by the fact that different institutions contract out various services, e.g., catering, cleaning, and security.

Finally, a brief overview is given to some State-funded activities, such as adult education officers, youth development officers and participants in employment training programmes.

The study concludes with a number of recommendations designed to improve the quality and relevance of the published sources of information on employment levels in the public domain.

INTRODUCTION

This paper, which focuses on employment in the public domain in recent decades, is the first part of a more general study of the public domain. Volume II is planned to cover the remuneration of public employees while Volume III will be devoted to employment and remuneration in State-sponsored bodies.

The concern of this paper with employment in the public domain poses a number of definitional and data issues, the solution of which are also relevant to the analysis in Volumes II and III. The two definitional tasks are (a) to set out the boundaries between the public and private domains to be followed in the text and (b), given such boundaries, to determine when a person may be deemed to be a public employee. The data issues pinpointed the inadequacies of the intermittent Census of Population as a source of detailed time series and sought to evaluate the worth of several published and unpublished series as alternative sources of information.

In defining the boundaries of the public and private domains it was found that the international demand for greater statistical information on the public domain was of such recent origin that international conventions for a standardised approach were still in the process of development. This fact suggested that some understanding be provided of current approaches and that a building block strategy be adopted which would permit differing methods of aggregating the basic components in accordance with preferred interpretations of the system. Much of this discussion is set out in an appendix lest it clog up the main text. A similar treatment is accorded to the definition of employment. Here the task was to select criteria to determine when a person selling his labour services to the government is to be deemed to be part of the public domain. This problem arises since a person's earned income may only be partly derived from his earnings from government sources.

An examination of data sources led to a listing of the many divisions of the public domain scattered among the numerous categories in the industrial classification of the Census of Population. This list was used to propose a framework for integrating such bodies into a new system which would correspond with the recommendations of international bodies concerned with public statistics.

The Census itself has not been used extensively in this report though its data have been used to check figures derived from other sources. Among the reasons why less reliance was placed on the Census as a primary source are the infrequency of publication, the fact that no analysis of the data distinguishes public and private domains and the manner in which current practice frequently leaves these domains inextricably interwoven in many of the classifications.

Instead greater reliance is placed on various departmental sources. The value of this paper is that for the first time it brings these sources together in a time series and supplements them where traditionally records have been sparse. These data are presented on a building block basis to facilitate aggregations differing from the framework approach which informs this study. Wherever possible reconciliations are given between any different sources used for the same data. One such reconciliation suggests that the records collected in the Civil Service Census (later the Staff Information System) possess a higher level of accuracy than is customary to credit them with.

Plan of the Paper

The paper begins with a definition of the public domain and an outline of the main categories considered in this report. A brief survey, given of some of the problems of defining employment, is followed by the main sections of the study. These examine in turn

> The Civil Service proper
> The former Department of Posts and Telegraphs
> Industrial Civil Servants
> The Judiciary and Oireachtas
> The Defence Forces
> The Gardai
> Local Authorities
> Health Boards and Voluntary Hospitals and
> Education

Two final sections then provide a synthesis of the material in the nine main sections and make recommendations for improved information.

SECTION I

DEFINITIONS

Chapter I.1

DEFINITION OF THE PUBLIC DOMAIN

The International Synthesis

As mentioned earlier in spite of the great international interest in the public domain in recent years the statistical bases for developing internationally comparable statistics on government are still in the early stages of formulation. One difficulty has been the need to integrate four major traditions in public accounting to which individual countries belong. These traditions vary in the use which administration and accounting made of budgetary, extra-budgetary, special account, decentralised agency, etc., approaches. The search for a common basis for delimiting the public domain has led to the selection of criteria which favour deciding this issue on the basis of the nature of the function and the derivation of authority rather than on the traditional criteria of legal standing or administrative conventions.

The major work internationally has been developed by the United Nations and by the International Monetary Fund (IMF). These works show clearly their evolution from the UN System of National Accounts (SNA) and their European equivalent (ESA) which were produced to harmonise both national accounts and the production of input-output tables. The IMF system differs from that of the SNA mainly to the extent that it seeks to avoid the consolidation of public financial enterprises within the public domain of general government and public enterprises. In other words, it seeks to identify the activities of these financial bodies separately. Apart from some minor conventional differences, the two systems can be treated as identical. In the employment area a detailed industrial classification of economic activities was evolved to parallel the EEC's ESA. Called NACE, it has been adopted by the Central Statistics Office since 1975.

Aggregation by Branches of Economic Activity

As Appendix I documents in some detail, the basic units of national accounting are aggregated following two different patterns in conventional national accounts. One approach focusses on classifying the atoms of activity into

14

kind-of-activity units (KAU) which are grouped into BRANCHES. This procedure circumvents the difficulties posed by vertical and horizontal integration of enterprises and by amalgamations and collects all similar activities (e.g., agriculture) irrespective of the institutional setting in which the activity occurs. In Irish accounts one major branch is entitled "public administration and defence" and acts as the kernel of the public employment matrix. However, since the public domain is not exclusively devoted to public administration and defence, some of its other activities, e.g., education, health, postal services, forestry and sanitation, are aggregated with similar kinds of activity provided by private interests and are included in other branches. The public element is rarely separately identified.

Aggregtion by Institutional Sector

A more important aggregation in the context of this study is that which starts from the institutional unit. Such a unit is defined in the ESA as "institutional if it keeps a complete set of accounts and enjoys autonomy of decision in respect of its principal function". The principal function provides the yardstick for aggregation which typically follows a sixfold subdivision of the economy. A secondary criterion of aggregation is the source of the principal resources used by the unit. Thus the institutional sector comprising "general government" derives its main resources from compulsory levies on units in other institutional sectors (often called sectors for short) whether received directly or indirectly. The main function of the general Government sector is the "production of non-market services for collective consumption and carrying out of transactions intended to redistribute national income and wealth".

Conventions cover what are deemed to be market and non-market services. Transport and finance are always market. Defence is always non-market. Others are deemed to be non-market only if more than half their resources are derived from Government transfers, e.g., education, research, health, cultural and recreational activities. Thus a University is deemed to belong to the Government sector irrespective of its legal status if the Government is the major source of funds.

Those institutional units, whose function is the production of goods and market services and whose resources are derived from the sales of output, belong to the enterprise sector. This sector may be subdivided into financial and other enterprises and the former between credit institutions and insurance enterprises since the sources of resources differ. The detailed taxonomy is given in Table A.1 of Appendix I. Some institutional units in the enterprise sectors will belong to the public domain if they are in accordance with the IMF definition of the nature of Government (see next section).

The ESA definition of institutional units referred to "residential" units —

those which were controlled by agents residing within the State. Foreign units operating within the State are deemed to belong to the "rest of the world" sector which could include units of supra national governments, e.g., EEC, as well as transnational enterprises, etc. Not all units are institutional in that they may lack either autonomy or a special set of accounts. By convention households are assumed to be institutional units in spite of non-compliance with this measure. Their main function is consumption. Their resources come from wages, property and transfers. Some enterprises are not institutional since they do not keep accounts, e.g., many farmers and self-employed. These units are also included in the household sector unless their very considerable size warrants their being deemed quasi-institutional. They are not likely candidates for inclusion in the public domain.

The household sector is often combined with private non-profit institutions whose resources are derived from voluntary contributions and property income[4] and which produce non-market services for particular groups of households, religious, clubs, trade unions, etc.

The New Classification

Aggregation by branches does not distinguish as public more than a small part of the public domain, i.e., public administration and defence. Aggregation by sectors gives a more comprehensive picture but presents the difficulty that some bodies in the enterprise sector are public. There is no public involvement with the household or private non-profit institutions.[4] To get the most complete picture a new term is needed, analogous to "branch" and "sector" in the other classifications and which segregates clearly public from private irrespective of branch or sector. In this report the term used is "domain".

The Nature of Government

The basic starting point for delimiting the public domain is the IMF definition of the nature of government.

> The government of a country consists of the public authorities and their instrumentalities, established through political processes, exercising a monopoly of compulsory powers within a territorial area or its parts, motivated by consideration of public purpose in the economic, social and political spheres and engaged primarily in the provision of public services differing in character, cost elements and sources of finance from the activities of other sectors. (IMF, 1964, p. 8).

---

[4]This is the international definition. In Ireland religious orders, engaged in health and educational services, derive funds from the State.

This definition provides a touchstone by which to classify activities and agencies between public and private, some key concepts being the idea of "instrumentalities" and the focus on "public purpose" in arriving at the dichotomy. Bodies in the enterprise sector belong to the public domain if the units concerned can be viewed as "instrumentalities" of the public authorities, "established through political processes" which were "motivated by considerations of public purpose in the economic, social and political spheres". The specific application of this rule has tended to be governed by two criteria — those of public ownership and control. By convention public ownership is assumed if the authorities hold a majority of the stock. Control is assumed if the authorities appoint the board.

The Outline of the Public Domain

The use of the new classification, based on this definition, gives us a public domain which is wider in coverage than that derived from the branch or sector approaches. The public domain is wider in extent than the Public Administration and Defence branch since it includes from other branches those bodies the majority of whose resources come from the State. These bodies are to be found in all the other branches — agriculture, industry, transport and commerce and other domestic. The public domain is wider than the government sector since it includes public bodies in the commercially-oriented enterprise sector.

In Appendix I the implications of the criteria for delimiting the public domain are spelt out in some detail. These criteria are then applied to various bodies in the Irish economy and about fifty of them classified as public bodies in the enterprise sector. These are classified by branch in Table A1.2 at the end of that appendix. In addition to State-sponsored bodies they include on the basis of their commercal activity the Forestry Division and the Department of Posts and Telegraphs prior to the latter evolving into three State-sponsored bodies.

Table A1.2 also itemises the constituent elements of the Government sector. There are a very great number of bodies enumerated and there are also many categories and types of organisation. A significant number of these bodies are State-sponsored and are classified as to whether they serve a Government function, e.g., Bord Pleanála, or else are designed to serve (a) enterprises or (b) households. State-sponsored bodies serving enterprises are to be found engaged in (i) research (e.g., An Foras Talúntais), (ii) training, (e.g., AnCO) and economic promotion (e.g., IDA). Those serving households are active in the fields of education, (e.g., Higher Eduction Authority) and health (Blood Transfusion Service Board). Some serve households in the latter's role of producers (e.g., Board for the Employment of the Blind) or consumers (e.g., Legal Aid Board). Closely analogous to these bodies are a small number of bodies not strictly speaking State-sponsored bodies but none the less heavily dependent on State

financing, i.e, the IPA, the ESRI and the Irish Productivity Centre. For our purposes these will be treated as if State-sponsored bodies.

The constituent State-sponsored bodies in the various cateories are, as stated
already, set out in Table A1.2 under the enterprise and general Government
sector headings. They will not be discussed further in this report since a separate
study is planned to deal with these numerous agencies.

The major elements in the general Government sector are (a) central and
local government and (b) public non-profit institutions in the fields of eduction
and health. To take the latter first, although secondary schools and voluntary
hospitals are not State-sponsored and operate with considerable independence
the fact that in virtually all cases they derive over half their operating costs from
the State warrants their inclusion in the public domain in accordance with the
IMF criteria. Local authorities are now divided between health boards and local
government. Harbour authorities are deemed to belong to the enterprise sector.

Central government consists of the Civil Service proper, the Gardai and the
defence forces. A small group are distinguished partly because they are remunerated from central funds, i.e., the Judiciary and the Ministers together with the
Comptroller and Auditor-General. For convenience members of the Oireachtas
are included with this group.

In keeping with international practice a number of "departmental enterprises" are distinguished in Table A1.2. These are public enterprises omitted
from the enterprise sector because they fall short in the measures for inclusion,
i.e., sales to the public on a large scale. These enterprises either do not sell to the
public or the scale is not large relative to their main work. The Office of Public
Works would be an example of the former; sales by the Brucellosis Laboratory
are an instance of the latter. The agencies concerned are listed in Table A1.2 but
in the report itself it is not proposed to identify them separately from other
departmental work. A similar observation applies to agencies, such as the
National Museum, listed in Table A1.2 serving households in their role as consumers. In general these bodies will be included with their parent departments.

To sum up, State-sponsored bodies are not considered in this report which
concerns all other bodies in the public domain. This means that study of public
enterprises is postponed. However, because of the nature of the historical time
series it is convenient to include from the enterprise sector in this report both the
former Department of Posts and Telegraphs and the Forestry Division. In the
general Government part of the public domain this report will examine:

1. The Civil Service proper
2. The Department of Posts and Telegraphs
3. Industrial Civil Servants
4. The Judiciary and Oireachtas

5. The Defence Forces
6. The Gardai
7. Local Authorities
8. Health Boards and Voluntary Hospitals
9. Education

In this examination the focus will be on employment. Costs and wage rates will be studied in a separate volume.

The Definition of Employment

In defining the public domain it was noted that modern international practice favoured criteria based on the nature of the function and on the derivation of authority rather than on legal standing or administrative conventions. A similar spirit is obviously called for in the definition of employment. Traditional conventions have tended to exclude from public employment those who sold goods and services to public authorities. Clearly a case can be made where such sales are once off or occasional. It is a different matter where the sale of a service occurs on a regular basis and accounts for a significant proportion of the vendor's income. Accordingly this study seeks to include as far as possible all those who derive more than half their earned income from public sources either directly or indirectly. The latter source refers to bodies, such as voluntary hospitals, which are included in the public domain. It is not always possible, however, to say how many members of a particular group are dependent ultimately on taxation for more than half their regular earned income. For example, it is not easy to determine how many doctors in the choice of doctor scheme are so dependent. Similar considerations apply to veterinary surgeons and barristers. In some areas numbers of fee paid staff have been recorded continuously, e.g., architects working for local authorities, lecturers in universities, doctors and pharmacists in the choice of doctor scheme, managers of sub-post offices and of social welfare branches. However, in other areas the use of contractors can change the classification of staff from public to private as when cleaning services are so obtained in the newer office blocks. Many third-level educational institutions contract out catering, security and other functions. It is important to form some ideas of such employment if a study aims at being comprehensive. In former decades those working on such bases for the civil service departments were recorded with distinctions made between regular and occasional workers "on piecework, task-work, capitation or fee terms". Subdivisions classified professionals, skilled tradesmen and others. Other censuses covered those employed on temporary schemes. It is regrettable that such practices have been discontinued since they gave valuable insights into the wider definition of public employment. In the case of many private and voluntary organisations in the areas of education, health and welfare, funding on a capitation basis provided resources to employ regular staff ultimately dependent on taxation. Many of these were unrecorded until inflation and other developments caused the organisation to seek funding on a budget basis. For our purposes such staff in "capitation" institutions are to be deemed as public employees if their public salary exceeds that derived from private sources. A similar observation would apply where the fees to the organisation are funded by grants, e.g., where scholarships enable students to pay college fees. Where public salaries are less than half the total income, records should also be kept since circumstances can change. Otherwise once a threshold is crossed all staff suddenly switch from private to public.

Where staff are clearly in the public domain the methods of recording can vary from organisation to organisation and present problems of aggregation. The advantage of a Census of Population is that it defines all workers in terms of a single occupation and industry on the Census date. Its disadvantages are that it includes foreigners temporarily in the country, excludes natives temporarily abroad and may misrepresent industries whose seasonal average differs in time of occurrence from that of the Census. This latter consideration applies also to the tendency of many public domain enumerations to settle for a count on a defined date. Unfortunately the choice of dates is not uniform though an increasing number of bodies favour either the last day of December or the first working day of January. This tendency makes for consistency but needs to be supplemented where seasonal employment is low at the turn of the year, e.g., in road construction or drainage schemes of the Office of Public Works.

A head count on a defined day presents only a partial picture. The staff needs to be classified into full time, permanent part time, regular casuals and occasional temporaries. Some agencies omit to include some of these non-full-time staff, whereas others include not only all of them but also their full-time equivalents (FTE). This latter practice is the most informative and is recommended for universal adoption. Some bodies settle for average numbers of part timers which may be better than the number on a specified day but will contain less information than FTEs. Other versions of these averages occur in those agencies which record either or both maxima and minima. Some documents, such as the Estimates for the Public Service, provide information on budgeted employment. These would be valuable indicators if the Appropriation Accounts in their turn were as detailed and also recorded actual employment. The practice of yet other bodies to record authorised levels of employment is advantageous for planning purposes. It would be more beneficial, however, if the number of vacancies were also noted.

It will be clear that the diversity of enumerating practices adopted by different agencies introduces some degree of fuzziness into the precision with which it was hoped to report on actual employment in this study.

A worthwhile supplement to any study of employment at a moment in time is a calculation of staff wastage and renewals. Wherever possible such information is included in the various sections.

Data Sources

It is not proposed to examine data sources in a single section. Each section will examine the relevant material at the outset of its investigation of employment levels.

The bulk of the study will now examine the various subgroups listed above in the outline of the public domain, starting with the Civil Service proper.

SECTION II

CIVIL SERVICE

Chapter II

THE ENTIRE CIVIL SERVICE

Introduction

The Civil Service is the body of staff which serves in a civil capacity the organs of State defined by the Constitution, i.e., the President, the Houses of the Oireachtas, the Judiciary, the Taoiseach and the Ministers, the Attorney General and the Comptroller and Auditor General (Finlay, 1966, p. 7). The Constitution (Article 28.1) provides that the Government shall consist of not less than seven members but not more than fifteen. These fifteen members comprise An Taoiseach and the Ministers of State. All except a small number of civil servants serve the Government as members of the staff of the various departments of State. These staff are known in the 1956 Act governing the Civil Service as "the Civil Service of the Government". In addition "the Civil Service of the State" are those who function independently of Ministerial control since they form the personnel of the Offices of the President, the Houses of the Oireachtas, the Attorney General and the Comptroller and Auditor General. The basic legislation on the regulation, control and management of the Civil Service is the Civil Service Regulation Act of 1956 which updated previous legislation. Some civil servants of the State are governed by separate legislation, e.g., the Comptroller and Auditor General Act 1923 or the Staff of the Houses of the Oireachtas Act 1959 and a similar observation applies to some civil servants of the Government, e.g., the Court Officers Act 1926. Both sets of civil servants are paid from moneys voted annually by Dail Eireann and provision for their remuneration is included in the annual Book of Estimates for the Public Service. This Book provides directly for certain other categories of personnel who are outside the Civil Service, i.e. the Defence Forces, the Gardai, National and Secondary teachers, persons employed on the basis of fees for work performed (often doctors or laywers), persons employed on a contractual basis (e.g., sub-post office managers) and tradesmen and industrial workers whose pay and conditions are closely related to those of their counterparts in industrial and commercial employment.

24

Normally, civil servants are not authorised to perform statutory functions in their own right; such powers are reserved to Ministers, and civil servants' statutory functions are limited to conveying Ministers' decisions as set out in general directives. In the current complexities of administration the interpretation of these directives must, perforce, be undertaken by civil servants. It would be wrong, however, to infer that statutory functions never vest in civil servants. The Oireachtas has created certain bodies of Commissioners who have received definite statutory functions which they exercise in their own rights. Although such Commissioners are appointed by the Government or by individual Ministers and their staffs are usually appointed and provided by Ministers and their offices form part of a Minister's Department, they are legally quite independent of Ministers in the performance of their statutory duties. Examples are the Revenue Commissioners, the Land Commissioners, the Civil Service Commissioners and the Commissioner for Valuation.[5] It is clear that the nature of their responsibilities requires that they be seen to be independent of political intervention.

Partly as a result of this arrangement and for other administrative reasons it will be found that some departments include separate offices which are usually self-contained and frequently largely independent of the headquarters' office. Certain of these self-contained offices may be larger than some full departments. Thus the figures for the Department of Finance include those of the offices of the Revenue Commissioners, the Office of Public Works and several other sizeable offices; the Department of An Taoiseach covers the Central Statistics Office; the Courts of Justice are included with the Department of Justice. A measure of the increasing independence of subsections is provided by the growth in the number of "accounting officers" from 22 in 1967 to 30 in 1982. Accounting officers are those persons who carry the ultimate responsibility under the Minister for authorising every expenditure under a particular vote for expenditure granted by Dail Eireann. In 1967 the Secretary of the Department of Finance, T. K. Whitaker, was accounting officer for 13 votes. His successor in 1982, M. Doyle, accounted for only six. The remainder had individual accounting officers.

The first section of this report is concerned with the Civil Service as understood in the above terms since the legal distinctions between civil servants, teachers, and industrial workers in the Service tend to be reflected in the statistical records which have accumulated over the years. Even within the Civil Service, application of the building block approach to the study of the public domain requires that the former Department of Posts and Telegraphs be treated

---

[5]The Social Welfare Act 1952 grants statutory powers of decision to "deciding officers" and "appeals officers" of the Department of Social Welfare relating to the benefits under the Act. These often quite junior staff are in an analogous position to those of the Commissions.

separately, both because its commerical activities mean that it belongs to the enterprise sector and also because its structure is substantially different from the other departments. Other blocks would separate out the industrial, fee paid, and casual workers and consider them separately. Where possible part-time employment is also distinguished from full-time working. This arrangement gives us four major groupings of civil servants:

1. The non-industrial Civil Service, apart from the Department of Posts and Telegraphs, which will be called in this study the Central Civil Service.
2. The Department of Posts and Telegraphs.
3. Industrial workers associated with 1 and 2.
4. Other workers.

Ideally the next sections should consider these groups seriatim. However, the surviving records for the period before 1950 do not permit such a disaggregation in each year. Thus the initial review of developments will concentrate on time series data up to 1957 which covers the entire Civil Service but does not distinguish the four groups listed above. This series is based on a memorandum which summarises the annual returns of the Civil Service Census (CSC). This census is the ultimate source of all employment data on the Civil Service and operated continuously from the establishment of the State until superseded by the computerised Staff Information System (SIS) in 1975.

The Civil Service Census

The Census was designed to record "all civilian personnel (except as shown below) whether whole-time or part-time" who were "required to carry out the normal functions of Departments". It excluded:—

(a) Persons holding Parliamentary Offices
(b) Persons paid out of the Central Fund
(c) Persons employed regularly and remunerated on a piece work, task work, capitation or fee basis.
(d) Professional classes paid on a fee basis for occasional services.
(e) Persons other than profession classes remunerated on a piece work, task work, or fee basis for occasional services.
(f) Foreman, Artisans, Gangers, Labourers, etc., employed on schemes or works of a temporary nature other than relief works.

In the earlier decades records were kept for each of these excluded categories. In the case of category (c) those employed regularly but not on a salary basis, the records contained both the number of persons involved and the fees, etc., paid. In the case of categories (d) and (e) only the outlays were recorded while with category (f) average numbers were recorded alongside the costs.

Given the nature of the records kept for many of these categories it proved difficult to include them with the returns of the Census in an extended time series. The difficulty, which the omission of these numbers avoided, is in part that of marrying numbers on a specified date with numbers which were annual averages. In part it may have also seemed inappropriate to combine numbers of regular employees with those who were regularly employed on a fee basis but whose main source of income was elsewhere. The Census itself records numbers on the first working day in January and has done so since 1924.

Total Employment in the Civil Service 1922 to 1957

A major reclassification of the CSC was applied to the January 1958 returns. This change afforded Finance an opportunity to review employment experience since the foundation of the State. The summarised material contained in an unpublished internal memorandum is reproduced in Table 1 and graphed in Figure 1. The totals in the first column can be regarded as fairly comprehensive since they include not only civil servants and industrial workers but also casuals attached to the Department of Posts and Telegraphs and the Land Commission (i.e. Forestry workers). Prior to 1958 it was the custom to include industrial workers as a set of grades within each department. Subsequently they were given a census of their own. All those recorded in the Census had individual cards returned for compilation. In the case of casual workers this was dispensed with and the total numbers involved in two Departments were appended to the regular Census. Given the comprehensiveness of the main column it is difficult at this stage to account for a total of 23,396 for 1932 given in a Finance analysis of the Census which was 1,603 higher than that in Table 1. That table also is interesting in that it provides, in addition, the monetary rewards of those explicitly excluded from the Census i.e. pieceworkers and temporary labourers.

On the first of April 1922 21,035 civil servants were recorded in the new State's employment. These numbers included 17,239 permanent civil servants transferred from the British Civil Service as well as a further 3,176 transferees who had been taken on for temporary war-time duties. This total also included 131 employees of Dail Eireann who had served that body prior to the Treaty as well as 88 British civil servants who had resigned their posts on political grounds. The transferred officers had their rates of pay protected under Article X of the Treaty. The Saorstat was powerless to modify these rates which had benefited "from the operations of Whitleyism" i.e., a reorganisation of the British Civil Service in 1920 which affected practically all classes increasing both existing pay and rates of pay. On 1 January 1934, 9,823 were still serving even though there had been many premature retirements.

Between April 1922 and October 1923 2,320 staff were taken on temporarily to cope with new duties. Of these 676 were needed to handle compensation in the

Table 1: *Numbers employed and remuneration of civil servants 1922–1958 giving separate expenditure for persons on piece rates, temporary workers and overtime*

Civil Service January 1	Nos.	Cost year ending December 31 previous year	Persons on piecework taskwork capitation or fee terms	Foremen, artisans, gangers, labourers employed on schemes or works of a temporary nature other than relief	Overtime
		£	£	£	£
1922 (Apr)	21,035	4,170,861	—	—	—
1923 (Oct)	22,269	3,943,985	—	—	—
1924	21,538	—	—	—	—
1925	21,758	—	—	—	—
1926	22,885	4,073,436	—	—	—
1927	22,708	4,061,667	—	—	—
1928	23,349	4,040,243	—	—	—
1929	23,796	4,074,587	—	—	—
1930	21,817	3,919,766	—	—	—
1931	21,616	3,818,897	—	—	37,189††
1932	21,793	3,819,542	100,393†	193,062	47,084*
1933	22,141	3,781,053	132,328	265,770	69,949
1934	22,037	3,791,353	146,544	221,500	81,621
1935	23,573	4,025,957	145,049	334,815	86,130
1936	24,549	4,321,105	159,494	348,965	86,811
1937	25,113	4,505,406	154,124	387,431	110,190
1938	26,023	4,882,816	168,836	349,367	104,141
1939	26,775	5,065,117	179,634	290,126	100,739
1940	27,411	5,383,768	174,787	343,610	89,663
1941	27,400	5,480,785	193,296	410,342	110,281
1942	28,176	5,629,041	190,007	235,533	127,964
1943	29,081	6,106,501	191,169	260,284	154,498
1944	29,546	6,472,323	196,098	236,882	171,213
1945	30,333	7,302,204	201,907	235,054	204,210
1946	30,489	7,655,575	204,335	280,807	242,464
1947	31,179	8,784,502	226,064	317,855	363,905
1948	32,171	9,129,849	260,739	384,104	389,913
1949	33,485	10,322,434	277,686	347,959	359,473
1950	33,975	10,664,966	297,592	493,396	365,161
1951	35,287	11,175,201	305,071	667,361	431,997
1952	36,512	13,260,712	330,849	976,206	430,734
1953	37,632	13,777,427	356,855	987,177	395,345
1954	37,731	15,043,777	411,468	1,015,116	400,546
1955	38,427	15,343,152	531,709	946,270	483,799
1956	38,645	17,255,351	601,540	1,040,921	526,982
1957	39,051	17,808,462	635,825[a]	864,736[a]	444,034
1958	38,471	17,847,873	—	—	—

Source: Special Report on Civil Service Census. (a) *Data not in Special Report.*

Note: Prior to 1930 Columns 1 and 2 include numbers and costs of certain staff recorded in Columns 3 and 4 after 1933. Figures for 1930, 1931 and 1932 exclude such staff.

— = not available

†Excludes classes other than professional for occasional services.

*Excludes £1,554 paid to industrial staff OPW.

††Excludes industrials in Defence and OPW.

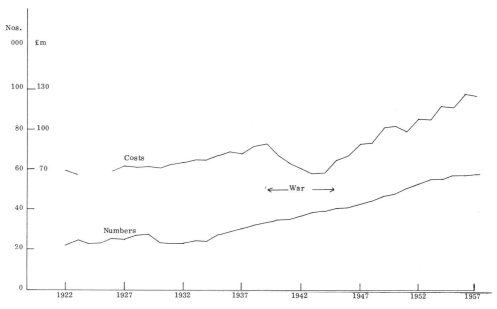

Figure 1: *Number and Costs (at constant 1981 prices) of Civil Service 1922–1957*

Note: Left scale gives numbers. Right scale gives costs in £m.

Office of the Public Works and 468 to cater for the new duties of the Revenue Commissioners. In 1926 approximately 2,000 were still temporary, though it was hoped to replace them by a smaller number of more efficient personnel recruited by open competitve examinations.

The figures show that the tendency for numbers to grow was arrested in 1929 when about 2,000 staff were let go or not replaced. It is not clear if these were the temporary staff referred to above or if the 1929 world crisis had any influence on this drop of over 8 per cent. During the 1932 to 1934 period when the Commission of Inquiry into the Civil Service was gathering evidence, numbers remained down but began an upward trend during 1934 which continued fairly steadily until the balance of payments crisis of 1952 put a brake on all Government expenditures. The only analysis of this growth was a partial one by Linehan in 1954 who wrote for a special group concerned with the rapidly rising cost of civil service employment which was no doubt inspired by the 1952 crisis. His analysis in terms of departmental growth will be deferred until the departments are examined in more detail later on in the study. It may seem strange in the light of today's concerns with the public sector pay bill to realise that concern was also deeply felt three decades ago. This is understandable since the annual compound rate of growth between 1934 and 1952 was 2.86 per cent or a much higher rate of growth than that recorded in the three subsequent decades. This may come as a surprise to those who regard rapid growth of public empoyment as a modern phenomenon. If we might anticipate later commentary, part of the reason for the public perception of growth in the 'seventies as being very rapid is due to the fact that 1952 deflected the early growth path downwards so that growth in the 'fifties and 'sixties was markedly below trend. Relative to these decades growth in the 'seventies appeared all the more explosive. Relative to the 'thirties and 'forties the *rate* was less remarkable. However, the absolute increases that the rate represented were becoming ever larger. At the latter end of the earlier period, annual increases were of the order of 1,300 at a time when the State's share of national income was less dominant.

While analysis of growth in terms of departmental change has been deferred, another dimension of change can be gleaned from the Report of the Commission of Inquiry into the Civil Service and from Linehan's (1954) analysis. This appears in Table 2.

Table 2: *Numbers of Civil servants in selected years 1927–1953 classified as established and unestablished officers, industrial workers and others*

Jan 1	Established	Unestablished whole time	Officers part time	Industrials	Other*	Total Table 1
1927	9,353	4,325	6,045	2,985		22,708
1931	10,027	3,118	5,963	2,508		21,616
1934	10,697	2,818	6,103	1,904	515	22,037
1935	11,679	3,153	6,152	2,589		23,573
1940	13,266	9,779		2,342	2,024	27,411
1947	13,407	12,165		3,260	2,347	31,179
1953	16,873	12,354		4,601	3,804	37,632

Sources: 1927–1935 Commission of Inquiry into the Civil Service 1935; 1934 and 1940–1953, Linehan (1954).

*These "other" figures are the residual when other items are subtracted from the final column. They appear to be casuals attached to the Post Office and the Forestry section of the Department of Lands.

Note: Industrials can be classified as established and unestablished and were predominantly the latter.

One striking feature of the table is the number of part-time officers — about 6,000 in each of the years where this total is recorded. A further breakdown of the 1934 figures shows that virtually all these — 5,705 (93.5 per cent) — were post office employees.

The distinction between established and unestablished has become relatively unimportant in the modern Civil Service. The term "established" is defined in the Department of Finance's Annexures to Circular No. 46 of December 1933 as "serving in a pensionable capacity under the Superannuation Acts". As Table 2 indicates unestablished officers can be either full time or part time. In the former case the term covers staff "employed on a quasi-permanent, unestablished, temporary or purely casual basis". The part-time staff "comprises unestablished officers who during the period of their employment are not required to give their whole time to the Public Service".

Over the growth period 1934 to 1953, 15,593 additional posts were created. Over 6,000, or 40 per cent of these, were in permanent pensionable posts associated in the popular mind with the Civil Service. Growth in the unestablished posts and "other" posts exceeded 3,200 each and combined accounted for more than did the rise in established posts, i.e., 22 per cent + 21 per cent, respectively. Growth in industrial employment was just 2,700 or 17 per cent. This pattern of growth was quite different from that associated with recent expansion.

Table 3: *Sex composition of non-industrial civil service in selected years 1934 to 1953*

	1934	1940	1947	1953
Total	19,618	23.045	25,572	29,227
of which men	14,759	16,635	17,865	20,001
of which women	4,859	6,410	7,707	9,226
% women	24.8	27.8	30.1	31.6
Established men	8,137	9,404	9,364	11,171
Established women	2,561	3,862	4,043	5,702
% women	23.9	29.1	30.2	33.8

Source: Linehan (1954).

An examination of the sex composition of change 1934 to 1953 is given in Table 3 for the non-industrial Civil Service. The absolute increase was greater for men than for women. Nevertheless, the proportion of women in the total rose. This growing share was more marked in the case of established posts where the absolute increase for women was higher over the two decades.

For the interested reader Appendix Table A2.1 gives a time series for 1938 and from 1945 to 1959 which distinguishes sex, established status and industrial grade. While established men increased in numbers continuously, unestablished

Table 4: *Numbers of civil servants serving on 1st January 1934 and 1953 by sex and grade group*

Grade Group		Established			Unestablished		
		Men	Women	% Women	Men	Women	% Women
1. Administrative and Executive	1934	1,684	43	2.5	13	—	0.0
	1953	2,554	141	5.2	29	2	6.5
	Increase	+ 870	+ 98	10.1	16	2	11.1
2. Clerical Writing Assistant	134	2,216	1,249	36.0	424	86	16.9
	1953	2,641	3,394	56.2	518	388	42.4
	Increase	+ 425	2,145	83.5	94	302	76.3
3. Typing Grades	1934	0	560	100.0	0	61	100.0
	1953	1	914	99.9	1	92	98.9
	Increase	1	354	99.7	1	31	96.9
4 and 5. Inspectorate and Professional	1934	855	61	6.7	533	126	19.1
	1953	1,459	113	7.2	1,304	144	9.9
	Increase	604	52	7.9	771	18	2.3
6. Supervisory Manual, etc.	1934	3,249	638	16.4	5,001	1,449	22.5
	1953	4,265	1,139	21.1	5,904	2,058	25.8
	Increase	1,016	501	33.0	903	609	40.3
7. Messenger/Cleaner	1934	133	10	7.0	651	576	46.9
	1953	251	1	0.4	1,074	840	43.9
	Increase	118	- 9	nil	423	264	38.4

Note: Inspectorate has been combined with Professional Scientific and Technical because all persons with degrees included in the Inspectorate in 1951 were subsequently transferred to Professional, etc.

Source: Linehan (1954).

men fell 17 per cent in numbers between 1952 and 1958. Numbers of established women peaked in 1953 and then fell over 4 per cent to 1958. Unestablished women tended to decline for more than the decade to 1958. Industrial workers were affected by the revisions of 1952 (see page 35).

The destinations of women arriving into the Civil Service are set out in Table 4 which classifies employees into broad grade groupings. The senior administrative group is called "administrative and executive". Representation of women in this group increased but not at a rate sufficient to give them anything like a proportionate share. Representation in the professional grades and in the inspectorate was only slightly better but the gains by women fewer. The bulk of the women found themselves in the grouping "clerical, writing assistants, etc." where over time they accounted for five out of every six additional posts and thus increased their share of the total by 20 percentage points to 56 per cent. A further major outlet for female talents was the grouping "supervisory, manual and manipulative" which is predominantly a set of post office grades, such as post office clerk. The proportion of women among messengers, cleaners, etc., declined in both established and unestablished posts because of the more rapid rise in employment of male messengers.

Chapter II.2

THE CENTRAL CIVIL SERVICE

Sources and Adjustments

The material presented in the last section was based perforce on a time series which gave the total number of civil servants. At the outset of that section it was acknowledged that a building block approach, which disaggregated this material, would be preferable and, to recapitulate, such blocks were identified as:

1. The Central Civil Service
2. The Department of Posts and Telegraphs
3 and 4. Industrial and casual workers.

When we turn to the sources seeking separate figures for the Post Office and industrial workers we find:

(a) Prior to 1950 data are scrappy, ill defined and emanate from a variety of sources so that figures do not always refer to the same aggregates.

(b) Between 1950 and 1975 annual reports of the CSC survive, the only difficulty being revisions of the recording procedures in 1952 and 1958. Unfortunately documentation on the 1952 revision does not exist and changes must be inferred from the records. The 1958 changes are well itemised.

(c) A more significant overhaul of the system occurred in 1975 when the CSC was computerised to become the Staff Information System (SIS). Unfortunately the transition was not as smooth as those in earlier revisions and serious lacunae resulted over the transition period to July 1977. In addition, considerable understatement was evident up to 1981 as indicated by a Dail statement in December of that year. One task of this study will be to remedy these deficiencies as far as possible so that a continuous time series is made available.

If we now take these periods in turn we find a list of sources, all derived ultimately from the CSC, for the period up to 1950 as follows:

(1) A brief Finance memorandum of 1926 which provides a separate but undefined total for the Post Office.

(2) A detailed analysis by Finance of the 1932 CSC from which some tables are missing.

(3) The Report of the Commission of Inquiry into the Civil Service 1935 which gives some detail of 1934 employment, distinguishing the Post Office but excluding industrials and casuals. It also gives more summary data from 1927, 1931 and 1935, distinguishing part-time and unestablished personnel.

(4) An article by Linehan (1954) which gives details for the years 1934, 1940, 1947 and 1953 by sex and grade groups (including industrials) but excluding casuals. The Post Office is not identified separately.

(5) Surviving records from the 1938 and 1940, CSC.

Of these sources only categories (2) and (5) give departmental detail.

If we link these sources to the general aggregates in Table 1 of the previous sections we can estimate the number of casuals. The broad results are given in Table 5.

Table 5: *Some estimates of Post Office, Industrial and Other employment in Civil Service in selected years 1926 to 1940*

Year	Total from Table 1	Post Office	Other Departments	Industrials	Casuals[e]
1926	22,885[a]	12,715[b]	10,170[b]		
1932	21,793[c]	11,316+641[d]	9,082	2,998	
1934	22,037	10,720	8,898	1,904	515
1938	26,023	12,269	10,486	3,185	
1940	27,411	11,285	11,760	2,342	2,024

[a]Memo gives 22,953. [b]Includes industrials and possibly casuals. [c]Finance analysis gives 23,396.
[d]Post Office element in 2,998 industrials. [e]Residual.
Sources: see text.

Precise figures are not available for 1922 but broadly speaking the Post Office employed 13,500 to 6,800 in other departments just after the transfer of sovereignty.

The 1952 and 1958 Reclassifications

The source of information for the period 1950 to 1975 is the CSC. However, recording procedures changed at least twice in this period, in 1952 and again in 1958. The main thrust of the 1952 revision was to halve the number of grade groups analysed from 98 to 50. In the process some reclassifications occurred. Degree holders in the Inspectorate group of grades were reclassified in the Professional grade grouping. A second reclassification affected the industrial grades. In 1952 a new grade, "non-professional staff in the Engineering branch of the Department of Posts and Telegraphs" was added to the grade grouping of Manipulative, Minor and Supervisory staff. The new total was 1,828. In 1951, 1,967 industrials were listed in the Engineering branch but only 134 a year later. The new grade must, therefore, have been once part of the industrial staff. Perhaps this helps to explain why Linehan's 1953 figures for industrials, i.e., 4,601 was 1,874 higher than the CSC's 2,727.

Other industrials were also divided between casuals, such as forestry workers who were no longer enumerated individually but as a block to be appended to the totals for departmental employment, and those industrials still listed with their departments but also recorded separately. These two changes were carried further in 1958 when both were formally excluded from the main CSC.

In 1958 others excluded from the CSC were (a) scale-paid staff formerly returned as part-time staff and now recorded separately and (b) a small number of miscellaneous staff excluded for various reasons. The effect of these reclassifications on the central Civil Service was not large and reduced the previous total by 448, or 3 per cent. Since 242 of these continued to be enumerated but separately, and so can be added back in, the change was only slightly more than 1 per cent. Those omitted were:

    162 non-industrial civilians with the Army
    80 branch managers of Social Welfare Offices
    206 whose *annual* remuneration was less than £50.

The first two groups are now recorded as "non-industrial workers outside the Staff Information System". The 206 last mentioned earned an average £9.75 in 1958 and were mainly employed by the Office of Public Works.[6] They were defined as "part-time staff not paid on an hourly basis who had received less than £50 in the year". They are not to be confused with staff "off pay" who for one reason or another, e.g., prolonged illness, were still on the staff but not in receipt of any salary, wages or allowances. In 1959 staff off pay numbered 92. The 1976 SIS recorded 951 off pay including 87 part timers.

The Staff Information System

In 1975 the system of recording was computerised. It was decided to push ahead with this programme and not delay so as to integrate the system with the pay-issuing mechanism which is still considerably decentralised among departments. As a consequence of initial teething troubles with the new Staff Informa-

[6]On 1 January 1958, 257 staff were returned as earning a total of £3,711 during 1957. The following year the number of staff had fallen to 47. The 210 omitted staff were distributed as follows: 184 at £1,323 in Office of Public Works; 11 at £360 Revenue Commissioners; 6 at £184 in Defence; 5 at £142 in Social Welfare and 4 at £176 in the provincial branch of P+T.

tion System (SIS) a break occurred in the time series. In the confusion of the transition period no records of part-time officials were collected between January 1975 and July 1977. No figures of any sort were produced for January 1977. Unfortunately this hiatus occurred in the period just after the Coalition Government introduced its 1975 go-slow on recruitment. The growth in numbers recorded over the period of uncertainty was considerably below that reported in the periods immediately before or after it. The difficulty has been to disentangle a genuine reduction in recruitment from a possible failure to pick up all the staff including the new arrivals.

An element of understatement became increasingly evident in the rapid expansion of the post-July 1977 period. The sheer volume of recruitment and departures made it difficult to keep records up to the minute. Understatement due to this factor was compounded by the fact that departments neither incurred any penalty nor lost out on any gain by neglecting to transmit careful and timely returns to the central co-ordinating agency in the Department of the Public Service. This situation changed dramatically in July 1981 when a fresh ban on recruitment only permitted one vacancy in three to be filled henceforth. It then became in the interest of departments to inflate historic numbers where possible. In the rush to provide maximum returns a gap became apparent between the new figures and the old, suggesting that the earlier returns were understated though the possibilities of overstatement in the new figures could not be ruled out. A Dail statement of 17 December 1981 opted for the former interpretation. "As a result of a special survey of numbers serving made in July 1981 it was found that the figures for previous years (which are compiled from returns by individual Departments and Offices) has been significantly understated".

This study seeks to adjust the figures for such understatements. The nature of the available data means that a two-stage approach must be adopted. At the first stage the understatements for the combined Central Civil Service and the Post Office are estimated. In the second stage the corrections are allocated between the two categories.

Corrections for Understatement

The understatement problems mean that the numbers actually reported as employed on the first working date of January are too low in a particular year. This situation could be remedied if we knew:

(i)   Numbers on the previous January (N_t)
(ii) Numbers recruited during the previous twelve months (R_t)
(iii) Numbers leaving the service during the previous twelve months (D_t)
since

$$N_{t+1} = N_t + R_t - D_t$$

For the purposes of this study it was decided to accept the numbers recorded on January 1975, i.e., before the SIS was launched, and thus, to assume that the major understatements occurred subsequently. Given this benchmark, numbers on each subsequent January could be developed if we knew the flows into and out of the service year by year.

For reasons that are unknown no record of recruitment has been developed on a regular basis. It might be thought that the publishing of statistics by the Civil Service Commission in recent years has altered this situation. Unfortunately these reports only give the numbers offered jobs. This tells us little for a number of reasons: Frequently a candidate would sit for and be offered more than one post. Some offers would be made to personnel already employed in the service. Many offers are rejected since the chosen candidates have found other employment or engaged in study courses by the time the offer was made. These rejections are not recorded. In brief recording levels of actual recruitment is only a very recent phenomenon and associated with the July 1981 brake on expansion in numbers.

Unlike recruitment, records of departures enjoy a long history and this study builds on this fact in tackling the problem of understatement. Not that the records themselves are free of difficulties. Here the problems are, first, that the records only relate to full-time employment. Second, although departures were reported by department, surviving material is frequently in aggregate form without any separate identification of Post Office departures. Third, the records of departures also suffered from the transition to the SIS and are not available for several years after 1974, i.e., when they were most urgently needed.

Recruitment prior to January 1975

The absence of recruitment data prior to January 1975 is not a serious one if we assume that the January counts were accurate and that departures were also accurately recorded. Recruitment is simply the change in numbers over the year plus departures, or in terms of our equation:

$$R_t = N_{t+1} - N_t + D_t$$

Using this formula estimates of recruitment were developed for each year starting with January 1958 and ending with January 1975. The results are shown in Table 6.

The next task is to use these recruitment data to project recruitment for the period of uncertainty which began in January 1975. Here use was made of the fact that the SIS classifies staff by year of recruitment. A printout was obtained of the January 1982 distribution. For each year prior to January 1975 it was now possible to relate numbers of survivors (i.e., currently employed) to the numbers in the original cohort of recruits. The percentages surviving were plotted and

Table 6: *Recorded terminations and implied recruitment of full-time staff in Civil Service (including P+T) 1958–1975*

	Number January 1	Left during year	Recorded increase	Implied recruitment	% of January total	
					Left	Appointed
1958	21,934	1,277	156	1,433	5.8	6.5
1959	23,990	1,370	101	1,471	5.7	6.1
1960	24,091	1,771[a]	-7	1,764	7.4	7.3
1961	24,084	1,396	887	2,283	5.8	9.5
1962	24,971	1,491	791	2,282	6.0	9.1
1963	25,762	1,685	583	2,268	6.5	8.8
1964	26,345	1,721	1,363	3,084	6.5	11.7
1965	27,708	1,777	953	2,730	6.4	9.9
1966	28,661	1,887	442	2,329	6.6	8.1
1967	29,103	1,851	761	2,612	6.4	9.0
1968	29,864	2,069	937	3,006	6.9	10.1
1969	30,801	2,251	1,839	4,090	7.3	13.3
1970	32,640	2,176[b]	1,768	3,944	6.7	12.1
1971	34,408	2,409	1,454	3,863	7.0	11.2
1972	35,862	2,086[c]	2,068	4,154	5.8	11.6
1973	37,930	2,625	3,449	6,074	6.9	16.0
1974	41,379	2,841	2,317	5,158	6.9	12.5
1975	43,696	2,281	1,378	3,659	5.2	8.4

[a]Includes an unusually high level of secondments, 368, perhaps due to the transfer of Broadcasting to RTE (see note 1, Table 13). Had a normal (i.e., average level for 1961–1972 inclusive) number been included the figure would have been 1,422 (a rate of 5.9%).

[b]This was due to an unusually low level of retirements. "Normal" level for 4 years 1968–69, 1971–72 would have made the figure 2,288.

[c]Number leaving for "other reasons" was exceptionally low: 482 below average 1970–74 excluding 1972.

Source: Civil Service Census.

found to be influenced by the time elapsed between the year of recruitment and January 1982. The data are set out in Table 7.

It appeared that there was a more rapid attrition rate from 1982 back to 1967 and a slower one before that. Two linear equations were fitted to the data with 1967 as the point of inflection. Equation one took the form:

$$Y = a - bX$$

where Y is the predicted surviving in January 1982 from an original cohort recruited X years previously. Recruits in 1981 were assumed to have averaged a service of six months by January 1982 and similarly for earlier years. The result obtained was:

% surviving after X years service = 100.5% – 4.57 (X years of service)

Table 7: *Number of full-time staff serving in January 1982 related to the cohort recruited in their year of entry into the Civil Service 1958 to 1974*

Year of entry	Cohort recruited	Still serving in January 1982		% Predicted by regressions
		Number	% of cohort	
1958	1,433	401	28	28
1959	1,471	426	29	29
1960	1,764	582	33	30
1961	2,283	619	27	31
1962	2,282	701	31	32
1963	2,268	759	33	33
1964	3,084	995	32	34
1965	2,730	973	36	35
1966	2,329	898	39	<u>37</u>
1967	2,612	956	37	34
1968	3,006	1,170	39	39
1969	4,090	1,695	41	43
1970	3,944	1,854	47	48
1971	3,863	1,911	49	53
1972	4,154	2,532	61	57
1973	6,074	3,651	60	61
1974	5,158	3,516	68	66

Sources: "Cohort recruited" is from Table 6, i.e., "implied recruitment". Other data from SIS. Predictions refer to regressions given in the text.
Note: Underlining in column shows changeover between regressions.

The r value was 0.974. It was gratifying to find that those just recruited, i.e., with no years service had a predicted survival of 100.5%!

The second equation took the form

$$Y = a + bX$$

where Y predicted the percentage survivors starting from a benchmark in 1957 and adding to it for each year after 1957. The result was:

% surviving in 1982 = 26.4 per cent + 1.143 (year of entry less 1957)

The fit was much poorer (r = 0.74).

The predictions of these equations are given in Table 7 and mapped in Figure 2. Both equations predicted 39 per cent for 1968 which corresponds with the calculated value.

The second equation predicts that about 9 per cent of a cohort will still be in the service after 40 years. There is no way to check this expectation against the facts. As it stands it would imply a recruitment of about 1,640 in 1941.

The essential message in the two equations is that there is a normal tendency

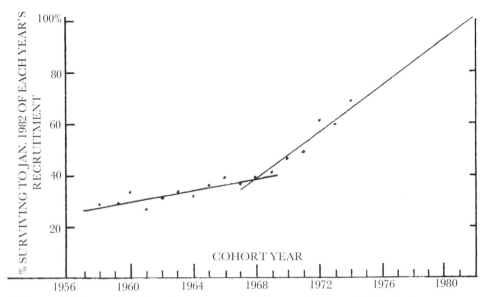

Figure 2: *Regression lines of percentage surviving to January 1982 of each year*

for about 4.6 per cent of a cohort to leave each year for the first decade or more, after which the rate of attrition moderates to about 1.1 per cent annually. Presumably a more sophisticated form of function would combine the two equations into a smooth curve.

As we have seen the first equation predicted no depletion from a cohort just recruited. This was an extrapolation of the data themselves. This result encourages us to believe that estimates from the equation for other years since 1975 are likely to be reasonably close to what actually happened. The value of this finding is that we now both know the number of survivors from each year's cohort and have an estimate of the percentage this represents of the original cohort. From these we can estimate the original cohort. In terms of the last equation the calculation is:

$$\text{total, year of entry} = \frac{\text{currently serving} \times 100}{100 - 4.67 \text{ (years of service)}}$$

In other words, we now have estimates of recruitment for the years of uncertainty after 1975. If we can also estimate departures our problem is solved and a time series of Civil Service numbers can be constructed.

Before taking steps to estimate departures one implication of the above work on recruitment may be noted. An attrition rate of 4.6 per cent per annum from a cohort will reduce it to half its size in little over a decade. This can be confirmed for cohorts where we have estimated their original strength independently from departures and annual change data. For example, there were in early 1982,

1,882 (48 per cent) surviving from a cohort of 3,944 recruited in 1970 and 1,917 (50 per cent) surviving from a cohort of 3,863 recruited in 1971. As a corollary of such a high rate of depletion, existing staff tend to include a large number of young people replacing the losses. This is a topic to which we shall return below.

Departures prior to 1975

Table 6 calculated recorded departures as a percentage of the initial January count. It was noted that special circumstances (e.g., setting up of RTE and the transfer of wireless staff in 1960) influenced the levels in three years 1960, 1970 and 1972 and these observations were excluded. This stratagem did not greatly alter the predictions of the subsequent equation from what it would have otherwise been but it improved the r value. The result was:

Percentage of January count leaving in year = 5.72 + 0.0815 (year – 1957) which had an R^2 of 0.83.

The predictions of this pre-1975 equation were tested against recorded departures for two years in the post-1975 period, i.e., 1978 and 1980. While there is no guarantee that these SIS departures were accurately measured they fit in fairly closely with those expected by applying the departures equation to the under-recorded January numbers of the SIS (i.e., to the numbers we are seeking to adjust). The outcomes were:

	Predicted	Recorded	Interpolated
1978	3,415	3,463	
1979	3,669	—	3,637
1980	3,747	3,811	

All this suggests that the departures equation broadly reflects the long-term trend of departures to rise as a proportion of the January count. This outcome seems to indicate that high intake is accompanied by high outflow, especially in those years when women civil servants were required to resign on marriage.

Calculating the Under-Enumeration

We now have two equations which give us the possibilities of estimating both recruitment and departures. There are two remaining difficulties. The departures equation gives us the general trend. As Table 6 shows, individual years may have special circumstances which cause them to deviate considerably from the trend. For example, 1972 was predicted to have an outflow at a rate of 6.9 per cent whereas recorded departures were only 5.8 per cent. The years of the recruitment go-slow, 1975 to 1977, could have influenced the rate of outflow downwards, as mobility would be expected to be less in a recession. In 1975 the records show 2,281 as leaving against an expected outflow of 3,140. It is difficult to know how to allocate the difference between SIS under-recording of the out-flow and deviations from the trend due to the intake go-slow.

The second difficulty relates to the recruitment side. The value of the recruitment equation depends on the surviving members of each cohort being accurately recorded. Examination of the files indicated that the January 1982 count had to be underestimated by a minimum of 1,327, or 2.2 per cent, to be consistent with the 1983 records. The deficiencies were pinpointed and yielded a total for the Civil Service of 60,166 in January 1982, which was somewhat (0.6 per cent) short of the DPS corrected figure of 60,500 for the same date. Nevertheless, this figure was accepted as a basis for the adjustments. The understatement phenomenon would also impinge on recorded departures. Before discussing this let us examine Table 8 which adjusts the data for understatement. The recorded level of staff on January 1 1982 was 58,839.

Table 8: *A reconstruction of January counts 1975 to 1982 to allow for understatement*

	Total number January 1st			Change during year			DPS adjusted SIS
	Calculated	Recorded SIS	Under-statement	Recruits	Losses	Increase	
1975	46,977	46,977	—	4,143	2,281[a]	1,862	46,977
1976	48,839	48,124	715	2,696	1,710[b]	986	48,372
1977	49,825	na	na	2,951	1,843[b]	1,108	50,000
1978	50,933	48,803	2,130	5,257	3,463[a]	1,794	50,200
1979	52,727	50,005	2,722	5,984	3,637[c]	2,347	52,100
1980	55,074	51,960	3,114	6,904	3,811[a]	3,093	54,900
1981	58,167	56,680	1,487	3,949	1,950[a]	1,999	58,700
1982	60,166	58,839	1,327	—	—	—	60,500

Note: Recruitment calculated from the survivorship equations:
[a] Recorded SIS. [b] This level was assumed to give required outcome. [c] Interpolated.

The 1982 SIS showed that over 45 per cent of these staff, i.e., 27,279, were recruited in the previous seven years. Grossed up, using the recruitment equation, these staff were calculated to be the survivors of the 31,884 staff actually recruited over this interval. Already 4,605 had left. The distribution by year of recruitment is given in Table 8.

In theory, the level of departures should have been calculated using the departures equation especially for the years 1978–1980. There is some doubt whether the equation would hold in years of low recruitment, as is instanced by 1981. Applying the equation to the years 1978 to 1980 would have yielded higher estimates of departures, viz., 3,785, 3,961 and 4,183, respectively. This would have increased aggregate departure rates by 1,048. A study of the files gives the strong impression that such levels were plausible. They would require levels of recruitment higher by 340 in each year to keep the balance right. Such higher levels of intake are also plausible and could even be on the low side. The table does not make these adjustments as there is no firm basis for recalculation, however strong the impression of its correctness might be. For that reason the levels of departure are based on those actually recorded. In the case of 1976 and 1977 the levels chosen are those which would keep the general balance correct. The results do not seem implausible. A separate study now seeks to examine the area of wastage rates in greater detail. The results of that study may enable us to produce more definitive estimates.

Table 8 also gives the adjusted SIS figures produced by the Department of the Public Service for the same years. The greatest discrepancy occurred in 1978 when the DPS estimate was lower than ours by 1.4 per cent. In other years the estimates were closer. It is also likely that the higher DPS figures for recent years are closer to the mark since the adjustments in Table 8 erred on the side of conservatism.

Disaggregation of the Figures Adjusted for Understatement

In theory the same procedure as that used for the global calculations could be used to adjust the figures for the Post Office and other departments separately. However, there was one major deficiency. Pre-1973 departures available to us, do not distinguish those leaving the Post Office from other departures. It was, therefore, necessary to estimate them. Such an eventuality inevitably adds a degree of tentativeness to the entire exercise.

Figures of departures are available for the years 1975, 1978 and July/June 1979/80 distinguishing both sex and department. These figures suggest that sex may be a more important determinant of departure rates than department, viz:

	1975		1978		1979/80	
	Male	*Female*	*Male*	*Female*	*Male*	*Female*
P+T	3.4	7.9	4.8	11.1	3.0	10.0
Other Depts.	3.5	7.0	4.9	11.1	4.5	11.0

It was decided to calculate departure rates, therefore, on the basis of the differing sex composition of the staff in the two groups. Here the Post Office displayed a pattern markedly different to that of the rest of the Civil Service. This was due to the fact that the Engineering branch of the Post Office accounted for a large part of the Department's total, but employed few women. This factor completely swamped the fact that in the smaller headquarters branch the proportion of women was above the average of other departments. Thus, in the last decade the ratio of women to men civil servants outside the Post

Office was 4:5. Inside the Post Office it was 4:12 (or 1:3) and these ratios did not alter much from year to year.

Since we know the sex composition of the two groups we can proceed if we can weight the women by their higher propensity to leave. Departure data by sex are, however, also rare. Apart from the figures cited already the only other record relates to 1957 when women had a proclivity to leave 1.6 times stronger than that of men. By the mid-'seventies this inclination exceeded 2.1 times and was rising. It was probably associated with the higher employment levels of young women and rising marriage rates. As a rule of thumb it was decided to apply ratio factors of 1.7, 1.8 and 1.9 to the periods around 1960, 1965 and 1970, respectively. When these weighted tendencies were applied to the female share of the staff in both groups the expected share of total departures from other departments yielded a figure which did not deviate much from 56 per cent over the entire period in spite of the changing sex composition of the groups. It was now possible to split departures for the pre-1975 period between the two groups. The stage was thus set to apply the methodology used in the previous section.

The data will be given later in the presentation of the time series. From the annual change and the calculated departures, estimates of the implied recruitment were formed. The number of survivors of each cohort still serving in January 1982 was, then, regressed on the estimate of total cohort size and two equations obtained analogous to the post-1967 equation obtained earlier. Predicted percentages of survivors were reduced by 4.91 per cent and 4.46 per cent for each year of service before January 1982, viz:

> Other departments   102.23 – 4.91 (years of service)
> P+T   100.45 – 4.46 (years of service)

R values were 0.972 and 0.901, respectively.

From these equations grossed up estimates of total cohorts were obtained from the information on survivors, as set out in Table 9. The combined results came within 1 per cent of reproducing the figures obtained in Table 8, i.e., before disaggregation. Both series were adjusted to eliminate this shortfall and the adjusted figures are given later in Tables 12 and 15.

The next step was to disaggregate departures between the two groups. The figures available for 1978 and 1980 indicated a split of 58:42 between other departments and the Department of Posts and Telegraphs and this was applied to other years as well. It was now possible to adjust both groups for understatement. To avoid repetition the estimated corrections are not given until we reach Tables 12 and 15. The precision of these figures of course, reflects the outcome of the calculations rather than constituting a claim of absolute accuracy. One attraction of the estimates is that they allocated 70 per cent of the

Table 9: *Estimates of recruitment in the Post Office and Other Departments 1975–1981*

| Cohort | Posts and Telegraphs | | | Other Departments | | | Total Civil Service | |
	Survivors	Predicted %	Grossed up	Survivors	Predicted %	Grossed up	Table 9	Table 8
1975	1,289	71.5	1,803	1,623	70.3	2,309	4,112	4,143
1976	894	76.0	1,177	1,124	75.2	1,494	2,671	2,696
1977	1,004	80.4	1,249	1,340	80.1	1,672	2,921	2,951
1978	1,736	84.9	2,046	2,680	85.0	3,151	5,197	5,257
1979	1,998	89.3	2,237	3,302	90.0	3,670	5,907	5,984
1980	2,806	93.8	2,992	3,624	94.9	3,820	6,812	6,904
1981	1,707	98.2	1,738	2,152	99.8	2,157	3,895	3,949

understatement in both 1980 and 1982 to the Post Office. This is the same proportion as was found in the special survey of late 1981.

Time Series for the Central Civil Service 1922–1985

For convenience and to cater for the differences in data quality the time series for departments other than that of Posts and Telegraphs is presented in three segments. These segments are divided by the reclassification of the Civil Service Census in 1958 and by the need to adjust the post-1975 SIS. Table 10 summarises our knowledge of the first period.

The central Civil Service doubled its employment levels between the foundation of the State and 1950 — an annual compound growth rate of 2.5 per cent compared with 2.2 per cent for the entire 36 years. Between 1922 the build-up of new departments and the expansion of others gave this initial period an above average growth, 2.9 per cent per annum but it is likely that were data available, the growth would be seen to have stopped midway through the decade. This possibility is supported by the decline between 1932 and 1934 and by the trends for all the Civil Service studied earlier. After January 1934 the new industrial and agricultural policy promoted an expansion of 4.8 per cent annually up to the outbreak of World War II. The next decade as a whole witnessed a reduced growth of 1.4 per cent annually but is likely to have contained accelerating growth for the last few years of the decade when social policy was being developed. Continuing such a hypothesised growth, employment levels in 1950 and 1951 experienced an absolute level of increase equal to that of the entire decade previously, or an annual rate of 6.3 per cent. Alarm was felt at such high rates of increase and a special study group met to consider its implication. One of the commentators, Linehan (1954) has provided us with a valuable source of insights into this rising employment. However, even as the group was convened the 1952 crisis halted the expansion and numbers declined on average by 0.6 per cent yearly between 1953 and 1958.

Table 10: *Employment in the central Civil Service 1922–1959*

January	Total	Part time	Whole time	Entered in year still serving Jan '82
1922	6,800(approx)	na	na	—
1932[a]	9,082	na	na	2
1934	8,898	398	8,500	24
1938	10,486	na	na	94
1940	11,760	na	na	62
1950	13,566	526[b]	13,040	260
1951	14,047	629	13,418	190
1952	15,332	607	14,725	200
1953	15,399	585	14,814	120
1954	15,015	555	14,460	112
1955	14,913	729	14,184	209
1956	14,872	725	14,147	194
1957	15,063	738	14,325	193
1958	14,929	734	14,195	243
1958 (revised)	14,481	na	na	243
1959 (revised)	14,551	951	13,600	262

[a]A figure of 10,170 was recorded for 1926 but obviously included industrials.
[b]Interpolated. 424 were recorded in 1949.

It is not possible to comment on increases in part-time employment from 424 in 1949 to 629 in 1951 or again to explain the recovery in this employment during 1954. It is also unfortunate that we do not have revised figures for part-time employment on 1 January 1958. The revisions of that occasion could be expected to reduce part-time employment so that the high level of January 1959 is difficult to account for, unless it is a repeat of the 1954 phenomenon.

The second segment is presented in Table 11 and covers the period between the 1958 reclassification and the introduction of the Staff Information System in 1975. As mentioned in the discussion of sources the reclassification caused a reduction of 448 staff. Of these 206 were to be no longer enumerated since their *annual* remuneration was less than £50. The other 242 continued to be enumerated but no longer as SIS non-industrial Civil Servants. Figures for these reclassified staff are presented later in this study and may be added to the figures in Table 11 should anyone wish for a more continuous series. For details see the previous section.

Table 11 shows a steady decline in part-time employment alongside a steady rise in whole-time employment. The rising trend in recruitment between 1960 and 1973 fits an exponential curve of the form

$$\text{Intake} = 913 \, e^{0.0857 \, (\text{year}-1959)} \qquad R = 0.932$$

Table 11: *Numbers, recruitment and wastage from the central Civil Service 1959–1975*

	January count			Calculated departures whole time	Implied whole-time recruitment	Serving January 1982 recruited in year
	Total	Part time	Whole time			
1959	14,551	951	13,600	605[a]	840	262
1960	14,742	907	13,835	800	878	286
1961	14,817	904	13,913	786	1,419	326
1962	15,425	879	14,546	841	1,169	305
1963	15,751	877	14,874	942	1,203	389
1964	16,004	869	15,135	962	1,584	456
1965	16,617	860	15,757	993	1,598	557
1966	17,218	856	16,362	1,062	1,372	464
1967	17,520	848	16,672	1,037	1,564	474
1968	18,060	861	17,199	1,159	1,596	627
1969	18,475	839	17,636	1,261	1,893	771
1970	19,042	774	18,268	1,219	2,123	964
1971	19,948	776	19,172	1,349	2,431	1,098
1972	20,955	701	20,254	1,168	2,439	1,418
1973	22,189	664	21,525	1,470	3,288	1,925
1974	23,998	656	23,342	1,591	2,579	1,757
1975	24,906	575	24,331	1,292	(2,326)*	1,623

*Recruitment in 1975 is taken from Table 12 since there was no record of whole-time staff in January 1976 to calculate an implied level.
[a]Some records show a different total.

indicating that an average initial intake of 913 in 1960 was increasing at the rate of 8.57 per cent per annum to reach a projected 2,553 by 1972. In fact the rate of increase in 1973 was even higher than projected, i.e., 35 per cent. This rapid rate of inflow caused the newly elected Coalition government to take alarm. Intake was curtailed and a ban on increases imposed in 1975.

The rise in 1964 reflects the feeling that financial constraints were easing after the initial period of the First Programme for Economic Expansion, when constraint had been urged.

The 1973 peak intake of about 3,300 was double that calculated for five years earlier. This was an annual rate of increase of 15.6 per cent and spread fairly evenly over the period. Given that recruitment was rising so fast net gains might have been expected to be larger. However, departures were also rising as a share of the January count, e.g., 5.8 per cent in 1960 and 6.8 per cent in 1973. Some of this trend can be attributed to the increasing share of young women among recruits and rising marriage rates.

Table 11 also gives the numbers from each year's cohort of recruits still serving in January 1982. These figures were used in calculating the regressions detailed in the section on sources.

The final segment relates to the SIS as adjusted for understatement and appears in Table 12. These figures are probably a little on the low side if we accept the adjusted figures of the Department of the Public Service (DPS) as given in Table 8.

Table 12: *Adjusted census data, recruitment and departures 1975–1985 compared with unadjusted SIS figures for central Civil Service*

	Adjusted January count	Estimates for year of		Unadjusted SIS		
		Recruitment	Departures	Total	Part time	Understatement
1975	24,906	2,326	1,323	24,906	575	—
1976	25,909	1,508	992	25,521	na	388
1977	26,425	1,689	1,069	na	na	(745)
1978	27,045	3,187	2,007*	26,114	415	931
1979	28,225	3,718	2,109	27,648	397	577
1980	29,834	3,872	2,231*	28,860	384	974
1981	31,475	2,187	1,131	30,824	276	651
1982	32,531	1,059*	1,610*	32,181†	315	350
1983	31,980	617*	1,191*	31,701†	300	279
1984	31,406	238*	1,140*	31,123†	271	283
1985	30,504			30,241	251	263

Note: There are no DPS adjusted figures comparable with that of Table 8.
*Recorded figures. Understatement in 1977 is a guess. Estimates of recruitment and departures in 1982 and 1983 are not consistent with the unadjusted SIS. †Revised March 1985.

Lower recruitment figures show the effects of the 1975 go-slow and also of the clamp-down of July 1981 after which only one vacancy in three could be filled. The rise in recruitment between January 1978 and July 1981 reflects the efforts made under Fianna Fail Full Employment Programme over that period. Inflows in 1980 reached a new peak. It would appear that in times of reduced inflow, outflow tends to fall in sympathy with it. Perhaps this means that mobility is lower and cutbacks in recruitment more likely when economic conditions are unfavourable. It will be noted that after July 1981 outflows began to exceed inflows so that total levels fell. Unfortunately levels of inflows and outflows since January 1982 appear to be inaccurately recorded.

Table 12 shows a continuous fall in part-time numbers.[7] This would appear to be connected to the tendency to engage cleaning contractors in many of the newer Government offices rather than employing staff directly.

[7] 1981 appears to be miscalculated as it is out of line with the trend.

Time Series for the Department of Posts and Telegraphs 1922–1985

The earlier discussion on sources found that the Post Office had to be discussed at the same time as other departments. It is, therefore, appropriate that a parallel series of tables for the Post Office be provided at this juncture. This series is given in Table 13.

Table 13: *Employment in the Post Office 1922–1959*

January	Total	Part time	Whole time	Wireless	Entered in year still serving Jan. 1982
1922[a]	13,500 approx.	na	na	na	1
1926[a]	12,715	na	na	na	1
1932[a]	11,316	na	na	31	14
1934	10,720	5,705	5,015	na	35
1938	12,269	na	na	83	81
1940	11,285	na	na	61	40
1950	14,374	5,657[b]	8,717	205	292
1951	14,795	5,551	9,244	210	230
1952	15,175	5,483	9,692	229	357
1953	15,650	5,395	10,255	252	210
1954	15,793	5,370	10,423	311	122
1955	15,630	5,326	10,304	326	129
1956	15,562	5,266	10,296	334	141
1957	15,494	5,229	10,265	338	157
1958	15,166	5,215	9,951	349	173
1958 (revised)	13,053	3,102(est)	9,951	349	173
1959	13,117	3,098	10,019	—	185

Note 1: Wireless was part of Posts and Telegraphs over this period. It is not included, however, in the total.

Note 2: The 1958 "reduction" in part-time employment was due to a reclassification of 2,109 managers of sub-post offices and their transfer to separate returns. cf. Table 39.

[a]Total Post Office including industrials given for 1922 and 1926. In 1932 the comparable figure would be 11,957. [b]Interpolated: 5,763 were recorded in 1949.

Since the wireless section of the Post Office was destined to become Radio Eireann the employment in this section is not included in the total.

After Independence employment in the Post Office was pruned so that about 1,600 jobs were shed in the first decade. Expansion resumed after 1934 and peaked two decades later. This expansion was confined to whole-time personnel. In 1934 part-time staff outnumbered whole time. In the two decades the latter doubled while part-time numbers contracted somewhat. Traditionally (e.g., in 1940 and in 1975) five out of six of all staff were in the grades covering postmen, sorters and counter clerks so that the total included a much smaller proportion of the higher paid posts compared with the generality of the Civil Service.

The figures for survivors provide a crude barometer of recruitment policy. Compared with 1938, 1940 had low intake. This was also true of 1951 compared with its neighbours. Cutbacks were imposed in 1953 and again in 1954. Intake over the remainder of the 'fifties never reached even half the 1952 level when allowance is made for length of service.

The 1958 reclassification had considerable impact on recorded staff levels. While the exact reduction is not known since the revised 1958 figures are not divided between whole time and part time, the estimate in Table 13 is fairly accurate. Four staff were no longer recorded since their annual income was below £50. The 2,109 managers of sub-post offices, who were paid on a fee scale basis, were no longer deemed to be part-time staff and transferred to a separate census for "Non-industrial staff not in the Civil Service Census". Subsequent trends in their numbers will be given later in this study.

Table 14 records the 1959 to 1975 segment of the time series. From 1960 to 1975 whole-time staff numbers expanded continuously and virtually doubled

Table 14: *Numbers, recruitment and wastage from the Post Office 1959–1975*

	Total	January count Part time	Whole time	Calculated departures whole time	Implied whole time recruitment	Serving Jan. 1982, recruited in year
1959	13,117	3,098	10,019	765[a]	630	196
1960	12,994	3,110	9,884	622	909	338
1961	13,264	3,093	10,171	610	864	350
1962	13,485	3,060	10,425	650	1,113	431
1963	13,977	3,089	10,888	743	1,065	419
1964	14,379	3,169	11,210	759	1,500	579
1965	15,058	3,107	11,951	784	1,132	444
1966	15,391	3,092	12,299	825	957	476
1967	15,445	3,014	12,431	814	1,048	508
1968	15,629	2,964	12,665	910	1,410	566
1969	16,031	2,866	13,165	990	2,197	957
1970	17,208	2,836	14,372	957	1,821	918
1971	18,071	2,835	15,236	1,060	1,432	819
1972	18,409	2,801	15,608	918	1,715	1,111
1973	19,151	2,746	16,408	1,155	2,786	1,728
1974	20,751	2,715	18,036	1,250	2,579	1,826
1975	22,071	2,706	19,365	958	(1,817)	1,289

Note: Recruitment in 1975 is from Table 5 since the 1976 Census was inadequate for calculating implied recruitment.

while part-time numbers contracted after January 1964. The latter's share fell from 23.9 per cent in 1960 to 9.4 per cent in 1975. Inflows over the period tended to be more erratic than for other departments. Large intakes occurred in 1964, 1969 and 1973. Considerably less recruitment occurred in 1961, 1966, 1971 and 1975. The reasons for these fluctuations are not apparent.

The final segment of the time series takes us up to 1984 and is set out in Table 15.

Table 15: *Adjusted census data recruitment and departures 1975–1985 compared with unadjusted SIS figures from the Post Office*

	Adjusted January count	Estimates for year of		Unadjusted SIS		
		Recruitment	Departures	Total	Part time	Understatement
1975	22,071	1,817	958	22,071	2,706	—
1976	22,930	1,188	718	22,603	na	327
1977	23,400	1,262	774	na	na	(859)
1978	23,888	2,070	1,456*	22,689	2,432	1,199
1979	24,502	2,266	1,528	22,574	2,276	1,928
1980	25,240	3,032	1,580*	23,100	2,238	2,140
1981	26,692	1,762	819	25,856	2,048	836
1982	27,635	659*	970*	26,687	2,022	948
1983	27,324	428*	880*	26,855	1,977	469
1984	26,872	na	na	26,605	1,767	267
1985†				26,282†	1,372	

Note: There are no DPS adjusted figures comparable with those of Table 3
*Recorded figures. Understatement in 1977 is a guess.
†On January 1 1984, Telecom Eireann and An Post took over the relevant staff except for a few officials incorporated in the new Department of Communications.

The Consequences of Rapid Growth

The last sections showed the rapid growth in staff numbers in the most recent decade and a half. As a consequence there was an increase in the proportion of staff whose appointment was of recent origin. Since there are upper limits on the age of recruitment, a corollary of large numbers of recent appointments is a lowering of the average age and an increase in the numbers of young people. Typically women enter the service at younger ages than men and thereafter are also more prone to leave again. Thus a more youthful staff implies a greater chance that the share of women in the total will rise. A greater share of young women raises the average departure rate expressed as a proportion of the January count. We have already seen such a rise. Higher departure rates increase the need for recruitment to fill the vacancies unless a policy of retrenchment is in vogue when an opposite circle of causation might take over. The following sections of this paper will examine these trends in turn.

Duration of Service in the Central Civil Service

Table A2.2 in the Appendix gives annual details of the number of people serving on the first of January 1982 who joined the service in each year since 1961 and gives five year totals for those who were recruited earlier. To facilitate comprehension of the data cumulative totals are also given. The figures also distinguish by sex.

The total number of men in the central group was 17,721 or almost 3,300 more than the total for women (14,431). However, those who joined in 1965 or afterwards were equally divided between women 12,801 and men 12,860. The greater number of men was due to their predominance in the long serving cohorts. In the nine most recent years women in each cohort were (with one exception, 1978) more numerous than men. Earlier than that the scales were tilted in the other direction for those still serving in 1982 so that by the 1965 cohort the cumulative totals were equal.

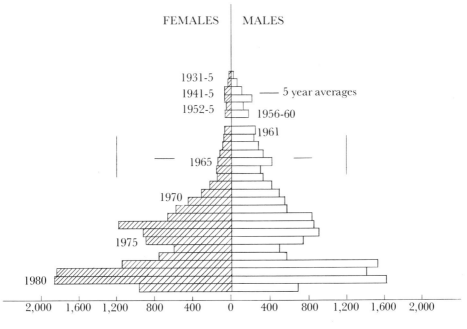

Figure 3: *Numbers of staff in central Civil Service serving in January 1982 classified by sex and year of recruitment.*

Figure 3 captures the material in the form of a pyramid in which the cutbacks after 1973 and 1980 are clearly visible. The greater numbers of women among recent entrants is also apparent as is their poorer representation prior to 1965.

Another way to highlight the recent origins of the staff is to calculate the dates after which each quartile arrived. (The calculations assume equal distribution of recruitment over the months of each year.)

Date after which the share of survivors was recruited	Female	Max. length of service (years)	Male	Max. length of service (years)
Last quarter of staff	24 July 1979	2.4	18 July 1978	3.5
Last half of staff	3 Dec. 1975	6.1	1 Jan. 1973	9.0
Last three-quarters of staff	18 Dec. 1971	10.0	15 Sept. 1963	18.3
All Staff	1 Jan. 1931	51.0	1 Jan. 1925	57.0

In other words, almost half the women had served less than six years and three-quarters less than ten years. The figures for men were not as concentrated. Half the men had served less than nine years in a service where at least 40 years' service was possible. However, a quarter of the men served more than 18 years but, as Table A2.2 shows, only 10 per cent of the women. These data are shown graphically in Figure 4.

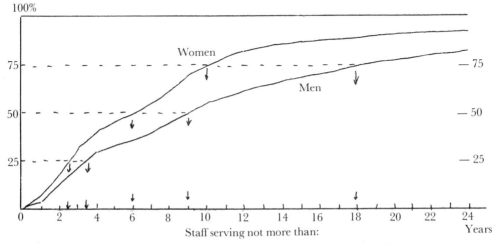

Figure 4: *Cumulative distribution of staff serving in the central Civil Service in January 1982 by years of service*

Duration of Service in the Post Office

Similar calculations for the Post Office are detailed in Appendix Table A2.3 and modelled in Figure 5. Compared to the profile for the central Civil Service,

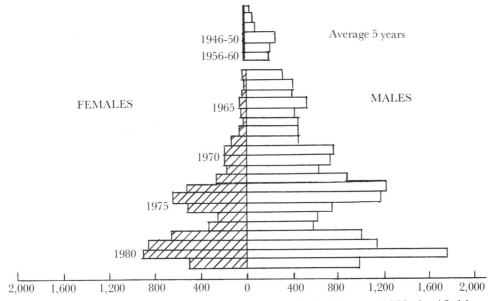

Figure 5: *Number of staff in the Post Office serving in January 1982 classified by sex and year of recruitment*

that for the Post Office shows a much lower intake of women and fewer survivors from earlier decades. Numbers of men in the Post Office, whose appointment was prior to 1970, form a large cohort and display less of the gradual attrition observed for similar men in the central Civil Service. The figure shows the effects of the 1975 and 1981 bans, as well as the cutback of the 'fifties.

If the staff are divided into quartiles on the basis of duration of service the cut-off dates for each quartile would be:

	Female	*Male*
1st quartile	3 September 1979	10 October 1977
2nd quartile	12 July 1976	28 February 1972
3rd quartile	17 March 1973	11 January 1963
4th quartile	1 January 1931	1 January 1922

Women in the Post Office were more recently appointed than those in the central Civil Service. Three-quarters of them had less than nine years' service on 1 January, 1982, whereas the cut-off point for the central group was 15 months more. In spite of the large increase in intake in 1980 Post Office men in each quartile were longer serving than men in the central Civil Service with the cut-off points being generally nine months more. Half the men in the Post Office had more than a year's longer service than three-quarters of the women but even so served less than ten years.

The Share of Youth in Employment

Given the upper age limit on recruitment a period of rapid staff increase can be expected to increase the share of youth in overall employment. Table A2.4 in the Appendix gives the end result of this process when it analyses the age distribution of the central Civil Service by sex as recorded in September 1982. Figure 6 drawn from these data, demonstrates the bottom-heavy nature of the age pyramid and also indicates the contrast between the sexes. Almost half the women were under 25 years of age and only one in six over 35 years old. Thus the median age for women was under 26 compared with 34 years for men. Three times as many men (48 per cent) were over 35 compared to the proportion of women.

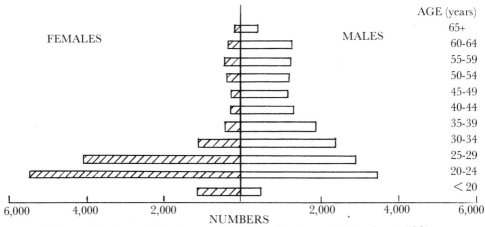

Figure 6: *Age profile of central Civil Service by sex (September, 1982)*

The pyramid shows that the smallest cohort for men in the age groups 20 to 64 occurs in the 45 to 49 age group. These would be the survivors of those seeking employment in the early 1950s. This was a time of low levels of recruitment. The larger size of the cohorts above this level may also be due in part to smaller wastage rates after recruitment during the war and post-war years when job opportunities outside the service were fewer. It also reflects the greater intake which occurred up to the end of 1952.

Another feature of the pyramid reflects the dramatic way that women departing have cut into the profile of female Civil Servants 30 years of age and older. The typical pattern for women seems to be to join in large numbers as clerical assistants but to leave again in considerable numbers as increasing family responsibilities weaken the attraction of humdrum clerical work. The high turnover of women does not, therefore, offer great scope for reductions by natural wastage since these clerical posts will continue to need staff. High intake, on the other hand, may not be such a threat for the future since, on past performance, a large number will be gone again within a few years.

Turning now to the Department of Posts and Telegraphs its major difference compared with the rest of the Civil Service in 1982 lay in the greater male share in its staff. Even though the proportion of females was increasing over time, e.g., from 17 per cent in 1960, it was still only 25 per cent in 1980. As a result the sex age profile was considerably different.

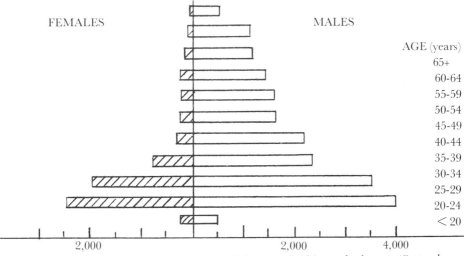

Figure 7: *Age profile of the Department of Posts and Telegraphs by sex (September, 1982)*

Compared to Figure 6 for the central Civil Service, Figure 7 shows much fewer females in the twenties age groups. In general there were more men employed in each age group in the Post Office compared with the central Civil Service even though total employment in the Post Office was lower. Under the age of thirty there were seven men to every four women. In the older age groups the predominance was much greater: sixteen men to every three women. This was in marked contrast to the situation in the central Civil Service where there were 50 per cent more women than men under the age of thirty; as many women as men under the age of 45 and three times more men than women over the age of thirty (see Appendix Table A2.4).

The situation in 1982 is the culmination of a long process promoted by rapid expansion. Table 16 takes a look at the growth in the share of staff under 21 years

Table 16: *Female and juvenile staff in non-industrial Civil Service (including P+T)*
1958 to 1985

January 1	All females				Staff under 21 years old				Females	Males
	All Depts.	% of staff	Central group	% of staff	Total	% of all staff	of which females	Females % under 21	% under 21 years	
1958	na	na	na	na	1,746	6	923	53	na	na
1959	7,364	26	na	na	1,782	6	1,005	56	14	4
1960	7,700	27	5,468	37	na	na	na	na	na	na
1961	7,673	27	5,356	36	2,386	8	1,457	61	19	5
1962	8,195	28	na	na	2,963	10	1,879	63	23	5
1963	8,647	29	6,051	38	3,322	11	2,161	65	25	6
1964	8,966	30	6,296	39	3,458	11	2,202	64	25	6
1965	9,592	30	6,696	40	4,084	13	2,538	62	26	7
1966	9,992	31	6,992	41	4,334	13	2,647	61	26	8
1967	10,109	31	7,186	41	4,208	13	2,516	60	25	7
1968	10,475	31	7,476	41	4,381	13	2,733	62	26	7
1969	10,912	32	7,665	41	4,651	13	2,970	64	27	7
1970	11,709	32	7,971	42	5,582	15	3,689	66	32	8
1971	12,533	33	8,532	43	6,347	17	4,247	67	34	8
1972	13,192	34	9,115	43	6,771	17	4,640	69	35	8
1973	13,954	34	na	na	7,327	18	4,943	67	35	9
1974	15,833	35	10,963	46	8,649	19	5,809	67	37	10
1975	16,820	36	11,312	45	8,517	18	5,492	64	33	10
1976	17,479	36	11,688	46	—	—	—	—	—	—
1977*	17,675	36	11,894	46	—	—	—	—	—	—
1978	17,727	36	12,040	46	—	—	—	—	—	—
1979	17,864	36	12,189	44	—	—	—	—	—	—
1980	18,596	36	12,870	45	—	—	—	—	—	—
1981	20,325	36	13,718	45	—	—	—	—	—	—
1982	21,252	36	14,431	45	—	—	—	—	—	—
1983	20,913	36	14,157	44	—	—	—	—	—	—
1984	20,126	35	13,767	43	—	—	—	—	—	—
1985	na	na	13,088	43	—	—	—	—	—	—

Note: "All Departments" include the former Department of Posts and Telegraphs which is omitted
from the "Central Group".
'—' means 'not recorded on previous basis'.
*July.

of age, or juveniles as they were formerly called. In the 1958 to 1974 period the
number of young people in all departments increased five-fold, from 1,746 to
8,649. Such a rapid growth increased their share of all staff, from 6 per cent to 19
per cent. Among female staff alone the share under 21 increased from 14 per cent
to 37 per cent. In the male camp, youths added to their share, going from 4 per
cent to 10 per cent. In this evolution girls increased their representation in the

under 21 group from 53 per cent in 1958 to 65 per cent in 1963. After a retreat to 60 per cent by 1967 a fresh increase brought their share to a peak of 69 per cent in 1972. The second trough had set in and the share fallen to 64 per cent when, with the transition to the SIS, this form of statistics was discontinued in its traditional form.

The Share of Women in Employment

Table 17 shows the continuous rise in numbers (apart from 1950) up to 1953 and a decline thereafter. The drop in women's share of total employment in 1952 was due to the transfer of 1,828 non-professionals in the engineering branch of the Post Office from being industrials. Excluding this all male transfer their share would have risen to 31.4 per cent.

Table 17 also gives the situation excluding scale-paid managers of sub-post offices since these staff were excluded in the 1958 reclassification. If we allow for

Table 17: *Number of women in the non-industrial Civil Service, selected years, 1927 to 1958 and their share of total employment (also excluding scale paid sub-post office mistresses) and of the central Civil Service*

| | | | Excluding scale paid sub-post office mistresses | | | |
| | | | | | Central Civil Service | |
January	Total number	Share of total	Total number	Share of total	Total number	Share of total
1927	4,355	22	—	—	—	—
1931	4,427	23	—	—	—	—
1932	4,597	23	3,433	19	2,127	27
1934	4,859	25	—	—	2,425	27
1935	5,449	26	—	—	—	—
1938	6,225	27	5,021	24	—	—
1940	6,410	28	—	—	3,774	32
1946	7,627	29	6,379	27	—	—
1947	7,766	30	—	—	—	—
1948	8,128	30	6,873	27	—	—
1949	8,488	30	7,217	28	—	—
1950	8,478	30	7,205	28	4,960	37
1951	8,811	30	7,510	28	5,255	37
1952	9,067	29	7,762	27	5,370	35
1953	9,226	29	7,930	27	5,427	35
1954	9,058	29	7,756	27	5,259	35
1955	8,802	29	7,497	26	5,082	34
1956	8,705	28	7,401	26	5,032	34
1957	8,790	28	7,483	26	5,143	34
1958	8,703	29	—	—	5,099	34

'—' means 'not now available'.

the transfer in 1952, the share held by women rose to 29 per cent on 1 January 1952 and subsequently declined. This phenomenon reflects the fact that women are more volatile staff members and large recruitments are necessary to replace large-scale departures. In a period of retrenchment, such as the post-1952 period, women are more likely to suffer than men. A similar experience can be seen at work in the recent 1981 clampdown.

Table 16 continues the picture starting from after the 1958 reclassification and giving more complete details of women in the central Civil Service up to 1985. By subtraction numbers of women in the Post Office can be determined. Between 1959 and 1982 total numbers almost trebled, going from 7,364 to 21,252. This represented an initial gain in employment share, which rose from 26 per cent in 1959 to 36 per cent in 1975. After this no gains or losses in share were made so that 36 per cent seemed to represent a steady state level for women, until the recruitment restrictions hit their chances disproportionately.

A parellel phenomenon was observed for the share held by women in the central Civil Service alone. Their share was between 36 and 37 per cent at the outset of the 'sixties and reached 46 per cent by 1974. After this a level of 46 per cent held for a few years and then a tendency to decline became apparent. This could, possibly, be partly due to the understatement in numbers affecting recorded female employment more than male. For example, 62 per cent of the understatement identified in recorded recruitment for 1981 related to girls omitted since girls made up 59 per cent of newcomers in that year. In other words, shortfalls in recent records are likely to understate women's position more than their share of total staff would suggest.

The recent tendency for women's share to fall may also reflect the uneven impact of the 1981 recruitment embargo on women. This embargo only permits one vacancy in three to be filled. Since women typically are much more prone to quit the Service, the greater outflow of women reduces their total and is not replaced by a corresponding inflow. Men are not subject to this outcome to the same extent. Thus in the central Civil Service the absolute number of women fell since 1982 but that for men rose slightly. Even before this the rate of increase of men — 30 per cent between January 1975 and 1982 — was greater. Add in 1982 to 1984 and the disparity became all the greater: 32 per cent vs. 22 per cent.

Since the increase up to 1983 for women in all departments was broadly the same as that for men, the Post Office experience had to differ from that of the central Civil Service, as indeed it does. Between 1975 and 1982 numbers of women increased 24 per cent while those for men by only 20 per cent. After 1982 these long-term rates in the Post Office reversed dramatically when absolute numbers of men rose 2 per cent those for women fell 7 per cent. The 1975–1984 rates were, therefore, 22 per cent for men and 16 per cent for women. Women are relatively much fewer, of course, in the Post Office.

The fact that the overall share of posts held by women stabilised at 36 per cent up to 1983 meant that the net additions to the women's group grew at about the same rate each year as did the net additions to the male workforce, i.e., 24 to 25 per cent. The significance of this finding is that the share of women in annual intake had to approximate the share of women in annual outflow. Since we know that women are more than twice as prone to leave as men they must be twice as likely to be offered and accept jobs in the Civil Service. One piece of evidence in this regard relates to the numbers of the central Civil Service staff who joined in 1981 who were still serving in January 1982. The 1,271 women represented 9.3 per cent of the initial January 1981 stock while the 881 men represented 5.2 per cent of the initial stock of men. Some 97 (at least) of the women had already left compared with 41 men, suggesting intakes of 10.0 per cent and 5.4 per cent, respectively. The figures for the Post Office were less convincing, 8.3 per cent vs. 6.1 per cent but the deficiency may be due to understatement. Before considering further how to use these insights to measure recruitment by sex it is necessary to look at the rates of outflow.

Wastage Rates among Women

Very little of the recorded data on departures gives a breakdown by sex. This was not true of the pre-1958 period when, unfortunately, other difficulties intervened. Such data as are available, are given in Appendix Table A2.5. The first difficulty is that departures were classified in four batches: (1) Full staff including industrials; (2) Part-time staff; (3) Casual staff excluding those employed by the Departments of Lands and of Posts and Telegraphs for whom individual records were not kept, and (4) Secondments. These were not categories for which total staff numbers were always available by which to calculate rates. However, taking terminations on a global basis the figures for 1953 and 1958 put female departures 1.3 times higher than those for men. The second problem with these data was that they refer to a period of retrenchment when departure rates would appear to be atypical of normal rates.

After 1958 and up to 1975 terminations were not classified by sex but rather by reasons for leaving. This in itself was a rather inadequate classification in which about half those leaving were recorded as going for "other" reasons. In the period up to 1973, when a marriage bar required women to relinquish their post on marriage, those who gave "marriage" as the reason for leaving were clearly women. The trend in this factor is given in the Appendix in Table A2.5 and shows that rising marriage rates in society in general since the early 'sixties were mirrored in the Civil Service. Marriage as a reason for leaving rose from 18 per cent in 1960 to double that share in 1972. The abolition of the bar caused marriage as a reason to plummet — from 36 per cent in 1972 to 25 per cent and 17 per cent in the next two years. However, as we shall see, the abolition of the bar did not reduce the relative propensity of women to leave. Departures presumably were in most cases merely deferred until family responsibilities made home life appear more attractive to many women.[8] The abolition of the marriage bar did not increase women's share of total employment, which stabilised at 36 per cent shortly afterwards (or 45 per cent in the central Civil Service).

Marriage was not the only reason for women leaving before the repeal of the bar though, in 1957 for example, 52 per cent of those leaving gave it as their reason.[9] When marriage as a reason is excluded women showed a lower propensity to leave than men for most specified reasons. The reasons given, excluding marriage, were distributed as follows:

	Men	*Women*
Death	14%	5%
Retirement	23%	23%
Discharged/Dismissed	24%	9%
Secondment/Religious vocations	1%	8%
Other	39%	54%

During 1957, 611 women and 1,049 men left or were seconded from the whole-time group including industrials. These were rates of 8.3 per cent and 5.2 per cent, respectively, or a ratio of 1.6 to 1 in favour of women.

No usable data were available for the period 1958 to 1975. Instead an attempt was made to determine the influence of the rising share of women in this period (see Table 16) on the overall departure rate (see Table 6). A regression of these data gave the following result:

Predicted Departure Rate (y) = 4.06 + 0.079 Percentage of Women

indicating that an all-male Civil Service would have a departure rate of about 4 per cent annually, whereas each percentage share of women in the staff would increase the rate of departure by just under 0.08 per cent. For example, predicted departure rates for a 20 per cent and a 40 per cent share would be 5.6 per cent and 7.2 per cent, respectively. While the result seems very plausible the R value was low: 0.393.

It would be expected that computerisation of the SIS in 1975 would have aided the analysis of departures. Unfortunately the three years for which analyses were available contained two that were unrepresentative in that

[8]Married women had to leave within a specified period after marriage if they wished to obtain a marriage gratuity.

[9]It is interesting to discover that one in every four of these did not wait to qualify for a marriage gratuity.

departure levels were considerably below trend, i.e., 1975 and the year July to June 1979/80. The other year, 1978, was more typical. Table 18 gives details for the central Civil Service.

Table 18: *Relative propensities of males and females to leave the central Civil Service in the late 'seventies*

| | Males | | Females | | Ratio of | Both Sexes | |
	Number	%	Number	%	rates	Average rate	% Female
1975	472	3.5	790	7.0	2.0	5.0	45
1978	683	4.9	1,324	11.1	2.3	7.8	46
1979	722	4.5	1,418	11.0	2.4	7.4	45

Although women were only four out of every nine staff over this period the number of them leaving was higher and their rate of departure was at least twice as high as for men. Because of the relative stability of the sex composition of the central Civil Service since 1975, it would seem reasonable to posit that recruitment of girls was at a very minimum about 60 per cent higher than recruitment of young men over this period. Further work is necessary to arrive at closer estimates. Thus a ban on recruitment is likely to hit female job opportunities more than those of males even if there is no bias in a period of retrenchment in favour of young men.

Part of the reason why so many girls leave may be due to their greater tendency to accept posts, such as those of typist and clerical assistant, for which boys did not generally compete and which were often better paid outside the Civil Service. Noirín O'Broin and Gillian Farren (1978) have recorded the dissatisfactions of Civil Service typists whose high rates of turnover led to the commissioning of their study. If girls enter in large numbers at these levels their chances of becoming career Civil Servants seem very limited even if their length of service were to become longer than it normally is. Women who enter as executive officers or higher can be expected to do better. Some tentative figures indicate that this is happening, albeit slowly.

Women in Senior Posts

After the abolition of the marriage bar in the early 'seventies women Civil Servants were eligible to continue in full-time employment after marriage. As promotion is generally closely related to seniority, the longer duration of female employment could be expected to influence the seniority of positions held by women. Table A2.6 in the Appendix sets out for some of the main General Service and Finance Grades in all departments, the numbers of males and females in administrative and clerical grades in 1932, 1972 and July 1982. This material can be analysed in two ways (a) the percentage of holders of a particular grade position who are female, and (b) the percentage of all females that hold that particular grade position. Both of these approaches are adopted in Table 19.

Table 19: *Proportion of each grade held by women and distribution of women Civil Servants by grade 1932, 1972 and 1982 (July) for Selected General Service grades*

	% of Grade held by Females			% of all Females in grade		
	1932	1972	1982	1932	1972	1982
Secretaries	Nil	Nil	2	Nil	Nil	Neg.
Principal Officer	Nil	1	3	Nil	Neg.	0.1
Assistant Principal Officer	Nil	4	25	Nil	0.2	1.6
Administrative Officer	12	17	30	0.2	0.2	0.4
Higher Executive Officer	1	13	35	0.1	1.1	3.8
Executive Officer	2	41	42	0.5	6.2	7.3
Staff Officer	13	60	61	1.5	4.1	4.9
Clerical Officer	17	63	65	21.5	14.9	18.8
Clerical Assistant	78	99	85	76.3	73.2	63.2

Neg. = negligible
Secretaries include deputy and assistant.

The vast majority of women have always been employed in the clerical assistant and clerical officer grades. Table 19 shows that in 1932, 98 per cent were so engaged. Fifty years later the share had dropped to 82 per cent. These grades are for clerks and for typists especially. Table 19 also shows that the share of all women who were in the lower post, i.e., the Clerical Assistant grade fell from 73 per cent to 63 per cent in the last decade. With the release of women from this lowest grade a very much improved distribution was developed. This can be seen as the number of all women who held higher posts improved between 1972 and 1982. Representation at Secretary and Principal Officer level is small but growing. The 25 per cent share of Assistant Principal posts and the 35 per cent of Higher Executive Officers are significant advances and probably entail a larger share than would be expected from the size of the population of long-serving women Civil Servants. Already in 1972, Executive, Staff and Clerical Officer posts had ceased to be the preserve of men which they were in the early 'thirties. The figures for Clerical Assistants in 1972 are a little uncertain as most males in the general group of grades were coded as "other" or miscellaneous (see Table A2.6).

The second half of Table 19 relates the grades to the population of females enumerated in the Appendix table. The reference group would be the distribution of males by grade. However, the huge number of female Clerical Assistants swamps all efforts at comparisons. If the distribution of males by grade is studied for 1972 and again for 1982 the two distributions are similar when Clerical Assistants are omitted. If a similar exercise is applied to women the incipient converging of the distribution of women by grade to that held by men can be seen in Table 20.

Table 20: *Changes in the distribution of women among specified general service grades in 1972 and 1982*

	Distribution by grade (excluding Clerical Assistants)		
	Men 1982	Women 1982	Women 1972
	%	%	%
Secretaries	2.1	0.04	Nil
Principal Officers	6.8	0.2	0.04
Assistant Principals	12.4	4.4	0.8
Administrative and Higher Executive Officers	20.2	11.5	4.9
Executive Officers	25.7	19.7	23.0
Staff and Clerical Officers	32.7	64.2	71.2
	100.0	100.0	100.0

As laid out above the pyramidal structure for males is fairly regular and even with each layer broadly in proportion to that above and below it. In 1972 the female pyramid could hardly be called a pyramid at all being virtually made up of the lowest two layers. Over the decade this structure changed as the base contracted and the upper layers came to fill out and height was added. A continuation of this trend over time, especially if accompanied by longer duration of service, could well reproduce the situation characterising teaching whereby merit criteria at entry and at promotion have produced a predominance of women. To test whether there is, in fact, equal opportunity in the Civil Service at present it would be necessary to classify staff by duration of employment and post first held.

In the schema above, Executive and Administrative Officers represent the basic career grades for those entering with Leaving Certificate and University degrees respectively.It will be noted that the above discussion focuses on that subset of Civil Servants who belong to "general service grades", i.e., grades common to several departments. It excludes grades such as professionals, checkers (called the Inspectorate) etc. The meaning of these grades is examined in a later section. If a pyramid was developed for all grades the position of women might not appear so unfavourable since in the Post Office, for example, there were large numbers of men, e.g., postmen, in low paid posts. However, the total also excluded female Clerical Assistants who made up 63 per cent of all women in 1982 (see Table 19).

The Grade Approach – General Service Grades

In the last section there was a suggestion that it would be useful to develop seniority pyramids for the entire Civil Service, distinguishing holders by sex. The difficulty with such an approach is the enormous number of grades in the Civil Service and the problems of equating the grades with each other. There are reported to be about 3,500 grades with different starting and maximum salaries, different numbers of increments and different titles. One dichotomy applied to this great heterogeneity is to distinguish general service grades, which are grades common to two or more departments, and departmental grades which are department specific. Since there are only a few dozen general service grades this core group is useful in that it enables analysis to focus on a small subset of grades, which none the less are representative, and comprised, for example, 36 per cent of the entire Civil Service in 1982. They form a much higher share of the central Civil Service, e.g., 56 per cent in January 1984, since the Post Office employs few staff in general service grades. Thus the opportunity to select a few grades with a higher degree of representativeness facilitates the study of salary trends over time. This representativeness is enhanced since many departmental grades use the general service grades as a point of reference.

Historically the division of posts into general service and departmental appears to have related to the career opportunities of the posts. The former permitted staff to be transferred throughout the Civil Service, and as such helps to establish the degree of flexibility, for example, within the Civil Service scheme of department restructuring. Those in many departmental grades tended to find their career prospects within the department itself. For several departmental grades this distinction seems less relevant today; for others, such as those in the Revenue Commissioners, the distinction has retained its pristine validity.

In some cases a departmental grade is identical with a general service grade apart from the title. For example, the Revenue Commissioners employ the Accountant General of Revenue and the Superintending Inspectors of Taxes. Both of these posts are equivalent to that of Assistant Secretary in the General Service. These Revenue grades are treated as "analogous to that of Assistant Secretary" and as such are included in a grade grouping "Administrative and Executive" which we shall study later.

A different situation arises where a professional qualification is required for a post. The Inspector of Mental Hospitals in the Department of Health has a rank analogous to that of Assistant Secretary but since his job requires a medical degree the post is not grouped in the Administrative and Executive category but with the Professional, Scientific and Technical category. The distinction is not always clear cut especially where similar posts are held by administrative and professional personnel. Thus some posts of Accountant, Welfare Officer, etc., are classified one way, others with the same title another way. Should a professional hold an administrative post, e.g., a doctor as Secretary of the Department of Health, the post is deemed administrative since the degree is not a *sine qua non*. Ideally it would be useful to equate all grades and reduce their number but this study makes only a small contribution in this regard. An indication of numbers in general service grades in recent years is given in Table 21.

Grade Groups

As hinted in the last section there is an alternative method of categorising grades. The traditional approach recognised eight broad categories, of which one group comprises industrial civil servants. The remaining seven groups were divided into 87 coded grades or grade groups in, for example, the *Annexures to Circular No. 46/33* issued by the Department of Finance in December 1933. Subsequently the number of grades was altered several times, for example as we have seen in 1952 and 1958, but the broad principles remained up to the computerisation of the SIS in 1975 when computer flexibility permitted a much greater variety of codes. Looking back on the grade groups, which persist in modified form today, it is not clear to an outside observer what function these groups served but this study will not seek to suggest any different structures. The account will follow the traditional approach.

Definitions of Grade Groups

The classification as originally coded was as follows:

I — *Administrative and Executive:*
This group covers all higher-grade officers and officers of the general Administrative and Executive grades and corresponding grades.

In practice this group includes all those career Civil Servants who would normally enter public service as Executive Officers after high performance in the Leaving Certificate examination or as Administrative Officers after obtaining a University degree. Some would enter these grades by promotion from lower grades. The more senior posts include in ascending order: Higher Executive Officers, Assistant Principal and Principal Officers, Accountants so called,[10] Commissioners, Secretaries, Deputy and Assistant Secretaries as well as a group

[10]That is a title of a post, not an indication of professional qualifications.

Table 21: *Numbers in the main grades in the general service, selected years (January) 1976 to 1984 (excluding finance grades)*

	1976	1977	1978	1979	1980	1984
Secretary	10	10	10	12	12	16
Deputy Secretary	5	10	12	13	12	9
Assistant Secretary	72	72	71	80	83	86
Principal Officer	212	217	223	239	256	281
Principal Officer Accounts	4	8	8	5	4	3
Assistant Principal Officer	466	497	510	557	608	680
Assistant Principal Accounts	5	6	6	6	6	1
APO Senior System Analyst	4	4	4	5	5	3
APO Programme Budgeting	6	6	4	4	4	4
Administration Officer	112	118	121	125	126	140
Higher Executive Officer (HEO)	993	988	996	1,089	1,158	1,340
HEO Systems Analyst	40	49	53	48	55	86
Executive Officer (EO)	1,670	1,645	1,617	1,810	1,850	2,184
EO trainee analyst	9	8	6	5	16	6
Staff Officer (SO)	741	777	787	835	867	899
SO Senior Programmer	15	18	18	19	26	30
SO Typist Superintendant	26	26	26	26	26	30
Clerical Officer (CO)	2,807	2,748	2,766	2,875	2,992	3,484
CO Programmer	55	68	64	57	55	83
CO Typist Supervisor	21	26	26	28	35	44
Temporary Clerk	20	12	12	9	7	1
Clerical Assistant (CA)	5,149	5,240	5,346	5,403	5,994	6,034
Clerical Asst. temp.	218	137	133	122	128	45
CA Programmer	1	3	3	7	4	4
CA Shorthand Typist	395	412	430	405	358	383
CA Shorthand Typist Temp.	7	3	3	3	4	5
CA Typist	1,072	1,093	1,141	1,183	1,343	1,716
CA Typist Temp.	8	3	2	7	22	5
Cleaner	80?	90	96	106	104	349
Messenger	689	717	731	707	738	742
Total above	14,912	15,011	15,225	15,790	16,898	18,693

of other posts with salaries at least as remunerative as those of Executive Officer. The group also includes grades specific to three departments, viz: — in the Revenue Commissioners, Assistant-Inspector to Chief Inspectors of Taxes as well as Officers, Surveyors, Collectors and Inspectors of Customs and Excise; in the employment branch of Industry and Commerce (now Social Welfare), First, Second and Third Class Officers; and in Posts and Telegraphs, grades including Assistant Controllers, Assistant Superintendants and Post Masters Class VI and above.

II — *Clerical and Writing Assistant:*
This group covers Staff Officers with maxima (below that of Executive Officer)[11] and officers of the clerical, writing assistant and kindred grades.

In practice these grades were those administrative and executive posts of lower rank than those in Group I.

III — *Typing Grades:*
This group covers Superintendents of Typists, Shorthand Typists, Typists, Clerk Shorthand Typists and Clerk Typists.

The content of this group is obvious from the definition.

IV — *Inspectorate:*
This group covers officers, whether having professional, scientific or technical qualifications or otherwise, charged with duties of inspection and report.

This nomenclature is unfortunate since it does not include many inspectors so-called. As we have seen above Group I includes Inspectors of Taxes and of Customs and Excise, as well as those of the Department of Social Welfare. The typical inspectors in Group IV are those whose job requires them to check whether regulations or conditions have been complied with. Some are furniture inspectors in the Office of Public Works, Probation Officers in the Courts and the familiar School Inspectors. The majority (59 per cent in 1980), however, who are in Agriculture and kindred departments, check the implementation of legislation and eligibility for grants. Others work in the housing section of the Department of the Environment, in Health or in Social Welfare. To avoid the ambiguity of the title "Inspector" this group is renamed "checkers" in this study. It will be noted that up to 1952 revisions the group included vets, engineers, architects, doctors, etc., who were then relocated in Group V.

V — *Professional, Scientific and Technical:*
The officers to be included in this group should generally be those, other than inspectors, in possession of certificates of qualification granted by some body outside the Civil Service, e.g., Doctors, Barristers, Solicitors, Architects, Engineers, etc. Officers qualified by experience and filling posts similar to some of those indicated should also be included in this group even though they may not actually possess the certificate of qualification mentioned.

Among those included here are Chaplains, Teachers, Translators, Verbatim Reporters and Draughtsmen.

[11]Original definition quotes a salary figure.

VI — *Subordinate Supervisory, Minor and Manipulative:*
This group includes Post Office manipulative classes and also minor supervisory and other grades which cannot appropriately be included in other groups, e.g., Stocktakers, Stewards.

The major sub-groups in this category are the Post Office employees — Postmen, Sorters, Post Office Assistants, Telephonists, Overseers and Supervisors. The group also includes preventive men and watchers in the Revenue Commissioners, Wardens in Prisons, Attendants in the Dundrum Asylum, Branch Managers Social Welfare (now excluded along with scale paid sub-post officers) and some others. In 1952 non-professional staff in the Engineering Branch of Posts and Telegraphs were relocated here from Group VIII, i.e., industrial.

VII — *Messengers, Cleaners and Subordinate Staff:*
This group covers Messengers, Attendants, Cleaners and similar subordinate classes.

The content of the group is obvious from this definition.

In summary, then, the classification distinguished the administrative and executive staff into an upper (I) and lower (II) group. Support staff were classified broadly into typists (III) professional and technical experts (V), those checking and reporting (IV) and non-administrative workers, cleaners and messengers (VII). Much of the Post Office, the prison staff and psychiatric hospital staff and some preventive men in the Revenue Commissioners were allocated to a separate group (VI).

Changes in Numbers by Grade Group
Table 22 orders the groups in descending order of average pay in 1980 which revealed a distinct break between the upper three groups and the lower four. The upper echelon presumably comes within the mandate of the Devlin Committee. No similar committee appears to report for the lower echelon.

In constructing the table 1932 presented a difficulty since the group classification was adopted in 1933. Surviving records from 1932 listed 6,828 staff as "other subordinate alongside cleaners and messengers" and 642 staff were listed "miscellaneous". These two categories have been arbitrarily allocated to the Post Office and Wardens group which only numbered 2,212 in that year. Because of the heuristic approach adopted the 1932 figures are to be treated with caution.

In 1952, 1,828 former industrials were added to the Group VI and degree holders in Group IV were transferred to Group V. In 1958 a second reclassification moved scale-paid staff out of Census reducing Group VI by

Table 22: *Employment levels by groups of grades 1932–1981*

Grade Grouping	1932	1940	1952	1961	1970	1975	1980	1981
I Administrative	1,453	2,218	2,684	2,857	3,729	5,262	6,095	7,521
V Professional	1,601	{1,111	2,074	2,369	3,176	3,792	5,503	6,793
IV Checkers		774	845	797	1,472	1,862	2,454	2,698
Upper echelon	3,054	4,103	5,603	6,023	8,377	10,916	14,052	17,012
VI Postmen, Wardens, etc.	9,682*	8,678	12,874	13,240	17,033	21,359	20,472	19,664
II Clerical	3,417	5,705	6,956	6,256	7,845	10,817	12,925	15,155
VII Messengers	1,044	1,644	2,145	1,833	2,189	2,445	2,597	2,756
III Typists	571	856	995	729	806	1,440	1,914	2,093
Lower echelon	14,714	16,883	22,970	22,058	27,873	36,061	37,908	39,668
Total	17,768	20,986	28,573	28,081†	36,250	46,977	51,960	56,680

*Includes 6,828 "subordinate" and 642 "miscellaneous" but excludes scale-paid staff, prices reporters and summons servers.
†Reduction of circa 800 due to 1958 redefinitions

about 2,113 managers of sub-post offices and 83 branch managers of Social Welfare offices. This would tend to cancel the 1952 additions to this group. Apart from these, a number of other minor deductions were made in 1958 from the lower echelon amounting to 372 in all, but the grade groups involved were not recorded.

Changes in the grading of posts over time reduce comparability. For example, in 1961 127 Executive Officers were returned after Finance Circular No. 3 of 1960 upgraded 127 Staff Officers. This involved a transfer to Group I which accounted for just three-quarters of the apparent increase in that group between 1952 and 1961. Group II "lost" these staff but they only accounted for 18 per cent of the fall in that group over the same period. The main cause was the reduction in female staff observed already over the crisis period of the 'fifties. A regrading of some typists on another occasion brought about a transfer from Group II to Group III but the extent of this change has not survived in the records.

Over the 'fifties the lower echelon suffered a drop in numbers at a time when the upper echelon rose by 5 per cent. Part of this drop can be attributed to the reclassification of scale-paid staff in Group VI. Even so reductions in the other groups were severe: 27 per cent for typists[12], 15 per cent for messengers and 9 per cent for clerical staff. A tendency to economise on lower paid non-pensionable staff is a normal feature of many cutback systems. It is less clear why Grade VI recorded declines between 1975 and 1981 at a time when the rest of the Civil Service expanded by over 44 per cent. This, however, may be due to under-statement which was heavily concentrated in the Post Office.

As it stands the immediate impact of Table 22 is to demonstrate a much more rapid growth in the upper echelon compared with the lower. The former's share of total employment was 17 per cent in 1932 but 30 per cent in 1981. Half the divergence occurred during the 'seventies. Since the central Civil Service and the Post Office exhibit greatly differing grade structures it is instructive to study these trends separately in the two aggregates.

The Grade Structure of the Central Civil Service

Table 23 repeats Table 22 for the central Civil Service alone.

Clearly the upper echelon grew much faster over the entire period compared with the lower. The overall rates of growth were 3.15 per cent and 2.0 per cent compound. Indeed in the first three decades the upper echelon grew more than twice as fast: 2.48 per cent vs. 1.17 per cent. If the period is subdivided it becomes apparent that the growth rates were growing rapidly in general and the divergence narrowing:

[12]This may include some reclassifications to clerical but the latter also fell in numbers.

Table 23: *Grade structures in the central Civil Service 1940–1982*

		1940	1952	1961	1970	1975	1980	1981	1982
I	Administrative	1,991	2,424	2,573	3,377	4,784	5,556	6,992	7,255
V	Professional	1,016	1,832	2,223	2,943	3,459	4,196	3,954	4,081
IV	Checkers	719	829	778	1,443	1,828	2,034	2,344	2,342
	Upper echelon	3,726	5,085	5,574	7,763	10,071	11,786	13,290	13,678
VI	Wardens, etc.	812	1,467	1,577	1,989	2,288	2,751	2,284	2,437
II	Clerical	5,058	6,089	5,358	6,734	9,216	10,770	11,370	11,988
VII	Messengers	1,278	1,688	1,648	1,828	1,996	1,753	1,945	2,024
III	Typists	796	923	660	738	1,335	1,800	1,935	2,029
	Lower echelon	7,944	10,167	9,243	11,289	14,835	17,074	17,534	18,478
	Total	11,670	15,252	14,817	19,052	24,906	28,860	30,824	32,156

	1940–1961	1961–1970	1970–1982
	%	%	%
Upper	1.94	3.75	4.72
Lower	0.72	2.25	4.19

To facilitate an appreciation of the trends, Table 24 gives both the share at points in time and the rates of changes in the intervening intervals. Because of reclassification between the groups in 1952 a joint rate of growth is given for professionals and checkers over the first interval. The negative rate for typists may be influenced partly by reclassifications to the clerical group which itself exhibited a slow growth.

In the 'sixties the highest rates of growth were in the upper echelon. In the 'seventies these rates were in those groups most associated with General Service Grades, Administrative, Clerical and Typing. Numbers in these groups almost doubled compared to a rise of less than a third for the rest, or in annual compound rates, 5.8 per cent vs. 2.4 per cent. The messenger and cleaners group was probably hit by the introduction of contract cleaning. Over the whole period the upper echelon grade groups increased their share of the total steadily from 31.9 per cent in 1940 to 42.5 per cent in 1982. In other words in 1940 lower echelon staff were more than twice as numerous. In 1982 they excelled by only a third.

If total staff in 1940 and 1982 are compared, the clerical and administrative grades accounted for 60.4 per cent and 59.8 per cent of staff, respectively, but within this total the senior group increased its share from 28.3 per cent to 37.6 per cent. This seems to lend credence to the charge made by those critical of the increasing cost of the Civil Service, i.e., that not only have rates of pay risen rapidly but the hierarchical structure has been modified so that higher grades have been created to do what was formerly associated with lower grade posts. In particular they allege that the most senior posts have proliferated. If this charge is substantiated it would be that this tendency would conceal real cost increases that would not be apparent from an examination of the rates for the grade on its own. A serious study of costs, therefore, would need to look both at regrading of posts as well as at rates of pay for a grade. These tasks will be deferred until later. First it is necessary to look at grade structures in the Department of Posts and Telegraphs.

Grade Structures in the Post Office

The dominant grouping in the Department of Posts and Telegraphs is that traditionally labelled "Supervisory, minor and manipulative" but which we have christened "Postmen, etc.". This group is made up of postmen, auxiliary and temporary postmen, allowance deliverers, boy messengers, post office clerks

Table 24: *Shares by grade-group and growth rates for the central group, 1940–1982*

		Share 1940	Annual growth*	Share 1961	Annual growth*	Share 1970	Annual growth*	Share 1982
I	Administrative	17.1	(1.2)	17.4	(3.1)	17.7	(6.6)	22.5
V	Professional	8.7		{15.0	(3.2)	15.4	(2.8)	12.7
IV	Checkers	6.2	(2.6)	5.2	(7.1)	7.6	(4.1)	7.3
	Upper Echelon	31.9	(1.9)	37.6	(3.75)	40.7	(4.7)	42.5
VI	Wardens, etc.	7.0	(3.2)	10.6	(2.6)	10.4	(1.7)	7.6
II	Clerical	43.3	(0.3)	36.2	(2.6)	35.4	(4.9)	37.3
VII	Messengers, etc.	11.0	(1.2)	11.1	(1.2)	9.6	(0.9)	6.3
III	Typists	6.8	(-0.9)	4.5	(1.2)	3.9	(8.8)	6.3
	Lower Echelon	68.1	(0.7)	62.4	(2.2)	59.3	(4.2)	57.5
	Total	100.0	(1.1)	100.0	(2.8)	100.0	(4.4)	100.0

*Annual growth refers to compound rates over the relevant interval.

and assistants, sorting assistants, learners, telephonists, supervisors overseers (and non-professional staff in the Engineering Branch since 1952). It accounted for five out of six in the Department in both 1940 and 1975 and four out of six in 1982. It would appear that much of the under-enumeration in the Civil Service can be traced to this grouping which may account in part for its apparent decline after 1975 when the computerised system was introduced. The details for the groups are set out in Table 25. The figures for 1982 do not cater for under-enumeration.

It is difficult to interpret the table because in 1952 the postmen gained 1,824 non-professional staff in the Engineering branch who were formerly classified as industrials and by 1961 this group had lost 2,107 scale-paid managers of sub-post offices. Over the years the major changes are largely of recent origin, i.e., since 1975. This was the period of a rapid rise in professional staff and also in clerical (mostly female) staff. These changes can be summarised by considering the shares held by the different groups:

		1940 %	1975 %	1982 %
I	Administrative	2.4	2.2	2.1
V	Professional	0.6	1.5	11.1
IV	Checkers	0.6	0.1	1.3
	Upper echelon	3.6	3.8	14.6
VI	Postmen, etc.	85.0	86.4	66.8
II	Clerical	6.9	7.3	14.6
VII	Messengers	3.9	2.0	3.4
III	Typists	0.6	0.5	0.6
	Lower echelon	96.4	96.2	85.4

The growing group would appear to have done so at the expense of postmen.

Employment in the Administrative and Executive Group

In an earlier section we noted the allegation that held that higher paid posts tended to multiply faster than lower paid. This study cannot attempt a complete review of this charge but makes a start by examining trends within the higher paid grouping, i.e., the Administrative and Executive Group.

A first necessity, however, was to establish inter-temporal comparability since the reporting of sets of grades has been by no means uniform over time. The biggest problem has been the varying numbers assisgned to the "other grades"

Table 25: *Grade Structure in the Department of Posts and Telegraphs 1940–1982*

		1940	1952	1961	1971	1975	1980	1981	1982
I	Administrative	225 + 2	250 + 10	284	352	478	539	529	565
V	Professional	52 + 43	100 + 142	146	233	333	1,307	2,839	2,971
VI	Checkers	52 + 3	16	19	29	34	420	354	348
	Upper echelon	329 + 48	366 + 152	449	614	845	2,266	3,722	3,884
VI	Postmen, etc.	7,865 + 1	11,365 + 42	11,663	15,044	19,071	17,721	17,380	17,818
II	Clerical	643 + 4	853 + 14	898	1,111	1,601	2,155	3,785	3,906
VII	Messengers	363 + 3	443 + 14	185	361	449	844	811	913
III	Typists	55 + 5	65 + 7	69	68	105	114	156	162
	Lower echelon	8,926 + 13	12,726 + 77	12,815	16,584	21,226	20,834	22,134	22,799
	Total	9,255 + 61	13,092 + 229	13,264	17,198	22,071	23,100	25,856	26,683

The separated figures for 1940 and 1952 refer to wireless broadcasting.

row.[13] Table A2.7 in the Appendix presents the categories (a) used in 1938 and 1940, (b) in 1952 and (c) in 1961, 1970 and 1975. In each case the central Civil Service and Post Office are identified.

The advent of computerisation in 1975 had led to a different approach being adopted to the staff files. In the development of programmes 167 grades are currently distinguished as members of Group I. Since such fineness of the grading would be unwieldy for this study the grades have been regrouped into categories reminiscent of the pre-1975 classification. The table is given in Appendix A2.8 together with an exhaustive set of notes as to how these grades were reduced to 17 categories within which the actual grade of the category had associated with it both equivalent and analogous grades. This table was prepared especially for this study and is not available elsewhere. The notes provide a valuable insight into the variety of grades covered by the Administrative and Executive grouping. These ranged from those on salary maxima of £28,499 in 1981 to those whose maximum was less than £8,000.

Table 26 presents a reasonable reconstruction of the composition of Group I between 1938 and 1981 as it emerges from the reconciliations of the material in Appendices A2.7 and A2.8. The 1938 data present some difficulties in allocation since it is not clear where to allocate 79 persons described as heads of division and branch. This group covers several levels and includes Assistant Secretaries, Directors, Chief Clerks and Superintending Officers. The 1938 breakdown also aggregates accountants of all grades. The Accountant General, who is currently of Assistant Secretary rank, is included with lower ranking Assistant and Deputy Accountants, some of whom (but not all) could probably be now classified under the "Professional, etc.," heading. For this reason greater confidence in general is attached to the post-1940 figures. However, the decline in the "Other" category between 1952 and 1970 raises problems as to whether some of this decline was recalssification into grades analogous to those in the general service.

The totals for Section A + B + C, i.e., Assistant Principal and higher, show an annual 4.3 per cent rise in these grades since 1938 though the rise was 5.4 per cent in the last twenty years. The pattern of change discernible from the table indicates similar annual rates of growth for the intervals 1938 to 1952 (4.8 per cent), 1961–70 and 1975–81 (both 4.6 per cent). The two intervening periods differ markedly. The 'fifties was a period of strong control by the Department of Finance during which annual growth was only a fifth of these rates. In contrast, the early 'seventies was a boom period for employment at higher grades with an annual average of 8 per cent. In part this could be due to the practice of guaranteeing promotion to Assistant Principal within a few years to Administrative Officers. Within this upper group, numbers of Assistant

[13]In earlier records 6 per cent were so designated; in later more than a quarter. It is not clear why a classification system should give minute detail in some areas and no detail at all in others.

Table 26: *Disaggregation of Group I by categories 1938–1981*

	1938	1940	1952	1961	1970	1975	1981
Dept. Sec./Commission Chairman	15	14	16	8	20	21	23
Secretary Equivalents					4	6	13
Deputy Secretary (DS)	24	23		22	5	9	12
	+	+					
DS Equivalents	79*	95*	72		21	23	14
Assistant Secretary				42	56	67	83**
Equivalents and Analogue				15	24	36	53**
Total Section A	39+79	37+95	88	97	130	162	198
Accountants***	34	35	n.s.		12	10	10
Analogue to PO Finance				24			
PO/Finance	40	48	135		27	46	61
PO/GS				94	152	210	278
PO/GS Analogue				20	23	36	57
Total Section B	74	83	135	138	214	302	406
Analogue APO/Finance					21	37	21
Asst. Principal/Finance	57	61	263	81	60	117	131
Asst. Principal/GS				172	294	443	662
Analogue	4	4		45	78	112	116
Total Section C	61	65	263	298	453	709	930
Totals A + B+ C	253	280	486	533	797	1,173	1,534
Administrative Officer				20	70	85	151
2nd and 3rd Secretaries	41	43	63	27	33	61	54
HEO	196	219	402	500	694	993	1,310
EO	626	616	641	628	998	1,543	2,147
EO upgraded†	—	—	—	127	119	96	
Total Section D	863	878	1,106	1,302	1,914	2,778	3,662
Total A to D	1,116	1,158	1,592	1,835	2,711	3,951	5,196
Other (including unclassified)	1,054	1,058	1,092	1,022	1,018	1,311	2,325
Total Group I	2,170	2,216	2,684	2,857	2,729	5,262	7,521

*Heads of Division and Branch, grade composition unclear.

**11 Assistant Secretaries in Dept. of Finance on general service scales are included in "equivalents" to preserve continuity.

***Accountants of all grades.

†Staff Officers II regraded EOs in Finance Circular 3/60.

Principals increased at an annual average of 9.4 per cent which was more than twice as fast as growth in number of Assistant Secretaries and higher grades. The rate of increase in employment of Principal Officers was intermediate to these extremes.

Section D displayed the same pattern as the upper group since 1961 with a very similar overall growth rate. It differed in that its annual growth between 1938 and 1952 was only 1.8 per cent whereas the upper group was 4.8 per cent — nearly three times as fast. In the 'fifties the lower group grew as slowly but now this was considerably faster than the upper group achieved. It will also be noted that the 1961 figure for Executive Officers contains 127 persons formerly holding the post of Staff Officer Grade II. This grade was converted to Executive Officer on 1 July 1960 under Finance Circular 3/60. The general impression emanating from this analysis is that growth at higher levels appears to have been, if anything, slower than that lower down the hierarchy.

The issue may be clouded by the inclusion of equivalent and analogous grades within the upper categories. Table 27 excludes these for the period after 1961 when a general rate of 5.5 per cent annually was recorded. These post-1961 rates of growth were not the isolated phenomenon which those, whose earlier memories relate to the 'fifties, might argue. If the figures (not shown in Table 27) are trustworthy, it would appear that in that decade Principal Officers, Assistant Principals and Higher Executive Officers recorded annual growth levels of 0.2 per cent, 1.4 per cent and 2.5 per cent, respectively. However, these rates were a considerable reduction on the rates of 3.5 per cent, 10.5 per cent and 5.3 per cent chalked up in the previous twelve years. Again it was the Assistant Principal cohort that showed the greatest increase. In marked contrast Executive Officer numbers were virtually stationary over the 23 year period of the 1938 to 1961 period until the influx of upgraded Staff Officers in the last six months added 20 per cent to this category. This decision reflected the new mood ushered in by the First Programme for Economic Expansion. It has been claimed that the new approach to economic development, by weakening the control of the Department of Finance, facilitated the growth in numbers.

Turning to the post-1961 period analysed in Table 27, we find a greater variety of trends. At the highest level studied — Assistant Secretary — both the long-term and short-term growth has been the slowest. In the immediate past Assistant Principal Officers recorded the highest growth apart from that by the small numbers of Administrative Officers. These were also the groups who were among those with the highest growth rates in the long term. Principal Officers in the Finance grade also displayed very high rates of growth but the data are less reliable. In the early 'seventies, Assistant Principals and Principal Officers in Finance grades grew extremely rapidly in numbers, perhaps due to the splitting up of Department of Finance functions, such as the Department of the Public

Table 27: *Annual rates of change in numbers in specific grades 1961–1981*

	Interval				
	1961/ 1981	1970/ 1981	1961/ 1970	1970/ 1975	1975/ 1981
Assistant Secretary*	3.5	3.6	3.2	3.7	3.6
Principal Officer (all)	6.0	6.0	6.0	7.4	4.8
Principal Officer GS	5.6	5.6	5.5	6.7	4.8
Principal Officer Finance	(8.5)	7.7	(9.4)	11.2	4.8
Asst. Principal (all)	6.3	7.6	4.8	9.6	6.0
Asst. Principal GS	7.0	7.7	6.1	8.5	6.9
Asst. Principal Finance	(4.0)	7.4	(0.0)	14.3	1.9
Administrative Officer	10.6	7.2	14.9	4.0	10.1
Higher Executive Officer	4.9	5.9	3.7	7.4	4.7
Executive Officer	5.4	6.1	4.4	7.8	4.6
All	5.5	6.7	4.5	7.8	5.0

*1981 figures exclude 11 Assistant Secretaries in Finance on the assumption that they were excluded in other years.

Figures in parentheses are estimates since 1961 records include analogous grades.

Service. In the long term, and also in the short term, numbers in the junior post of Executive Officer grew at below average rates as did those holding jobs as Higher Executive Officer. The conclusion would, therefore, appear to be that there has indeed been a remarkable burgeoning of higher level posts but mainly in middle management positions.

Employment by Department

The Civil Service is an organic structure whose evolutionary nature is well illustrated by development since Independence as it affected the division of the Civil Service into Departments of State. The chief new feature introduced by the transfer of the State service into the control of a native Government was the constitution, in relation to each of the ministries, of a fully organised Department of State with adequate headquarters machinery, etc. Effective headquarters already existed in respect of Education, Agriculture and Local Government, but in other fields, e.g., Finance, Revenue, the Stationery Office and the Post Office, the real headquarters were in London. Furthermore, completely new services, consequent on self-government, e.g., External Affairs, Defence, etc., had to be inaugurated. The Ministers and Secretaries Act 1924 provided for eleven such departments — those of the President of the Executive Council (which became that of An Taoiseach under the subsequent new constitution of 1937), Finance, Justice, Local Government and Public Health,

Education, Lands and Agriculture, Industry and Commerce, Fisheries, Posts and Telegraphs, Defence and External Affairs.

An analysis comparing 1926 with 1922 showed an increase of 1,918 over the four years. Twelve cases of increases totalling 2,644 were offset against reductions, of which some 800 in the Post Office was the major one. This analysis showed half the increase to be due to entirely new services. The 1,274 new posts were: Defence 849, Finance 190, Oireachtas 80, External Affairs 57, Exchequer and Audit 29, State Laboratory 26, Civil Service Commission and President's Office 15 each and Office of the Minister of Education 13. A further 1,370 were accounted for by increased activities of existing offices. An extra 860 were required in the Revenue Commissioners due to the imposition of customs with the United Kingdom and the need to man the land border. The Board of Works found its duties almost doubled and needed 460 more to reconstruct war damaged public buildings such as the Four Courts or the numerous police statons. Fifty extra staff were needed in the independent Stationery Office to handle contracts. Apart from these, other departments increased staff to cope with new legislation. The 1923 Land Act added 150 more to the Land Commission. The Agricultural Acts affecting dairying, eggs and livestock added 90 to the existing Department of Agriculture. It is greatly to be regretted that later expansions in the Civil Service were not equally minutely documented as an aid to evaluation.

Changing Departmental Structures 1928–1985

The first change in departmental structures occurred in 1928 when Lands separated from Agriculture and attached to Fisheries. The outbreak of World War II in 1939 saw a new Department of Supplies which performed some functions of Industry and Commerce as well as war-time controls until reincorporated in its parent department on the cessation of hostilities in 1945. Thus the number of departments reverted to the original eleven. The rise in social expenditure saw two new departments hived off in 1947, mainly from the Departments of Local Government and Public Health (subsequently the Department of Local Government) and of Industry and Commerce. These were the Departments of Health and Social Welfare. In 1956 Roinn na Gaeltachta separated from the Department of Lands. The Department of Transport and Power brought the number to fifteen in 1959 when it was set up from Industry and Commerce. This number coincided with the Constitutional limit on members of the Government. Henceforth, additional departments meant that some Ministers controlled more than one department with the aid of Parliamentary Secretaries, or Ministers of State as they became later called. In 1966 the Department of Labour was launched, taking with it some functions of Social Welfare. In 1973 the growing size of the public employment caused the

Department of Public Service to be given a separate identity having previously functioned within the Department of Finance. In 1977 the agricultural departments were re-arranged with the Department of Lands rejoining Agriculture but leaving Forestry behind in a new Department of Fisheries and Forestry. The following year another reshuffle on the industrial side led to new alignments, "Industry, Commerce and Energy" and "Transport and Tourism". Another change in the same realignment occurred in 1980 when Energy became a separate Department and Tourism replaced it to create the Department of Industry, Commerce and Tourism. This was not the final change. The establishment of two new State-sponsored bodies, An Post and Telecom Eireann left a residual group of policy makers in the old Department of Posts and Telegraphs. These amalgamated with the Department of Transport to form the Department of Communications in 1984. The other part of the old Industry and Commerce Department was redesignated the Department of Industry, Trade, Commerce and Tourism. For a brief period between 1978 and 1980 a new Department of Economic Planning and Development took some of the functions of the Department of Finance. After its demise its functions were distributed to the Departments of Finance and An Taoiseach. Other changes were in title. External Affairs became Foreign Affairs and Local Government became the Environment.

The creation of a new Department does not necessarily mean that additional functions are to be taken on by the Civil Service. It may be that a Department's functions have become too burdensome for one Minister to carry. The creation of Transport and Power to take on some of the functions of the Department of Industry and Commerce perhaps exemplifies such a development. Again it may have been deemed desirable to concentrate functions of a similar character which had been dealt with by a number of departments, or even by non-Civil Service bodies. The setting up of Social Welfare was primarily such an operation. In general, however, the need to set up extra departments reflects the expanding activities of the Civil Service arising from the entrusting of additional powers and functions to Ministers under legislation passed by the Oireachtas.

Analysis of the First Period of Growth to 1952

No detailed analysis has been made of the reasons for this growth apart from that by Linehan (1954) who wrote at the end of the first growth period. He divided the Civil Service into three groups — the Post Office, the historic departments, i.e., Departments of An Taoiseach, Justice, Defence, External Affairs and Finance and the modern departments, i.e., those engaged in economic and social development. In broad terms their proportions at the launching of the Saorstát were 13,500: 2,600: 4,200. Almost immediately the historic departments increased by 1,600 due to the expansion in the Revenue

Commission and the Office of Public Works. This produced approximately equal numbers in the historic and modern groups. Both these groups increased by 5,000 between 1922 and 1953 but the timing was different. After the initial spurt the historic departments experienced a fairly steady increase of 100–150 annually up to 1953. Thus the group doubled in size between 1922 and 1934 and increased by half subsequently. In contrast the modern departments were relatively static up to 1934 and more than doubled subsequently. Numbers in the Post Office fell below 12,000[14] by 1934 and then grew to almost 16,000 by 1953. In the initial period there was a shift in favour of headquarter staff matched by a decline elsewhere.

Linehan looked in detail at the Departments of Industry and Commerce and Agriculture. The former started with approximately 500 staff in 1923 and increased to 1,800 in 1953. (These figures were adjusted for the loss of the Central Statistics Office and for transfers to Social Welfare.) Growth did not start until 1934 when the new policies of protectionism added 300. After 1940 meteorological and other airport services expanded continuously to reach 700 in 1953. The other development was the rise and demise of the Department of Supply which added some 700 more but 300 of these posts disappeared with the disappearance of the Department's functions.

Agriculture, too, was slow in starting on its growth path. Numbers in 1932 and 1923 were broadly similar and under 800. New legislation caused numbers to jump to 2,000 by January 1935 and by a further 1,300 in the subsequent year. After 1940 compulsory tillage, etc., and the acquisition of the National Stud added 500 more. After the war the Land Rehabilitation Project, the Poultry Development Scheme and the Soil Centre at Johnstown Castle added a further 350.

Linehan tried to relate these changes to various indices of output. For example, his rough estimates of letters delivered, phones installed, etc., matched Post Office growth. He came under considerable fire for noting that, as the Department of Agriculture expanded, agricultural output remained static and 25 per cent of farmers left the land. Clearly this criterion may have been over simplistic. It is not proposed to develop Linehan's study in this present study though clearly such an analysis must be a longer-term objective.

Numbers in Departments 1932–1985

Surviving records give a breakdown of total numbers in each department for 1932, 1938, 1940 and from the late 1940s onwards. This study does not reproduce all that material. Such a reproduction would be more relevant in a detailed study of departmental expansion. Instead, some benchmark years are

[14]11,316 in 1932.

given in Table 28. Interested readers are referred to Humphreys (1983) who gives a series for the years 1970 to 1983 inclusive. More recent revised estimates were given in the Dáil on 6 March 1985.

Although data are plentiful the departmental approach gives rise to several difficulties in making comparisons over time. One of these arises from the decision to omit or include categories of staff not previously so treated. Recent examples are the decisions to exclude State solicitors and the local staff employed in embassies abroad. In the 1958 reclassification, as we have seen, several others were excluded. The most notable of these were the more than 2,000 people responsible for sub-post offices which were previously classified as part-time employees. Earlier censuses included large numbers of summons servers and reporters of prices at fairs and markets.

Apart from those who were omitted or reclassified another source of difference arose where staff remain in the public domain but are no longer included in the departmental returns due to the establishment of, for instance, semi-State bodies. Thus a major change occurred when the staff of the Department of Posts and Telegraphs became employees of one of two new semi-State bodies or were transferred to the newly named Department of Communications. The hiving off of wireless broadcasting from the same department in the early 'sixties was a forerunner of such reorganisation. This is now under the aegis of the semi-State body — Radio Telefís Eireann. Other examples are numerous. The establishment of Aer Rianta, The IDA, An Foras Talúntais, AnCO, etc., involved transfers from certain departments. The Department of Education was once directly involved with the Metropolitan College of Art and the Irish Folklore Commission. The 1938 returns of that Department have an old world ring about them. They included departmental employment in the Irish Training School of Domestic Economy and the Killarney School of Housewifery. A perusal of old books of *Estimates for Public Services* will give other illustrations.

A final source of potential misinterpretation arises from the tendency to reorganise and regroup departments to meet the changing priorities of society. The evolution of the Department of Industry and Commerce is a striking illustration of the chameleon character of economic departments. In earlier arrangements this department dealt with not only industry, trade, prices, mining, transport, meteorological services, aviation and power, but also unemployment assistance, unemployment benefit, the Central Statistics Office and vocational training. On the wind up of the war-time Department of Supply, its staff were for a time incorporated into Industry and Commerce. At various times sections of the Department were reallocated. The Central Statistics Office was made independent under the Department of An Taoiseach. Unemployment payments went to either the Department of Labour or of Social Welfare.

Table 28: *Non-industrial employment by department, January 1932–1985*

Department	*1932*	*1940*	*1952*	*1960*	*1970*	*1975*	*1980*	*1981*	*SIS*	*July 1981 Survey***	*1985*
President	5[a]	8	6	8	9	11	10	12	11	10	10
Oireachtas	81	81	85	84	120	140	175	153	159	189	202
Taoiseach	14[a]	22	22	21	35	46	50	154	165	172	156
Finance	175[b]	177[c]	237	169	409	328	} 382	468	473	465	430[aa]
Paymaster General	25	26	33	34	33	54					
Auditor General	40	50	60	48	60	72	84	101	100	96	85
Revenue Commissioners	1,986	2,631	2,654	2,786*	3,810	} 5,448	6,748	7,441	7,665	7,218	6,818
Finance Solicitor	14	17	14	14	31						
Civil Service Comm.	37	83	87	73	104	174	240	204	193	222	138
Public Service	—	—	—	—	—	286	418	452	458	449	404
Economic Planning	—	—	—	—	—	—	110[d]	(181)[d]	7	—	—
Total Core	2,377	3,095	3,198	3,237	4,611	6,559	8,217	8,003	9,231	8,821	8,243
Public Work	330	499	625[e]	833[e]*	754	824	959	934	1,057	1,090	981
State Laboratory	23	30	26	37	33	53	63	70	67	63	65
Stationery Office	112	134	146	145	155	157	167	187	185	178	161
Valuation Office	93	98	100	103	125	177	} 485	210	205	209	190
Ordnance Survey	179	116	109[f]	147	154	221		316	349	394	363
Total "Finance Industrial"	737	877	1,006	1,265	1,221	1,432	1,674	1,717	1,863	1,934	1,760
Defence	273	548[g]	729	491*	495	557	632	674	692	658	609
External Affairs											
home }	94	36	137	118	147	331	402	524	588	708	531[bb]
abroad }		85	137	141	195	285	372	excl.	excl.	excl.	excl.
Total Defence/Foreign	367	669	1,003	750	837	1,173	1,406	1,198	1,280	1,366	1,240

Table 28: *(cont'd.)*

Department	1932	1940	1952	1960	1970	1975	1980	1981	SIS	July 1981 Survey**	1985
State Solicitors	27	27	27	28	—	31	excl.	excl.	excl.	excl.	excl.
Chief State Solicitor	20	25	35	36	61	73		60	59	95	83
Attorney General	9	11	12	11	15	23	98[h]	22	23	22	24
Director Public Prosecutions	—	—	—	—	—	—	14	10	10	16	16
Justice	104	111	118	112	164	276	452	549	551	633	640
Public Record Office	17	15	20	17	15	26	29	29	28	35	31
Gardai	87	91	107	86	127	289	307	314	339	374	439
Prisons	309	259	295	243	336	647	1,140	1,397	1,419	1,536	1,565
Courts:											
Metropolitan	16	22	39	33	44	96	72	93	104	76	85
District	149	133	113	89	102	103	153	140	141	147	139
Supreme + High	160	151	151	147	161	167	145	185	178	197	179
Circuit	169[j]	204	216	192	192	247	184	221	226	287	278
Registry:											
Lands	107	105	129	137	229	274	416	501	507	513	468
Deeds	64	63	63	61	53	60	68	86	88	86	71
Charitable Donations	9	10	8	9	8	11	8	10	10	12	11
Total Law Enforcement	1,247	1,227	1,333	1,201	1,507	2,323	3,086	3,617	3,683	4,029	4,029
Education[k]	74	63	64	133	245	255					
Education Misc.[l]	21	25	22	23	37	excl.					
Primary	242	299	286	197	200	223					
Secondary	40	53	63	62	138	353					
Vocational	81[m]	71[m]	70	59	82	10	1,127	1,081	1,052	1,213	1,076
Reformatories	14	10	13	13	16	15					
National Museum	45	46	49	47	54	61					
National Library	31	35	45	49	51	61					
National Gallery	16	16	16	17	41	47	49	49	49	57	47
Total Educational	564	618	628	600*	864	1,025	1,176	1,130	1,101	1,270	1,123

Table 28: (cont'd.)

Department	1932	1940	1952	1960	1970	1975	1980	1981	SIS	July 1981 Survey**	1985
Fisheries	225	32	43	71	106	114	147	159	175	⎫ 1,302	206
Forestry	792	151	277	601	959	1,048	1,068	1,044	1,066	⎭	981
Agriculture		1,039	1,842	1,995*	2,866	3,645	4,649	4,916	4,974	5,123	4,487
Land Commission	799[n]	1,088[n]	1,091	941	892	888	71	81	80	74	64
Gaeltacht	–	128	136	55	66	70					
Total Rural	1,816	2,438	3,389	3,663	4,889	5,765	5,935	6,200	6,295	6,499	5,738
Industry, Commerce	788[o]	718	949	512	558	762	934	989[p]	1,000[p]	1,051[p]	949[p]
Transport, Tourism		56[q]	536[q]	645[q]	1,061[r]	1,132[r]	1,180	1,238[s]	1,227[s]	1,226[s]	1,227[z]
Central Statistics		above	307	231	314	407	415[t]	556[t]	541	648	464
Total "Economic"	788	774	1,792	1,388	1,933	2,301	2,529	2,783	2,765	2,925	2,640
Environment	250	434	334	337	643	840	1,033	1,132	1,140	1,094	939
Health			193	182	259	323	338	396	404	376	354
General Registry Office	44	42	48	44	76	excl.	excl.	excl.	excl.	excl.	excl.
Dundrum Asylum	57	61	73	74	excl.	excl.	excl.	excl.	excl.	excl.	excl.
Social Welfare	198[u]	1,435[v]	2,255[v]	1,880*	1,361	2,699	2,760	2,928	3,203	3,289	3,358
Labour	–	–	–	–	851	466	706	720	720	854	817
Total Social	549	1,972	2,903	2,517	3,190	4,328	4,837	5,176	5,467	5,613	5,468
Post Office HQ	9,292[y]	702[w]	917	931	1,142	1,733	1,861	2,491	2,545	28,220	26,282
Metropolitan		1,870[y]	2,678[y]	2,681	3,860	4,801	5,029	5,587	5,642		
Provincial		6,205[y]	7,178[y]	6,762	7,518	8,727	8,303	8,493	8,647		
Stores		245	302	378	409	473	471	500	517		
Engineering		233	2,017	2,242†	4,269	6,337	7,436	8,785	9,027		
Wireless Broadcast	31	61	229	372	–	–	–	–	–	–	–
Total P+T	9,323	9,316	13,321	13,366	17,198	22,071	23,100	25,856	26,378	28,220	26,282
Grand Total	17,768	20,986	28,636	28,108	36,250	46,977	51,960	56,680	58,063	60,677	56,652

Notes:

(a) Prior to the new constitution in 1938 figures for President and Taoiseach relate to Governor-General and President of Executive Council, respectively.

(aa) Includes 19 Ombudsman's Office.

(b) Includes Tariff Commission (7), Central Savings Committee (11).

(bb) Includes 34 seconded.

(c) Includes Central Savings Committee (8).

(d) Alternative estimates put figures 141 and 163. Of 1981 figure only 18 included in total.

(e) Includes Special Employment Schemes Office 107 and 98, respectively.

(f) Includes Place Names Commission (1).

(g) Includes Co-ordination of Defence Office (5).

(h) Includes Law Reform Commission (1).

(i) Figure given was 660 from which 491 part-time summons servers were arbitrarily deducted to maintain comparability with other years.

* Redefinitions in 1958 (see text) reduced 1960 totals by 71, 184 and 150, respectively. Smaller changes occurred in some other departments.

** Figures from special survey, following recruitment ban July 1981.

(k) Headquarters, Accounts, Publications and Development Branches.

(l) Included under Education up to 1970 were Metropolitan School of Art: 19, 22, 22, 23 and 25, respectively. The Irish MSS Commission 2, 3, 2 and Irish Folklore Commission 1970 (12).

(m) Included are Irish Training School of Domestic Economy 16, 13 and Killarney School of Housewifery 3, 2, respectively.

(n) Includes Quit Rent Office (11).

(o) Excludes 35 Reporters at Fairs, 80 Branch Managers (Unemployment Exchanges). The Reporters may be in 1940 returns.

(p) Department of Energy (106, 162, 226, 320), Industry, Commerce and Tourism (883, 838, 825, 669).

(q) Transport, Meteorology and Marine branch; Railway Tribunal (2) in 1940 only.

(r) Transport and Power.

(s) Transport.

(t) Alternative figures presumably including part timers would make totals 562 and 610, respectively.

(u) National Health Insurance Commission: Industry and Commerce includes Unemployment Insurance.

(v) Excludes (90, 80, respectively) Branch Managers for comparability with later figures. 1940 Total made up of National Health Insurance Commission (301) plus Unemployment Insurance and Unemployment Assistance Branch of Industry and Commerce.

(w) Includes Post Office Savings Bank (85).

(y) Excludes, for comparability with later figures, scale paid subpost officers 2,024 (1932), 1969 (1940) and estimated 2,083 in 1952 of which 153 attributed to Metropolitan Branch.

(z) Communications.

† Redefinitions in 1958 (see text) reduced 1960 totals by 35, 188, 35 and 114, respectively. Smaller changes occurred in some other departments.

Transport and Power became a separate Department. At different times a Department of Energy has been separately identified. For a time it left Transport and Power to join Industry and Commerce leaving a department exclusively devoted to Transport, or to Transport and Tourism. Another reshuffle produced three departments, of which one was Trade, Commerce and Tourism. Another example is provided by the Department of Economic Planning which, like the Department of the Public Service, was an off-shoot of the Department of Finance. Its creation reduced staff in the Department of Finance; its abolition strengthened the Department of An Taoiseach. Even where Departments do not change their names, their roles can differ over time as when the Department of Labour (a relative newcomer) was for a while responsible for the local offices run by the Department of Social Welfare. A more subtle redistribution of responsibility can occur relatively unnoticed as when the Department of Education assumed responsibility for school buildings previously under the care of the Office of Public Works.

For all these reasons the changes in departmental strength over time require careful interpretation. This is shown to some extent by the copious footnotes attached to Table 28. This table shows over more than half a century the evolution of departments, broadly grouped to overcome the problem of interdepartmental reorganisation.

In his 1954 study Linehan grouped departments into three; commercial — the Post Office; traditional — Taoiseach, Justice, Defence, External Affairs, Finance; and modern, i.e., economic and social development. This classification anticipated that of Rose (1980) by a quarter of a century. The latter noted that the traditional could be found, for example, in early Victorian Britain and dubbed this group as the "defining role" of government. He divided Linehan's "modern" between those with an economic developmental role and those with a social services role. In Table 29 the nine broad groupings of Table 28 are assembled to approximate Rose's definition. Like Table 28 there are two sets of figures for July 1981. One gives the normal SIS return. The other — in parentheses in Table 29 — gives the results of a special survey of staff at the time of the recruitment ban. This second set provided the evidence of under-enumeration but it appears that it may not have covered the same ground as the SIS.

A few points only have been selected from the great variety of changes over the long time span of Tables 28 and 29. In general the average annual overall growth rate was 2.2 per cent compound. The first and second groups chalked up slightly higher rates: 2.3 per cent. The third group, services, grew at 3.5 per cent but this was made up of 1.3 per cent for Education — the lowest growth of the nine and 4.5 per cent for the social category. The higher rate of growth of the latter category is largely attributable to a 17.3 per cent growth in the first period

Table 29: *Changes in staffing levels by departmental groups 1932–1985*

January	1932	1940	1952	1960	1970	1975	1980	1981	1981	July	1985
Core	2,377	3,095	3,198	3,237	4,611	6,559	8,217	9,003	9,231	(8,821)	8,243
Finance/industrial	737	877	1,006	1,265	1,221	1,432	1,674	1,717	1,863	(1,934)	1,760
Defence/Foreign	367	669	1,003	750	837	1,173	1,406	1,198	1,280	(1,366)	1,240
Law Enforcement	1,247	1,227	1,333	1,201	1,507	2,323	3,086	3,617	3,683	(4,029)	4,029
Defining Role	4,728	5,868	6,540	6,453	8,176	11,487	14,383	15,535	16,057	(16,150)	15,272
Rural	1,816	2,438	3,389	3,663	4,889	5,765	5,935	6,200	6,295	(6,499)	5,738
Economic	788	774	1,792	1,388	1,933	2,301	2,676	2,783	2,765	(2,925)	2,640
Developmental Role	2,604	3,212	5,181	5,051	6,822	8,066	8,611	8,983	9,060	(9,424)	8,378
Education	564	618	628	600	864	1,025	1,176	1,130	1,101	(1,270)	1,123
Social	549	1,972	2,903	2,517	3,190	4,328	4,837	5,176	5,467	(5,613)	5,468
Services Role	1,113	2,590	3,531	3,117	4,054	5,353	6,013	6,306	6,568	(6,883)	6,591
Post Office	9,323	9,316	13,324	13,366	17,198	22,071	23,100	25,856	26,378	(28,220)	26,282
Total	17,768	20,986	28,576	28,108	36,250	46,977	51,960	56,680	58,063	(60,677)	56,523

Note: Figures for July 1981 represent the situation at the peak of employment before the recruitment ban was imposed. Those in parentheses are derived from a special survey.

which may reflect inadequate data. The high rate should be linked with the slight fall in the economic group since some of the social expenditure was originally the responsibility of the Department of Industry and Commerce and the table may not have apportioned these adequately to the social group. After 1940 the rate was the same as for the first two groups. The growth of the Post Office was only 2.0 per cent though it is possible that if underenumeration was rectified the rate would approach 2.2 per cent. The broad picture, then, is a fairly similar rate of expansion in seven groups with a substantial lower rate in Education and to a lesser extent in the Finance Industrial group (1.7 per cent), i.e., Office of Public Works, Stationery Office, etc.

The phasing of these growth rates have been widely different. Between 1952 and 1960 a negative rate of growth was recorded, only partly due to reclassifications. Otherwise the pre-1970 period had an average growth of 2.4 per cent which was the same as the average between 1975 and 1984. The 1970 to 1975 period had a particularly high rate of 5.3 per cent though subsequently 1980 clocked up an amazing 9.1 per cent and 4.9 per cent for the first half of 1981. The overall slower growth after 1975 includes the effects of the 1975 and 1981 bans on recruitment. In absolute numbers the average increment was just 780 annually. Pre-1970 this average was 486 compared with 1,897 for the post-1970 period up to July 1981. The 1975 to 1980 average was 997. Prior to 1970 the fastest growth sectors, apart from the social group, were the rural development group followed closely by those responsible for economic development. Law enforcement made little increase (0.5 per cent) though staff in the Department of Defence had been built up somewhat as a result of World War II.

These earlier trends contrasted with the post-1970 situation. Law enforcement departments (and these did not include the Gardai) had more than double the average rates 6.8 per cent while rural departments had less than half the average of 3.0 per cent (1.1 per cent). The core group of departments expanded over 30 per cent faster than average — Finance, Revenue Commissioners, Taoiseach, etc. Social departments also expanded at high rates. The lower showing of the Defence/Foreign Affairs group may be due to an "apparent" drop in 1980 of almost 15 per cent when other departments grew by over 9 per cent. This could be due to the omission of overseas staff of Foreign Affairs. Education continued to lag behind. Its above average growth in the late 'seventies was eroded by falls in both 1980 and early 1981. It may be that these falls were due to underenumeration since the department had a little "compensatory" growth rate subsequently, i.e., after the ban on recruitment. Even so the overall growth rate for this department was only three-fifths the average for the fourteen years beginning January 1970.

This sketchy account can be fleshed out for individual departments by reference to the detail in Table 28. A few items call for comment. The

Department of Finance had fewer staff in 1960 than in 1952 though no hiving off had occurred in the meanwhile. This reduction was due partly to the disbanding of the Exchange Control section. Figures for the Office of Public Works in 1952 and 1960 included the Special Employment Schemes Office. Figures for the former year for the Central Statistics Office included temporary staff concerned with processing the 1951 Census of Population. Figures for Industry and Commerce in 1952 contained perhaps 250 staff associated with war-time supplies office which was wound up before 1960. The returns for the Department of Social Welfare for 1950/51 in the Book of Estimates was shown as 1,688 in the 1950–51 Estimates but the next book of Estimates increased this figure by a net 535 due to the absorption of the National Health Insurance Fund staff into the Department. These staff were not returned in the previous years but were included in the 1940 returns. During the 'fifties employment in Social Welfare was reduced considerably, e.g., 152 during 1953. The simultaneous decline in the Department of the Gaeltacht is probably related to the launching of Gaeltarra Eireann as a State-sponsored body. The factory employment of Gaeltacht industries was previously returned as public employment but was not recorded here but under "industrials". Within the Post Office group employment in the provincial branch grew slowly, only 0.8 per cent annually since 1940, compared to a growth rate of 1.8 per cent in the metropolitan branch. Faster growing than this was the engineering branch with a rate of 3.7 per cent so that it had become the largest employer within the P+T group with one-third of the total by 1984. In 1932 its staff were very few. Employment at headquarters had also risen substantially. These few scattered remarks indicate the need for a more detailed appraisal of growth patterns. In such an exercise it is important to allow for the hiving off of responsibility to semi-State bodies. For example, it is clear that the growth of the Industrial Development Authority reduced the need for some expansions in its parent body — the Department of Industry and Commerce and similarly for Aer Rianta, etc. Such a study will be postponed until after the State-sponsored bodies have been examined.

Part-time Staff

Table 2 gave figures of part-time employment contained in total employment before World War II. Table 30 continues the series from 1949 to 1985 with some exceptions. The records for 1950 are missing. Computerisation of the SIS in 1975 broke the continuity by omitting 1977. The same cause meant that the Post Office was not distinguished from other departments in a number of Censuses. Table 30 also gives the average earnings of part-time staff as a percentage of all average earnings. This gives a broad indicator of full-time equivalents. However, this indicator probably underestimates the real equivalent, especially outside the Post Office. This is so because part-time staff can generally be

Table 30: *Part-time officials in the Post Office and other departments 1949 to 1985 distinguishing sex and providing estimates of full-time equivalents*

| January | Total | Post Office | | Other Departments | | Average part-time earnings as a % of average total earnings | |
		Male	Female	Male	Female	Post Office	Other Depts.
1949	6,187	—	—	—	—	—	—
1950	—	—	—	—	—	—	—
1951	6,180	4,130	1,421	443	186	61	52
1952	6,090	4,042	1,441	430	177	60	50
1953	5,980	3,978	1,417	401	184	61	51
1954	5,925	3,953	1,417	367	188	61	49
1955	6,055	3,911	1,415	520	209	60	39
1956	5,991	3,867	1,399	515	210	59	37
1957	5,967	3,829	1,400	523	215	59	36
1958	5,949	3,809	1,406	521	213	58	36
1959*	4,049	3,013	85	283	668	53	33
1960	4,017	3,030	80	267	640	54	33
1961	3,997	3,021	72	252	652	54	33
1962	3,939	2,992	68	236	643	55	35
1963	3,966	3,020	69	215	662	55	34
1964	4,038	3,089	80	209	660	54	34
1965	3,967	3,023	84	200	660	56	30
1966	3,948	2,988	104	198	658	54	30
1967	3,862	2,912	102	194	654	54	35
1968	3,825	2,858	106	192	669	53	39
1969	3,705	2,757	109	195	644	55	38
1970	3,610	2,706	130	192	582	56	41
1971	3,611	2,688	147	179	597	58	43
1972	3,502	2,641	160	168	533	56	45
1973	3,410	2,548	198	153	511	58	46
1974	3,371	2,463	252	149	507	59	50
1975	3,281	2,307	399	132	443	58	50
1976	3,050	2,140	471	82	357	—	—
1977 (July)	2,899	1,933	535	76	355	57	43
1978	2847	1,888	544	74	341	57	43
1978 (July)	2,751	1,804	554	69	324	—	40
1979	2,640	1,715	561	77	320	—	—
1980	2,622	1,683	555	70	314	50	45
1980 (July)	2,465	1,527	553	70	315	—	—
1981	2,324	1,404	604	54	262	—	—
1982	2,337	1,352	670	55	260	—	—
1983	2,277	1,274	703	53	247	—	—
1984	2,038		1,767		50	221	—
1985	1,623		1,372		43	208	—

*Prior to 1959 scale-paid staff were included as part timers.

Note: By 1985 the traditional Department of Posts and Telegraphs had ceased to exist.

'—' means not available.

expected to cluster in low paid grades, such as cleaners, whereas the general average would include senior posts.

As Table 30 shows most of the part-time staff are Post Office employees. Among these auxiliary postmen in the provincial branch were a dominant group whose significance has declined over time more rapidly than the decline in part-time employment in general. Prior to the 1958 reclassification the Post Office group included more than 2,100 scale paid managers of sub-post offices (in 1957 1,307 female and 806 male) whose level of remuneration varied enormously. The reclassification almost eliminated female part-time staff in 1959. However, numbers subsequently expanded especially during the 'seventies against a background which more than halved male numbers.

Outside the Post Office numerous departments returned a few part-time workers. For example the 431 recorded in the SIS of July 1977 were distributed among the major employers as follows:

Agriculture	106	(85)	Foreign Affairs	19	(9)
Social Welfare	104	(65)	Houses of the Oireachtas	16	(9)
Revenue Commissioners	40	(38)	Prisons	16	(12)
Industry and Commerce	34	(14)	Courts	9	(3)
Office of Public Works	28	(5)	Valuation and Ordnance	12	(12)
Environment	22	(6)			

The remaining 25 were scattered among ten other votes. By 1984 the total had dwindled to 271. The figures in parentheses above indicate the departmental distribution in 1984 apart from 13 in 7 other departments.

One difficulty remains with Table 30 and relates to the reclassification of 1958. As explained elsewhere 80 scale-paid managers of Social Welfare branches were reclassified from being hitherto deemed part time. In addition a number of staff earning less than £50 per annum (and prima facie part time) were also deducted. This would account, perhaps, for the drop in males from 521 to 283 but no explanation is available for the abrupt rise in part-time female staff from 213 to 668. It seems more likely to be another case of reclassification. In 1975 the transfer to the SIS coincided with another set of falls in numbers. In the case of females the change from 1975 to 1976 is plausible, being not out of line with the fall in the previous year. Males were also declining over the 'seventies though the fall in 1975 was exceptionally large. It is not easy to say whether the computerisation of the SIS involved a reclassification, an under recording or merely happened to coincide with a genuine reduction.

In 1985 the bulk of the part-time staff outside the Post Office were cleaners and the fall in numbers over time undoubtedly reflects in part the tendency to replace cleaners by cleaning contracts to outsiders which characterised, in particular, the newer Government offices. Apart from cleaners, prisons employed part-time mess attendants. Social Welfare employed part-time local agents, etc. Table 30 also suggests that inputs of hours worked may have changed over time. Average earnings were compared rather crudely with all average earnings to obtain an approximate index of the fraction of normal hours worked by part timers.

Chapter II.3

PIECE WORKERS

Table 1 represents a historical overview of payments to pieceworkers up to year 1957. In these records a distinction was made between those employed on a regular basis compared with those whose employment was only occasional. Each sub-group was subdivided into industrial, professional and other workers. The broad categories of expenditure during 1956 are given in Table 31 which only records numbers employed in the case of regular employees.

Table 31: *Employment and remuneration of persons employed on piecework, taskwork, capitation or fee basis during 1956*

	Regulars		Occasionals	Total
	Nos.	*Remuneration*	*Remuneration*	*Remuneration*
		£	£	£
Industrials	785	3,612	1,298	4,910
Professionals	834	73,858	257,077	330,935
Others	1,212	148,937	116,758	265,695
Total	2,831	226,407	375,133	601,540

The industrial workers in this group are different from industrial civil servants or temporary industrial workers employed by the Civil Service. They are essentially outside the public domain but earn a fee. All but six of the 785 regulars were voluntary crews of lifeboats. One of these six was at the College of Art and earned a fee of £104. The five regulars with Roinn na Gaeltachta had a combined annual earnings of £25 compared to £1,254 earned by occasional industrials with the same department. Occasional work at the Department of Justice accounted for the remaining £44.

97

Fees are a more normal source of income for professionals. Table 32 provides an expanded version of Table 31 above but excludes industrials. This table shows that almost two-thirds of the fees were paid by Agriculture. These were earned by veterinary surgeons, mostly as occasional workers under the Bovine Tuberculosis Eradication Scheme then starting to get seriously under way. Others were retained on a more regular basis under the inspection requirements of the Fresh Meat Acts. The Department regularly employed a large number of "others" as judges at agricultural shows, as livestock inspectors, teachers at agricultural schools, but here the average fees were small (£26). Another major department paying professionals on a fee basis was the Department of Education where examiners, especially in the secondary branch, accounted for much of the occasional employment. Woodwork and Rural Science teachers in technical schools and art teachers in the National College of Art made up most of those regularly in receipt of fees. Doctors' fees were important in the Garda vote (and also in Defence). The Office of Public Works, however, paid out twice as much to its professional advisers. Industry and Commerce made fee payments to the Chairmen of its Committees and Commissions. Posts and Telegraphs had 516 professionals averaging £21 each in fees. The Circuit Court retained stenographers and interpreters.

Non-professionals were also in receipt of fees. Important among the regular workers were 65 Collectors of Taxes whose fees were more than three-fifths the total. Social Welfare paid 325 people £47 a piece in 1956. Roinn na Gaeltachta had five agents averaging £2,700 each which were considerable fees in that year. The Circuit Court had 414 summon servers. The general registry office of the Department of Health retained 47. The Central Statistics Office paid out over £7,000 in fees, presumably to those returning prices, etc. On the Occasional employment account £5 out of every £6 were disbursed by the Department of Posts and Telegraphs and of these almost three-quarters were fees connected with broadcasting, then a branch of that Department. The most significant other spenders were Roinn na Gaeltachta and the Civil Service Commission.

The collation of these fee records was very valuable. After 1958 the practice was discontinued so that the very considerable fees associated with, for instance, livestock disease eradication are not now separately recorded. Since the veterinary surgeons involved have been in regular receipt of fees over several decades it is difficult to see why they are treated differently from scale-paid managers of sub-post offices who are not included in this category of pieceworkers. Evidence that the line of demarcation has proved difficult to draw is provided by the case of State solicitors. In recent practice, these solicitors, who also have private practices, have been omitted from the lists of those in the public sector, through heretofore they had always been included. As a result, they are now treated like other lawyers who sell part of their services to the State.

Table 32: *Departmental breakdown of persons in receipt of fees, piece rates, etc., during 1956 omitting industrial workers*

Department	Type of contract	Professionals		Others	
		Nos.	*Fees (£)*	*Nos.*	*Fees (£)*
Agriculture	Regular	106	38,713	195	5,093
Agirculture	Occasional	—	177,035	—	140
Lands/Forest	Occasional	—	1,403	—	199
Education	Regular	62	10,586	13	552
Education	Occasional	—	45,970	—	584
Wireless	Occasional	—	—	—	71,500
P+T	Occasional	—	404	—	28,312
P+T	Regular	516	10,927	2	38
Finance	Regular	2	4,354(Fin.)	65	91,905(Rev.)
Revenue C.	Occasional	—	1,442	—	239
Gardai	Regular	135	5,580	—	—
Gardai	Occasional	—	1,241	—	—
Courts	Occasional	—	1,230	—	532
Courts	Regular	5	1,856	414	12,575
Social Welfare	Regular	2	289	325	15,178
Social Welfare	Occasional	—	815	—	644
Health	Both	(1)	357	(48)	1,449
Defence	Both	(2)	6,309	—	—
Industry + Commerce	Regular	1	32	145	1,886
	Occasional	—	9,439	—	764
Gaeltacht	Both	—	—	(5)	22,071
OPW	Occasional	—	11,521	—	32
CSO/CSC	Regular	—	—	—	7,050/4,734
Others	Both	(2)	1,432	—	218(LG)
Total		834	330,935	1,212	265,695

Figures in parentheses mean that these only earned part of the fees shown.
Abbreviations: CSO Central Statistics Office; CSC Civil Service Commission; LG Local Government; OPW Office of Public Works.

That the fees earned can be considerable was revealed in answers to Dail questions concerning the disastrous fires in the Stardust Dance Hall and on the Betelguise Oil tanker. The inquiries held both cost approximately a million pounds. In accordance with the criteria used for deciding whether a person belongs to the public domain, i.e., whether over half his income was derived from the State it would be necessary to relate the fees to other private fees earned. In the Stardust enquiry eleven counsel earned almost a quarter of the total in fees with individual fees in about half the cases exceeding £25,000, i.e., the highest salaries in the Civil Service. Three sets of solicitors' fees were not included in this calculation.

In the enquiry into the Whiddy oil tanker disaster consultants and assessors earned between them more than a quarter of a million pounds. These were only two inquiries. On another occasion the Dail was informed that 59 senior counsel and 115 junior counsel were paid £362,300 and £287,700, respectively. Clearly average payments of £6,140 and £2,500, respectively, would not constitute the major part of the average incomes of these individuals. However, an examination of the distribution of payments shows that in 8 cases, or 5 per cent of those listed, payments were in excess of £15,000.

Range	Senior Counsel	Range	Junior Counsel
Over £45,000	2	Over £30,000	2
Over £35,000	1	Over £10,000	1
Over £25,000	1	Over £5,000	14
Over £15,000	2	Over £2,500	13
Over £10,000	4	Over £1,000	27
Over £5,000	9	Over £500	13
Over £1,000	21	Over £250	13
Over £500	4	Over £100	18
Under £500	15	Under £100	14
	59		115

Better records are kept in the case of doctors who derive a substantial part of their income under the choice of doctor scheme since the numbers involved are recorded by the General Medical Services (Payments) Board. It is regretable that there is no longer any attempt to list all those in receipt of some payments from the State directly or indirectly. Perusal of the public accounts reveals many instances, such as those engaged in consultancy work for different departments, and the many examiners correcting and supervising public examinations. Volunteer defence forces are paid for attending summer camps and AnCO trainees for engaging in job training schemes. A number of people perform minor services for State bodies for which they are paid a small retainer. Local agents, for example, report prices in shops to the Central Statistics Office on a regular basis for the compilation of quarterly Consumer Price Indices. The Office of Public Works rewards "river watchers" whose job it is to give early warning of critical river levels. Aer Lingus takes on extra staff during the peak tourist season. Bord na gCon and the Racing Board employ very many staff during race meetings. A major Census often causes the Central Statistics Office to expand its team of enumerators. Universities afford teaching opportunities to occasional lecturers. On a more permanent basis secretarial assistants have recently been provided for members of the Dail. Although their saleries derive ultimately from taxation there has been a tendency to deem them to be employed by the TD rather than by the State. In this study that practice will not be followed. Nor will we exclude for analogous reasons caretakers employed by national schools.

Where the accent is on the measurement of governmental impact it would be useful to continue the pre-1958 practice and widen the scope of the enquiry to all those whose livelihood is obtained largely from the sale of goods and services to Government. This extension is likely to be more significant in countries where there are large-scale contracts for research and also for the production of armaments. Even in Ireland the exsistence of contracts as an alternative to direct employment can obscure comparisons. For example, on the NIHE campus at Limerick much of the maintenance and catering is undertaken by contract firms whereas at some other Universities such staff are directly employed. Both groups are ultimately dependent on State finances. Local authority housing is another example where contract building offers an alternative to direct construction. As already noted numbers of part-time staff have fallen in the Civil Service generally, as contract cleaning made its inroads into department after department. This study will, in a few cases, make up for the failure to continue the pre-1958 series but clearly an adequate treatment would be a major project in itself.

Chapter II.4

WORKERS NOW RECORDED OUTSIDE THE SIS

While the piece workers reported in the last section have not been recorded since 1958 in any form, other workers, who were excluded from the Census prior to 1958 (see Table 1), have continued to be enumerated but outside the Censuses and Staff Information System (SIS). Since 1958 these excluded staff have been referrred to as (a) industrial workers and (b) non-industrial workers outside the Staff Information System.

The antecedents of these workers in the pre-1958 records are varied. One group, separately identified prior to 1958, were "workers on temporary schemes other than relief", as set out in Table 1. A second group were casuals employed by the Departments of Lands and Posts and Telegraphs. These casuals were not returned individually to the Civil Service Census but were appended *en bloc* to the returns compiled for the individual departments. A third group were industrial civil servants, who were included in the Civil Service Census up to 1952 under four grade codes in a manner analogous to that for, e.g., postmen, and who were subsequently afforded a census of their own. By and large these three groups became the industrial civil servants of the post-1958 period. A fourth group consisted of civilians attached to the Defence Forces, who have always been separately identified. Most of these were industrial civil servants but not all. The fifth group were fee-paid staff in the Departments of Posts and Telegraphs and in Social Welfare, who were returned as part-time staff prior to 1958. These formed the bulk of the category described currently as "non-industrial staff not in the SIS". The remainder of this category is made up of a miscellaneous group of staff, the reasons for whose separate treatment is obscure unless it is based on the manner of payment. A large part of these staff are employed by the Department of Posts and Telegraphs.

The analysis, which follows, will use the post-1958 categories, starting with industrial civil servants. After a brief definition of industrials, this group will be related to industrials as recorded in the Census of Industrial Production, before employment levels are reported.

Chapter II.4A

INDUSTRIAL CIVIL SERVANTS

Definition

Industrial civil servants have been traditionally defined as "manipulative and operative staffs in factories and workshops", and also "foremen, artisans, gardeners, gangers, labourers and other manual workers employed regularly and directly by the State". The 1953 returns show the variety of occupations of industrial workers. They included printers, engineering fitters and guillotine operators (Revenue Commissioners), typewriter mechanics (Stationery Office), bookbinders and carpenters (Museum), deer and vermin trappers (Forestry), forestry trainees, gamekeepers, water bailiffs, river watchers (Fisheries), coach painters and viewers (P+T), rock gardeners, harbour constables and assistant to dairy maid (OPW).

Broadly speaking industrial civil servants are people who follow a normal industrial occupation but whose employment happens to be in the public sector. Their employment is often governed by different regulations and catered for by different trade unions. However, this definition is not complete because to some degree there are other workers within the Civil Service proper whose work is similar, e.g., staff in the engineering branch of the Post Office but who have been traditionally treated differently in the records. At first sight industrials would appear to qualify for the United Nations category of "departmental enterprises" since the staff concerned produce marketable goods and services which are sold exclusively to the public sector. While the parallel is obvious it is not clear what the original rationale for the classification of industrials has been. If the parallel was to hold we would expect that industrial civil servants would also correlate with those civil servants included in the industrial branch of the National Accounts and also with those industrial workers which the annual Census of Industrial Production (CIP) described as belonging to "Local Authorities and Other Government Departments" up to 1977. In practice there is little relationship between these categories and industrial civil servants.

Comparison with CIP – "Workers in Government Departments"

In the section on local authorities Table 61 reveals that the bulk of workers in the CIP group "Local Authorities and Other Government Departments" were in fact employed by the local authorities though the share of Government departments was rising up to the time when this category was reclassified in accordance with NACE in 1978. Examination of Table 61 shows that about 10 per cent of these latter workers were in fact salaried. This marks the first difference between the two series. Industrial civil servants are a group sharing a common grade in the public domain. Industrial workers in the CIP "Government departments" share a common activity but different grades. Within the Civil Service salaried workers would probably belong to the "administrative and executive" or "professional" grade groups.

The second difference lies in the composition of the two series. This can only be illustrated for 1974, a year for which details of the CIP composition were available.

	CIP	CSI
Post Office	6,422	177
(of which assembly of telephone equipment)	(159)	(134 stores)
Office of Public Works	1,781	2,231
(of which part timers)	n.a.	(1,500 approx.)
Defence	nil	1,418
Forestry	24 (sawmills)	2,811
Land Commission	25 (wood)	241
Agricultural Schools and Farms	nil	490
Ordnance Survey (printing)	48	nil
Revenue Commissioners (printing)	nil	38
Irish Lights (other machinery)	125	excluded
Others (Justice, Transport, etc.)	nil	46
Total	8,425	7,452

The CIP does not include agricultural activities, such as forestry, except where they involve manufacturing, e.g., sawmilling. Such activities are included in the agricultural branch of the National Accounts and as such do not form part of "Public Administration and Defence". The Civil Service Industrials, on the other hand, include few in the Post Office which looms large in the CIP. The two series are closest together in their account of the Office of Public Works which, in the case of the CIP, included 37 in furniture making and 109 in engineering in 1974. However, the OPW industrials would appear to contain about two-thirds of their number as "casual and seasonal" workers. It is strange that the CIP includes printers in the Ordnance Survey but excludes those in the Revenue Commissioners. Irish Lights staff are not included in the Civil Service at all, be they industrial or otherwise.

Given that the composition is so different it is no surprise that the evolution of employment levels of the two series, as mapped in Figure 8, shows no similarities. The rise of CIP employment reflects the growing importance of the engineering branch of the Department of Posts and Telegraphs. The reasons for the decline in numbers of industrial civil servants will be taken up in the next section.

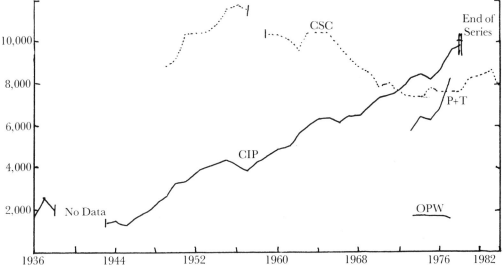

Figure 8: *Comparison of the levels of employment of industrial workers in Government departments as recorded in the Census of Industrial Production and the Civil Service Census 1936–1982*

As is clear from Figure 8, which is based on Table 61, the Census of Industrial Production series enjoyed a long history. In 1974 the CIP was reformulated to conform with the international NACE classification developed by the United Nations (see Appendix I). The old classification was finally superseded in 1978. One casualty of the reformulation was the dispersal of Government industrial activities and their incorporation into the appropriate industrial classifications. In fact the bulk of the Post Office employment and of the Office of Public Works were deemed to be construction and were no longer included in Industrial

Production but relegated to a separate Census of Building and Construction. Thus, 97.5 per cent of the 8,425 quoted above for 1974 was transferred in this manner, i.e., 6,263 (P+T) + 1,635 (OPW). The remaining 2.5 per cent, or 527 workers, were allocated to industrial production as indicated above. Two categories of mechanical engineering incorporated activities of Irish Lights and the Office of Public Works. Electrical engineering now includes the assembly of communications equipment by P+T. Forestry sawmills and the manufacture of wooden furniture by the Office of Public Works are now under the Wood "46" code numbers while the printing of maps by the Ordnance Survey is included under Paper and Printing. The virtues of this rationalisation are obvious. It is, however, unfortunate that there is no longer any published source of public industrial activities so defined with which to meet the growing needs of analyses of the public domain.

Regular Industrial Workers and Casuals pre-1958
   Up to the reclassification of 1952 industrial workers were included in the Civil Service Census in one of four grade codes. These distinguished in, for example, 1950

			of whom women
Code 107	General Industrials	3,438	97
Code 108	Crews of Boats	74	—
Code 109	Dublin Parks and Gardens	183	2
Code 110	Other gardens, Agricultural and Forestry, Labourers	2,135	3
		5,830	102

It proved possible to rearrange codes 108 to 110 to comply with the post-1952 classification which distinguished casuals from other industrial workers, i.e., those not individually returned in the Census. Thus Code 110 included 1,979 forestry casuals. The Office of Public Works employed 23 crew. Agriculture employed 148 in Dublin Parks and 55 in other gardens. Agriculture employed 35 and 101 in Dublin and other parks. Other crew worked for Industry and Commerce (11) and Defence (40). On this basis Table 33 was developed for the 1932 to 1958 period.

Some points are worth noting about Table 33. As we have seen earlier non-professional industrials in the engineering branch of the Department of Posts and Telegraphs were transferred to the "manipulative" grade group in 1952 and no longer deemed industrials. Second, the P+T casuals also include indus-trials. Non-industrial casuals who numbered 661 in 1951 clearly do not belong to

Table 33: *Industrial workers by department, 1932††, 1940 and 1949–1958*

Department	1940	1949	1950	1951	1952	1953	1954	1955	1956	1957	1958
Revenue Commissioners	7	10	11	10	11	12	12	34	33	32	32
Office of Public Works	553	608	623	641	724	751	713	641	626	531	524
Stationary Office	4	3	4	4	3	4	4	12	10	8	4
Valuation and Ordnance	12	13	13	14	14	14	17	—	—	—	—
Justice	2	3	3	3	3	—	—	3	3	3	3
Gardai	16†	12	16	17	—	—	—	—	—	—	—
Courts	—	—	—	—	—	—	1	1	1	1	1
Education	11	1	1	1	—	—	—	—	—	—	—
Museum	13	7	8	7	5	5	5	5	4	5	5
College of Art	—	—	—	—	3	3	3	3	3	3	3
Agriculture	129	163	159	181	191	189	197	224	248	252	251
Fisheries	35*	17	18	18	16	15	14	12	11	5	4
Forestry	40*	27	30	44	35	42	59	22	24	8	7
Gaeltacht	24*	64	56	69	65	65	44	41	52	51	55
Industry and Commerce	—	66	83	89	147	149	144	162	173	178	176
P+T Provincial		4	4	4	4	4	4	2	2	2	1
P+T Stores		114	116	113	134	141	138	106	99	97	93
P+T Engineering	829	1,352	1,483	1,697	(a)	—	—	5	5	4	4
P+T Wireless		38	37	37	(b)	—	—	—	—	—	—
Defence	667	1,126	1,076	1,073	1,080	1,123	1,172	1,232	1,471	1,415	1,258
Officers Abroad	—	—	—	—	—	—	—	1	1	1	1
Social Welfare	—	—	—	3	3	3	3	—	—	—	—
Dundrum Asylum	—	3	3	4	4	7	8	8	8	6	6
Total Industrials	2,342	3,631	3,744	4,029	2,422	2,527	2,538	2,514	2,779	2,602	2,428
Casuals employed											
Lands	n.a.	1,786	1,979	2,121	2,769	3,187	3,402	4,302	4,448	5,107	4,934
P+T (Industrials only)	n.a.	135	107	85	50	77	156	158	201	51	247
All Industrials	n.a.	5,552	5,830	6,235	5,241	5,791	6,096	6,974	7,428	7,760	7,609

Notes: †Include 6 workers in prisons.

*Breakdown between sections uncertain. (a) Reclassified in 1952; (b) Transferred to Radio Eireann.

††The 1932 figures were: Total 2,990 — OPW 1,298; P+T 641; Agric. 609; Defence 433 and 3 each Justice, Museum and Ordnance.

Totals for 1938 and 1945 were 3,185 and 4,583 respectively.

this table. Third, Radio Eireann became independent of the Civil Service Census in 1952. In 1958 the Army employed 150 non-industrial civilians. Perhaps these were included in the 1956 and 1957 returns. Figures for 1932, given as a footnote, show a substantial drop in employment in the Office of Public Works and Agriculture over the 'thirties. The War of Independence and the Civil War had inflated staff levels in the former during the 'twenties. The entry of the Department of Industry and Commerce into the areas of aviation and meteorologial services can be traced in the employment levels of that department. In general, employment in 1938 and 1945 was 3,185 and 4,583, respectively.

Table 34: *Numbers employed on temporary schemes other than relief by department, 1948 to 1957*

Department	1948	1950	1951	1952	1953	1954	1955	1956	1957
Office of Public Works	228	753	928	911	997	1,069	1,102	1,225	1,023
Agriculture	156	312	750	1,636	1,041	575	605	582	521
Fisheries	6	2	4	4	21	12	12	12	4
Land Commission	2,130	1,756	1,795	1,996	1,685	1,888	1,888	1,670	1,600
Forestry	147	240	398	275	499	319	354	350	267
Gaeltacht	—	41	41	45	35	32	4	5	5
Industry and Commerce	86	68	22	21	—	—	6	7	7
P+T (Engineering)	63	63	68	46	72	174	197	147	110
Defence	351	225	243	257	410	729	410	313	315
Education	—	2	2	2	2	2	—	2	2
Museum	—	—	2	—	—	—	—	—	—
Wireless	—	—	—	—	1	1	1	1	1
Total	3,167	3,462	4,253	5,193	4,763	4,801	4,579	4,314	3,855

Workers on Temporary Schemes pre-1958

The second category excluded from Table 1 were workers on schemes which were essentially temporary in their particular area but which might move around the country. Table 34 gives the picture up to 1957 while Table 35 uses the pay levels of 1956 to give some idea of the duration of this employment by department.

Numbers of All Industrial Workers post-1958

The left hand columns of Table 36 give the evolution of industrial employment between 1959 and 1985 distinguishing three major groups of departments. Appendix Table A2.9 gives the same totals up to 1982 but disaggregating seasonal and casual workers from others. This classification in Table A2.9 enables us to link the post-1958 series with its antecedents. Table A2.9 does not always agree with Table 36 because of some revisions made by the author. These are generally small except in recent years when differences of about 350 were recorded, perhaps due to changes in approach to staff at the Office of Public Works. That body was unable to provide a continuous series since 1968 separating casuals and seasonals from others. It would appear that such distinctions are not easily made in practice.

Table 35: *Foremen, artisans, gangers, labourers, etc., employed on schems or works of a temporary nature other than relief during 1956 (average numbers)*

Employer	Average numbers	Total pay	Pay per head
		£	£
Office of Public Works	1,225	394,172	322
Land Commission	1,670	269,934	162
Agriculture	582	131,237	225
Forestry	350	90,930	260
Defence	313	72,432	231
Posts and Telegraphs	147	53,726	365
Others*	27	2,685	99
Total	4,314	1,015,166	235

*Fisheries £251 (12); Industry and Commerce £890 (7); Gaeltacht £1,147 (5); Education £124 (2).

A set of Appendix Tables A2.10 to A2.12 gives a breakdown of industrial employment but by department and by casual and seasonal vs. permanent. These tables form an expansion of both Tables 36 and A2.9. Inspection of these tables and relating them to Table 33 indicates that the latter, broadly speaking, provides the pre-1958 series for industrial workers other than casual and seasonal. Table 33 gives totals of 7,760 and 7,609 for 1957 and 1958 and Table A2.9 continues with 7,206 and 7,313 for the two subsequent years. A decline in "casuals" in the Department of Lands accounts for the fall in the totals. It is unfortunate that Table 33 refers to such "casuals" in the last two rows since, after the 1958 classification, the workers concerned are clearly defined as industrial workers *other than casual and seasonal*. Perhaps these workers should have continued to be defined as casuals, or, as seems to have happened more recently, they could have been deemed to be non-industrials. In our tables they are part of the non-casual industrials in accordance with SIS practice.

The antecedents of the casuals and seasonals so described in Table A2.9 appear to be those employees engaged in temporary schemes other than relief as set out in Table 34. Figures for 1958 do not exist but if we compare 1957 with 1959 the major difference over the transition is a drop in Land Commission employment of almost 600 — from 1,600 to 1,006 (see Table A2.10). This accounts for most of the difference between the 1957 total on Table 34, i.e., 3,855 and the 1959 total in Table A2.9, i.e., 3,110 — a decline of 745. The other major break was in defence from 315 to 56 (Table A2.13).

Table 36: *Employment recorded outside the Staff Information System (or Census) 1959–1985*

Jan. 1	Industrial				Non-Industrial				Grand Total
	P+T	Defence	Others	Total	P+T	Defence	Others	Total	
1959	246	1,462	8,608	10,316	2,641	153	210	3,004	13,320
1960	223	1,473	8,634	10,330	2,647	150	408	3,205	13,535
1961	280	1,444	8,386	10,110	2,796	149	331	3,276	13,386
1962	232	1,486	8,065	9,783	2,620	155	258	3,033	12,816
1963	292	1,491	8,866	10,649	2,766	167	243	3,176	13,825
1964	280	1,507	8,685	10,472	2,764	167	210	3,141	13,613
1965	290	1,408	8,852	10,550	2,875	168	221	3,264	13,814
1966	232	1,434	8,329	9,995	2,940	162	180	3,282	13,277
1967	207	1,340	7,583	9,130	2,810	167	225	3,202	12,332
1968	209	1,330	7,291	8,830	2,858	188	142	3,188	12,018
1969	187	1,327	6,971	8,485	2,779	187	161	3,127	11,612
1970	178	1,323	6,400	7,901	2,843	192	137	3,172	11,073
1971	197	1,322	6,569	8,088	2,870	194	146	3,210	11,298
1972	175	1,344	6,245	7,764	2,716	194	175	3,085	10,849
1973	170	1,397	5,859	7,426	2,901	194	168	3,263	10,689
1974	179	1,418	5,857	7,454	2,899	201	163	3,263	10,717
1975	184	1,741	5,913	7,838	2,805	202	158	3,165	11,003
1976	179	1,754	5,863	7,796	2,682	210	171	3,063	10,859
1977	179	1,650	5,607	7,436	2,713	308	218	3,239	10,675
1978	179	1,683	5,387	7,249	2,806	294	173	3,273	10,522
1979	190	1,770	5,891	7,851	2,850	298	236	3,384	11,235
1980	202	1,798	6,056	8,056	2,703	327	247	3,277	11,333
1981	230	1,786	6,397	8,413	2,720	317	225	3,262	11,675
1982	238	1,727	6,362	8,327	2,765	302	505	3,572	11,899
1983	241	1,687[e]	6,464	8,392	2,657	258[c]	539	3,454	11,846
1984	240	1,646	6,267	8,153	2,543	215	470	3,228	11,381
1985	238[a]	1,369	5,742	7,349	2,415[a]	462	591	3,468	10,817

[a] =not included already in totals for Bord Telecom and An Post.
[e] = estimate.

Departmental Composition of Industrial Employment

Marrying up the pre- and post-1958 series gives us a broad classification of industrials as set out in Table 37 for a set of years.

Table 37: *Composition of industrial employment, selected years 1951 to 1985*

	1951	1957	1959	1964	1974	1981	1985
OPW	1,569	1,554	1,711	2,573	2,231	3,109	2,455
Forestry	2,563	5,382	4,658	4,685	2,811	2,867	2,512
Lands	1,795	1,600	1,053	868	241	130	536
Agriculture	931	773	867	338	490	156	154
Defence	1,316	1,730	1,462	1,507	1,418	1,786	1,369
P+T	270	264	246	280	179	230	excl.
Other	310	311	319	221	84	135	85
Total	10,451†	11,614	10,316	10,472	7,454	8,413	7,111

Note: For complete series see Appendices; wireless not included (i.e., 37 in 1951 and 1 in 1957).
†1,697 staff transferred from engineering branch in 1952 reclassification included in total.

(a) Agricultural Departments

Table 37 showed that the major employers have been the rural departments: Agriculture, Lands and Forestry; and the Office of Public Works, which is also rural to the extent that a major responsibility has been drainage. Apart from temporary schemes in 1949, the pre-1958 details of employment in rural departments can be found in Tables 33 and 34. These are summarised here:

1949	4,347	1952	6,902	1955	7,395
1950	4,476	1953	6,643	1956	7,322
1951	5,289	1954	6,440	1957	7,755

This group contains three separate activities (a) Forestry workers including sawmilling; (b) workers (almost exclusively casual) employed by the Land Commission largely in the "improvement of estates" and (c) workers employed by the Department of Agriculture at schools, farms, gardens, laboratories, etc. All three activities involve both whole-time and casual workers.

The post-1958 levels of employment are given in Appendix Table A2.10. The overall levels are graphed in Figure 9. In Forestry, employment has stabilised in recent years at about 2,850 but informed opinion is that productivity gains have been inadequate in the late 'seventies and further cutbacks would be appropriate. This is sobering news in view of the generally favourable climate for increased production over the 'eighties documented by Convery (1979).

Figure 9 reflects the diminishing activities of the Land Commission which had caused the work to shrink to one-eighth of its size in 1960 by January 1978. The Commission was recently abolished.

The rise in Agriculture in the early 'fifties probably reflects the intensive drive under the Land Project. Between 1959 and 1961 and again in 1980 reorganisations of the institutional arrangement catering for farmers caused a change of employer rather than a loss of jobs. The occasions were the establishment of An Foras Talúntais which took over facilities, such as Johnstown Castle soil research station, and of ACOT, the State-sponsored body for farm advisory services. The Munster Institute has been earmarked for transfer to University College, Cork. Currently, the Department retains a number of responsibilities, such as the Botanic Gardens, Backweston Farm, the laboratories at Thorndale and Abbotstown, the bull station at Tully, Kildare, Spike Island quarantine station and Raphoe potato station.

(b) The Office of Public Works

This office has difficulty in presenting an accurate account of its employment levels for a number of reasons. To begin with, much of the work is seasonal and is unlikely to be undertaken on January 1st when the Census is normally taken. Drainage schemes are not usual when rivers are in spate. In addition some employees are of a very peripheral nature, being paid very small sums for activities like watching an unmanned beacon for malfunction, reading river flow gauges and caretaking. Others are engaged in very minor marine works. An estimate of the numbers involved put these numbers at 350. They appear to be returned as casual and seasonal workers.

Perhaps as a consequence of these difficulties the distinction between whole time and part time was not reported for many years after 1967. Indeed the levels of employment in general have been variable. Estimates of industrial employment for the five years ending January 1981 were extracted specially for this study. However, returns made later to another agency gave a different level of employment for January 1981. This latter return of 2,753 full time and 356 casual and seasonal totalled 3,109 which was almost 500 more than the 2,613 provided by the special study.[15] Such a difference in interpretation may have bedevilled the records over a considerable period of time. A study of employment fluctuations shows swings of comparable magnitude, e.g.,

Jan 1962	compared with	1963	+628	(+34%)
Jan 1965	compared with	1966	−398	(−15%)
Jan 1970	compared with	1971	+413	(+21%)
Jan 1980	compared with	1981	+540	(+21%)

[15]Similar discrepancies were found for 1977 and 1978: 2,835 and 2,750 vs. 2,163 and 2,210.

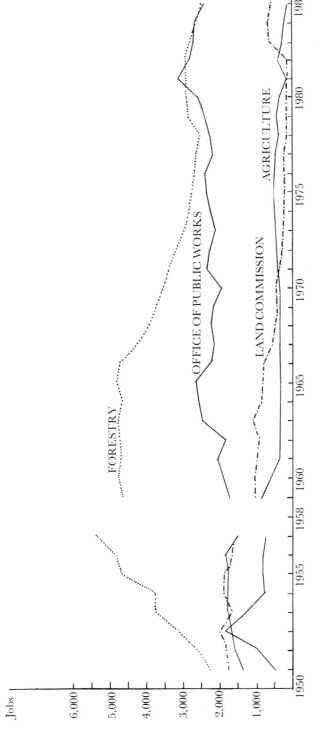

Figure 9: *Industrial workers by major areas of employment 1950-1985*

It is not clear if such shifts in employment actually occurred or if the change is due to differing interpretations of employment levels. The evolution of employment is graphed in Figure 9 and the data given in Appendix Table A2.12.

(c) Other departments

Figures for the Post Office are given in Appendix Table A2.11 for the post-1958 period and were generally about 200. They reached 290 in 1965 and dropped to 152 by 1981. Of these, workers in the stores branch maintained a fairly steady level of about 140. This level was somewhat less before 1958. In the early 'fifties totals included about 37 staff transferred later to Radio Eireann and a large number of non-professionals in the Engineering branch later regraded out of the industrial group. The decline in casual employment has been partly due to Trade Union representations whereby casual watchmen were upgraded to quasi-permanent status and their duties extended to include office security.

Employment by other departments has never been large, as Appendix Table A2.12 shows. Some considerable employment by Industry and Commerce in the early 'fifties was reduced to negligible proportions with the establishment of Aer Rianta — the State body in charge of airports. In a like manner the establishment of Gaeltarra Eireann to promote Gaeltacht industrial development caused the elimination of the industrial employment hitherto given by the Department of the Gaeltacht. The only sizeable staff otherwise consists of printers with the Revenue Commissioners.

Chapter II.4B

NON-INDUSTRIAL STAFF NOT IN THE SIS

This rather cumbersome title refers to a new category of staff which amalgamated all the loose ends following the 1958 reclassification. As Table 38 shows, a major element was the scale-paid staff formerly included in the Civil Service Census as part timers. These were the managers of sub-post offices and also of Social Welfare branches. Another element was the pre-1958 casuals in the Department of Posts and Telegraphs who were not industrial workers. These were groups of workers whose members were not recorded individually but in blocks. Typically they were auxiliary postmen and boy messengers though there was some ambiguity here in that in the Department of Posts and Telegraphs casual referred to the mode of appointment rather than the duration of employment used in other departments. Many P+T casuals were, therefore, virtually permanent.

A special category was comprised of "civilians in defence". This category arose because the Department is unusual in that it has two components. First, there are the normal Civil Service staff whose employment is governed by the Civil Service Employment Acts. A handful of these staff are classified as industrials. The second component is made up of the armed forces, whose employment is governed by the 1954 and other Defence Acts. Among these are a large number of civilians who are neither established civil servants nor Defence Forces. The bulk of these civilians are also industrials. Indeed on 1 January 1958, as Table 33 indicates, more than half of all industrials other than casuals were defence civilians. Some civilians were not industrials, e.g., 162 in 1958. In the revised classification these non-industrial civilians were included in the non-SIS non-industrial category. Sometimes, given the separate regulations applying to the armed forces, Civil Service procedures tend to treat all civilians with the defence forces as a separate category.

All the above categories were identifiable in the pre-1958 records and surviving data from this period are provided in the Appendix Table A2.14. Apart from these groups the 1958 reclassification opted to transfer to this cate-

Table 38: *Employment levels of non-industrial workers not in the Staff Information System by major categories, 1950[a] to 1985 excluding defence*

	Sub-post officers	Casuals in Post Office	Social Welfare[b]	Other	Total
1950[a]	2,035	n.a.	n.a.+84	n.a.	n.a
1955[a]	2,108	742	na+83	n.a.	n.a.
1960	2,162	297+188	14+103	285+6[c]	3,055
1965	2,173	483+219	12+100	72+37	3,096
1970	2,104	442+297	6+100	31	2,980
1975	2,073	492+240	12+95	51	2,963
1980	2,075	427+201	13+104	(53+77)	2,950
1984	2,077	466	14+110	236+110	3,013
1985	2,078[d]	337[d]	16+106	728+203	3,468[e]

[a] The non-industrial non-SIS category only dates from 1959. These are some pre-1958 elements.
[b] Includes about 80 part-time Managers of branch offices.
[c] Agriculture returned 188 but only 69 a year later. Presumably the balance had transferred to the newly established An Foras Talúntais.
[d] Now part of semi-state bodies, Bord Telecom and An Post.
[e] The rise during 1984 was part due to the inclusion of Garda yardmen formerly overlooked. Defence categories may also have been reclassified.

gory such staff as happened to be at work on the Census data but whose work would terminate before three months had elapsed from date of appointment. These included in 1960, 188 employees of the Department of Agriculture (due to be transferred to the new An Foras Talúntais?) 60 with the Revenue Commissioners and approximately 35 each in the Departments of Education and Labour.

Appendix Table A2.13 gives the distribution of non-industrial non-SIS apart from the Post Office for the post-1958 period. The Post Office groups are detailed in Appendix Table A2.11. Table A2.13 reveals that more than three quarters of these staff are part time. The broad picture is summarised in Tables 36 and 38. The latter includes some pre-1958 data on the employment levels in certain major categories and excludes defence.

Reconciliation of the Pre- and Post-1958 Series

Having completed an examination of all the major constituents of the central Civil Service and of the Post Office let us now demonstrate how to reconcile the series preceding and following the 1958 reclassification. The necessary steps are set out in Table 39.

Table 39 gives the old and the new series for the central Civil Service on lines 11 and 15 and for the Post Office on lines 6 and 9. The old series for industrials and casuals are given on lines 2 to 4 and the new series on line 17 but for 1958.

Table 39: *Link between the pre- and post-1958 series for the Civil Service*

Grand Total 1 January 1958 *(Table 1)*		38,471
Deduct pre-1958 categories		
(a) Industrials (Table 33)	-2,428	
(b) Industrials, casual, (Table 33)	-5,181	
(c) Non-industrials casuals (Table A2.14)	-418	
Total Deduction (a)+(b)+(c)		-8,027
Non-Industrial pre-1958 Civil Service		=30,444
Deduct from Pre-1958 P+T		-15,166
(d) Those earning under £50 pa	-4	
(e) Sub-Post Office Managers (Table A2.14)	-2,109	
Deduct Post-1958 P+T (i.e.) 15,166 -(d)-(e)=13,053		
Deduct Wireless Broadcasing (Table 13)		-349
Pre-1958 Central Civil Service (Table 10)		=14,929
Deduct		
(f) Those earning less than £50 pa	-206	
(g) Non-industrial civilians in Army (Tables A2.14)	-162	
(h) Branch Managers Social Welfare (Table A2.14)	- 80	-448
=Post 1958 Central Civil Service (Table 10)		=14,481
Total of Column	=10,588	
of which:—		
those not enumerated after 1958 (i.e. (d)+(f))	-210	
Pre 1958 Industrial Employees other than casual and seasonal		
i.e. (Table 33) (a)+(b)+(c)+(e)+(g)+(h)	-7,609	
New Balance		
Post-1958 Non-SIS Non-Industrials (part) (See Table 38).	2,769	

The origin of the post-1958 group, non-SIS non-industrials, is given on line 18. The table also shows that those who earned less than £50 annually before 1958 were excluded totally in Censuses after that date. The total for the non-industrial non-SIS groups in Table 38 was about 300 short of its normal post-1958 whereas the 1958 level for industrials newly defined was about 400 higher than the 1959 level. This suggests that there was probably a transfer between the two groups. It is unknown how many staff were enumerated in the Census for 1958 who were found to be in the class of those whose work would terminate before three months had elapsed from the date of appointment. After 1958 it was found that 212 workers were included in the new non-industrial non-SIS category who were not separately identified previously. These included 82 workers in the

Engineering Branch of the Post Office, 31 in Education, 29 in Social Welfare and 70 elsewhere. These would perhaps help to account for some of the implied transfers.

Employmint in Wireless Broadcasting

Table 39 shows that the 1958 total included employment in Wireless Broadcasting. This activity was performed by a division of the Department of Posts and Telegraphs up to January 1954. Subsequently it was allocated a vote of its own. By January 1961 the responsibility had passed to the State-sponsored Radio Telefis Eireann. Since it is more appropriate to consider this employment with that of the State-sponsored bodies it was removed from the series which documented employment in the Post Office.

SECTION III

LAW AND ORDER

Chapter III.1

AN t-OIREACHTAS AND THE JUDICIARY

In earlier sections we have examined trends in the central Civil Service, the Department of Posts and Telegraphs, the industrial Civil Service and in other employment not recorded in the Staff Information System. All of these were remunerated from funds voted annually by the Oireachtas. We must now look at those whose funding was not from voted money or whose appointment was due to public election. The latter comprise

(a) The President (Uachtarán) and
(b) Members of the Houses of An t-Oireachtas, i.e., Dail and Seanad

The former comprise

(i) The Judiciary and
(ii) The Comptroller and Auditor General

The last named civil servant is not included with the voted budget of the Civil Service since his function requires that he be independent of such votes to ensure the faithful discharge of his responsibilities. Similar rationale applies to the Judiciary.

Members of An t-Oireachtas
The Constitution regulates the numbers of members of the Dail in line with the size of the national population. The fall and rise in the numbers reflect the population turnaround since 1960.

In 1975 secretarial assistants were provided to deputies who were not office holders and since then numbers have increased until each deputy has his or her own. In 1981 assistants were paid for on the basis of one to each three Seanadoiri. Political parties also got some.

The Judiciary
The President of the High Court is, *ex officio,* an additional judge of the Supreme Court. The Chief Justice and the President of the Circuit Court, are *ex*

120

Table 40: *Numbers in An t-Oireachtas and in the Judiciary 1949 to 1985*

	An t-Oireachtas		Judiciary (Courts)					
	Dail	Seanad	Supreme	High	Circuit	District	Special Criminal	Total
1949/52*	147	67	5	6	11	42	—	64
1952/3	147	67	5	6	10	42	—	63
1953/4	147	67	5	7	10	42	—	64
1954/5	147	63	5	7	10	42	—	64
1955/6	147	63	5	7	10	42	—	64
1956/7	147	63	5	7	10	41	—	63
1957/8	147	60	5	7	10	41	—	63
1958/9	147	60	5	7	10	39	—	61
1959/60	147	60	5	7	10	38	—	60
1960/1	147	60	5	7	10	38	—	60
1961/2	144	60	5	7	10	38	—	60
1962/3	144	60	5	7	10	35	—	57
1963/4	144	60	5	7	10	35	—	57
1964/5	144	60	5	7	10	35	—	57
1965/6	144	60	5	7	10	35	—	57
1966/7	144	60	5	7	10	35	—	57
1967/8	144	60	5	7	10	35	—	57
1968/9	144	60	5	7	10	35	—	57
1969/70	144	60	5	7	10	35	—	57
1970/1	144	60	5	7	10	35	—	57
1971/2	144	60	5	7	10	35	—	57
1972/3	144	60	5	7	10	35	—	57
1973/4	144	60	5	8	10	35	—	58
1975	144	60	6	8	10	35	1	60
1976	144	60	6	8	10	35	1	60
1977	144	60	7	10	12	40	1	70
1978	148	60	6	10	12	40	1	69
1979	148	60	6	12	12	43	1	74
1980	148	60	6	12	12	40	1	71
1981	148	60	7	13	13	43	1	77
1982	166	60	7	16	13	41	2	79
1983	166	60	7	16	13	46	3	85
1984	166	60	6	18	14	44	4	86
1985	166	60	6	15	13	40	4	78

*No change in these years.

Source: Finance Accounts for Judiciary who are governed by Acts:

No. 8 of 1949	No. 39 of 1961	No. 21 of 1968
No. 32 of 1953	No. 18 of 1962	No. 11 of 1977
No. 35 of 1959	No. 9 of 1964	No. 15 of 1979

Note 1: An t-Uachtaran is not included in these numbers.

Note 2: Dail membership was 153 from 1923, 138 from 1935 and 147 from 1947.

Note 3: In 1975 clerical assistants were introduced for deputies who were not office holders and later for senators. Figures were 14 in 1975, 15 in 1977, 37 in 1980, 56 in 1981 and 151 in 1982: 12 assistants to Senators from November, 1981, later 20.

Note 4: The Finance Accounts may overstate the number of judges since the number includes all those paid in a year. A new appointment and a retiring judge could count as two although only one post was involved. Temporary judges are paid by the Department and appear in the SIS, i.e., 2 circuit and 5 district in 1985.

officio additional judges of the High Court. The Special Criminal Court, set up in May 1972, is composed largely of members of other courts but in 1984 also included three retired judges. Table 40 sets out the numbers in each court eliminating *ex officio* members. The District Court, which accounted for all the variation in numbers in the two decades 1953/4 to 1972/3, comprises a President, who is assigned to the Dublin Metropolitan District and 39 other justices, (22 are permanently assigned to the provincial districts, 10 to the metropolitan district and 7 are movable justices). Law provides for temporary increases in certain circumstances in the District Court. In June 1985 there were 5 temporary justices. This section does not consider them as they are paid from the Court Vote of the Department of Justice and returned in the Staff Information System. Conditions in the Courts are governed by Acts, of which eight were introduced since Act 8 of 1949 (see Table 40).

Chapter III.2

DEFENCE

Defence is outside the Staff Information System since the staff concerned are governed by the Defence Act 1954, etc., whereas the SIS Civil Service comes under the provisions of the Civil Service Commissioners Act, 1956, etc. The Defence Acts recognise permanent military personnel, the reserve and civilians. The latter may be subdivided into industrials and others. "Others" might include quasi-civil servants, such as typists.

The Permanent Defence Force

Regular monthly returns are available for the Permanent Defence Force (PDF) and these give details by rank. A time series from the Statistical Abstracts is provided in Table 41 up to April 1971 and supplemented by more recent data from the Department of Defence. To fit in with the Civil Service Census the later data are based on the situation on 1 January (or more correctly on the previous day).

Between 1950 and 1970 numbers were fairly constant except for a sudden increase during 1951 and 1952 which subsided rapidly during 1954 and 1955. The causes of this rise and fall are not clear unless they are related to the economic crisis of the same period. The growth in the Defence Force was rapid following the outbreak of community violence in Northern Ireland. Strength increased from 8,232 in 1969 to 14,662 in 1977, an annual rate of 7.5 per cent compound. Calculated from 1971 it was 9.2 per cent compound each year. This expansion was not affected by the 1975 Coalition ban since expansion was 16 per cent during 1975 — almost 2,000 extra men. During 1976 growth was over 9.5 per cent. Only during 1977 were there signs of a halt since outflow exceeded inflow in that year. However, this trend may have been independent of Government policy. The full employment programme of late 1977 failed to arrest the fall in numbers[16] so that January 1980 had 8.7 per cent fewer recorded in the

---

[16]Soldiers enlist initially on a three year engagement and many probably do not renew it in a period of boom.

Defence Force compared with three years previously. The recovery in numbers during 1980 and 1981 enabled the Defence Force to reach a new peak of 15,318 by end December 1981 when the recruitment ban was imposed. During 1982 average monthly intakes of 29 were swamped by average monthly losses of 117 so that numbers fell in each month except September. In June 1984 the Dail was told that in the five years 8,902 men and 66 women were recruited. Since the net gain was only 373 in this period 8,595 must have left. This implies a high level of wastage of one in eight per year.

In spite of the fluctuating levels in the strength of the Defence Force, establishment levels have continued to grow in recent years. There has, thus, been a considerable shortfall between permitted levels and recorded strengths, as the figures for recent years illustrate:

31/12	Establishment	Strength	Shortfall (%)
1976	15,493	14,662	5.4
1977	16,533	14,750	10.8
1978	16,589	13,752	17.1
1979	16,802	13,372	20.4
1980	17,926	13,764	23.2
1981	18,025	15,318	15.0
1982	18,064	14,457	20.0
1983	18,236	14,125	22.5
1984	17,962	13,891	22.7

Changes in Defence Structures by Rank

The purposes that Irish Defence Force serves might, presumably, be to provide a core of experienced personnel who could provide the nucleus of a larger force should national security call for a rapid build-up of military strength. If so, the *a priori* expectation would be for a high proportion of higher ranks to enlisted men. Figure 10 plots the trends for those ranks given in Table 41. It will be noted that the brunt of the fluctuations was borne by "privates and cadets" and, as we have seen in the 'seventies and up to December 1981, tended to be trending in the opposite direction to general Civil Service trends. The numbers of commissioned officers were virtually identical in 1952 and 1974 and grew slowly thereafter. In contrast NCOs (non-commissioned officers) grew 35 per cent in numbers over the same period and by 50 per cent more by December 1982. Officer numbers since 1974 are up by over a third. The result produced 3.3 NCOs to each officer in 1984 compared with 2.1 in 1952, 2.8 in 1962 and 1972 and 3.0 in 1977. Compared to the Gardai, the Permanent Defence Force has a higher ratio of higher ranks to enlisted men. In 1969 the two groups were equally numerous but rapid intake subsequently produced a ratio of 1.1 men to higher ranks in October 1984. The 1953 ratio of 1.9 was, thus, very unusual.

Table 41: *Strength levels in the Defence Force 1950-1985*

April/ January*	Commissioned Officers	Non-Commissioned Officers	Privates	Cadets	Grand total
1950	1,048	2,426	4,639		8,113
1951	1,101	2,418	4,361		7,880
1952	1,148	2,458	6,398		10,004
1953	1,162	2,524	6,876		10,562
1954	1,177	2,845	6,390		10,412
1955	1,181	2,856	5,655		9,692
1956	1,181	2,756	4,798		8,735
1957	1,185	2,731	4,930		8,846
1958	1,152	2,756	4,222		8,130
1959	1,131	2,808	5,249		9,188
1960	1,087	2,858	5,020		8,965
1961	1,055	2,956	4,857		8,868
1962	1,045	2,933	4,473		8,451
1963	1,072	2,904	4,473		8,449
1964	1,080	2,863	4,278		8,221
1965	1,102	2,872	4,225		8,119
1966	1,122	2,968	4,069		8,159
1967	1,128	3,009	4,194		8,331
1968	1,113	3,043	4,156		8,312
1969	1,094	3,076	4,062		8,232
1970	1,072	3,029	4,473		8,574
1971	1,106	3,025	4,532		8,663
1972	1,114	3,021	4,848	67	9,050
1973	1,118	3,181	6,041	126	10,466
1974	1,159	3,293	6,010	192	10,654
1975	1,234	3,486	6,726	156	11,602
1976	1,323	3,860	8,333	137	13,653
1977	1,391	4,157	8,979	135	14,662
1978	1,432	4,304	8,896	118	14,750
1979	1,449	4,284	7,856	87	13,676
1980	1,470	4,363	7,441	98	13,372
1981	1,452	4,512	7,682	118	13,764
1982	1,478	4,733	8,990	117	15,318
1983	1,512	4,955	7,874	116	14,457
1984	1,530	5,065	7,428	102	14,125
1985	1,559	5,032	7,230	70	13,891

Sources: Statistical Abstract to April 1971. Departmental Records afterwards.
*1 April up to 1971. 1 January afterwards.

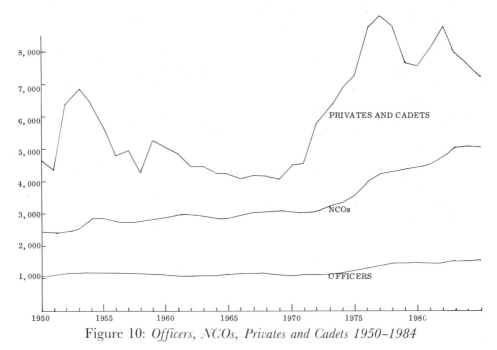

Figure 10: *Officers, NCOs, Privates and Cadets 1950–1984*

Cadets are the major source of officer recruitment. The variability of annual intake is brought out in Table 42.

Table 42: *Numbers of cadets commissioned and in training 1970–1984*

Year	Commissioned during year			In training at end of year		
	Army	Air Corps	Naval Service	Army	Air Corps	Naval Service
1970	31	3	2	55	5	2
1971	26	5	—	59	6	2
1972	29	—	—	112	10	4
1973	78	3	1	171	13	8
1974	100	2	4	131	17	8
1975	92	6	3	114	15	8
1976	70	5	4	111	17	7
1977	67	3	—	72	23	23
1978	41	14	11	64	7	16
1979	30	6	6	75	—	23
1980	21	7	10	100	—	18
1981	39	8	16	106	—	11
1982	34	8	8	107	—	9
1983	45	4	9	89	8	5
1984	48	8	5	66	—	4

Source: 1970–79 Dail Debates, 4 June 1980 and Departmental Records.

Changes in Defence Force by Corps

A very considerable amount of detailed information on the Defence Force can be gleaned from published sources. Much of this material is on a more exact basis than is normal for many other branches of the public domain and covers such material as levels of recruitment, reasons for and methods of retirement by rank, etc. Space and other considerations do not permit its reproduction here. One piece of analysis, however, is given below because it shows how the 1969 to 1977 expansion was distributed by corps. Figures for other years in the 'seventies are available from the same source.

Table 43: *Corp Strength in the Permanent Defence Force 31 December 1969 and 1977*

	1969			1977		
Corp	Officers	O/Ranks	Total	Officers	O/Ranks	Total
Staffs	186	330	516	214	390	604
Infantry	182	1,294	1,476	421	5,360	5,781
Artillery	63	411	474	89	885	974
Cavalry	44	275	319	71	717	788
Engineer	61	360	421	67	599	666
Signal	43	203	246	61	543	604
Ordnance	44	275	319	63	442	505
Supply & Transport	59	398	457	91	700	791
Medical	45	239	284	49	377	426
Military Police	19	317	336	36	520	556
Air	76	422	498	69	618	687
Naval Service	32	439	471	60	569	629·
Observer	10	9	19	6	13	19
Special Establishments	110	1,148	1,258	135	1,467	1,602
Total	974	6,120	7,094	1,432	13,200	14,632

Source: Dail Debates, 4 June 1980.

The major inflow of men was into the Infantry Corps which quadrupled in size. Cavalry and Signals more than doubled and Artillery doubled. Increases between 50 per cent to 75 per cent were recorded in Engineers, Ordnance, Transport and Supply, Medical and Military Police. The growth in the Air Corps and Naval Service were approximately half these levels. The last statement needs qualification. The strength of other ranks in the Naval Service was particularly high at the end of 1969 and declined 36 per cent during 1970. After the period shown in the table enlargement of the Naval Service continued, no doubt to meet the needs of fishery policy *inter alia* so that at the end of 1981 it contained 105 officers and 950 men before recruitment was halted and wastage took its toll. This level of the service was almost 70 per cent higher than that shown for end 1977 in Table 43.

The Air Corps strength level, on the other hand, was higher at end 1976 by about 4 per cent *viz* 716. Air Corps strength rallied during 1981 and unlike the Army the recovery brought it to a new peak of 825 by the end of the year. It was 873 at the end of September 1984 (Dail Debates 14/11/84).

A Note on the Reserve and Civil Defence

This study is primarily concerned with public employment, i.e., those who receive at least 50 per cent of their income from taxation, directly or indirectly. Some public moneys are paid out to others in connection with security duties, which in themselves would not qualify the person to be deemed a public employee. This note is included in the same spirit that professional fees were discussed and relates to the reserve and civil defence.

First Line Reserve

Officers and men enter the Reserve in the following manner. Officers who retire or resign from the Permanent Defence Force, other than those who retire on age grounds, may apply for appointment to be an officer of the Reserve Defence Force. Other ranks personnel, who, on termination of their period of service in the Permanent Defence Force have a Reserve commitment, are transferred to the Reserve Defence Force. All Reservists are liable to undergo a period of Annual Training, and are paid a small gratuity in addition to the payment they receive for their training. The decline in numbers in the years up to 1980 was caused by the abolition of the Reserve commitment for some years prior to that date, in an effort to increase recruitment. The re-introduction of this commitment in 1978 has led to an increase in the strength of the Reserve of other ranks since 1981.

Table 44: *Strength levels in the First Line Reserve, selected years 1954–1985*

	Officers	NCOs	Men	Total
31 Dec. 1954	534	424	3,145	4,103
31 Dec. 1959	511	496	2,668	3,675
31 Dec. 1969	377	283	1,207	1,867
31 Dec. 1979	128	100	198	426
31 Dec. 1980	139	109	290	538
31 Dec. 1981	138	107	428	673
31 Jul. 1985	127	135	906	1,168

These changing fortunes are also reflected in the numbers attending annual training as reported in the Dail (24 June 1982)

	Officers	NCOs	Men	Total
1959	426	191	976	1,596
1969	256	98	377	731
1981	107	63	167	337

It will be observed that, in spite of other commitments, a high level of officers participated. Perhaps the nature of the employment makes it less easy for NCOs and men to do so?

Second Line Reserve

The second line reserve consists of An Forsa Cosanta Aitiuil (FCA) and its naval equivalent, An Slua Muiri. Like the first line reserve gratuities are related to annual training. In 1981, 11,129 received full gratuity. This was half the numbers eligible. Details of the effective strength of the FCA by corps were published for each year of the 'seventies in the Dail Debates of 29 April 1980. These Debates also gave the ranks of the Permanent Defence Force personnel employed on duties with the FCA under the newly re-organised structures. This information was updated in the Dail Debates of 6 May 1982 which also included An Slua Muiri.[17] The effective strength of the FCA can be measured by the numbers who completed a minimum 14 days annual training. Some details are set out in Table 45. Numbers of privates have declined but overall participation has risen. However, since twice as many received the full gratuity as completed at least 14 days annual training, this might be a better measure of effective strength.

Table 45: *FCA personnel who completed at least 14 days annual training in selected years 1959–1981*

	Officers	NCOs	Privates	Total	Total Strength at Jan. 31
1959	—	53	3,788	3,841	18,821
1969	—	426	3,706	4,132	17,574
1981	549	1,883	3,489	5,921	18,416 (1982)*

Source: Dail Debates 6 May 1982, 21 June 1984.
*A year later there were 16,361, of which 6,361 were effective.

Table 46 documents recent inflows and outflows in the FCA. The strength levels of An Slua Muiri are small but were as high as 537 at the end of 1977. Like the FCA, An Slua Muiri is tending to increase the ratio of other ranks to enlisted men.

[17]FCA effective strength on Jan. 1, 1985 was 15,834 of whom 723 officers, 2,913 NCOs and 12,198 privates.

Table 46: *Enlistments and discharges in the FCA 1980–1984*

Year	Enlistments	Declared non-effective and discharged
1980	5,431	4,978
1981	5,770	5,403
1982	3,935	6,488
1983	336	5,036
1984	1,455	1,655

Table 47: *Strength of An Slua Muiri and Civil Defence Volunteers 1959 to 1982*

Jan. 31	An Slua Muiri	(Seamen)	Civil Defence Volunteers*	(Attendance at Courses)
1959	351	(277)	4,858	(n.a.)
1969	297	(197)	n.a.	(235)
1982	320	(213)	38,156	(618)

*.*Note:* Civil Defence strength refers to 31 December 1959 and 1981.
'Attendance at Courses' gives numbers at full-time Civil Defence School courses in the financial year concerned. (cf. Dail Debates, 6 May 1982).

Civil Defence

Civil Defence outlays are also small but nevertheless were almost £1 million in 1981. Civil Defence rolls are maintained by the local authorities. Those 113 members of the FCA who had been engaged in whole-time security duties prior to 1982 were in that year enlisted in the Permanent Defence Force.

Women in the Permanent Defence Force

On 31 March 1980 the establishment figures for the Women's Service Corps were set at 43 officers and 234 other ranks but at that date no women were actually serving. Since then recruitment has begun and it is hoped to provide an "expanded role" for women in both the Permanent Defence Force and in the reserve. Later the setting of a special establishment for women was abolished and opportunities for women were equated to those for men. In May 1983 numbers totalled 60, of whom 40 were NCOs and privates. Eighteen months later there was one extra in a complement of 25 officers, 16 NCOs and 20 privates. Due to the recruitment go-slow enlistment was by interview. This put a damper on general intake but, in the case of women, these difficulties were compounded by priority being given to combatant, i.e., male roles. There are no target numbers for women nor are there any serving in the naval and air corps.[18]

[18]Mr Barrett did not accept (Dail Debates 28/11/84) that former Minister Molloy was engaging in a cosmetic [sic] exercise when he permitted the recruiting of females!

Professional Qualifications in the Pemanent Defence Force

Under the University Scheme cadets, other than those in the Air Corps, attended either University College, Galway or Thomond College under contract from the academic years 1969/70 to 1978/79 inclusive. On June 4, 1980, the Minister of Defence provided the Dail with the numbers involved in each year and the faculty attended. However, 1980/81 marked a policy change in that cadets were trained and commissioned before attending university as officers. Choice of faculty was and is confined to Arts, Commerce, Science and Engineering at UCG and choice of subject was also restricted. All attending university are contracted for up to twelve years in the PDF and a further ten years in the reserve from the date of completion of the course or graduation. The University Scheme has provided graduates with technical and other qualifications. Prior to the University Scheme graduates coming on stream in sufficient numbers and graduates with certain qualifications were recruited directly to such corps as Ordnance, Engineers, Signals and Medical without being contracted for any length of time. Certain graduates are still recruited directly, e.g., doctors, dentists, and are commissioned on entry. The Minister on the same date provided detail on the current "stock" of such professionals.

Civilians with the Defence Force

As we have seen already, the criterion defining "civilians with the Defence Force" refers to those non-military personnel whose conditions of employment are governed by the 1954 Defence Act. This distinguishes them from other civilians whose conditions of employment come under the Civil Service Employment Acts. Some few industrial workers in the Department of Defence are in the latter category as are, of course, the departmental staff themselves.

Employment of civilians by the Defence Force was strongly influenced by the Second World War. None the less the peak employment level occurred a decade after hostilities ceased as figures in a 1957 Defence memorandum revealed:

1st January	*Number Employed*	*1st January*	*Number Employed*
1932(April)	410	1954	2,077
1939	627	1955	2,183
1949	1,642	1956	1,993
1952	1,531	1957	1,870
1953	1,565		

Total numbers in 1959 were 1,615, i.e., a fall of 255 in two years which was consistent with the fall of 313 in the previous two years. Thus there is no need to seek for explanations of the fall in terms of the 1958 reclassification. Appendix Table A2.13 gives the series from the first of January 1959, while some of the turning points are given in Table 48.

Table 48: *Civilians in Defence 1959 to 1985*

| | Industrials | | Non-Industrials | | |
Jan 1	Full time	Casual	Full time	Casual	Total
1959	1,406	56	136	17	1,615
1964	1,479	28	149	18	1,674
1971	1,315	8	169	25	1,516
1976	1,741	13	185	25	1,964
1977	1,640	10	287	21	1,958
1980	1,788	10	301	26	2,125
1982	1,703	17	289	12	2,021
1985	1,191	178	452	10	1,831

The first column of Table 48 is a continuation of the series for industrials given in Table 33 which recorded 1,415 in 1957 but only 1,258 in 1958. The second column would appear to be related to Table 34 which gave numbers employed on temporary schemes other than relief. However, there is a difficulty here in that in the 'fifties numbers in Table 34 were usually in excess of 300. The total in the two tables for 1957 was 1,730 which was 140 short of the numbers quoted in the Defence memorandum given above. These extras would appear to be the non-industrials given in Table 48. However, the suspicion remains that some of these may have been included with industrials in the returns of certain years. For example, the 1958 industrial total 1,258 was similar to that of 1955, 1,232 and 157 lower than that of 1957, i.e., 1,415. Perhaps this is merely a coincidence. Given the passage of time it is impossible to be more definite at this stage.

Composition of the Civilians in the Defence Group

As a consequence of some questions in the Dail a detailed breakdown is available of the trades and occupations of these civilian workers. A reply of 15 April 1980 listed the 40 occupations involved in the naval service and 11 in the Air Corps. On 10 June 1980 a further reply gave the establishment level and actual level on 1 June 1980 of 45 trades in the Army, 25 in the Navy and 12 in the Air Corps. A perusal of the list indicates the variety of jobs involved including such unexpected jobs as those of bath attendant, firelighter, tentmaker, labourer, kitchen and mess helper. On 30 October 1980 the Minister of Defence gave establishment levels, posts filled and technicians in training for the technician complement in the naval service, detailing the 12 posts involved. On June 4 yet another set of replies gave for each year in the 'seventies the number of apprentices enlisted in the Army Apprentice School (AAS) and in the Air Corps, the number in training at the end of each year, the number of applicants, the number of apprenticeships offered by trade distinguishing air corps mechanics, motor mechanics, fitters, electricians, carpenters and radio mechanics. The number in each trade who completed their apprenticeships and their distribution between the army, navy and air corps was also given. Space does not permit the reproduction of this wealth of information here.

Annual enlistments in the Army Apprentice School were generally about 60 and about 35 in the Air Corps, though the latter was as high as 56 in 1978. Over the 'seventies numbers in training in the AAS rose from 151 to 177 but doubled in the Air Corps — from 609 to 123. In the AAS the demand for places was about 160 in the first three years, under 300 in the next two, exceeded 600 in 1975 and then shot up to 1,463 and 1,807 in 1976 and 1977. In 1979, 1,356 applied. The big increases in applications to the Air Corps apprenticeships scheme occurred modestly in 1974 with a rise to 181 from levels around 140 previously. In the next three years applications trebled, doubled and doubled to reach 2,060 in 1977. Numbers were still high in 1979 in excess of 1,800. Since the apprenticeships offered were about 100, only one in twenty was accepted and this screening probably explains why about 90 per cent completed the course.

Chapter III.3

GARDAI

The Gardai resemble the Defence Force in that they also employ industrial and civilian staff but differ in that early retirement is not so much the norm. In this section only the Gardai themselves are considered since their support staff have been catered for under the Civil Service proper, or have been included in the treatment of industrials. The evolution in numbers is presented in Table 49

Table 49: *Employment in the Police Force 1950–1985*

June	*Gardai*	*All Police*	*June/January**	*Gardai*	*All Police*
1950	5,533	7,083	1968	4,973	6,546
1951	5,360	6,904	1969	4,985	6,543
1952	5,182	6,724	1970	4,977	6,532
1953	5,147	6,691	1971	5,036	6,612
1954	5,208	6,774	1972	5,350	6,961
1955	5,261	6,826	1973	6,035	7,794
1956	5,259	6,800	1974	6,216	7,990
1957	5,041	6,568	1975	6,567	8,419
1958	4,959	6,481	1976	6,575	8,449
1959	4,981	6,492	1977	6,608	8,485
1960	5,034	6,580	1978	7,241	9,182
1961	5,045	6,612	1979	7,334	9,396
1962	4,966	6,531	1980	7,568	9,693
1963	4,821	6,401	1981	7,737	9,882
1964	4,878	6,452	1982	7,770	9,943
1965	5,002	6,568	1983	8,621	10,831
1966	4,970	6,545	1984	8,951	11,232
1967	4,962	6,536	1985	9,129	11,387

Source: Statistical Abstracts to 1978, Departmental records subsequently.

*To ease comparison with other public employment the figures on 31 December have been given as applying on the following day for 1981 and subsequent years.

and graphed in Figure 11. Table 49 gives the employment of Gardai and other ranks. Calculations will show that, unlike the Defence Force, there is no tendency for An Gardai Siochana to become more officer intensive. In fact the trend could be slightly in the opposite direction. In 1950 there were 3.6 Gardai for each officer. Of late the ratio has been 4.0 to 1. Other ranks are 80 per cent Sergeants, which is a higher proportion than obtains in the Permanent Defence Force. Figures in recent years were as follows:

		Sergeants	*Officers*
1 January	1981	1,734	411
	1982	1,744	429
	1983	1,771	439
	1984	1,847	434
	1985	1,828	430

Figure 11 contrasts the experience of the Gardai with that of the Defence Force. Between 1950 and 1963 a slight annual decline of 0.8 per cent brought strength to a nadir of 6,401 in 1963. The impact of communal violence in Northern Ireland began to be felt during 1971 which had opened with strength at the same level as 1960. A rapid growth of 6.5 per cent compound was halted in 1975. This was not due to the 1975 recruitment ban, which applied to the Civil Service, nor was the recovery due to the 1977 full employment programme. The absolute decline in 1976 and the fact that only 20 recruits were in training in June was due to there being few suitable candidates in the 1974 recruitment competition. Due to the new regulations the next competition was not held until 1977. The 1982 rise likewise reflects the outcome of the July 1981 competition. Recruitment embargoes have not applied to the Gardai. Thus by November 1984 strength was almost 60 per cent above the level of June 1970 level which was typical of the stability in numbers of the previous five years. The expansion rate of almost 4 per cent in the years of growth was low relative to general Civil Service experience just as the previous stability has also been unique.

Any expansion of the Gardai numbers is governed by the strength currently approved in the Estimates and by the maximum establishment authorised by the Garda Siochana Acts. The relationship of these levels to actual strength levels in recent years is set out in Table 50. At the end of 1977 the rapid expansion, noted in the second part of the year, pushed actual strength, including trainees, above the level currently approved in the Departmental Estimates and very close to the maximum establishment level authorised under the Acts. The close relationship between the three figures continued up to the end of 1981. The decision to resume recruitment caused the gaps to widen temporarily.

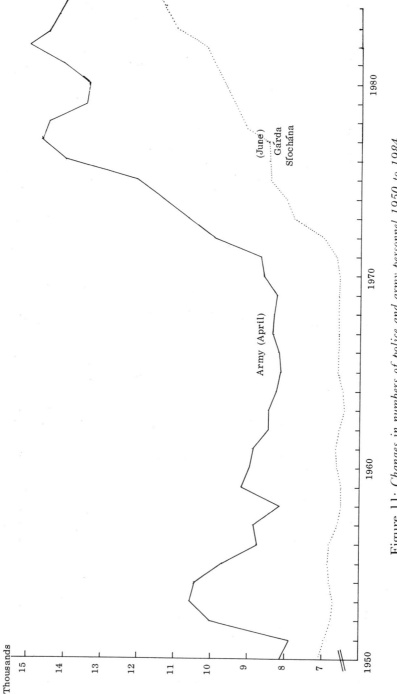

Figure 11: *Changes in numbers of police and army personnel 1950 to 1984.*

Note: Numbers on left start at 6,000

Table 50: *Actual and potential strength levels in An Garda Siochana 1971–1985*

Last day of year	Actual strength	Strength currently approved in Estimates	Maximum establishment authorised by Garda Siochana ranks order
1971	6,710	n.a.	7,723
1972	7,441	n.a.	8,002
1974	8,215	n.a.	8,502
1976	8,456	8,494	8,994
1977	8,821	8,575	8,994
1978	9,387	9,485	9,502
1979	9,569	9,499	10,002
1980	9,882	9,982	10,002
1981	9,943	10,000	10,002
1982	10,831	10,853	12,000
1983	11,232	11,715	12,000
1984	11,387	11,400	12,000

Garda Recruitment and Wastage

One index of recruitment would be to look at the numbers in training. However even in a period of growth these levels can change monthly. For example, November 1980 recorded 115; December 1980, 230 and June 1981, 105. Numbers training were down to 25 in early 1982 but when the 1981 competition results became available numbers in training were restored to ten times this level in May, i.e., 252. Levels of 500 were normal in the latter part of that year.

A Dail statement of October 21, 1980 permits us to adopt a more complete approach and to build on it for recent years. The numbers are given in Table 51 and the major elements are graphed in Figure 12. The latter clearly illustrates the variability of recruitment over the last decade and a half. These fluctuations tend to set up bunching in the personnel profile which can have detrimental effects on Garda promotion expectations and so breed discontent.

Table 51 reveals the changing pattern of losses. Tragically some of these have been murders of Gardai on duty as the Northern violence spilled over into the Republic. The pattern of retirement seemed to be displaying a tendency to fall from the levels achieved when numbers were more static and could be attributed to the growing youthfulness of those serving. This observation, however, has been upset by the recent upswing in retirements which also increased loss levels.

The period of non-expansion would appear to have led to a very considerable amount of overtime working which affected the take home pay of Gardai almost universally. The Devlin enquiry reports that in 1977/78, 95 per cent of all

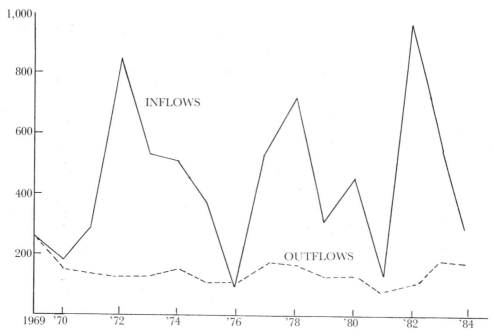

Figure 12: *Recruitment and wastage in the police force 1969–1984*

Gardai, Sergeants and Inspectors received overtime payments which were a substantial proportion of basic wage rates. This phenomenon will not be discussed here except to note that the substitution of extra staff for overtime could also affect the attractiveness of the job for individual Gardai.

Women in An Garda Siochana

At the end of 1984 it was 25 years since the "first 12 Ban Gardai took to the streets of Dublin".[19] At that time and up to 1978 their role was almost entirely confined to cases involving women and children. The first real breakthrough came in 1978 when equal pay in the force coincided with a substantial increase in the number of women recruits taken in. The first extension of duties involved liaison with, and then transfer to, the drug squad, the juvenile liaison scheme and public relations. In most recent years all branches of police work have been thrown open to them — investigation, the Murder Squad, the Central Detective Unit, Mobile patrol in both cars and on motor cycles, computers, the Control Room in Dublin Castle and especially in the expanding area of community relations.

The original 12 in 1959 increased to 35 in 1977. With the change in approach the Dail was told this had risen to 135 by 2 February 1981. These were 5 banshairsinti and 130 ban gardai, of whom 41 were recruits in training. The total

[19]See Heather Parsons, *Irish Independent*, 3 Jan. 1985.

Table 51: Recruitment and wastage in An Garda Síochána, 1969-1985

Year	Strength opening, i.e., 31/12 previous year	Recruitment plus reappointments	Losses	Net Change	Retirement	Resignation under 5 yrs	5 yrs+	Dismissal	Death
1969	—	253	259	-6	155	50	32	11	11
1970	6,514	181+3	147	+34	67	33	16	14	17
1971	6,551	292+3	137	+155	84	19	14	9	11
1972	6,709	854+3	125	+729	66	22	17	3	17
1973	7,441	536+1	125	+411	65	29	9	15	7
1974	7,853	510	148	+362	47	45	24	14	18
1975	8,215	366+4	104	+262	38	26	12	12	16
1976	8,481	86+1	104	-18	46	16	14	13	15
1977	8,464	535+2	172	+363	82	44	25	7	14
1978	8,829	718+4	164	+554	71	41	33	3	16
1979	9,387	305+4	127	+178	45	26	35	3	18
1980	9,569	446	133	+313	55	17	20	10	31
1981	9,882	134	73	+61	22	17	9	3	22
1982	9,943	986	98	+888	50	11	8	8	22
1983	10,831	581	180	+401	116	18	15	6	25
1984	11,232	367	212	+155	146	11	15	16	24
1985	11,387								

Source: Garda records.

"Resignations" are retirements which do not benefit from either pensions or gratuities, though nowadays those with 5 years service obtain preserved superannuation benefits.

ban gardai was 86 the previous October. The expansion continued after the lifting of the recruitment ban. In April 1983 there were 3 inspectors, 3 sergeants and 242 ban gardai. At the beginning of 1985 the latter numbered 330.

It is clear from information provided to the Dail (10 Oct. 1984) that there is a greater demand for posts than vacancies. For example, 3,122 applied in the 1983 Recruitment Competition and 987 were successful in their interviews. However, only 35 of these were to be appointed by October 24, 1984. This contrasts with the experience of 5,979 male applicants who had a similar success rate at the interviews but whose appointment rate of 593 was almost nine times higher than that of women.

Chapter III.4

PRISONS

Information about prisons is already included in the survey of the non-industrial Civil Service and is set out, for example, in Table 28. However the discussion of security in the last sections naturally suggests that it might be helpful to take a special look at the Prison Service. Table 28 gives the total employment under the vote for Prisons. Since the figures are incomplete Table 52 fills in the picture from 1949 to 1975, i.e., up to when the records were computerised.

After computerisation it was convenient to give a detailed analysis of the various grades which had heretofore been amalgamated in the Civil Service Census. Thus, Governors prior to 1975 included Deputy Governors. Prison Officers included in addition Chief Officers, Assistant Chief Officers, Matrons and Assistant Matrons. Clerks included Assistant Clerks. The "other" category up to 1958 apeared to have included workers in quasi-industrial categories who were excluded from the main Civil Service Census in the 1958 reclassification but who continued to be enumerated in the Directory of State Services. The 1970 Directory lists 353 staff, all in departmental grades of the Prison Service. This was 17 more than those recorded in the Census. Apart from vacancies, which may have been listed in the Directory, the latter listed 3 stewards, 1 foreman of works, 3 chief artisans, 2 workmen and a cook — 10 staff which may have been excluded from the main Civil Service Census. Thus the Directory and Census show a close correspondence in that year. The 2 "other" in the Census may be the two probation and welfare officers of the Directory and (?) the psychologist. In the Civil Service Census these "others" were classified as "lower inspectorate" without further explanation.

In the light of the volatility of employment in the 'seventies it is useful to be able to form an impression of recruitment and wastage before that decade began. Recruitment must be inferred in relation to terminations of employment and annual changes in numbers. The annual detail is given in Table 53. In the years for which data were available since 1959 average departures were 21 and average recruitment 25, if the exceptional recruitment in 1967 is omitted. This

141

Table 52: *Composition of employment in Prisons 1949–1975*

Year	Governors	Prison Officers Male	Prison Officers Female	Mess Attendants	Clerks	Chaplain	Medical	Other*	Total
1949	6	229	40	7	20	11	7	7	327
1950	6	223	35	7	20	10	7	6	314
1951	7	218	38	7	20	10	7	6	313
1952	5	208	39	5	18	n.a.	n.a.	6	295
1953	5	190	32	5	19	10	7	9	277
1954	5	195	32	5	20	10	7	9	283
1955	5	188	29	5	20	10	6	9	272
1956	5	185	26	5	20	10	6	9	266
1957	5	173	24	4	19	8	3	8	244
1958	5	173	22	4	20	7	3	—	234
1959	5 (est)	n.a.	n.a.	4 (est)	20 (est)	n.a.	3 (est)	—	234
1960	5	183	20	4	20	8	3	—	243
1961	5	191	19	4	20	8	3	—	250
1962	5	205	16	4	20	8	3	—	261
1963	5	202	17	4	20	8	3	—	259
1964	5	222	16	4	20	8	3	—	278
1965	5	223	17	4	21	8	3	1	282
1966	5	222	17	4	21	8	3	2	282
1967	5	219	17	3	21	8	3	2	278
1968	5	249	18	4	25	8	3	2	314
1969	6	261	20	5	25	8	3	2	330
1970	6	268	20	5	24	8	3	2	336
1971	6	288	17	6	25	7	3	3	355
1972	7	305	21	6	25	10	3	9	386
1973	11	484	25	7	24 (est)	11	5	9	576
1974	10	537	25	7	24	11	4	25	643
1975	10	536	25	10	24	11	4	27	647

Note: The medical staff may be unestablished and "visiting" or established and resident; usually the former.
*Up to 1957 these were classified as "other manipulative workers" and seem to have been transferred out of the Census in the 1958 reclassification, probably to become industrials. After 1965 "others" refers to staff graded as "lower inspectorate" up to and including 1970. Subsequently the total included typists viz 1,2,2,2 and 3. Apart from these and prison officers 1972 to 1975 figures included 2,2,7 and 6 women.

Table 53: Recruitment and terminations in employment among Prison staff 1948 to 1969

Change During	Prison Officers Male	Female	Mess Servants	Chaplains	Other	Total	Total Recruitment
1948	20	4	—	1	2	27	n.a.
1949	13	6	1	1	2	23	10
1950	9	2	3	1	1	16	15
1951	n.a.	n.a.	4	—	3	n.a.	-12+?
1952	13	3	1	—	2	19	1
1953	9	1	—	2	—	12	18
1954	15	4	2	—	1	22	11
1955	7	3	1	1	2	14	20
1956	12	5	1	3	5	26	4
1957	13	3	—	2	—	16	14
1959*	8	1	—	1	2	12	21
1960	13	1	1	—	1	16	23
1961	14	3	—	—	—	17	28
1962	20	2	—	1	2	25	23
1964*	30	—	2	1	1	34	38
1965	20	1	1	1	—	23	23
1966	20	5	1	1	—	27	23
1967	13	4	2	—	—	19	55
1969*	11	1	1	3	2	18	24

*No records survive for 1958, 1963 and 1968.

slow rise in staff numbers was subsequently disrupted by the high levels of resignations recorded since the outset of the 'seventies. The details were captured in replies to two Dail questions during 1980 and have been supplemented from departmental records for more recent years. The series is set out in Table 54.

It is difficult to be clear what is meant in Table 54 by total personnel. The 272 at the end of December 1970 can be compared with those for January 1 1971 in Table 52. This records a larger number, both for prison officers and for total personnel. Table 52 is not very different from the State Directory of 1971 which gives the permissable establishment level of 379 and includes vacancies. Similar difficulties occur in other years. However, after computerisation the numbers in Table 54 are higher than those in the Staff Information System. The differences are smaller. For that reason the main interest in the table focusses on the inflows and outflows and the ratio of staff to the average number of prisoners.

Table 54: *Developments in the Prison Service in relation to average number of Prisoners 1970–1985**

		Terminations due to:		Strength at end Dec.		
Year	Recruits	Resignation	Retirement	Prison Officers	Total Personnel	Prisoners Average Daily No.
1970	28	3	2	264	272	749
1971	48	13	3	295	303	893
1972	203	13	3	477	485	1,035
1973	152	51	5	568	582	963
1974	94	53	2	588	602	961
1975	175	39	5	711	725	1,019
1976	128	50	11	774	789	1,049
1977	164	51	9	875	891	1,029
1978	320	91	10	1,094	1,123	1,179
1979	138	71	11	1,143	1,181	1,140
1980	362			1,444	n.a.	1,215
1981	74			1,490	n.a.	1,196
1982	118			1,555	n.a.	1,236
1983	31			1,560	n.a.	1,450
1984	31			1,535	n.a.	1,590 (prov.)

Sources: Dail Debates, 20 May and 30 October 1980, Departmental Records, Rottman, 1984.
Note: Prisoners are those in prisons and places of detention. Loughan House was a special school and so excluded. Total Personnel is not defined.
*Strictly speaking 31 December 1984.

In the table it is noted that Loughan House, now closed, was not a place of detention but rather a special school. The State Directory gives separate establishment levels for it, i.e., 113 in 1979 and 109 in the four subsequent years. In 1979 the actual manning was reported in the Dail as 67 prison service staff catering for the 17 boys at the school on January 1st of that year.

Table 54 illustrates the rise in manning levels relative to average prisoner levels which resulted in there being more prison officers than prisoners for the first time in 1979. The rise in manning levels appears to be in response to the high levels of departures recorded in Table 54, e.g., 8 to 9 per cent in 1974 and in 1978. In 1980 difficulties over manning came to a head when the Prison Officers Association complained of the excessive amounts of overtime at Mountjoy Prison and called for a prison officer strength of 2,000 for the service as a whole to correct the "dangerously low levels" of manning. The 1980 recruitment campaign brought numbers in general to 1,450. It was hoped that this expansion would facilitate the reduction of overtime by permitting changes in rosters.

Prison Officer ratios vary by prison. Statistics on this were given to the Dail in 1979 and recapitulated in Table 55.

Table 55: *Location of Prison Officers and Prisoners on 1 January 1979*

	Officers	*Prisoners: Men*	*Prisoners: Women*
Mountjoy	299	379	11
Limerick	107	79	7
Cork	44	40	—
Arbor Hill	73	65	—
Portlaoise	268	176	—
Glengariff Training Unit	53	63	—
Shelton Abbey	29	28	—
St. Patrick's Institution	116	164	—
Shanganagh Castle	34	32	—
Total	1,023	1,026	18

Note: In addition 4 officers were engaged full time in staff training and 67 serving at the special school, Loughan House.

During 1979 the number of female prison officers rose from 47 to 60 catering for 18 women prisoners. This restored the situation obtaining in 1958 when 59 women officers were recorded. It was customary to record women officers, etc., separately up to the mid-1970s when they were put on the same pay scales as men. Presumably women, formerly described as matrons and assistant matrons, are now included with their male equivalents, chief officers and assistant chief officers. In these roles women would clearly have responsibilities *vis-à-vis* male prisoners.

As the numbers of staff expanded considerable adjustments were made to staffing structures as reported in the State Directory and as returned in the Staff Information System. The former has not recorded welfare officers, psychologists or clerical assistants in the last five years. The latter has tended to omit chaplains, visiting medical officers, and housekeepers over the same period. An attempt to capture the changes is given in Table 56 which updates the material in Table 52.

Apart from mess servants, temporary nurses, etc., the basic entry grade is that of prison officer. Promotion can either be via the administrative side grades of Clerks II and Clerk I to Assistant Governor or via the custodial side to the same post passing through Assistant Chief Officer and Chief Officer II. Chief Officer I is equivalent to an Assistant Governor. For women the same goal could be achieved via assistant matron and matron and at various times one or two Chief Officers I were women. Depending on the size of the prison, Governors and Deputy Governors could be on higher or lower scales.

Table 56: *Composition of Prison Staff on January 1 1976 to 1984*

	1976	1977 July	1978	1979	1980	1981	1982	1983	1984
Governor	11	9	9	9	9	8	8	8	14
Deputy Governor	3	3	3	3	5	5	6	5	7
Assistant Governor	9	13	13	13	14	13	12	13	22
Clerk I	30	27	28	28	30	38	38	38	50
Clerk II	74	71	73	72	123	166	174	176	193
Prison Officer (PO)	585	669	658	920	920	1,134	1,146	1,214	1,304
of which female	(20)	(48)	(46)	(47)	(60)	(57)	(60)	(61)	(n.a.)
Temporary PO	16	11	11	11	11	4	4	3	3
Typist	1	2	1	1	1	1	1	1	1
Mess Servants	13	13	13	13	13	15	15	14	14
Welfare Officer	—	7	6	6	6	4	4	4	6
Chaplain	4	4	4	4	4	n.a.	n.a.	n.a.	n.a.
Medical (visiting)	2	2	2	2	2	n.a.	n.a.	n.a.	n.a.
Other	1	1	1	1	2	9	9	9	—
Total	749	832	822	1,083	1,140	1,397	1,417	1,485	1,614

Notes: Some Governors and Deputy Governors are on higher scales. Co-ordinators of Education are included with Deputy Governors. Assistant Governors includes Chief Officer I and Industrial Training Officers I, Chief Trade Officer I. Stewards were also included in 1976. ClerkI includes Chief Officers II (including Trade) and Matrons and Chief Artisans up to 1980. Clerk II includes Assistant Chief Officers and Assistant Matrons. Welfare Officers include psychologists. "Other" up to 1979 refers to a housekeeper and an installer in 1979. Subsequently 3 temporary nurses, 5 kitchen helps and a laundress.
Source: Staff Information System.

SECTION IV

LOCAL BODIES

Chapter IV.1

BACKGROUND TO LOCAL BODIES

At the end of the Second World War local authority auditors audited the accounts of over 400 local bodies. These were:—

27 County Councils
 4 County Borough Corporations
 7 Borough Corporations
51 Urban District Councils
25 Town Commissioners
 3 Boards of Assistance
 2 Boards of Public Assistance
 4 Port Sanitary Authorities
11 Joint Mental Hospital Boards

36 Joint Drainage Committees
 7 Joint Burial Boards
15 Miscellaneous (incl. Library) Bodies
23 Boards of Conservators of Fisheries
38 Vocational Education Committees
27 Committees of Agriculture
26 Harbour Authorities
97 Education Endowment Bodies

Of these the 97 Endowed Schools, audited under the Educational Endowment (Ireland) Act of 1885, do not refer to local authorities.

Such a variety of bodies complicated the collection of statistics and subsequent re-organisations have affected the continuity of the time series. This wealth of organisations arose as the modern concept of local government evolved on a piecemeal basis during the nineteenth century and the whole trend of post-war development has aimed at streamlining these bodies in the light of modern management methods and to meet the very changed requirements of modern times. This section gives a brief overview of the historical evolution and the more recent synthesis.

* * *

In the eighteenth century various towns and boroughs had some limited powers over their own affairs derived from their charters. Elsewhere impermanent Grand Juries, set up for criminal control in judicial counties, were encouraged to take on other duties for which they raised a cess. Each barony made presentments twice yearly seeking to finance public works especially roads but also extra police, coroners, courthouses, etc. Corruption was rife. Three acts' involved these juries in maintaining some health services:—

1765 — County Hospitals Act made capital funds available for 36 county and 5 town infirmaries for the sick poor to be managed by elected governors.

1818 — Hospitals (Ireland) Act set up a network of fever hospitals to combat infectious diseases under local boards of health responsible for preventive services.

1821 — Lunacy (Ireland) Act established district lunatic asylums for which the government appointed the governing body and chief executive.

1828 — In urban areas the Lighting of Towns Act gave the town commissioners power to finance schemes for water, sewerage, cleansing, lighting and fire brigade. These powers were amended in the Towns Improvements Act, 1854.

In 1838 the Poor Relief Act was passed which had a major impact on local government thinking and practices for at least 115 years. This was to be the first step to implement a plan for local government devised by Jeremy Bentham under which the county would be divided into districts, each of which would have a popularly elected assembly. These assemblies would employ salaried executive officers, and both the assemblies and their officers would be strictly accountable to Government departments to be newly created. Applying the principles of strong central direction, strict accountability (to Poor Law Commissioners), salaried management and uniformity of service a network of 126 unions was drawn up, each having a workhouse controlled by a board of guardians (justices of the peace and elected ratepayers) who levied a poor rate. The decision to set up harsh workhouses unattractive to all but the most destitute explicitly rejected the findings of a Commission of Inquiry which favoured development works and aroused such hostility that the other parts of Bentham's visionary scheme were abandoned. Instead subsequent reforms and extensions formed a patchwork in which "each service, as it was introduced, was made the responsibility of whichever of the existing set of local authorities was considered to be the most convenient" (Hensey, 1979, p. 4).

1840 — Municipal Corporations Act defined the modern boroughs and abolished all but 10 corporations whose administration had fallen into varying degrees of disrepute.

1842 — Drainage Act gave drainage works executed by the Commissioners of Public Works over to drainage boards to maintain (Act amended in 1866).

1846 — All policing became a charge on central government. This trend was continued when local prisons were also transferred from the Grand Juries in 1877.

Between 1838 and 1878 the responsibilities of Boards of Guardians were increased but in some cases central funding was provided to encourage expansion:—

1846 — Poor Law Hospitals were to supplement workhouses and infirmaries.

1851 — Medical Charities Act required the boards to establish dispensaries and appoint district medical officers. Boards also ran schools for workhouse children. Boards were also given responsibility for nuisance removal and disease prevention.

1856 — Boards became burial authorities in rural areas.

1862 — Boarding out system introduced due to high child mortality in workhouses.

1863 — Dispensary doctors became responsible for registry of births and deaths.

1866 — Sanitary Act made boards sewer authorities in rural areas.

1868 — Central government contributed all the salaries of workhouse teachers and half that of dispensary and workhouse doctors.

1872 — Irish Local Government Board, appointed by the Government, took over from the Poor Law Commissioners. This Board was also made responsible for non-poor law preventative services but not for mental health. The board was unable to marry the two traditions adequately and has no access to legislation.

1875 — Central Government provided maintenance grants for lunatics.

1878 — The Public Health Act attempted to marry the poor relief and preventive systems by creating urban and rural sanitary districts from the poor law unions and by consolidating previous legislation. Even though the act provided for grants towards the salaries of sanitary officers the development of health administration was retarded by being subordinated to poor relief in practice.

Subsequently power to engage in a number of other services, provided to local authorities, met with little response in spite of increasing State contributions:—

1883 — Labourers Act — Rural Sanitary Authorities could provide agricultural labourers with a cottage and a plot if existing accommodation was unhealthy.

1888 — Local Taxation Accounts launched a complex system whereby local authorities could benefit increasingly from State funding.

1889 — Sanitary authorities were empowered to levy rates for technical or manual instruction. Like the 1855 provision for town libraries it was little availed of.

1890 — Housing of the Working Classes Act consolidated existing urban housing legislation and empowered urban authorities both to regulate housing and to build. However no subsidies were offered for this purpose.

Collins (1963, p. 25) summed up the need for reform at this time in the following words:

> Parliament in its legislation had not produced a system of local government. It had adopted expedients to meet difficulties as they arose or as the political complexion of Parliament changed. There was no unifying conception running through its local legislation. The principle of representative institutions had been applied in the towns but not in the counties.... The picture that local government presented was a picture of authorities operating independently of one another and operating in overlapping areas. In the counties were the grand juries ... in the boroughs the town councils, in the smaller towns the town commissioners, some of which were urban sanitary authorities. In the poor law unions which covered counties, cities and town the boards of guardians acted as poor law authorities and in the rural part of the unions as sanitary authorities. In the asylum districts, which were single counties or combinations of counties boards of governers nominated by the government and bound by the rules of the Privy Council managed the district asylums. Besides these authorities there were trustees for drainage districts and navigation, harbour and pier authorities, burial boards and governors of the eighteenth century system of county infirmaries. Some of the authorities were subject to control by the central authorities and some were not.

The first step towards sorting out this jumble of authorities, taken in 1898, set in motion a trend towards a reduction in the number and types of authority and towards the abolition of legal distinctions between different branches of the services which is still continuing at present.

1898 — The Local Government Act limited Grand Juries to their judicial functions and the boards of guardians to poor (including medical) relief. The remaining functions were to be run by elected councils. The functions of baronial presentments and of rural and urban sanitary districts were given to elected rural and urban councils while the administratively defined county replaced and revised the former judicial counties. The elected county councils had few functions initially, apart from levying rates, maintaining roads and appointing the boards of management of mental hospitals. In this democratic spirit justices of the peace lost their *ex officio* entitlement to membership of the board of guardians.

1899 — Agriculture Act established the Department of Agriculture and Technical Instruction, which led to committees for technical and agricultural instruction.

After 1900 the idea of the State as a promoter of social welfare became manifest in several statutes and in the reduction in the burden of local financing:

1908 — Old Age Pensions Act and 1911 National Insurance Act reduced the need for poor relief.

1914 — Education (Provision of Meals) Act gave power to urban councils to provide meals to necessitous children in national schools.

1915 — Notification of Births (Extension) Act introduced a scheme for expectant mothers.

1919— Public Health (Medical Treatment of Children) Act provided for the schools medical service.

1920 — The Blind Persons Act catered for the needs of the blind.

After independence a number of schemes, advanced by Sinn Fein, were implemented which had the effect of strengthening the county councils and eliminating the smaller bodies.

1923 — The boards of guardians were abolished and replaced by boards of public assistance appointed by the county councils.

1924 — The Department of Local Government and Public Health took over from the Irish Local Government Board, and from the Privy Council in respect of mental health. Unlike its predecessors the Department could initiate legislation.

1925 — Rural District Councils were abolished and their sanitary responsibilities discharged through county boards of health i.e., the boards of public assistance. Road responsibility were assumed by the county councils. County medical officers of health were appointed.

— The Fishery Act removed local rates from fisheries and imposed special rates levied by boards of conservators.

1926 — Local Authorities (Officers and Employees) Act began the process of regularising the appointment of officers by giving the selection of some officers to a Local Appointments Commission.

1930 — Vocational Education Act set up Vocational Education Committees under the aegis of the Minister of Education — a transfer from Agriculture.

1931 — County Committees of Agriculture set up under the Minister for Agriculture as an extension of the 1899 Act.

1932 — Housing Act provided subsidy to recoup to Local Authorities part of loan charges in providing houses subject to the rents being approved.

1933 — Unemployment Assistance was introduced and reduced the cost of public assistance though some local authorities were required to contribute.

— The Hospital Thrust Fund was established under the Public Hospitals Act to help with the capital costs of any hospital, clinic or nursing organisation.

1940 — The County Management Act revolutionised local management by giving power to a salaried manager to discharge executive functions and formulate policy. As a consequence the stratagem of appointing boards of councillors was no longer necessary. Thus the boards of health and of public assistance and the mental hospital committees were dispensed with where a single county was involved and their responsibilities returned to the county council itself where the legal distinctions were still preserved. Some committees remained obligatory and for these the manager had no role since they were not under the aegis of the Minister for Local Government and Public Health, e.g., the Vocational Education Committees, the School Attendance Committees, the County Committees of Agriculture and the Old Age Pension Committees. Visiting Committees of Mental Hospitals and Consultative Health Committees were also obligatory.

1941 — Local Government Act continued the work of the 1926 Act by distinguishing major and minor officers from servants under the aegis of the Department. The general effect was to continue the assimilation of the system of recruitment and conditions of service to those operating in the civil service.

— Due to the war-time unavailability of bitumen local authority engineers supervised turf production to meet the fuel shortage and to give employment to redundant staff.

1945 — Mental Treatment Act introduced a totally new concept of mental illness permitting voluntary admissions to mental hospitals.

— Arterial Drainage Act abolished drainage boards and gave the responsibility to county councils.

— The Tuberculosis (Establishment of Sanatoria) Act caused the central authorities to build 3 sanatoria from Hospital Trust Funds and transfer them to their local authorities.

1947 — Health Act reduced the number of health bodies from 90 to 31 by transferring the health aspects of sanitary services (infectious diseases, food hygiene, etc.) from urban district councils to county councils. The State agreed to meet the cost of all improvements in health services until local and state contributions were equal.

— At the national level the growing complexities of the work of the Department of Local Government led to the creation of three departments: those of Local Government, Health and Social Welfare. As a result, the Health and Social Welfare Orders transferred from the Minister of Local Government responsibilities for certain local activities. These were:

Health:
1. Prevention of infectious diseases
2. Establishment and supervision of hospitals, etc.
3. Control of health personnel
4. Food hygiene
5. Health research and statistics

  6. School medical service, maternity and child welfare,
   free milk scheme
  7. Registration of births, deaths and marriages
  8. Public assistance and administration of Children Acts.

Social Welfare: 1. Old age, Widows' and Orphans' pensions
  2. National Health Insurance and Blind Welfare
  3. School meals, fuel and footwear schemes
  4. Home assistance, supplementary cash allowances, etc.

These tasks themselves continued to be performed by the local authorities as before.

1949 — Local Authorities (Works) Act extended powers for flood relief and the Oireachtas made available substantial grants for this purpose between 1950 and 1957.

1953 — Health Act transferred responsibility for hospitals and dispensaries to the county councils and ended the legal distinctions between sanatoria and county and district hospitals. The new terms of eligibility for health services replaced assessment of need with entitlement and ended the poor law ethos. Choice of doctor and hospital were introduced in the maternity service.

1954 — Connaught Health Authorities combined to manage a sanatorium as the Western Health Authorities Board.

1960 — All health authorities in each of the county borough counties came together as United Health Authorities. Now 27 health authorities nationally.

1971 — The launching of 8 regional health boards "split locally what had been split centrally" since the partition of the Department of Local Government and Public Health in 1947.

1973 — Agreement was reached with voluntary hospitals to fund most of their costs on an agreed basis to replace the variety of sources of income which they had derived from the State since the 1953 Act came into effect. Public nature of these hospitals now recognised:

 — The Joint Board Hospitals, St James's and the James Connolly Memorial Hospital, became state-sponsored bodies independent of the Eastern Health Board.

 — A phasing out period of 4 years began which removed the rates contribution to housing and health services.

1974 — Local Government (Roads and Motorways) Act designated national primary and secondary roads and made their upkeep and improvement a national charge.

1977 — Department of Local Government renamed Department of the Environment.

— Social Welfare (Supplementary Welfare Allowances) Act abolished home assistance — the last relic of the poor relief — and gave a new uniform national scheme to the health boards to administer. This applied also the footwear scheme.

1978 — Local Government (Finance Provisions) Act removed the rates from householders.

This short summary demonstrates the growth of public provision. It also shows how the system evolved from one run by a muiltiplicity of independent local bodies financing their own services to a situation where most local finance was abolished. Staffing levels in a much smaller number of larger authorities were subjected to central control and the State assumed responsibility for the planning and financing of many services.

Chapter IV.2

LOCAL BODIES INCLUDING HEALTH

Exluded Bodies

In this section we shall not consider those local authorities which fall outside the scope of the County and City Management Acts. These are the Vocational Education Committees, to be covered under Education; the Harbour Authorities and the boards of conservators of fisheries, whose employment will be treated with that for State-sponsored bodies in general and the County Committees of Agriculture, which have a separate section to themselves.

The Earlier Records

The earliest surviving departmental records in the present series for employment by all local authorities relate to County Borough Councils, County Councils, Urban District Councils, Town Commissioners, Mental Hospital Committees, and the Dublin and Cork Boards of Public Assistance. These early records cover the years 1938 to 1944 inclusive. Records for 1945 have not survived. In subsequent years the records available cover in addition the Boards of Assistance of Waterford, Balrothery and Rathdown, the Joint Boards of the Dublin Fever Hospital and the Cork Sanatorium, the Joint Burial Boards and the four Port Sanitary Authorities. The collective employment of these additions amounted to 637 in the year 1947/48 and added only about 1 per cent to total employment levels. Thus their absence does not significantly distort the earlier records.

Total Local Employment

Given the intertwined nature of responsibilities outlined in the background section above it would have been useful if, after the 1947 re-organisation of local government, staff had been classified by reference to their responsible Minister. The 1947 Act had divided up the old Department of Local Government into three departments: those of Local Government, Health and Social Welfare and transferred responsibility for particular local activities to each of these departments. No complete classification on this basis appears to have ever been done.

156

This means that it is not possible to extend back the statistics for health boards with any degree of certainty earlier than their inception in 1971.

A second difficulty is that the Department of Local Government ceased to include information on local health employment in its overall totals once the responsiblity for health was given to the health boards and it was some time before a good quality series was developed by the Department of Health.

Table 57: *Total local authority employment 1938–1984*

March 31	Year ended Nos	March 31	Year ended Nos	
1938*	56,000	1961	45,420	
1939*	56,000	1962	47,658	
1940*	57,300	1963	48,105	
1941*	51,900	1964	47,618	
1942*	66,900	1965	47,351	
1943*	59,600	1966	48,341	
1944*	55,538	1967	49,722	
1945	n.a.	1968	52,004	
1946	46,276	1969	52,527	
1947	50,028	1970	54,489	
1948	53,972	→1971	55,746††	
1949	56,339	Reconstituted**		
1950	55,751	1973	57,367	(55,568)
1951	60,142	1974	61,033	(59,279)
1952	62,486	1975	62,665	(60,865)
1952 Dec.	62,266	1976	n.a.	n.a.
1953 Dec.	55,739	1977	67,466	(65,636)
1954 Dec.	57,438	1978	68,908	(67,024)
1955 Dec.	56,461	1979	71,374	(69,354)
1956 Dec.	53,337	1980	75,100	(72,892)
1957	n.a.	1981	77,747	(75,350)
1958	47,367	1982	n.a.	(75,385 est)
1959	46,389	1983	n.a.	(74,745)
1960	44,056†	1984	n.a.	

Source: Departmental enumerations. Average monthly payroll used in earlier records.

†Another earlier return gave 46,721. Reasons for the revision are unknown.

*Totals for these years do not include the Boards of Assistance of Waterford, Balrothery and Rathdown, the Dublin Fever Hospital, the Cork Sanatorium, Waterford Port Sanitary Authority and the Joint Burial Boards. Separate figures for the excluded bodies show the following totals subsequently for 1946 to 1949:— 630, 663, 637 and 696.

**From 1973 onwards the series combines data collected by the Department of the Environment on local administration and by the Department of Health on (a) Regional Health Boards and (b) the joint body hospitals in Dublin, i.e., St. James's and the James Connolly Memorial Hospital. Unfortunately the dates of collection of the figures differ. Figures in parentheses omit (b).

††Devlin estimate including part timers substituted for departmental enumeration.

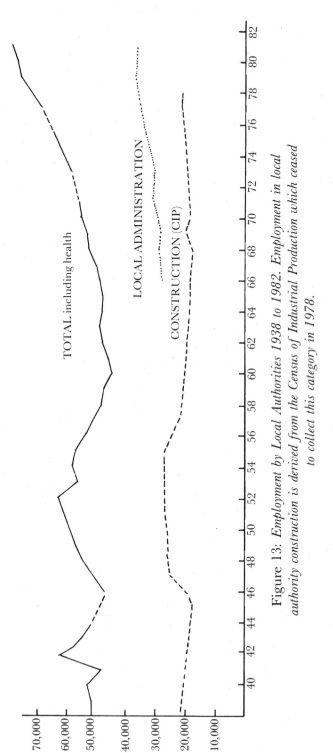

Figure 13: *Employment by Local Authorities 1938 to 1982. Employment in local authority construction is derived from the Census of Industrial Production which ceased to collect this category in 1978.*

Lacunáe, thus, occur for the mid-seventies. This complicates extending the old series forward from 1971. Nevertheless, a good overview of the development of total local employment can only be obtained if the post-1971 series can be made to contain the same elements as were included in the pre-1971 totals. In adding back employment hived off to the regional health boards it is also necessary to include two joint body hospitals, St. James's and the James Connolly Memorial Hospital which were in the pre-1971 series but became independent of the Eastern Health Board in 1973. Both are now, strictly speaking, state-sponsored bodies.

The reconstituted series is represented in Table 57 and graphed in Figure 13. Both representations show a rapid post-war rise which mirrors the developments in the Civil Service as does the peaking in 1952 when the economic crisis hit. However the rapid rate of decline (4.4 per cent annually) which caused numbers to shrink from 62,700 in 1952 to 44,000 by 1960 was exceptional. The subsequent rise of 2.8 per cent annually was slower than for the Civil Service so that it was the mid-'seventies before the 1952 level of employment was surpassed. In the course of these changes internal redistribution occurred, e.g., as between the shares going to local government and to health and also within each area itself, e.g., in the share held by salaried officials. In the cycle of change Figure 13 indicates that the contribution of local authority construction workers to the changing total was more significant before 1960. The upsurge since 1966 was, to a considerable degree, due to the rise in health services. It is proposed to study these shifts in some detail.

Chapter IV.3

EMPLOYMENT IN LOCAL GOVERNMENT

The previous section gave the aggregate level of local employment. After April 1 1971 this aggregate was divided in two and separate series published for local administration and for health boards. The next two sections attempt to trace back the antecedents of these two series.

Sources of Local Employment Data
(a) Departmental Enumeration

Three sources of data are available for this purpose. The first source is the Departmental Enumeration (DE) reported in aggregate in the last section. This enumeration became associated with the needs of a local government input into the calculation of National Accounts from 1947 onwards. For this purpose it was sufficient to record total payments of wages, salaries and other emoluments but as a check that the totals were comprehensive numbers employed were also recorded. These totals were published most years from 1952 onwards up to 1970 together with the number of "officers" for whom the Minister for Local Government was the responsible Minister. The concept of officer will be explored later. At this stage it is sufficient to note that these staff are, very broadly speaking, the equivalent of the non-industrial Civil Service. Unfortunately for our purposes figures for "servants" for whom the Minister for Local Government was responsible are rarer and, when available, present some difficulties in reconciling with other sources due to the seasonality of such "industrial" employment. Numbers of servants are also several times larger than numbers of officers.

The departmental enumeration was not undertaken purely for national income purposes, as the survival of pre-war aggregates indicates. The annual reports thus contain information on specific activities over time — all of which relate to aspects of the local government side of local activities. These would be work on (a) Roads and bridges, (b) Special employment schemes, (c) Turf production, (d) Housing and (e) Fire Brigades (see Table 58). Some series relate to average employment, others to peak employment and yet others to a specific

160

Table 58: Employment in specified local authority activities† 1944–1971

Year	Roads and bridges (average)		Employment schemes (peak)	Turf (peak)	Works act (average)	Housing (average)	Fire Brigade	
	Direct	Contract					full time	part time
1944/45	n.a.	n.a.	n.a.	31,032	—	n.a.	n.a.	n.a.
1945/46	13,808	n.a.	7,809	17,970	—	n.a.	n.a.	n.a.
1946/47	18,609	n.a.	6,147	17,382	—	n.a.	n.a.	n.a.
1947/48	21,148	n.a.	867	n.a.	—	n.a.	n.a.	n.a.
1948/49	24,239	n.a.	1,013	5,563*	—	n.a.	n.a.	n.a.
1949/50	18,314	n.a.	3,165	—	n.a.	n.a.	n.a.	n.a.
1950/51	17,927	n.a.	1,592	n.a.	8,121	n.a.	n.a.	n.a.
1951/52	17,460	n.a.	2,779	9,981	4,751	n.a.	n.a.	n.a.
1952/53	17,949	1,623	6,300	2,888	1,840	n.a.	n.a.	n.a.
1953/54	20,528	1,630	7,012	569	1,155	n.a.	n.a.	n.a.
1954/55	19,855	1,414	5,708	neg.	1,332	n.a.	n.a.	n.a.
1955/56	18,808	1,424	6,015	—	1,783	n.a.	n.a.	n.a.
1956/57	16,693	1,405	4,369	—	1,408	n.a.	257	1,821
1957/58	14,964	1,228	5,682	—	n.a.	n.a.	263	1,775
1958/59	14,193	1,292	5,625	—	—	n.a.	267	1,920
1959/60	13,960	1,093	5,212	—	—	n.a.	n.a.	n.a.
1960/61	13,805	891	5,306	—	—	1,626	n.a.	n.a.
1961/62	13,703	940	4,751	—	—	1,803	n.a.	n.a.
1962/63	13,194	1,017	4,556	—	—	2,181	286	1,834
1963/64	12,728	899	3,772	—	—	2,434	411	1,645
1964/65	12,547	929	3,515	—	—	3,291	418	1,804
1965/66	12,543	965	2,750	—	—	3,982	482	1,821
1966/67	12,283	305	800	—	—	3,146	498	1,840
1967/68	n.a.	n.a.	—	—	—	4,524	n.a.	n.a.
1968/69	n.a.	n.a.	—	—	—	5,077	n.a.	n.a.
1969/70	n.a.	n.a.	—	—	—	4,585	n.a.	n.a.
1970/71	n.a.	n.a.	—	—	—	3,738	527	1,919

Source: Annual Reports, Department of Local Government.

†For explanations see text.

*Employment schemes for former turf workers after cessation of scheme. Scheme recommenced 1950/51.

Note: The peak period for employment schemes is a week in December or January and June/July for turf production. Monthly figures are available for direct and contract work on roads and bridges and in some years for housing and other categories.

Table 59: *Officers and servants of local authorities responsible to the Minister for Local Government for selected years 1958–1971*

Year	Total	Officers	Road workers average	Other servants average	Total servants average
1958/59	28,817	5,212	14,510	9,095	23,605
1965/66	27,824	5,232	12,973	9,619	22,592
1967/68	28,298	5,883	11,086	11,379	22,415
1968/69	28,082	6,070	10,859	11,153	22,012
1970/71	30,526	6,444	9,483	14,599	24,082
(part time)	(3,510)	(564)	(1,160) est	(1,786) est	(2,946)

Sources: Unpublished Departmental Memoranda. The 1970/71 figures are derived from a Devlin survey for January 1 and include partimers. For this reason they are not strictly comparable with earlier figures. Part-time servants were allocated to road works proportionate to their share of full-time workers.

date. In no case was a complete breakdown given of the composition of all staff reporting to the Minister for Local Government. Broad subclassification were calculated for a few years — see Table 59. The figures for roadworkers in 1958/59 and 1965/66 differ slightly from those given in Table 58.

(b) The Census of Population (CP)

The Census of Population published figures under a variety of headings for the years 1946, 1951, 1961, 1966, 1971 and 1981. Since there is no industrial classification for local authority *an sich*, the material must be collected from under a number of headings and there is no guarantee that some groups of local authority workers might not be overlooked. Several of the industrial classifications included the words "Local authority" in their title. These varied from census to census but generally included mental hospitals, county hospitals and homes, other medicine and care of the sick, house construction, civil engineering and other local authority employment. This last group included county committees of agriculture. In 1946 and 1951 local authority turf production was listed as a separate item. More recently recording of such turf provision was included in "Turf production" but it is not clear if anyone was so described in 1971. A local authority label was not attached to "water" even though it is clearly an exclusively local authority activity. In 1951 this category was described as "Waterworks and Sanitary Services" and therefore may contain more than "water" in subsequent census records. If so, this would help to explain its very much higher employment levels in 1951. Some other categories may also contain a local authority element, notably gasworks and quarries. If so there is no way to determine the numbers included. On the basis of what is clearly identified Table 60 was constructed.

Table 60: *Employment by local authorities (excluding harbours and education) as returned in the Census of Population 1946–1981*

	1946	1951	1961	1966	1971	1981
1. Mental Hospitals	n.a.	4,192	4,637	5,181	18,646	30,356
2. Other Hospitals	n.a.	6,343	10,031	10,972		
3. Other Medicine	n.a.	2,208	2,303	1,995	2,761	3,327
Subtotal above	n.a.	12,743	16,971	18,148	21,407	33,683
4. Waterworks	n.a.	1,473	521	682	823	968
5. Local Government nes	n.a.	8,277	9,298	11,360	13,740	11,154
Subtotal above	17,283	22,493	26,790	30,190	35,970	45,805
6. House Construction	24,043	32,955	2,379	2,736	14,479	19,036
7. Civil Engineering			5,753	13,474		
8. Turf Production	5,045	1,132	n.a.	n.a.	n.a.	n.a.
Subtotal 6 to 8	29,088	34,087	18,132	16,210	14,479	19,036
Total	46,371	56,580	44,922	46,400	50,449	64,841

Table 61: *Employment figures from the Census of Industrial Production 1936–78 distinguishing salaried workers and total engaged in (a) local authority building and construction (b) local authority waterworks and (c) industrial work in Government Departments*

| | Local authority | | | | | Government Departments | |
| | Building & construction | | Waterworks | | Both | | |
Year	Total	Salaried	Total	Salaried	Total	Total	Salaried
1936	18,257	781	1,113	200	19,370	1,766	193
1937	23,453	857	1,192	216	24,645	2,695	245
1938	21,384	876	1,309	250	22,693	2,024	253
1943	18,384	810	945	150	19,329	1,399	229
1944	n.a.	n.a.	1,111	n.a.	n.a.	1,526	239
1945	17,256	863	1,124	197	18,380	1,278	243
1946	19,583	946	1,126	207	20,709	1,684	296
1947	24,179	1,030	1,151	200	25,330	1,931	296
1948	25,283	1,071	1,281	216	26,564	2,326	339
1949	25,334	1,168	1,301	253	26,535	2,763	352
1950	25,938	1,248	1,270	254	27,257	3,242	408
1951	26,698	1,282	1,316	283	28,014	3,406	415
1952	26,391	1,416	1,363	310	27,754	3,941	450
1953	26,328	1,488	1,339	307	27,667	4,021	485
1954	26,544	1,498	1,384	324	27,928	4,218	472
1955	26,607	1,495	1,568	334	28,175	4,354	484
1956	23,695	1,574	1,555	353	25,250	4,068	513
1957	21,601	1,513	1,297	305	22,898	3,950	490
1958	20,528	1,474	1,274	245	21,802	4,287	502
1959	20,402	1,408	1,329	257	21,731	4,579	506
1960	19,400	1,431	1,424	264	20,824	4,837	502
1961	19,406	1,527	1,427	240	20,833	4,945	519
1962	19,140	1,447	1,316	255	20,456	5,671	588
1963	18,509	1,536	1,313	184	20,822	6,022	597
1964	18,449	1,556	1,350	190	19,799	6,351	594
1965	18,303	1,649	1,500	217	19,803	6,403	658
1966	18,119	1,664	1,423	217	19,542	6,095	686
1967	17,479	1,647	1,436	204	18,915	6,440	666
1968	17,504	1,745	1,443	216	18,947	6,462	726
1969	19,965	2,035	1,472	243	21,437	6,842	827
1970	18,053	1,888	1,620	243	19,673	7,372	826
1971	18,689	2,032	1,601	252	20,290	7,416	834
1972	18,902	2,128	1,734	259	20,636	7,703	887
1973	19,278	2,172	1,782	221	21,060	8,244	895
1974	19,817	2,436	1,782	201	21,599	8,419*	962
1975	20,302	2,645	1,794	249	22,096	8,197	987
1976	20,908	2,815	1,865	269	22,773	8,680	1,015
1977	21,574	2,606	1,920	263	23,494	9,619	1,104
1978	21,237	2,697	1,976	300	23,213	9,864	1,180
	End of Series					End of Series	

*Figures for Government Department engaged in manufacturing included in their own NACE group from 1974.

(c) The Census of Industrial Production (CIP)

The third source relates to part of local government employment — that which involves industrial activities. Each year up to 1978 the Census of Industrial Production recorded the numbers engaged in industrial activities in local authorities and in government departments. Due to the courtesy of the Central Statistics Office a series is available, in Table 61, which refers to local authorities alone. A separate series records employment in waterworks. These series give the annual levels for salaried staff and the number of other workers on a defined week generally in September or October. Thus the total refer to all staff involved in the activity and not just to the industrial workers.

Estimating Local Government Employment
(a) Before 1972

Although the Census of Population (CP) total for 1946, 46,371, is very similar to that in the Departmental Enumeration (DE) in Table 57, 46,276, the level of disaggregation does not permit any estimates of the local government element so that year can be disregarded. Table 62 collates the data for other years as derived from Tables 57 to 61. There is, of course, no reason why the figures should all agree with each other as they were compiled at different times, include different entities and use different criteria for recording. It is, however, useful to try to decide which of these is to be preferred for our purposes.

If we accept that the aggregate figures in Table 57 are correct we need to divide these totals into two parts such that each is a precursor of the post-1971 series for local government and health. The first difficulty is that we have no clear statement anywhere of the exact composition of the Table 57 totals. This complicates our difficulty in explaining the balances left over after the CP totals have been deducted from the Table 57 aggregates.

The second difficulty is that the Ministers for Local Government and for Health are not the only ones with responsibility for local activities. The Minister for Social Welfare is the Minister for assistance officers who numbered 154 whole time and 213 part time on 31 December 1958 and similar numbers six years later. In addition the Minister for Justice controls coroners, courthouses, etc, the Minister for Defence civil defence, the Minister for Energy gasworks, the Minister for the Gaeltacht housing and sanitary services, all activities quite apart from the major inputs of the Ministers for Agriculture, Education and Transport which relate to County Committees of Agriculture, Vocational Education Commitees and Harbour Authorities. Employees of these latter bodies are, hopefully, not included in the Table 57 totals. It will be noted, however, that County Committees of Agriculture were included in the 1971 CP total listed under Local Government in Table 62. Presumably they were also included in previous Censuses. This means that where the 1958/59 depart-

Table 62: *Composition of local authority employment (various sources) 1951–1971*

Date	Total Table 57	Source	Responsible Minister Local Govt.	Health	Balance 1–2–3	Industrial Employment Table 58	Table 61	As source
	1		2	3	4	5	6	7
1951	60,142	CP	43,837	12,743	3,562	27,640	28,014	34,428
1958/59	47,367	DE	28,817	16,532[a]	2,018	21,110	21,802	23,605
1961	45,420	CP	27,951	16,971	498	21,628	20,833	18,653
1966	48,341	CP	28,252	18,148	1,941	20,240	19,542	16,892
1965/66	48,341	DE	27,824	20,517		20,240	19,542	22,592
1967/68	52,004	DE	28,298	23,706		n.a.	18,947	22,415
1968/69	52,527	DE	28,082	24,445		n.a.	21,437	22,012
1971	(54,489)	CP	29,042	21,407	4,040	n.a.	20,290	14,479
1971	55,746	Dev.	30,526[b]	25,220[c]	−1,257	n.a.	20,290	none

Included parttimers were (a) 2,953; (b) 3,510 and (c) 1,177.
Note: CP = Census of Population; DE = Departmental Enumeration; Dev = Devlin Report 1972. In column 7 CP gives construction and water figures from Table 60; DE = Servant figures from Table 59.

mental enumeration gives figures for staff for whom either the Ministers of Local Government or of Health were the responsible Ministers we should like to know how to account for the balance of 2,018 *vis-à-vis* Table 57. It appears to be too large to be staff of other Ministers.

The third difficulty is the large number of part time staff who numbered almost 3,000 in health in 1958/59. These may not have reported themselves as local authority health staff in the self-reporting of the CP. Allied to that is the problem of servants whose employment levels fluctuate from month to month. A series is available for those recorded at work directly or under contract on roads and bridges for each month in the years recorded in Table 58. In three-quarters of the cases the months of minimum employment were March or April, i.e., near th edate of the CP. Maximum employment displayed less regularity, 27 per cent of years it occurred in November/December, 55 per cent of the time in June/July. Thus the CIP returns for September or October were more likely to be nearer the maximum. Examples of the range are as follows:

	Average	*Minimum*		*Maximum*		*Range*
1950/51	17,927	14,263	March 1951	21,245	July 1950	6,982
1958/59	14,193	11,997	March 1959	15,523	Nov. 1958	3,526
1960/61	13,805	12,607	Jan. 1961	14,407	Sept. 1960	1,800
1965/66	12,543	11,435	Feb. 1966	13,244	June 1965	1,809

As the average decreased the range narrowed more rapidly. This could account for the large balance reported for 1951 except that in that year the CP reported a massive 32,955 in local authority construction — the only time that the CP figures exceeded the CIP. The same phenomenon can be observed with water-works where in other years the CIP was several times higher than the CP levels.

In summary then, there exists a considerable degree of ambiguity in employ-ment levels for local government staff which reference to the sources was unable to dispel. On balance it was decided to accept the Devlin division for 1971. When allowance is made for 464 staff in County Committees of Agriculture the DE and CP figures for 1966 are virtually identical. The CP figure for 1961 was accepted net of 354 agricultural staff, i.e., 27,617 and DE figures for later years. The figures for the 'fifties are more problematical. The DE total showed a drop of 14,722 between 1951 and 1961 which was over a thousand less than the 15,775 fall recorded by the CP categories construction and waterworks. The difference can be explained as a difference between the CP and CIP records for waterworks employment viz -952 vs. +111. In local government the rise of a thousand in "Local government not elsewhere stated" was cancelled by a similar sized fall in turf production. This suggests that the bulk of the balance in Table 62 can be attributed to the local government elsewhere with an estimated 350 assistance officers added to health. On this rather arbitrary basis, Table 63 gives the division of the Table 57 totals. The higher estimates in Table 63 can be assumed to be seasonal roadworkers and other servants.

Table 63: *Estimates of local goverment and health employment 1951–1971*

Year	Total Table 57	Local Government	Health
1951	60,142	47,049	13,093
1958/59	47,367	30,485	16,882
1961	45,420	27,617	17,803
1966	48,341	27,824	20,517
1967/68	52,004	28,298	23,706
1968/69	52,527	28,082	24,445
1971	55,746	30,526	25,220

These figures link in with those given in Table 59 except for the year 1958/59.

(b) 1972 and After

In 1976 regular local authority staffing returns had to be submitted to the Department for the first time and were subjected to rigorous appraisal by the Department's personnel section. In the process some discrepancies were revealed in the more traditional time series collected for National Income estimation purposes which placed the accent on costs. While the traditional series may have contained an element of double counting, since the multiple tiers of government often resulted in the same officer holding several responsibilities, such an explanation cannot explain the major difference in the two series at the end of 1978, i.e., 3,436. The reason appears to be the inclusion or exclusion of part timers since a survey by Devlin for March of the same year recorded 37,131 staff made up of 33,290 whole-time employees and 3,841 part time.

The two series were as follows:—

	National Income	Personnel
End March 1972	30,199	30,154
End March 1973	30,454	30,667
End March 1974	31,635	31,993
End December 1974	31,453	31,692
End December 1975	33,060	32,149
End December 1976	33,954	n.a.
End December 1977	34,494	32, 658 August
End December 1978	36,019	32, 583 August
End December 1979	36,747	34,834

	National Income	*Personnel*
End December 1980	36,666	35,710
End December 1981	36,296	35,885
End December 1982		36,261
End December 1983		35,598
End December 1984		35,400 (est)

Note: The Personnel series are based on independent enumerations since 1976 and recalculations for the earlier period.

Part of the differences could be that the National Income Series used annual averages for certain categories of workers who are unlikely to be engaged on Summer road work or drainage schemes in the middle of Winter. If that is indeed the case it is interesting to note that the NI series peaked in 1979 just after rates had been removed from residences and local sources of financing thus became fewer. The lower "personnel" estimates did not show this trend. The personnel series showed a greater response to the full employment programme launched in 1977. Neither series appears to have been greatly influenced by the recruitment go slow which hit the general Civil Service in 1975 and while no formal recruitment ban was instituted in 1981 restrictions on staff numbers were put into operation at that time.

Trends in Local Government Employment

Taking Tables 57 to 63 together with Figure 13 we can form some impressions of change over almost fifty years. As we have seen, the situation prior to 1951 is less well documented and does not permit the exclusion of health employment. Even so it is apparent that much of the fluctuation in this period is due to activities on the local government side. Table 57 shows total employment to have been approximately 56,000 in 1938, 1939, 1944, 1949 and 1950 with considerable annual fluctuations in between e.g. 67,000 in 1942 and 46,000 in 1946. The background section indicated that scarcity of tar inhibited road making from 1941 onwards while the scarcity of fuel caused a major swing towards local authority turf production. Table 58 shows 31,032 men engaged in this activity in 1944 but due to bad weather numbers were less than 60 per cent of this level in the next two years. Numbers were not reported for 1947/48 and the requirement to engage in turf production was abolished at the outset of 1948. Since large numbers of men were displaced 5,563 ex turf workers were found employment in 1948/49 even though road works had expanded by more than 10,000 men between 1945/46 and 1948/49.

Apart from these activities special employment and emergency schemes were operated by the Special Employment Schemes (SES) Office under a separate vote until April 1967. These schemes were for men receiving employment assistance and were allocated in accordance with the levels of local unemployment. They were classified as Urban and Rural Employment Schemes, Rural Improvement Schemes, Minor Employment Schemes and Bog Development Schemes. When the SES Office and Vote were transferred to Local Government in 1967 similar work continued for another three years when accommodation and bog roads were grant aided where a group of landholders were involved. Peak employment under these schemes was generally reached in January or December. In the initial stages men were recruited on a rotational basis for 6, 8 or 12 weeks depending on whether they lived in rural or urban areas or in county boroughs. Peak levels of employment varied widely as Table 58 shows, e.g., 7,809 in 1945/46 and 867 two years later.

A further source of employment was the Local Authorities (Works) Act of 1949 under which the Oireachtas voted substantial sums for flood control over the first half of the 'fifties. Average employment in 1950/51 was unusually high, 8,121 men.

The coming together of these various schemes transformed the 1946 employment levels from the lowest on record, before the decline in 1959 and 1960, to produce the highest ever recorded in 1952, i.e., 62,486, a figure which was only surpassed in 1975. The record year of 1952 was the last year of post-war growth and the balance of payments crisis of that year affected all public expenditure. The sharp fall in 1953 was continued until the trough of 44,056 was reached in 1960. In terms of local government employment Table 63 suggests a fall of almost 20,000 at a time when health employment was rising almost 5,000. The contrast was continued over the 'sixties when local government employment was fairly stable while health employment rose a further 7,000. This was also the experience of the 'seventies, as Figure 14 clearly graphs.

At first sight it would appear that the employment experience of local authorities was at variance with that of the Civil Service. However when the differing experiences of industrial and non-industrial civil servants are noted the parallels become more apparent. In general industrial staff have tended to decline in number while non-industrial expanded rapidly. The overall experience of the local authorities was due to the predominance of such industrial staff who were not so dominant in the Civil Service. This can be seen when employment trends of officers and servants are studied separately.

Officers and Servants of Local Government

As is brought out in the background section the whole trend in recruitment has been to eliminate the possibilities of local jobbery and to institute procedures by which staff would have the same professional qualifications as was taken for granted in the Civil Service. The first step towards Arthur Griffith's ideal was the establishment of the Local Appointment Commission in 1926 to fill chief

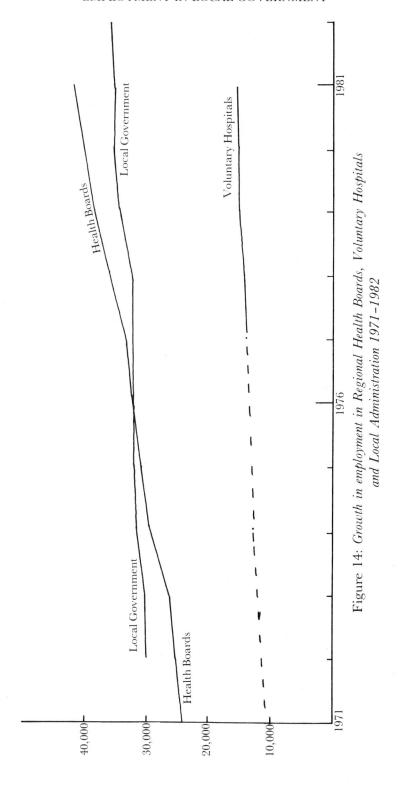

Figure 14: *Growth in employment in Regional Health Boards, Voluntary Hospitals and Local Administration 1971–1982*

executive, professional and technical offices. The Local Government Act 1941, following on the repeal of the Poor Laws (under which local bodies appointed their own staff), empowered the Minister to fix the size of local authorities and provided for a reduction in their size. The Act also distinguished three types of office: major, minor and other. Major offices were filled by the Local Appointments Commissioners alone and applied to all senior offices excluding staff officer, senior library assistant, rates collector, rates inspector. Both creating the post and making the appointment required ministerial sanction and could only be filled after sitting for an examination. Creating minor posts had to be sanctioned by the Minister but not the choice of appointee. The posts involved included clerical officer, library assistant, clerk typist, store-keeper, draughtsman and clerk of a lesser town. Other[20] staff became known as "servants". Their mode of appointment was at local discretion and their job security more precarious.

During the mid-1970s the clerical and administrative structure comprising staff officers, clerical officer and clerk typist was replaced by a seven grade structure with clerical officer, clerk typist and clerical assistant as the entry grades and the promotion grades being administrative officer, senior staff, staff and assistant staff officer. Other higher grades on the administrative side are manager, secretary and accountant or finance officer. As we shall see the new grading structure was responsible for the rise in administrative and executive posts in the period immediately before 1978.

Although the distinction between officer and servant is of long standing few early records survive. Writing in the mid-'fifties the former secretary of the Department of Local Government, D. Turpin, commented on the ambiguity of the term "officer". At the time of writing he noted that of the 62,000 currently employed about 40,000 were

> manual (mainly road) workers and about 18,000 (described as officers) in a class corresponding to the non industrial class in the Civil Service. In addition there were about 4,000 'officers' whose duties were closer to those of manual workers than those of officers as normally understood.... About 4,000 officers were part time only.

The point being made here was that "officer" referred to the normal civil service type jobs as distinct from jobs held in the Civil Service by industrial workers. It did not convey the idea of leadership but merely the idea of filling an office.

The point made by Turpin can be grasped by studying the composition of the officer group at the time he penned the above comment:

[20]That is non-officers, not "other" types of office above.

Administrative	211
Executive: Indoor	370
Executive: Outdoor	1,950
Clerical (incl. library)	2,350
Professional higher	4,095
Professional other	7,500
Domestic and ancillary	4,600
Total (approx.)	21,076

The listings brings out the strange fact that domestic staff in institutions — wardsmaids, kitchen staff, farm workers, tradesmen attached to institutions, etc., are deemed to be officers. The title "servant" is reserved for road workers and other manual workers.

It might be noted in passing that in the above listing the other professional group were largely comprised of nurses; furthermore, that the total did not include about 1,200 part-time doctors, who might otherwise have been included in the higher professional grouping. The only other record of the total number of officers is given by Roche (1982) in 1961 as 16,750 including both whole time and part time.

This section is more concerned with officers under the control of the Minister for Local Government. Broadly speaking the pre-war staff of 3,300 reached 5,000 by 1950 and, as Table 59 showed, remained at about that level up to April 1966. Within this stability a degree of oscillation occurred, e.g., 5,134 in 1952 and 5,198 in 1963; 5,366 in 1956 and 5,379 in 1965; 5,233 in 1959 and 5,232 in 1966. After April 1966 a period of rapid increase began:

March 31 1967	5,762
March 31 1968	5,883
March 31 1969	6,070
March 31 1971	6,444

Of the 6,444 surveyed by Devlin in 1971 only 5,880 were full-time officers and of these only 5,362 were contributors to superannuation. Table 64 documents the continuation of their upward march which stopped just short of 10,000 by the end of 1982. This rate of 3.9 per cent shows that, for the local equivalents of the non-industrial Civil Service, job opportunities were in no way inferior to those facing their opposite numbers in central government.

The brunt of the lack of general expansion in local government was borne by the more numerous "servants" category. In the post-1966 period this group grew at less than 1 per cent annually. Two short periods accounted for more than this total increase. Table 59 showed a rise of more than 2,000 during the period

Table 64: *Officers and servants of local authorities 1972–84**

Year	Month	Officers	Servants	Total
1972	March	6,802	23,352	30,154
1973	March	7,093	23,574	30,667
1974	March	7,544	24,449	31,993
1974	Dec.	7,667	24,025	31,692
1975	Dec.	7,812	24,337	32,149
1976	Dec	n.a.	n.a.	n.a.
1977	Aug.	8,070	24,588	32,658
1978	Aug.	8,521	24,068	32,583
1979	Dec.	9,068	25,766	34,834
1980	Dec.	9,038	26,672	35,710
1981	Dec.	9,597	26,288	35,885
1982	Dec.	9,883	26,378	36,261
1983	Dec	10,095	25,503	35,598

*Striclty speaking December 31 1983.

1968/69 to 1970/71 and a similar increase is recorded in Table 64 between August 1978 and December 1980. The cause of the first rise is unclear but it is reported in both the CIP returns and in the Departmental enumeration. The later increase may have something to do with the full employment pogramme, though the rise in road employment from 9,540 to 11,000 occurred in the previous two years. In general, servants as a group showed little tendency to increase in numbers. August 1978 figures were only 2 per cent above those two decades earlier.

Details of long-term trends in the Census of Industrial Production activities are provided in Table 61. These tend to confirm the upward trend in the proportion of jobs going to officers. These figures show that the ratio of wage to salary earners has dropped dramatically in construction: 26.4 (1937), 19.8 (1950), 12.8 (1960), 8.8 (1969) and 6.4 (1976) when the CIP series was about to be discontinued. This took place against a general background of decline. The 26,607 of 1955 had fallen to 17,479 by 1967 and rallied to 21,237 when publication of the series ceased in 1978.

Table 61 also records employment in local authority waterworks. Here the long-term trend in employment has been upward but, unlike the local authorities in general, there has been little evidence of any tendency to substitute salaried workers for wage earners. In 1950 the 254 salaried employees were 20 per cent of the 1,270 staff. In 1975, 249 catered for 1,794 staff—i.e., 14 per cent.

The Composition of Local Government Employment

Initially it was hoped that a study of the occupational structure of local government employment would benefit from the fact that the Census of Population classifies jobs both by industry and by occupation. In practice the CP classification by occupation proved to be less useful due to problems of reassignment and of aggregation. Thus in 1951, 44 per cent (3,627) of the total were classified as "local authority officials" most of whom it would appear were reclassified later as "clerks and typists" but even this category included draughtsmen in some censuses who were subsequently deemed to be "professional and technical". Similar difficulties can be found in the case of "unskilled workers" and "engineers".

Other sources have been somewhat more rewarding. An analysis for 1958/59 enables us to capture the general composition of that year's officer group:

Managers, county secretaries, town clerks	145
Accountants, staff officers, etc.	446
Professionals: Engineers, architects, town planners, quantity surveyors, solicitors, draughtsmen	733
Rent and Rates Collectors (outdoor staff)	1,064
Library staff, clerical officers, typists	2,499
Miscellaneous	325
Total	5,212

This can be supplemented by the analyses published in the two Devlin Reports of 1972 and 1979 reproduced in Table 65.

Broadly speaking the message in Table 65 is: the higher the post the more rapid the increase in numbers, e.g., managerial, etc., +115 per cent, clerical +40 per cent, servants +16 per cent, part timers +9 per cent. Were it not for the rapid growth (82 per cent) in numbers of unskilled workers other than road workers the industrial worker group in general would have only had a 2 per cent increase in whole-time employees in contrast to the 44 per cent chalked up for officers in general.

Table 65 showed that between 1971 and 1978 unskilled workers were continuing to move towards other activities rather than road works. Fewer road-making jobs may reflect technological change especially in urban areas, e.g., although Dublin employed 27 per cent of all local authority staff on 1 January 1971 only 7 per cent of all whole-time unskilled roadworkers were engaged by that county. The rise in the number of other unskilled workers may be associated with non-industrial services of local authorities such as litter collection, fire fighting, swimming pool attendants, traffic school wardens and the general cleaning, messenger, porter and security staff of the various authorities.

Table 65: *Changes in the composition of the local authority workforce between 1971 and 1978*

	1971	1978	% change
Managerial, Administrative, Executive: higher*	139	299	115
Managerial, Administrative, Executive: other	489	796	63
Professional and Technical: higher*	432	578	34
Professional and Technical: other	1,088	1,823	68
Clerical and Allied	3,732	5,211	40
Officers whole-time total	5,880	8,707	48
Officers part-time total	564	562	—
Officers all	6,444	9,269	44
Supervisory Manual	2,245	2,776	24
Skilled	2,564	2,516	-2
Semi-skilled	2,340	2,816	20
Unskilled: Road Workers	8,323	8,198	-2
Unskilled: Other	3,621	6,590	82
Other whole-time employees	2,043	1,687	-17
Servants whole-time total	21,136	24,583	16
Servants part-time total	2,946	3,279	11
Servants all	24,082	27,862	16
All whole time	27,016	33,290	23
All part time	3,510	3,841	9
Grant total	30,526	37,131	22

Source: Devlin Reports 1972 and 1979.
*Above maximum pay of £2,500 (1970), £7,000 (1978). These are roughly equivalent, being at or slightly above the maximum earnings of the higher executive officer in the Civil Service.

A rich if random source of information on the local authorities are the Dail Debates. For example, in June 1980 numbers of craftsmen were given distinguishing foremen, assistant foremen, chargehands and ordinary craftsmen plus road gangers, road foremen and road overseers. These numbers were detailed by individual authority. In the same month similar detail was provided for part-time and whole-time veterinary officers distinguishing permanent and temporary. The previous month details by authority of architects, civil engineers and town planners was provided. Interested readers are referred to these sources.

Local Employment by Type of Authority

Another traditional method, by which to classify local authority jobs, has been by type of authority, e.g., county council, town commissioners, etc. As we have seen statistics for these categories extend back to the Second World War. However, the re-organisations, which ultimately led to the creation of the eight health boards in 1971, have tended to disrupt the continuity of the series.

Among the mosaic of bodies functioning in 1947 there was some with no longer any health responsibility so that their employment levels enjoy a continuous 'series unaffected by compositional changes due to health re-organisations. These were the urban district councils and the town commis-sioners. Certain counties had also found it advantageous to come together to create joint bodies to manage cemeteries, libraries and drainage. In these cases the discharge of these functions was kept independent of the parent bodies and a series of records endures to this day. For other bodies the situation was more complex. Seven counties traditionally reserved to themselves the function of Mental Hospital Authority (Donegal, Mayo, Clare, Kerry, Wexford, Kilkenny and Louth) rather than form joint boards. In these counties employment included that for mental health care. In other counties employment was recorded for the joint mental hospital boards separately.

In 1954 control of Merlyn Park Sanatorium was handed over to the Western Health Institutions Board, on which all Connacht counties were represented. This Board could take over other bodies as well but no records show if it did so. It was altogether different in 1960 when four United Health Authorities merged all the health activities in the counties of Dublin, Cork, Limerick and Waterford. In the process the three public assistance boards covering County Dublin, i.e., Dublin, Balrothery and Rathdown, the South Cork Board of Assistance and the Board for County Waterford lost their separate identity. Mental health, hospital and other health functions were also transferred so that from 1960 employment

Table 66: *Employment by type of local authority in years ended March 31, 1947, 1954 and 1959*

	1947	1954	1959	Change 1947/54	1954/59
County Councils	37,223	39,702	29,482	+7	−26
County Boroughs	5,537	8,113	7,022	+47	−13
Urban District Councils	1,897	2,142	1,892	+13	−12
Town Commissioners	109	123	104	+13	−15
Joint Burial Boards	41	42	46	+2	+10
Joint Drainage Boards	—	259	236	—	−9
Subtotal	44,805	50,381	38,782	+12	−23
Boards of Public Assistance	1,954	2,707	3,987	+39	+10
Mental Hospital Boards	3,015	3,510	3,722	+16	+6
Joint Hospital Boards	239 ⎫				
Port Sanitary Authority	15 ⎬	840	898*		
Other	— ⎭				
Subtotal	5,223	7,057	7,607	+35	+8
Total	50,028	57,438	46,389	+15	−20

*Includes Joint Library Committees, Western Health Institutions Board.

in county boroughs (and their neighbour counties) was purged of its health element. The series continues unbroken up to the present. In contrast the local government element in county council employment is only separately identifiable in 1972, after the setting up of the regional health boards in 1971.

Prior to the 1960 re-organisation, the broad picture can be gleaned from two years for which complete records are still available; 1946/47 and 1954. In 1954 employment levels were below those of the peak year of 1952 but none the less mark a point before the crisis of the mid-'fifties caused the severe retrenchment which put numbers down a further 23 per cent below 1954 levels.

In the 'fifties the slowest growth and the severest reductions were borne by the county councils. Those lost more than 10,000 staff in the late 'fifties, or more than a quarter of their numbers. County Boroughs and their neighbours in the same counties, the Boards of Public Assistance, made considerable advances in the early 'fifties which persisted for the latter over the late-'fifties. As a result, their share of employment rose from 15 per cent in 1947 to 24 per cent in 1959. Surviving records are inadequate to determine the influence of Dublin in these differing patterns.

The year of minimum local authority employment was 1960. It was also the year when the four United Health Authorities were created reducing staff levels in four county councils and their associated county boroughs. Available data for the new series are collected in Table 67.

The pruned county boroughs of 1964 employed almost 6,500. By 1982 the payroll extended to almost 11,000. Another fast growing group of bodies were the urban district councils which included the borough corporations. In contrast Table 67 shows growth in county council employment to have been sluggish, even after three out of every eight staff were transferred to the Regional Health Boards in the 1971 reshuffle of responsibilities. The changing structure of local employment appears to be a reflection of the growing urbanisation of Irish society in general.

The decline in employment by town commissioners may be due in part to the more rigorous statistical procedures of the Department aimed at avoiding double counting where some officers have joint responsibilities. Similar considerations may apply to some of the other small bodies.

It will be noted, however, that even where employment level has been relatively static the composition of staff has usually continued to shift in favour of officers. This aspect of the change is brought out in Table 68. Some additional information has appeared in the Dail Debates. In November 1982 details of non-permanent officers and servants were listed by authority for 1979, 1980 and 1981. All servants were so described as were a declining number of officers: i.e. 867, 850 and 756, respectively. Another Dail question (October 1980) showed 917 temporary officers in county councils and county boroughs alone at end

Table 67: *Local government employment 1964–1984 by type of authority*

Year ended Mar.	Total	County Councils	County Boroughs	Urban District C	Town Commiss.	Drainage	Joint Bodies Library	Burial
1964	47,618	27,150	6,491	1,799	79	193	n.a.	n.a.
1967	49,722	27,595	7,293	1,822	79	188	52	96
1968	52,004	28,337	7,658	1,997	79	455	52	43
1969	52,527	28,928	7,914	2,014	85	207	54	45
1970	54,489	29,263	8,076	2,002	72	219	58	17
1971	41,387	30,427	8,497	2,052	138	183	45	45
1972	30,154	19,094	8,682	2,099	76	90	67	46
1973	30,667	19,315	8,867	2,152	66	154	67	46
1974	31,993	20,494	8,877	2,401	66	41	74	40
Dec. 1974	31,692	19,811	9,158	2,488	63	60	72	40
Dec. 1975	32,149	20,083	9,333	2,480	70	60	80	43
Dec. 1976	[33,954]	[21,093]	[9,842]	[2,775]	[55]	[73]	[78]	[38]
Dec. 1977	32,658	19,799	9,815	2,864	72	24	46	38
Dec. 1978	32,583	19,303	9,793	3,192	52	134	80	35
Dec. 1979	34,834	21,294	10,386	2,908	47	94	74	31
Dec. 1980	35,710	22,171	10,313	3,023	51	16	102	34
Dec. 1981	35,885	22,145	10,453	3,072	23	73	87	32
Dec. 1982	36,261	21,977	10,908	3,117	29	104	100	32
Dec. 1983	35,598	21,401	10,982	2,938	51	93	103	30

Note 1: In 1964, 11,906 staff were unidentified in the records. In the last years of the 'sixties the balance unaccounted for above was made up of:

	United Health Authorities	Mental Health Boards
1967	10,512	2,089
1968	10,612	2,771
1969	10,469	2,811
1970	11,592	2,890

These bodies are omitted from the 1971 total.

Note 2: Some details for years prior to 1964 are given in the text.

Note 3: Figures for 1976 are from the less reliable National Income Series (see text). Figures for 1977 are based on this source also.

Table 68: *Officers and Servants by Type of Local Authority 1972–1984*

Year ended March 31	County Council		County Borough		Urban District Council	
	Officers	Servants	Officers	Servants	Officers	Servants
1972	4,124	14,970	1,978	6,704	570	1,529
1973	4,420	14,895	1,998	6,869	553	1,599
1974	4,752	15,742	2,108	6,769	577	1,824
1974 Dec.	4,803	15,008	2,160	6,998	594	1,894
1975 Dec.	4,898	15,185	2,180	7,153	616	1,864
1976 Dec.	n.a.	n.a.	n.a.	n.a.	n.a.	n.a.
1977 Dec.	4,978	14,821	2,374	7,441	629	2,235
1978 Dec.	5,061	14,242	2,641	7,152	700	2,492
1979 Dec.	5,612	15,682	2,669	7,717	680	2,228
1980 Dec.	5,603	16,568	2,635	7,678	699	2,324
1981 Dec.	5,981	16,164	2,800	7,653	742	2,330
1982 Dec.	6,232	15,739	2,820	8,088	724	2,393
1983 Dec.	6,288	15,113	2,903	8,079	769	2,169

Table 68: *(cont'd.)*

| | Town Commissioners | | Drainage | | Joint Bodies | | | |
| | | | | | Library | | Burial | |
	Officers	Servants	Officers	Servants	Officers	Servants	Officers	Servants
1972	40	36	23	67	59	8	8	38
1973	36	30	19	135	59	8	8	38
1974	36	30	16	25	47	27	8	32
1974 Dec.	36	27	20	40	46	26	8	32
1975 Dec.	40	30	20	40	50	30	8	35
1976 Dec.	n.a.	n.a.	n.a.	n.a.	n.a.	n.a.	n.a.	n.a.
1977 Dec.	41	31	7	17	36	10	5	33
1978 Dec.	36	16	1	133	76	4	6	29
1979 Dec.	30	17	1	93	69	5	7	24
1980 Dec.	36	15	—	16	56	46	9	25
1981 Dec.	12	11	—	74	56	31	6	26
1982 Dec.	14	15	—	104	87	13	6	26
1983 Dec.	37	14	2	91	90	13	6	24

Note: For totals and comment see previous table: Figures from 1978 onwards have been more closely scrutinised especially for officers in lesser bodies.

1979. The difference appears to be whether it was a permanent post filled temporarily, etc. The same sitting was told that as a result of the restrictions on recruitment 463 vacancies in permanent posts were unfilled at end December 1981.

Recent Monitoring

The crisis in state finances has led to the development of a monitoring system recording local authority employment on a monthly and quarterly basis since April 1982. The monthly exercise involves the provision of a detailed breakdown of building employment (involving local authority direct labour) in major functional areas. The quarterly exercise treats total direct employment. The coverage includes County Councils, County Boroughs, Borough Corporations and one Urban District Council. A typical example of the average monthly return is provided for December 1982:

Monthly	*Housing*	*Roads*	*Sanitary Services*	*EIS**	*Miscell.*	*Total*
Total	2,705	9,146	2,597	1,312	465	16,225
Construction	412	2,353	487	—	—	3,252
Maintenance	2,293	6,793	2,109	—	—	11,195

*Environmental Improvement Schemes.

For the same date the quarterly return was:

Management/Clerical	6,286
Professional/Technical	2,661
Others	22,686
Total	31,633

These new series will be an important source of up-to-date information when the methods of linking them to the total series have been perfected. For example, in October 1980, 6,790 and 6,648 workers were recorded, respectively, as engaged in the construction of local authority housing at 30 September 1979 and 31 August 1980. This included those employed by contractors. The 412 above only referred to direct labour.

Chapter IV.4

HEALTH

Introduction

As outlined in the background section the legacy of the nineteenth century was three separate services — those relating to mental health, public assistance and preventive health services discharged by numerous, often small-scale, bodies. Financing was generally up to these bodies apart from some capital resources provided by Hospitals Trust Fund. After the Second World War the State took a more active role symbolised by the building of three sanatoria in 1945 — the first State hospitals in over a century. This was followed by partnership with the local authorities in 1947 when the State, through the newly established Department of Health, agreed to meet in full all increases in the costs of local health services until the State contribution matched that financed locally. Thus 1947 marks a milestone in the development of the health services (and in the escalation of local rates charges).

The 1953 Health Act defined those *entitled* to health care and thus removed the last vestiges of the Poor Law ethos. In the Dublin area the absence of public acute hospitals led to an increased acceptance by local authorities of responsibility for the costs of treatment in voluntary hospitals. These hospitals are to be found mainly in urban areas and many of them date back to the eighteenth century, though those of Catholic nursing orders are post-Catholic emancipation. In the East region 41 hospitals were voluntary and only 7 were local authority hospitals. In the rest of the country the ratio was 24 to 91. The facts of geographic concentration were to bring the voluntary hospitals increasingly into the public ambit and this was formally recognised in an agreement to fund these hospitals costs reached in 1973/74. Statistics on voluntary hospitals employment tend to date from this agreement though clearly there was no sudden leap in public subsidies.

Apart from the voluntary hospitals the employment levels in public health were clarified when in 1971, 8 regional health boards were hived off from other local administration. All health functions were transferred and in addition the

Central Mental Hospital was placed under the Eastern Health Board and was no longer part of the Civil Service. The dispensary system was abolished and replaced by a "choice of doctor" scheme which was expected to be more cost effective and better suited to individual needs. Since the dispensary doctors had been permitted to have private practices the change was not so major from the point of view of recording employment levels.

A number of specially set-up hospital authorities cut across the neat dichotomy presented above. St. Laurence's Hospital Act 1943 gave its control to a statutory board appointed by the Minister. The Health (Corporate Bodies) Act 1961 regulates the administration of 5[21] specific hospitals: St. Luke's Board is appointed by the Minister; the National Medical Rehabilitation Centre is a joint venture of the Sisters of Mercy and the National Rehabilitation Board. St. Kevin's Hospital, Dublin, is managed by St. James's Hospital Board jointly controlled by the Eastern Health Board and the Federation of Dublin Voluntary Hospitals. A similar board, called the James Connolly Memorial Hospital Board, manages Blanchardstown sanatorium as a joint venture of the Eastern Health Board, the Mater, St. Laurence's and Jervis Street Hospitals. The last two hospitals will be replaced by a new hospital at Beaumont, while other developments will cause the closure of yet other voluntary hospitals. Since the St. Kevin's and Blanchardstown hospitals are neither public nor voluntary, the statistics tend to treat them separately.

Levels of Health Employment

The difficulties of disentangling health employment from other local authority staffing has been adequately discussed in the previous section where Table 63 presents some global estimates of health employment up to 1971:—

1951	13,093
1958/59	16,882
1961	17,803
1966	20,517
1967/68	23,706
1968/69	24,445
1971	25,220

This series was chosen because it links in well with the Devlin estimate of 25,220 for 1971 made up of 24,043 whole-time employees and 1,177 part-timers. Support for the general level of the Devlin estimates is provided by an exceptionally thorough survey by Donal Murphy of the Institute of Public Administration. His survey of training needs in the health services established an employment level of 24,403 in 1971. It will be observed that both Devlin and

[21]One body was set up to build a hospital for the Southern Health Board.

Murphy were considerably higher than the CP 1971 figure of 21,407. This latter can be regarded as a minimum figure since it would omit administrative staff in local authority offices with special responsibility for health or public assistance.

Even though the Census of Population figures are minimal ones they have an interest in their own right as they document some trends within the health services. The figures, given already in Table 60, are:

	1951	1961	1966	1971	1981
Mental Hospitals	4,192	4,637	5,181	18,646	30,356
Other Hospitals	6,343	10,031	10,972		
Other Medicine	2,208	2,303	1,995	2,761	3,327
Total	12,743	16,971	18,148	21,407	33,683

These figures reflect the division in legal responsibility outlined above by which mental hospitals were separate from other local authority hospitals until the establishment of the health boards in 1971. Other medicine presumably relates to dispensary doctors, midwives, district nurses, etc. These Census figures probably exclude most part timers. Even so, they show a substantial rise in health employment which increased by 164 per cent overall. This growth rate was unlike the experience in other areas of local authority employment in general which fell 24 per cent in the three decades.

Table 69: *Employment in Health Services distinguishing health boards and public hospitals 1971–1983*

				Hospitals			
Year	Date	Source	Health Boards	Joint Board		Voluntary	Total
1971	31/3	IPA	24,403[a]			10,672	35,075
1973	n.a.	RDH	24,901[b]	1,799		—	—
1974	28/2	CH	27,286	1,754		12,913	41,953
1975	26/2	DQ	29,173	—		—	—
1977	28/2	CH	31,682	1,830		13,984	47,496
1977	31/12	H	33,038		16,417		49,455
1978	28/2	CH	34,366[a]	1,884		14,672	50,922
1979	28/2	CH	36,771	2,020		15,100	53,891
1980	28/2	CH	38,058	2,208		15,381	55,647
1981	28/2	CH	39,640	2,397		15,993	58,030
1982	Sept.	CH	39,285		18,721		58,006
1983	Mar.	CH	38,860		18,640		57,560

[a] Devlin Surveys at these dates gave 25,220 and 34,439 respectively (i.e., 24,043 and 32,589 whole time; 1,177 and 1,850 part time).

[b] A Dail question of 18/7/73 elicited a total of 26,070 (including Joint Board Hospitals).

Sources: CH: Census by Dept. of Health; H: Books by Hensey former Secretary of Health; IPA: Survey by Donal Murphy; DQ: Dail Question; RDH: "Restructuring the Department of Health".

The year 1971 saw the establishment of eight regional health boards. A Dail statement of July 1973 estimated the numbers of "additional staff necessitated by the setting up and operation of each board" as 212, i.e., 36 managerial team posts, 5 administrative, 54 executive and 117 clerical. Post 1971 health employment is set out in Table 69. A hiatus occurred between the time the Department of the Environment ceased to record health employment and a very comprehensive series was firmly established by the Department of Health in 1977. An isolated record of that Department also surveyed the situation in 1974. Material from other sources varies in quality. Surprisingly enough undated data in a report on "Restructuring the Department of Health" and in two Dail questions appears to be somewhat less precise.[22] The high quality of the Devlin figures applies only to health boards. Donal Murphy's IPA study included details of 42 voluntary hospitals and summary figures for 17 others. Both the IPA and Devlin figures[23] for 1971 would appear to have included the Joint Board Hospitals with the Eastern Health Board since their independent status was only recognised from 1973 onwards. In fact enquiries revealed that, when these hospitals were reconstituted, a considerable number of staff were reluctant to sever their connection with the Eastern Health Board and insisted on being returned as EHB staff. In this circumstance a strong possibility exists that double counting occurred by both bodies returning the same staff. The figures for the voluntary hospitals reflect their inclusion in the records due to the new deal negotiated in 1973/74. Data earlier than 1971 are not available.

The data in Table 69 can be expressed in growth rates for the period 1971 to 1981 as follows:

		Hospitals	
	Health Boards	*Joint Board*	*Voluntary*
1971/74	6.0		6.6
1974/75	6.9 ⎫	1.3	0.6
1975/77	4.2 ⎭		
1977/78	8.5	3.3	11.6
1978/79	7.0	7.2	2.9
1979/80	3.5	9.3	1.9
1980/81	4.2	8.6	4.0
1981/83	–1.0	1.0	

[22]The RDH report had a misprint of +1,000 for the North Western Health Board (H.B.). A Dail reply in July 1973 gave the Eastern H.B. as 5,934, perhaps a misprint for 5,134 (CH). In addition the Southern H.B. was overestimated 400 and South-Eastern H.B. underestimated by a like amount.

[23]Devlin 1979 did not advert to this fact and gives the Eastern H.B. as 5,801 in 1971 and 5,830 in 1978. Other boards at the same time increased 47 per cent. In reality the EHB increase was 33 per cent.

The overall rate from 1974 to 1981 peak was 5.5 per cent for Health Boards and 3.1 per cent for voluntary hospitals. These trends are graphed in Figure 14 above. By end 1985 employment levels are required to be 5 per cent below the peak level.

Occupational Composition of Health Employment
(a) Pre-1971

As we have seen the local authority health figures tend to be a minimal estimate since some elements of administration are not included in those categories identified. With this reservation in mind we can list the occupations as in Table 70. Because of the varying degree of aggregation by subcategory from Census to Census the content of "others" may be eligible for inclusion elsewhere in the table, especially in the earlier years.

Table 70: *Local authority medicine in the Census of Population 1951 to 1981*

	1951	1961	1966	1971	1981
Doctors	856	1,202	1,122	1,420	1,806
Religious	410	605	558	528	498
Nurses	7,155	9,432	9,916	11,280	16,698*
Other Profesionals	290	520	573	674	2,363
Typists and Clerks	125	374	474	568	1,791
Domestics, etc.	2,716	3,669	4,295	5,336	7,938
Maintaining and producing	559	582	644	866	1,664
Transport workers	158	157	212	360	740
Others	474	430	354	375	185
Total	12,743	16,971	18,148	21,407	33,683

*Including 135 Dentists.

The CP data shows almost equal numbers being added to the total in the first two decades: 4,228 and 4,436. Some of the smaller categories had the largest growth, typists and clerks, other professionals and transport workers. It is noteworthy that some religious were engaged in local authority work. These were nuns in "other" hospitals (i.e., not mental health hospitals). The rise in domestic and allied staff was much more rapid than that of nursing staff (9.4 per cent annually vs. 2.3 per cent). Numbers of doctors also grew somewhat faster than the corresponding number of nurses. The overall growth rate for the two decades was 2.6 per cent, which was relatively high.

The 1958 total in the departmental enumeration was not very different from the total from the 1961 Census of Population. Table 71 gives its composition for

Table 71: *Numbers employed by Health and Mental Hospital Authorities February 1958 distinguishing institutional and non-institutional staff*

A. Institutional Staff

Category of Staff	Health Authorities	Mental Hospital Authorities	Total
Medical	424	90	514
Medical Auxiliaries[a]	204	22	226
Nursing	3,446	3,613	7,059
Domestic[b]	3,428	301	3,729
Other[c]	865	829	1,694
Total A	8,367	4,855	13,222
of which part time	452	101	553

B. Non-Institutional Staff (under the Health Authorities)

	Whole time	Part time	Total
Medical	133	692	825
Midwives	—	551	551
Nursing	254	3	257
Dentists	71	119	190
Health Inspectors	156	—	156
Sanitary Sub-Officers	160	—	160
Caretakers	—	985	985
Others	136	50	186
Total	910	2,400	3,310
Total B	12,669	553	13,222
Grand Total A+B	13,579	2,953	16,532

[a] Pharmacists, radiographers, physiotherapists, laboratory staff, etc.

[b] Wardsmaids, attendants, cooks, gardeners, porters, laundry workers, etc.

[c] Tradesmen, ambulance drivers, boilermen, labourers, telephonists, clerical staff, almoners, chaplains, etc.

the only year available: 1958, and permits comparison with Table 70. Presumably institutional staff in the table referred to hospitals whereas non-institutional referred to dispensaries, district nurses, midwives, etc. It is noteworthy that the non-institutional staff were predominantly part time while part-time working by institutional staff was much rarer.

(b) Health Board Employment

The Department of Health survey is comprehensive so that it is possible to obtain a series on the occupational structure of health boards since February

1974. Donal Murphy's study fills the gap for the early 'seventies. The picture; detailed in Table 72, differs from the 1981 data in Table 70, perhaps indicating the latter excluded administration.

Table 72: *Occupational structure of health boards 1971–81*

	1971*	1974	1977	1978	1979	1980	1981
Medical and Dental	1,555	1,400	2,040	2,019	2,318	2,395	2,437
Nursing and Allied	11,710[a]	16,286	17,000	18,650	19,725	20,611	21,144
Paramedical	576	730	1,145	1,283	1,430	1,455	1,695
Catering/Housekeeping	5,714[a]	3,467	4,882	5,308	5,563	5,731	6,095
Maintenance	1,488	1,548	1,642	1,763	1,746	1,685	1,837
Administration	1,687	2,308	2,874	3,318	3,692	3,834	4,119
Other	1,673	1,547	2,098	2,025	2,297	2,347	2,313
Total	24,403	27,286	31,681	34,366	36,771	38,058	39,640

Source: Dept. of Health Census, except 1971 IPA.

*Includes Joint Board Hospitals.

[a]Donal Murphy's grouping appears to differ from that of the department. The totals are 17,424 (1971); 19,753 (1974) and seem to be broadly comparable.

The IPA 1971 Survey appears to confine those classified as nurses to nurses and probationers. The Departmental Census includes "Allied", presumably located under "housekeeping, etc." by Donal Murphy. Combining the two categories is probably a good strategy for 1971/1974 comparisons.

The average annual compound rate of growth between 1974 and 1981 was high at 5.5 per cent. However, within the group the largest contingent was one of the slowest growing, i.e., nursing at 3.8 per cent. Maintenance staff grew slower in numbers (2.5 per cent) but were not a major category. The relatively slow growth of nursing staff meant other groups displayed above average rate of increase. For doctors, administrators and catering/housekeeping staff the pace was high at 8.4 per cent annually while the small group of paramedicals grew by the phenomenal rate of 12.8 per cent on average each year.[24]

An alternative classification was provided by the two Devlin reports and summarised in Table 73.

The classification of servants was not entirely satisfactory in 1971 hence the large numbers of "others". The use by Devlin of "officers" and "servants" permits a link-up with the pre-reorganisation data.

Among the officers the increase of other professionals, e.g., nurses, was not as marked as the rapid growth of administrators and clerks. The latter increased 2.5 times in seven years while higher professional numbers almost doubled.

[24]See 'other professionals' in Table 70 which included more than 512 social workers in 1981.

Table 73: *Classification of officers and servants in Health Boards in 1971 and 1978*

Officers	1971	1978	Servants	1971	1978
Managerial etc. higher*	55	155	Supervisory Manual	61	344
Managerial etc. other	206	872	Skilled	661	1,132
Professional, higher	691	1,352	Semi-skilled	406	521
Professional, other	13,299	15,636	Unskilled	3,450	9,348
Clerical	1,389	3,072	Others	3,825	157
All whole time	15,640	21,087		8,403	11,502
Part time	575	915		602	935
Grand total	16,215	22,002		9,005	12,437

*See note on Table 65.

Change among servants was much slower, a phenomenon also observed in the case of local government servants.[25]

Dail statements are an important supplementary source of additional information on the occupational structure of individual health boards. In June 1980 data for twelve categories of employee were given. These were hospital consultants, junior hospital and public health doctors, hospital, public health, and other nurses, social workers (a) in community care areas, (b) medical, (c) psychiatric and (d) other; physiotherapists and home helps. The total of 601 social workers of all types employed was greater than the 538 posts funded directly or indirectly by the Department of Health. The Eastern Health Board employed 311 — no doubt a reflection of the higher levels of urbanisation in the board's area. In March 1977 the Dail was told that the EHB social workers numbered 75 as compared with 28 in 1972. The massive increase between 1977 and 1980 was in part the outcome of the full employment programme. Prior to its commencement 370 social workers were employed but only 75 in the EHB. The Coalition Government had plans for 38 more. The 370 in actual employment were employed as follows:

(a) By health boards   173
(b) By voluntary groups engaged in Community care services
    in concert with health boards   61
(c) By national voluntary organisations   65
    and
(d) By voluntary hospitals   71

[25]A Dail statement in October 1981 gave the June numbers for servants by health board in 1979, 1980 and 1981. The totals were 12,321, 12,691 and 13,084.

The expansion in the number of public health nurses was on a more scientific basis. Complaints of overload were investigated by a study group set up in 1971 whose report in 1975 laid the basis for the complement of 1,152 at work in February 1981.

Home helps were one of the innovations of the 1970 Health Act. These staff were predominantly part time, the Dail was told in April 1982. The totals for the health boards were:

	Whole time	*Part time*
1978	180	5,039
1979	211	5,840
1980	172	6,356

Later in the year (November) the Minister for Health detailed by health board the 2,532 manweeks of employment created under the Community Care Employment Scheme. This Scheme, and many of the extra jobs arising from the full employment programme are being reviewed closely in the light of the current financial difficulties.

(c) Voluntary Hospitals[26]

Since 1973/74 these hospitals have been directly dependent on State sources for all but a small fraction of their financing. In presenting their occupational structure in Table 74 Joint Board Hospitals are included from 1974 onwards. In 1971 they were part of the Eastern Health Board.

Table 74: *Occupational Structure of Voluntary Hospitals 1971–1981*

	1971	*1974*	*1977*	*1978*	*1979*	*1980*	*1981*
Medical Dental	476	1,359	1,698	1,816	1,881	1,953	1,999
Nursing	5,498	7,814	8,146	8,355	8,625	8,861	9,289
Paramedical	660	1,054	1,225	1,275	1,314	1,359	1,457
Catering/Housekeeping	2,118*	2,615	2,749	2,924	2,966	3,075	3,113
Maintenance	252	381	396	445	465	473	500
Administration	859	1,286	1,391	1,503	1,543	1,609	1,772
Other	809	228	227	238	241	259	260
Total	10,672	14,737	14,972	16,556	17,120	17,589	18,390

Note: 1971 is based on IPA sources. The other years are from the departmental census. For this reason the categories are not comparable. An additional difference is that 1971 does not include Joint Board Hospitals, then with the health boards.
*This total is made up of catering 262, domestic 1,491 and portering 365.

[26]See Table 110 for note on pre-1971 employment.

These public hospitals had some special features. They employed virtually no psychiatric nurses and, as Donal Murphy documented, their hospital staff are predominantly students. The difference was as follows in 1971:

	Health Boards	Voluntary Hospitals	Both
Trained Nurses	9,359	2,427	11,786
Student Nurses and Pupil Midwives	2,351	3,071	5,422
Total	11,710	5,498	17,208
Percentage Trained	80	44	68.5

Perhaps part of the reason for this difference is that voluntary hospitals are frequently teaching hospitals. Thus, more than half the nursing staff are not yet trained. This factor should help to moderate costs.

Like the health boards, nurses, the largest group, grew second slowest in numbers. Unlike the boards, doctors grew fastest, 5.7 per cent annually, but even this high rate fell short of the 8.4 per cent of the health board doctors. Catering and housekeeping grew at the nurses' rate, i.e., much slower than in the health boards. Paramedicals and administrators grew at 4.7 per cent per annum. These were high rates but appear less so when set alongside health board rates of 12.8 per cent and 8.4 per cent annually.

Choice of Doctor Employment

Among major developments on the services side of the Health Act 1970 was the abolition of the dispensary system and the introduction of the "choice of doctor" scheme. The health boards availed themselves of the facility under Section II of the Act to establish the (GMS) General Medical Services (Payments) Board for paying doctors and pharmacists in the new scheme. This approach avoided the need for the boards themselves to add to their staff since it involved making agreements with individuals to provide services on a contract basis.

The employment given by the GMS (Payments) Board is not dealt with here since corporate bodies under the Health Act are generally considered under State-sponsored bodies. (The Joint Board Hospitals are an exception.) The Payments Board itself in its annual report records the number of doctors and pharmacists contracting and provide information of their services and of their fees. It seems unlikely that more than a fraction of these contractors receive over half their income from this source. This would rule out their inclusion as State employees by our criterion. The figures[27] are as follows:

---

[27]It is not clear why the figures in the Annual Reports are lower than these supplied figures.

December 31	Doctors	Pharmacists
1973[27]	1,123	1,176
1974[27]	1,144	1,199
1975	1,270	1,145
1976	1,296	1,146
1977	1,302	1,106
1978	1,313	1,117
1979	1,303	1,110
1980	1,319	1,106
1981	1,375	1,116
1982	1,418	1,115
1983	1,440	1,114
1984	1,463	1,110

These doctors can be related to the old dispensary doctor system which permitted dispensary doctors to have private practices of their own. I have seen no record of the number of dispensary doctors but a note on Table 71 indicates that it did not include about 1,200 part-time doctors who were presumably such dispensary staff in 1958. If so, the numbers involved did not change greatly over the 'sixties.

Homes for the Mentally Handicapped

Before 1975 homes for the mentally handicapped were grant-aided on a capitation basis. Since this arrangement minimises the need to supervise the budgets of the individual homes, statistics on their operations tend to be sparse. In 1975 the funding system was changed, partly because capitation rates were proving uneconomic and partly to upgrade the service levels in response to Mental Handicap Year 1975. More comprehensive data on employment than became available to the Department of Health:

end 1976	2,808	end 1980	4,070
end 1977*	3,334	end 1981	4,460
end 1978	3,510	Sept. 1982	4,611
end 1979	3,787	Mar. 1983	4,579

*Excludes alcoholic unit at Belmont Park, Waterford; Hensey (1979) gives 3,195.

The increase in 1981 was due to the changed status of St. Michael's House which previously at end 1980 employed 330 without any State funding. In 1981 St. Michael's House accepted State funding. The Department of Health noted that the increase in employment in 1977 could be divided between 190 jobs in new units commissioned in the year and 340 others developed under the job creation programme. The composition of the staff is set out in Table 75.

Table 75: *Occupational Structure of Homes for the Mentally Handicapped, including St. Michael's House Jan. 1977 to Jan. 1984*

	1977	1978	1979	1980	1981	1982	1983	1984
Medical and Dental	25	25	33	33	33	34	27	40
Nursing and Allied	2,134	2,295	2,416	2,586	2,599	2,600	2,663	2,859
Paramedical	195	217	237	247	247	247	225	256
Catering and Housekeeping	593	625	672	681	681	681	720	774
Maintenance	92	126	126	130	130	130	140	140
Administrative	253	264	264	290	292	292	278	315
Others (incl. Chaplains)	268	295	314	356	356	356	340	369
Total	3,560	3,846	4,061	4,322	4,338	4,341	4,393	4,753

Figures include full-time equivalents of part-time staff but exclude sessional staff. Totals may not agree due to rounding.

Other Health Bodies

In his book Dr. Hensey gave a figure of 1,400[28] as the employment in other health bodies on 31 December 1977. Presumably this total referred to semi-State bodies, such as the Voluntary Health Insurance Board, the National Rehabilitation Board, the Blood Transfusion Service Board, etc. Employment in these bodies is discussed in the special study of semi-State bodies. Here it should merely be noted that setting up a semi-State body is one way in which employment in central services can be affected. Such alternative forms of employment need to be kept in mind in any discussion of public employment in general.

[28]Specialist Agencies employed 1,425 in March 1983.

Chapter IV.5

COUNTY COMMITTEES OF AGRICULTURE

The Minister for Agriculture was the responsible Minister for these committees and their employees. The establishment of ACOT under the Agriculture Acts of 1977 and 1979 led to most of the functions and employment of the Committees to be transferred to this new State-sponsored body.

During the years of their separate identity technical employment by the Committees was faithfully recorded annually by the Department of Agriculture. The annual changes in numbers of instructors in (a) agriculture, (b) beekeeping and horticulture and (c) poultry keeping are set out in Table 76. Details of support staff are more sparse and only recorded sporadically in the 'seventies. The estimates are as follows:

1958	41	1974 (1 Jan)	120
1966	50	1975 (1 Jan)	123
1971 (1 Jan)	105 (approx)	1976 (31 Dec)	n.a.
1972 (1 Jan)	110	1977 (31 Dec)	125
1973 (1 Jan)	115 (approx)	1978 (31 Dec)	n.a.
		1979 (31 Dec)	127

On the 1st July 1980 these 840 staff (713 Technical and 127 Clerical) were transferred to a newly established State-sponsored body, ACOT — Council for Development in Agriculture.[29] At that time the composition of the 840 staff was slightly different:

[29]It might be noted in passing that 280 staff were also transferred from the Department of Agriculture, i.e., 65 Head Office, 18 Western Regional Office, 4 Botanic Gardens as well as from the centres at Athenry (62), Ballyhaise (51), Clonakilty (27), Kildalton (53).

Table 76: *Technical Staff of County Committees of Agriculture 1944 to 1979*

| Year ending March | Chief* Agri. Officers | Instructors† in | | | | Total |
		Agri.	Horticulture and Beekeeping	Poultry	Home Econ.	
1944	58		48	55		161
1945	65		46	61		172
1946	68		46	62		176
1947	67		46	64		177
1948	71		46	68		185
1949	74		46	78		198
1950	83		49	80		212
1951	88		51	80		219
1952	105		46	79		230
1953	118		50	79		247
1954	129		51	81		261
1955	142		50	81		273
1956	152		55	80		287
1957	166		56	79		301
1958	178		57	78		313
1959	191		59	78		328
1960	213		62	77		352
1961	217		59	78		354
1962	217		59	79		355
1963	220		63	79		362
1964	250		69	83		402
1965	277		72	89		438
1966	34	264	73	93		464
1967	38	291	74	93		496
1968	38	292	78	94		502
1969	40	298	83	88		509
1970	51	333	82	89		555
1971	53	361	79	100		593
1972	55	370	82	117		624
1973	57	398	87	112		654
1974	57	399	86	30	80	652
1974 Dec.	66	400	87	31	83	667
1975 Dec.	81	393	81	31	84	670
1976 Dec.	82	418	84	29	85	698
1977 Dec.	83	409	83	27	84	686
1978 Dec.	85	421	84	28	85	703
1979 Dec.	85	436	81	28	83	713

Source: Department of Agriculture Reports.

*Includes Deputies.

†Includes Senior Instructors.

Technical		*Clerical*	
Chief Agricultural Officers	27	Senior Staff Officer	1
Deputy Agricultural Officers	58	Staff Officer	26
Senior Instructors	73	Clerical Officer	43
Instructors in Agriculture	366	Clerk Typist	55
Instructors in Horticulture	80		
Instructors in Poultry	27		
Farm Home Management			
Advisers	84		

The growth in numbers shown in Table 76 has tended to differ from that of the Civil Service in general and resembles more closely the rates of change of the Department of Agriculture itself. Numbers trebled between 1944 and 1967 and grew more slowly subsequently. Growth between the end of 1975 and 1979 was less than 6 per cent *in toto*.

SECTION V

EDUCATION

Chapter V.1

BACKGROUND TO EDUCATION

The current structures of Irish education have been deeply influenced by the historical circumstances under which they arose. In this regard Tussing (1978) found two themes recurring since the time of Henry VIII until Independence.

> One is the use of the British and by the Irish Protestant ascendancy of their control over the education system ... for political and sectarian proselytism. The other, a reaction to the first, is the tendency (in the schools and outside) of Gaelic Catholics to associate nationalism with Catholism, and to associate both of them with hostility to an active State role in education (p. 44)

When this struggle intensified in the nineteenth century much of the education was provided without any State involvement and it is therefore interesting to trace the steps by which the current situation evolved with its heavy dependence on State financing for all levels of educational provision.

Phase One: The three centuries before Catholic Emancipation in 1829 saw the rise and decline of the legal obstacles to Catholic education. Towards the end of the period the teaching orders and seminaries had begun their work replacing the Irish schools in Europe. Some of today's learned bodies were already contributing to Irish development.

1541 — Honorary Society of Kings Inns, financed by dissolution of the monasteries, took over legal education from earlier bodies dating back to 1292.

1578 — Irish college opened in Paris, Salamanca (1592), etc. By 1789, 478 students were studying abroad, 348 in France. Many schools were closed by French Revolution.

1591 — A charter of Elizabeth I enabled citizens of Dublin to set up Trinity College (TCD) as a first college in a University of Dublin. The purpose was to promote Anglicanism and funding was from confiscated rebel estates.

1637 — To enter TCD Catholics must renounce popery.

1657 — Erasmus Smith of London, anticipating the Restoration, gave confiscated estates given to him by Cromwell to set up schools to educate the poor of Ireland — the endowed schools of today.

1692 — Charter for Royal College of Physicians (examining body). New charter 1878.

1731 — Royal Dublin Society (RDS) founded.

1749 — RDS set up Metropolitan School of Art which was aided by the South Kensington Department of Science and Art in 1854.

1775 — Presentation Sisters began their work in Cork, Killarney 1793, Dublin 1794.

1782 — Relief Act restored, to Catholics, the right of teaching lost in Penal Laws.

1784 — Surgeons in the city of Dublin decided to "establish a liberal and extensive system of surgical education" — the College of Surgeons.

1785 — Royal Irish Academy founded.

1792 — Catholics' right to teach no longer needed a licence from the Protestant Bishop of the diocese. Hedge schools began to become pay schools.

1793 — St. Patrick's, Carlow and St. Kieran's, Kilkenny founded as diocesan colleges and secondary schools.

1794 — Catholics could get degrees from TCD but not fellowships or scholarships.

1795 — Maynooth College set up to wean Irish from Continental Irish schools (many were closed in the French Revolution) with their dangers of radicalism. Maynooth was open to the laity from 1800 but this section had failed by 1817.

1802 — Christian Brothers began in Waterford.

1811 — Society for the Promotion of the Education of the Poor — the Kildare Place Society — established to promote non-sectarian bible reading. The society's schools were grant-aided by Peel from 1815. Although their schools were secular the society became suspect to Catholics by subsidising other proselytising schools.

1828 — Royal Hibernian Academy of Arts set up — new charter 1861.

1830 — Law Society founded. Incorporated by Charter in 1852.

Phase Two 1831–1883: Active promotion of State-supported secular education began with primary schools, 1831, and universities, 1845. Opposition proved so strong that clerical management of national schools was conceded in 1861 and the Catholic University implicitly recognised by 1879. A small beginning was made in 1878 to support denominational secondary schools on the basis of payment by results.

1831 — At this time there were in Ireland 9,657 "daily schools" of which 5,653 were maintained by parental subscription and 4,404 were endowed. It was now proposed to establish a multi-denominational non-sectarian system of national schools (forty years earlier than in Britain). If the locality provided the sites and a third of the building costs the State undertook to build and maintain the schools, pay the teachers and pay half the cost of books, etc. The property had to be vested in approved trustees. Teacher training was provided in the central training establishment in Marlborough Street, Dublin where three model schools were built in 1838. Teacher training stressed agriculture with a Farm Training Institute at Glasnevin. It was envisaged in 1835 that an "academy" would be built in each county as well as a farm school and a "college" in each province. By 1870 the Board ran 19 model agricultural schools, and recognised 18 others under local management. At 83 national schools, farms or gardens were attached.

1837 — Mechanics Institute set up in Dublin; in Clonmel by Bianconi 1845.

1838 — Church Education Society set up by Church of Ireland to provide alternative national schools where all pupils were required to read the bible. Schools gradually joined national system especially in 1860s.

1839 — National Education Board classified teachers on a basis which survives up to today. Assuming local contributions to teachers' salaries the Board paid gratuities of £10 per 100 pupils to male teachers, £8 to females.

— Royal Institute of Architects set up.

1845 — Queen's University established with colleges at Cork, Galway and Belfast as part of Peel's plan to weaken the Repeal Movement.

— National Education Board directed that national schools be henceforth vested in itself. At both primary and university level there was growing Catholic hostility to Protestant control, British emphasis and secularism. Model schools, teacher training and universities were boycotted and became *de facto* Protestant.

— Robert Kane set up Museum of Irish Industry which became the Royal College of Science in 1867 when less than half the students were Irish.

1849 — School of Design set up in Royal Cork Institution.

1854 — Catholic University, headed by Newman and founded by public subscription, was modelled on Louvain. Its associated colleges were St. Stephen's Green College, Maynooth, Clonliffe, St. Patrick's Carlow and the French College (1860). Its medical school at Cecilia's Street was recognised by professional bodies and became the fourth largest medical school in the UK by 1905. The other colleges were finally refused a charter in 1860 and did not thrive.

1855 — School of Art set up by Athenaeum Society of Limerick.

1858 — Reformatory Schools Act provided for certification of already existing reformatories; 10 were certified by 1865.

1861 — The National Education Board recognised the principle of clerical management of national schools and abandoned its model school programme.

1864 — National Gallery founded.

1869 — Irish Church Act disestablished Church of Ireland and made funds available for education.

— Irish National Teachers' Organisation (INTO) founded.

1872 — School managers were given the power to appoint and dismiss teachers subject to 3 months notice. Teachers' salaries were to be based on a class salary, a good service salary, results, gratuities and local contributions.

1873 — Last religious tests abolished at TCD.

1874 — The Catholic University now recognised 37 secondary schools as providing teaching up to university entrance standards.

1875 — Average Irish teacher's salary was £43/6/0 compared with £83/0/4 (England) and £84/11/1 (Scotland). The National School Teachers (Ireland Act) gave Boards of Guardians power to levy rates for national school funding, i.e., salaries and teachers' residences but most boards would not, partly because Christian Brothers Schools (CBS) could not benefit. None the less 950 residences were built. Any rates levied were transferred to technical education after 1889.

1877 — National Library and National Museum opened.

1878 — Up to this date there was no State involvement in secondary education which was provided by diocesan colleges, military and commercial colleges, select academics, etc. The Intermediate (i.e., Secondary) Education Act now afforded these establishments an opportunity to gauge their excellence by appointing 7 Intermediate Education Commissioners to conduct public examinations. Although the Commissioners did not interfere with schools or teachers, apart from small sums of prizes, etc., the conditions of entry and competition imposed uniformity.[30] There was no co-ordination of primary and secondary education, apart from in CBS schools. Secondary tops in national schools were excluded from the terms of the Act.

1879 — University Education Act imitated the 1878 Act by setting up a Royal University purely as an examining and degree conferring body. The Queen's University was dissolved and half the new fellowships given to the Catholic University, renamed University College, Dublin. Others went to the Queen's Colleges and Magee College.

1880 — Poor results and *laissez faire* hostility to State expenditure halted the National Education Board's experiment with agricultural schools and all were closed except the Albert College and the Model Farm School in Cork (now the Munster Institute).

[30]Denis Gwynn wrote "The formation of character, the cultivation of taste, the disinterested love of learning not being capable of being tested by examination were disregarded in the sordid race for results fees". W. S. Armour wrote "Let the Jeremiahs in kid gloves, like Matthew Arnold, and damaged Solomons, like Mr Mahaffy, say what they will, it has on the whole improved the quality of the article" (quoted in McElligott, 1966, p. 60).

1883 — The National Education Board was faced with the fact that only 2,142 out of 7,904 Catholic teachers and 1,412 out of 2,714 Protestant teachers were trained. It decided to recognise denominational training colleges. In that year St. Patrick's, Drumcondra (1875) and Our Lady of Mercy, Baggot Street (1877), now Carysfort College, immediately availed of recognition. The Kildare Society College of 1811 and that of its successor, the Church Education Society, was renamed the Church of Ireland College in 1884 and was recognised. (It is in Rathmines since 1968.) Waterford (1891) and St. Angela's Limerick (1901) came later.

Phase Three 1883–1924: The modern university system was launched and technical education promoted. Conditions of employment for primary and secondary teachers improved. Primary education was compulsory.

1884 — Technical education advances produced Crawford Municipal School of Art in Cork and Cork School of Music; Kevin St. (1885), Pembroke (1892).

1886 — Royal Institute of Chartered Surveyors established.

1892 — Compulsory attendance at school was introduced for urban children. Accordingly national schooling became totally free.

1898 — Apart from private schools little instruction in technical education existed. Some schools had been getting some finances for teaching science and art from the Department of Science and Art in South Kensington. Now the Local Government (Ireland) Act, which set up elected County Councils, empowered the latter to levy rates for the purposes of agricultural and technical education (under Acts of 1889 and 1891). This proved popular and 65 technical schools were set up by 1925.

1899 — Department of Agriculture and Technical Institute, set up under an act of 1898, took over the South Kensington schemes via a Board of Technical Instruction. The following year it took over the Albert College and Model Farm Cork from the National Education Board.

1901 — The system of paying national teachers by result was abolished. Class salaries were increased 20 per cent and a capitation grant paid based on class attendance.

1908 — The Irish Universities Act abolished the Royal University and established two universities: Queen's University Belfast and the National University of Ireland; the latter with colleges at Cork, Dublin and Galway. Maynooth became a recognised NUI college in 1910. NUI received £300,000 from the Church Disestablishment Fund. This ended the Catholic objections to university education.

1914 — The Intermediate Education (Ireland) Act set up a Registration Council for secondary teachers effective from August 1918. Teachers had seven years to qualify for registration and 3,130 did. The aim was to raise and secure the status of secondary teachers. Since only 398 of the 1,142 lay teachers in 1915 had security of tenure and minimum salaries, the act began the process of grant aiding secondary teachers' salaries. This it did by making teachers' salaries grants to schools where there was one lay teacher per 400 scholars, provided the school paid a minimum of £120 to men and £80 to women.

1917 — National teachers were paid directly by the State on a monthly basis.

1920 — The Government of Ireland Act awarded an annual £30,000 to TCD to make up for a fall in its rental income. In the first decade after Independence the Free State could only afford £3,000 (later increased by £2,250).

1921 — Teachers' Training College at Marlborough Street was closed. Primary teachers' salaries were cut 10 per cent.

Phase Four 1924–1961: Under the new Department of Education the basis for modern systems of secondary and vocational education were laid.

1924 — Department of Education took over the functions of the National Education Board, the Board of Technical Instruction and the Intermediate Education Commissioners. It inherited the Model Schools as well as the Metropolitan School of Art, the Irish Training School of Domestic Economy at Kilmacud, Co. Dublin, (closed 1941) and the Killarney School of Housewifery with their 470, 30 and 20 pupils, respectively. The Royal College of Science, which had been under the Department of Agriculture and Technical Instruction from 1900 to 1924, was transferred to it briefly. Other areas of responsibility were the National Museum, the National Library, the National Gallery and the National College of Art. The Department also had responsibility for reformatories, industrial and endowed schools.

— Under the Intermediate Education (Ireland) Act 1921 payment to secondary teachers on results was abolished and from 1924/25 the present scheme of incremental salaries was introduced. Provided lay recognised teachers were paid at least £200 (if male) and £180 (if female) by the school, capitation grants of £7 and £10 were paid to the school per recognised pupil (later increased to £11 and £16 respectively) subject to agreed staffing ratios, etc. From primary education 188 scholarships were made available and 75 scholarships on the results of the Intermediate Certificate Examination (raised to 112 in 1929). Prescribed texts were abolished (but reintroduced in 1940). Since no provision was made for building and maintenance grants there was an imbalance in the provision of schools only partially cured later by the VECs. This factor hit especially small schools, usually in the South West, built and staffed by lay teachers.

1925 — Christian Brothers joined national school system.

1926 — Seven Preparatory schools were set up to teach Irish to teachers.

— School Attendance Act, more effective than its predecessors, produced 73.5 per cent attendance in 1926.

— University Education (Agriculture and Dairy Science) Act transferred College of Science to UCD and set up the faculty of Dairy Science in UCC.

1929 — Superannuation Scheme introduced for secondary teachers, 5 per cent each teachers and schools.

1930 — Vocational Education Act replaced the Technical Instruction Committees with 38 Vocational Education Committees to run vocational schools (including 10 trade preparatory schools). These schools combined both technical and continuation education.

1937 — Secondary teachers get contract of employment.

1947 — TCD grant increased to £35,000 plus £2,250 for the medical school.

1956 — Army Apprenticeship School at Naas was set up with staff seconded from the VEC.

1960 — UCD moved to the Belfield campus.

— Academic work of Department of Agriculture's Veterinary College transferred to UCD and TCD.

1961 — Local Authorities (Education Scholarships) Amendment Act led State to supplement local authority expenditure on a matching basis. Local Authority scholarships awarded to second-level schools rose from 621 in 1960/61 to 2,318 in 1966/67 and to third level from 107 to 274. In 1964/65 the latter constituted half of all awards to undergraduates. A further 20 per cent came from the universities and 10 per cent from the Department of Education.

— Preparatory colleges, except the Protestant Colaiste Moibhi, became ordinary secondary schools.

Phase Five 1962 to 1980: These decades saw the development of a binary system at third level and a revolution in the provision of second-level schooling partly by free education and partly in new forms of school. Management of schools was modified to include teachers and parents.

1962 — "Investment in Education" team was appointed.

— Grant provided for maintenance costs in national schools.

— Pupil/Teacher Ratio of 15:1 set for schools of the blind.

1963 — Plans announced for Comprehensive Schools (first in 1966) and Regional Technical Colleges (first five founded in 1969).

1964 — Scheme of building grants for secondary schools announced.

1965 — Plans to close most one- and two-teacher national schools announced.

1966 — Maynooth opens its courses to lay students.

1967 — "Free" secondary scheme announced, including free school transportation, secondary courses for vocational schools and expanded building grants for secondary schools. Proposal to merge UCD and TCD.

— AnCO takes over industrial training from An Ceard Comhairle set up in 1959.

1968 — Higher Education Authority set up as *ad hoc* body: Permanent from 1972.

— First of Regional Technical Colleges opened.

1969 — Higher Education Grants scheme introduced.

— Rutland Street pre-school project began with aid of Van Leer Foundation.

1970 — Thomond College set up. National Institute for Higher Education (NIHE) at Limerick received its first students. Ban on Catholics attending TCD ended.

— Reform of national school curriculum, special classes for handicapped.

— Vocational Education Amendment Act permitted VEC's to co-operate with other schools to provide community schools and colleges.

— Kennedy Report on Industrial Schools and Reformatories.

1972 — School leaving age raised to 15. National Council for Education Awards established.

1973 — First Community School opened.

1974 — Last Comprehensive School opened.

— Three Colleges of Education recognised by NUI to award B.Ed. to national teachers.

1975 — New scheme of expanded aid to national schools announced for schools adopting the Committee of Management system.

1976 — Central Applications Office for university places opened in Galway.

1977 — Royal College of Surgeons joined NUI.

1978 — Dublin VEC forms the Dublin Institute of Technology from its 6 colleges.

— Clerical Assistants were provided for primary schools and full-time caretakers if staff numbered 16 or over.

1980 — Dalkey project (primary school) opened, Bray 1981.

— NIHE at Dublin opened.

— All special schools and residential homes except St. Joseph's Clonmel were transferred to Health.

Chapter V.2

PRIMARY EDUCATION

The next Statistical Report of the Department of Education is expected to show 949,497 persons in full-time education in September 1983. Of these, 575,478 were at first-level schools, 324,147 at second level and 49,872 at third level. The Department knew of 13,201 who were attending schools which received no public funding but acknowledged that there could be more, 1,686 others were aided by public funds but through departments other than Education, notably Agriculture and Defence. These figures excluded children in care in either residential homes or special schools for which the Department of Health held the responsibility. In September 1982 these numbered 1,015.

The structure of the schools system can be summarised as follows for September 1983:

First Level		*Third Level*	
National	3,270	Universities	2
Special (Handicapped)	115	Other HEA institutions	5
Private*	75	Teacher Training	
		— Primary	6
Second Level		— Home Economics	2
Secondary	511	Vocational Technological	9
Secondary Tops	2	Regional Technical Colleges	9
Vocational	248	Military Cadets	1
Comprehensive	15	Private*	13
Community	42		
Preparatory College	1	*Other*	
Domestic Economy, etc.	4	Special Schools	6
Agricultural, etc.	22	Residential Homes	26
Private*	12		

*i.e., non-funded.

While this is a total of 4,397 schools, not all of them are of direct interest to this study, i.e., the private schools can be omitted because they are not state funded in any way and, therefore, their staff cannot be deemed to be public employees. Among the others are some where the level of funding is not sufficient to constitute over half of salary costs. These are also omitted. Among the funded schools, as we shall see, the method of funding and its source differed, with 23 schools relying on Departments other than Education for their financing. This shall become clearer as we examine each level in turn.

Staff at First Level

On June 30 1984, 3,387 national schools were recorded and can be classified as follows:

Ordinary National Schools		*Special Schools for the Handicapped*	
Convent	382	Convent	27
Monastery	135	Monastery	12
Model	9	Lay	82
Other Lay	2,740	Total	121

Of these ordinary schools 133 had special classes for the handicapped. Two of them had a section where secondary level instruction was given, mainly to girls — the secondary tops schools. Among the ordinary schools were a number of national schools associated with residential homes and special schools which have not been separately identified since the mid-forties when their system of grant aid was put on the same basis as for other national schools. Also included is the Rutland Street special project which began in 1969 under joint sponsorship of the Department of Education and the Van Leer Foundation and aimed at research into the problem of social and economic deprivation. There were also four youth encounter projects seeking to cope with the problems of mitching.

Before looking at these schools more closely it is relevant to note the recent tendency for private primary schools to decline. Such a development will increase the demands on the funded system. The first record of pupil numbers in February 1965 gave 23,269 or 4.6 per cent of all primary school pupils. A decade later the same number was recorded, 23,260. Numbers then began to contract both absolutely and as a proportion:

Year	Numbers of Pupils	% of all primary	Year	Numbers of Pupils	% of all primary
1975	22,849	4.2	1980	18,311	3.2
1976	21,680	3.9	1981	17,045	3.0
1977	21,072	3.8	1982	15,351	2.7
1978	20,244	3.6	1983	14,077	2.4
1979	19,105	3.4	1984	11,969	2.1

Some of this decline was hastened by recent pay awards to teachers in non-aided schools which have still to work their way through the system. Coupled with the general recession this should lead to further reductions among the 77 surviving schools outside our consideration.

The aided sector includes 9 model schools. These are owned directly by the Department of Education and are relics of the old National Education Board scheme which was launched in 1831. Eighteen such schools were recorded in 1946/47 apart from 9 schools which were also "special Irish schools". Of the 18, 9 were recorded at three locations, since infant, boys and girls schools were separately recorded. Apart from model schools and some recent experiments, such as the multi-denominational Dalkey project, national schools are owned either by Church bodies or religious orders and managed since 1975 with the aid of school boards of management. These schools may be vested in trustees, in the Department of Education or unvested as a result of nineteenth century controversies. Such records, as were published up to the end of 1963, showed a rise in trusteeships from 2,666 in 1946 to 3,394 in 1963 with falls from 395 to 355 in Department schools and from 1,896 to 1,115 in unvested schools. This occurred in a period when 1,108 new schools became operational and 1,210 schools closed.

Tussing (1978) noted that national schools "in spite of their names, they are not public educational institutions in the usual sense ... Their principals and teachers, however, are paid directly by the State. The theory is that the State acts as 'agent' for the Management Committee in paying teacher salaries. In a practical, if not nominal, sense the teachers are State employees". Schools where all the teachers' salaries were paid directly by the State have been known historically as "classification" schools to distinguish them from a different type of school, extinct since 1981, referred to as a "capitation" school.

The strictly secular spirit enforced by the nineteenth century National Education Board caused certain religious orders to prefer to finance their own schools. Thus the Christian Brothers only joined the system in 1925 though other orders were in it from the beginning. In 1946 all monastery schools were in the classification scheme and all teachers in receipt of personal salaries with the exception of all the CBS schools and two of those of the Presentation Brothers. Among the convent schools, individual schools of the same order were often in differing categories and the tendency was to opt increasingly for personal salaries. This fact casts doubt on Tussing's view that schools opted for the capitation scheme to get around the vow of poverty taken by individual religious teachers. Capitation schools must employ minimum levels of staff to be recognised. Capitation grants per recognised pupil were then calculated to fund the salaries of these minimum staff exclusive of any lay staff salaries. These lay salaries were paid directly as in classification schools and omitted from the calculations. Once the minimum staff requirements were met the school was free to employ untrained members of the religious community and to avail of other staff for which the state made no contribution. Thus the system included religious supernumeraries, perhaps retired teachers, some of whom were trained (about 30 per cent in 1954).For the purposes of this study these are not included since they received no pay though their numbers are recorded in Table 84.

Numbers of Schools

A number of factors influence the number of teachers employed in the system even though there may be standard calculations of target pupil-teacher ratios at any moment in time. One of these is clearly the size of the school while another is the number of special schools and special classes, where better than normal ratios prevail. Other major factors are clearly the change in the targeted pupil-teacher ratios, the total size of the school-going population and the duration of their stay in national schools.

In connection with the last topic Coolahan noted that there were 20,800 pupils aged 14 and over in national schools in February 1944.[31] Excluding handicapped the number in January 1982 was 670 even though the school leaving age had been raised to 15 in 1972. This change was due to the revolution in post-primary provision. In the nineteenth century the absence of local secondary schools or their cost had led some national schools to provide "secondary tops" classes to compete in the examinations held by the Intermediate Education Board. In 1944 there were still over 4,000 pupils in such classes in spite of the developments in post-primary education. In spite of the introduction of the "free" second-level education programme in 1967, 400 pupils, mostly girls, were recorded in 3 secondary tops schools on 1st January 1982. These numbers will tend to reduce as alternative schools become available and one school has since closed. More important than this development has been the growing recognition of the age of 12 as the transition to post-primary education and the growing demand for such education. Thus in 1964 national schools had 37,176 pupils on their rolls aged thirteen and over and only 5,873 on January 1 1982 (excluding special schools and secondary tops).

In the reforming spirit of the 'sixties, especially after the report on Investment in Education, strenuous efforts were made to upgrade the physical quality of schools and to reduce the number of one-teacher schools. A school transport scheme was introduced in 1965 to facilitate such a programme. Thus the number of 1 and 2 teacher schools was brought down from 3,194 in 1962 (66 per cent of the total) to 949 ordinary schools in June 1983 (29 per cent). Of these 117

[31]These were up to 16 years of age and more numerous than the corresponding age group attending secondary schools.

were one-teacher schools. An example of what this meant for teacher numbers and pupil-teacher ratios was reported in the Dail in June 1980 for County Mayo when 118 such schools closed between September 1967 and 1979. Before closure 172 teachers taught 3,611 pupils — an average ratio of 21 but in single teacher schools ratios could vary generally between 12 and 30. At the extreme, one school in Ballindine had 77, another in Derrymore only 6. Presumably small class size is less attractive if the one teacher teaches several classes. In these cases amalgamation could be expected to increase class size.

The number of national schools rose rapidly throughout Ireland after their inception in 1831: 1835 1,106, 1850 4,547, 1900 8,684. This happened in spite of much clerical hostility which caused the Church of Ireland to build its own schools through the Church Education Society and caused religious orders to remain aloof in many cases. Thus, 2,661 primary schools were unassociated in 1871 though with disestablishment in 1869 Church of Ireland schools were participating to an increasing degree. The Christian Brothers also joined but only in 1925. Early on local contributions were expected but in 1892 in view of compulsory attendance, participation was declared free. Grants for maintenance of schools, however, were only provided in 1962. School attendance presented problems and was only 30 per cent of enrolments in 1870. This increased especially after an effective Act of 1926 and had reached 85.1 per cent by 1950 when Table 77 begins its record of the change in school numbers. By 1982 attendance rates were 91.5 per cent of enrolments.

Table 77 shows that by 1965, when bussing was introduced, the decline in total school numbers was negligible[32] even though within this apparent stability large numbers of new schools had been opened — mainly to replace antiquated buildings. Subsequently a fall of 30 per cent occurred, or an annual decrease of 2.1 per cent compound. Schools run by religious orders increased in numbers up to 1967 when the rationalisation programme gradually eliminated most of these gains. Table 77 shows the increased tempo of closures after this watershed.

National Teachers

The Killanin Committee of 1918 awarded the 12,000 lay teachers in the Free State area a significant improvement in their salaries which did not survive the coming of Independence. In line with public spending cutbacks teachers' salaries were reduced by 10 per cent in 1923. They were further reduced by 10 per cent in 1933 and 1934 and, although one of these latter cuts was later restored and the other linked to new pension arrangements, teachers pressed without success for a restoration of the 1922 situation. Their bargaining power

---

[32]There had been an earlier decline from 5,361 in 1932, 5,034 in 1942 and 4,876 in 1952 with pupil populations of 503,017; 460,199 and 460,845, respectively.

Table 77: *Numbers of National Schools 1950–1984 by category together with new schools and closures*

June	Total	Lay	Convent	Monastery	Model	Special Irish*	Change in Previous Year Openings	Change in Previous Year Closing and Amalgamation
1950	4,886	4,332	393	146	17	8	53	63
1951	4,879	4,313	394	147	17	8	54	61
1952	4,876	4,308	395	148	17	8	53	56
1953	4,880	4,308	398	148	17	9	58	54
1954	4,874	4,302	398	148	17	9	64	58
1955	4,872	4,296	401	149	17	9	65	69
1956	4,871	4,290	407	149	13	12	64	69
1957	4,869	4,287	408	149	13	12	81	83
1958	4,869	4,277	417	150	13	12	37	37
1959	4,878	4,278	426	150	12	12	100	91
1960	4,882	4,270	433	153	12	14	90	86
1961	4,881	4,245	452	155	12	16	74	75
1962	4,867	4.231	453	155	12	16	91	104
1963	4,864	4,224	457	154	14	15	93	96
1964	4,848	4,204	457	158	14	15	88	104
1965	4,847	4,205	454	158	14	16	23	24
1966	4,797	4,158	454	159	10	16	15	65
1967	4,685	4,039	462	161	9	14	16	128
1968	4,450	3,806	460	161	9	14	12	247
1969	4,294	3,655	458	159	8	14	20	176
1970	4,117	3,489	448	158	8	14	17	194
1971	4,012	3,387	446	157	8	14	23	128
1972	3,879	3,260	443	154	8	14	17	150
1973	3,776	3,154	446	154	8	14	17	120
1974	3,688	3,059	448	155	8	18	34	122
1975	3,585	2,978	438	154	15	(16)	29	87
1976	3,508	2,907	433	153	15	(18)	38	52
1977	3,468	2,873	429	152	14	(18)	40	63
1978	3,449	2,860	426	150	13	—	37	43
1979	3,432	2,846	424	149	13	—	34	51
1980	3,415	2,833	420	149	13		40	57
1981	3,402	2,824	417	148	13		29	42
1982	3,397	2,823	414	148	13		32	37
1983	3,393	2,823	410	148	12		39	43
1984	3,387	2,822	409	147	9		26	32

Source: Statistical Reports of the Department of Education.

*Note: In 1966, 9 of these schools were noted to be also model schools. Up to 1960 1 fosterage school (Rinn) was included; afterwards 3.

was weakened by over supply of teachers in the 1930s and 1940s which led to great problems for teachers getting permanent employment. From 1 October 1933 until repealed in 1958 a ban was imposed on the continued employment of female teachers after marriage. To aggravate the situation pupil numbers fell from 513,349 in 1933 to 444,132 in 1947. The surplus of teachers was not used to reduce pupil teacher ratios in large schools since the criterion for employment up to 1948 was average daily attendance rather than average enrolment. This caused some teachers to be teaching up to eighty or ninety pupils at certain times of the year. The dissatisfactions of teachers boiled over into a long and bitter strike lasting seven months in 1946 which the teachers finally called off without achieving any results. In these circumstances student numbers in training colleges were drastically reduced and some colleges were actually closed for periods in the 1940s (see Coolahan, p. 49).

Table 78 takes up the story when pupil numbers were slowly recovering but numbers of new teachers were few. In the early part of the 'fifties the scarcity of teachers meant that pupil numbers grew faster than the teacher population even though there were considerable numbers of untrained teachers in schools. The rapid rise in pupil numbers ended in the mid-'fifties when mass emigration was at its height. Although there was a population turn around in 1960, and a renewed upsurge in births, pupil numbers were fairly static between 1960 and 1968, perhaps due to increased transferrals to post-primary schools from age 12 onwards. Some benchmarks in the annual compound rates of change in pupil and teacher numbers are:

	Teachers %	Pupils %	
1950–56	0.5	1.34	
1956–60	1.1	0.26	
1960–68	0.8	0.04	
1968–70	0.2	0.87	
1970–75	2.4	0.71	
1975–80	2.4	1.20	
1980–85	2.2	0.69	(4 years only)

Overall the compound annual rate of growth in teacher numbers (1.4 per cent) was twice that for pupil (0.7 per cent). The implication of these changes for pupil-teacher numbers will be discussed later.

The rapid growth in teacher numbers occurred principally since 1970. The general 1975 recruitment civil service go-slow appears to have affected increases somewhat after June 1975. However the scope for curtailment was limited by the continuous upward pressure of student numbers. The increase in the year following June 1978 was substantial — 792 extra teachers or 4.5 per cent. This

Table 78: *Teachers and pupils at national schools 1950–1985*

Date	Total in June†	Of which untrained†	Of whom women	Junior assistant mistress	Temporary unqualified not included	Pupils†† average on roll	Average pupils per teacher
1950	12,870	n.a.	8,674	1,370		449,421	34.9
1951	12,792	n.a.	8,602	1,358	n.a.	452,114	35.3
1952	12,883	n.a.	8,695	1,388	n.a.	460,845	35.8
1953	13,000	n.a.	8,788	1,435	n.a.	468,707	36.1
1954	13,144	3,059	8,903	1,393	n.a.	472,536	36.0
1955	13,231	3,064	8,949	1,393	n.a.	479,487	36.2
1956	13,262	3,018	8,965	1,356	n.a.	486,634	36.7
1957	13,402	3,011	9,067	1,329	n.a.	488,197	36.4
1958	13,554	2,991	9,195	1,338	n.a.	490,700	36.2
1959	13,753	2,797	9,367	1,272	n.a.	492,315	35.8
1960	13,866	2,648	9,457	1,242	n.a.	491,851	35.5
1961	14,032	2,523	9,553	1,221	n.a.	490,016	34.9
1962	14,091	2,454	9,608	1,178	n.a.	484,618	34.4
1963	14,218	2,275	9,721	1,206	n.a.	484,393	34.1
1964	14,297	2,033	9,802	1,186	n.a.	487,178	34.1
1965	14,469	1,860	9,943	1,075	n.a.	490,168	33.9
1966	14,614	1,858	10,066	1,036	n.a.	493,249	33.8
1967	14,672	1,740	10,142	1,045	n.a.	496,516	33.8
1968	14,794	1,545	10,196	—	n.a.	493,549	33.4
1969	14,733	1,265	10,101	—	n.a.	497,541	33.8
1970	14,859	1,040	10,182	—	n.a.	502,158	33.8
1971	15,080	900	10,510	—	603	507,406	33.6
1972	15,450	742	10,802	—	n.a.	512,370	33.2
1973	15,612	689	10,920	—	444	510,550	32.7
1974	16,137	598	11,420	—	455	515,126	31.9
1975	16,718	390	11,880	—	335	520,542	31.1
1976	17,055	169	12,156	—	249	530,075	31.1
1977	17,273	157	12,360	—	279	536,429	31.1
1978	17,595	113	12,683	—	208	547,790	31.1
1979	18,387	111	13,329	—	85	550,819	30.0
1980	18,811	118	13,766	—	191	552,079	29.3
1981	19,356	124	14,303	—	109	555,780	28.7
1982	19,876	117	14,793	—	50	559,095	28.1
1983	20,381	107	15,216	—	54	564,889	27.7
1984	20,732	n.a.	15,663	—	n.a.	567,495	27.4
1985	20,933	n.a.	15,816	—	n.a.	n.a.	n.a.

†Includes teachers in Special Schools for the Handicapped, special classes and secondary tops. Excludes temporary unqualified teachers and supernumeraries.

††If instead of average numbers on the rolls, we use numbers at the end of the year, the total would usually be 15,000 higher; see *Statistical Abstract* 1970-71, page 190.

was probably associated with the full employment programme. In fact the Minister for Education, Mr Wilson, detailed for the Dail in March 1979 the 2,530 jobs which he had created since taking office, both in terms of jobs created and jobs filled. The details for primary education were as follows: it will be noted that not all posts involved teachers; nor does the list include 150 jobs on school construction:

		Jobs Created	Jobs Filled
Improved pupil/teacher ratio, increase in enrolments and provision for remedial teachers	1978	824	696
Improved pupil/teacher ratio, increase in enrolments and provision for remedial teachers	1979	650	—
Secretarial Assistance (Primary and Secondary Schools)		600	243
Scheme for caretakers		300	—
Special education for physically and mentally handicapped (mh)			
(a) improve pupil/teacher ratio for moderately mh		22	4
(b) visiting teachers for deaf and blind		8	8
(c) special classes for mildly mh		15	15
(d) youth encounter projects		9	9
(e) Vocational Training Centres for mh		10	10
(f) child care assistants in special schools		70	—
(g) extra classes for travelling children		22	18

Women and Untrained Teachers

One outcome of the growth in teacher numbers over the three decades has been the rise in share of staff posts held by women. As we have seen the dearth of teaching posts in the 'thirties led to a ban in 1933 on women teachers continuing to work after marriage. This ban was only repealed in 1958 even though the scarcity of teachers would have dictated its abolition a decade sooner. Over the 'fifties women's share was fairly static at about 67.6 per cent. Following the repeal of the ban it eased up slightly to 68.1 per cent for a few years. It peaked at 69.1 per cent in 1967 but really began to move upwards in the last decade from 69.9 per cent in 1973 to 75.6 per cent in 1985.

Another bonus of the increase in teacher numbers was the reduction in the number of untrained teachers. Excluding supernumeraries the 3,059 untrained teachers working in 1954 constituted almost a quarter of all teachers. Untrained supernumeraries numbered 467 in the same year (see Table 81). By 1983 qualified untrained teachers had decreased in numbers to 107, or an insignificant 0.5 per cent of all teachers. However, in March 1979 the Dail was told that 50 male and 610 female substitute teachers were employed on an average working day and of these only 130 were fully trained. One special group, listed in Table 78, were the Junior Assistant Mistresses (JAM), who were largely untrained. Numbers fell away from the 1953 peak of 1,435 to 1,045 in 1967 when a programme of retraining altered their classification and they ceased to be recorded. The fact that in 1963, 3,198 two-teacher schools consisted of a principal and a JAM was probably one of the powerful incentives for promoting larger schools in the late 'sixties.

Recruitment and Wastage

In any study of employment it would be useful to have analysis of recruitment and wastage. Information on these lines is, however, scrappy and discontinuous. Up to 1967 the Department of Education Reports recorded the number who received their first teaching post. This can be taken as a partial proxy for recruitment since it excluded those who had left the system but who were now reappointed. It also gave the number of Junior Assistant Mistresses separately. On the wastage side numbers were probably more complete though departures in many cases were not permanent. The total recruitment can be calculated as departures plus changes in the inventory of teachers. Table 79 provides these, exclusive of Junior Assistant Mistresses. These calculations permit reappointments to be estimated.

Table 79 shows the great reliance placed on Junior Assistant Mistresses up to 1955/56 when 139 were appointed, of whom only ten were trained. By the early 'sixties most JAMs were in fact trained. The classification of JAMs ceased after a special training programme had regraded them as ordinary teachers. It will also be observed that first time appointees only exceeded departures in numbers in 1963/64. The high level of female appointments reflects partly the vacancies created by the marriage bar for teachers which was abolished in 1958. This change may account for the fall in departures subsequently. The high level of female appointments also reflects the growing attraction of primary teaching for women.

It is disappointing that this valuable source of information was no longer published after 1967. Subsequently wastage data only refer to new normal and disability pensions awarded. The only index of appointments came to be the numbers who passed the final examinations in the teacher training colleges. It would be preferable if this material could be supplemented by data on deaths, resignations and appointments which are probably collected but not published. Recent published material is given in Table 80. No explanation is available for the high level of retirement in 1974/75 but it will be noticed that retirements have got fewer which probably reflects the impact on the age profile of the teacher population after a period of rapid recruitment.

Table 79: *Recruitment and Departures of Primary Teachers 1948–1967*

Year ended June	First Time Appointments			Junior Assistant Mistresses Appt.		Departures				Recruitment
	Male	Female	Total	Total	Trained	Retirement	Death	Other	Total	
1948	32	111	143	20	1	167	41	159	367	112
1949	91	196	287	79	14	129	49	234	412	553
1950	81	190	271	82	14	147	45	208	400	372
1951	88	177	265	84	10	137	37	210	384	261
1952	117	247	364	125	8	159	40	230	429	421
1953	112	218	330	132	9	199	39	269	507	485
1954	150	238	388	129	6	120	45	343	508	586
1955	143	247	390	108	5	119	44	340	503	468
1956	132	263	395	139	10	128	48	391	567	521
1957	130	299	429	118	12	182	32	398	612	668
1958	165	356	521	98	11	229	50	467	746	737
1959	122	332	454	32	9	213	41	339	593	759
1960	135	299	434	23	17	194	30	287	511	578
1961	122	304	426	27	19	210	50	254	514	624
1962	138	267	405	35	19	209	50	240	499	536
1963	107	262	369	26	21	215	30	173	418	445
1964	142	342	484	—	—	211	38	218	467	546
1965	203	388	591	—	—	214	32	252	498	670
1966	239	433	672	—	—	240	42	304	586	731
1967	195	414	609	—	—	238	29	336	603	661

Source: Dept. of Education Statistical Reports. (except Recruitment).

Note 1: First Time Appointments excludes Junior Assistant Mistresses, JAMs, the number of whose appointments is given separately, together with the number of them who were trained. Separate figures are available for the departures of JAMs who are included above.

Note 2: Except for the last four estimates recruitment figures do not refer to JAMs and are calculated as the sum of changes in teacher populations from Table 78 and departures excluding JAMs.

Table 80: *Newly qualified national teachers and retirements July 1974–June 1985*

June	Trainees who passed final examination	Teachers who retired	Teachers pensioned by disablement
1975	1,084	568	22
1976	270	200	21
1977	741	392	10
1978	968	300	20
1979	1,053	310	19
1980	904	265	22
1981	1,055	260	18
1982	925	237	39
1983	961	244	42
1984	826	n.a.	n.a.
1985	673	n.a.	n.a.

Source: Department of Education Statistical Reports.
Note: The paucity of qualified trainees in 1976/77 was due to a year's "production" being lost because of the introduction of the 3 year training course in 1974.

An unexpected source of recent experience for teachers leaving the service was that given in the Dail in February 1985, which showed the impact of the recession. From these figures it is possible to deduce some data on recruitment. The fall in departures limited the opportunities for recruitment which had already been curtailed by the financial problems of the 'eighties. Low levels of recruitment raised fears about the ease of re-entry of teachers who temporarily retired and tended to reinforce the tendency not to leave. In 1983/84 only two women teachers gave up their posts on marriage and both were leaving Europe. A complicating factor has been the redundancies caused as suburbs move into new stages of the life cycle — a phenomenon long familiar in many rural areas.

Table 81: *Recruitment and departures from primary teaching July 1978–July 1984*

School Year	Teachers leaving service	Change in stock†	Estimate of recruitment
1978/79	996	669	1,665
1979/80	982	530	1,512
1980/81	801	463	1,264
1981/82	688	411	1,099
1982/83	780	559	1,339
1983/84	699	297	996

Source: Based on Dail question, 5 February 1985.
†Differs somewhat from Table 78 above.

Table 82: *Special Schools*: number, pupils and teachers 1950 to 1984, also numbers of capitation schools*

June	Special Schools for the Handicapped			Convent Schools		Monasteries	
	Number	Pupils	Teachers††	Capitation†	Personal	Capitation	Personal
1950	10	n.a.	n.a.	337	56	89	56
1951	10	n.a.	n.a.	338	56	90	57
1952	12	n.a.	n.a.	340	57	91	57
1953	15	n.a.	n.a.	340	59	91	57
1954	15	1,173	n.a.	340	58	88	60
1955	16	1,283	n.a.	339	62	89	60
1956	20	1,463	n.a.	342	65	89	60
1957	24	1,820	n.a.	344	65	89	60
1958	26	1,923	n.a.	350	67	90	60
1959	28	2,024	n.a.	353	73	90	60
1960	33	2,185	n.a.	358	75	92	61
1961	33	2,202	n.a.	360	92	92	63
1962	35	2,360	n.a.	362	91	92	63
1963	40	2,563	n.a.	354	103	91	63
1964	43	2,768	193	347	110	92	66
1965	48	3,246	224	336	118	90	68
1966	54	3,700	262	329	125	90	69
1967	60	4,223	299	326	136	91	70
1968	65	4,603	336	318	142	91	70
1969	69	5,066	369	257	201	89	70
1970	70	5,408	415	208	240	88	70
1971	76	5,826	470	183	263	88	69
1972	80	6,081	495	117	326	87	67
1973	85	6,535	521	96	350	86	68
1974	89	6,816	558	53	395	87	68
1975	88	7,066	614	32	406	84	70
1976	92	7,303	671	7	426	84	69
1977	96	7,547	726	5	424	17	135
1978	104	8,148	751	1	425	—	150
1979	108	8,083	817	1	423	—	149
1980	112	8,220	881	1	419	—	149
1981	113	8,233	857	1	416	—	150
1982	116	8,455	852	—	414	—	149
1983	120	8,595	864	—	410	—	148
1984	121(115)*	(8,453)*	(780)*	—	409	—	147

†Schools paid on a capitation basis as distinct from those where all teachers received personal salaries.

††In 1979, 70 child care assistant full-time posts were created and these increased to 85 by 1982 and remained at that level since.

**Note:* The concept of special schools only dates from 1962 when the blind got a special arrangement. Other types of school followed. The schools include some for able-bodied but disadvantaged groups, e.g., travellers. Figures in parentheses for 1984 refer to the handicapped alone.

Source: Department of Education Statistical Reports.

Special Schools for the Handicapped

One of the sources of increased job numbers, noted by Mr Wilson above, was the provision of special facilities for the physically and mentally handicapped. Table 82 documents the rise in the number of special schools since 1950. It does not record the numbers of special classes in ordinary schools since the extra teachers for these are not separately identified. There were 133 schools providing such classes in June 1983. In April 1985 there were 169 classes for mildly- and 7 for moderately mentally handicapped.

There were some schools for deaf mutes in the early nineteenth century and schools for the blind after 1870. Care of the mentally handicapped was left to voluntary organisations. Coolahan (p. 185) noted one such school, St. Vincent's, in 1950 but 33 in 1960. A ferment of interest at the end of the 'fifties led to a special inspector being appointed in 1959; special teacher training for mentally handicapped at Drumcondra in 1960 and a White Paper on the same topic in the same year. The breakthrough was in 1962 when schools for the blind were given a special pupil-teacher ratio of 15:1. The deaf won a similar arrangement soon afterwards. In 1963 official recognition was given for the first time to a school for maladjusted children and the moderately mentally handicapped schools received special status the following year. Following the report of the Commission on Mental Handicap in 1965 the emphasis was put on special transport and on re-organising residential schools so that as many pupils as possible spent the weekends at home.

Continuous progress was made in the 'seventies. Special classes were arranged in ordinary schools in 1970. A visiting service was introduced in 1974 for children with impaired hearing and in 1978 for the partially sighted. Stricter criteria for special classes had been introduced the previous year. At present, apart from special schools and special classes, educational services are also provided in certain voluntary centres appropriate to the needs of the children attending them. Furthermore "many children are catered for by part-time teaching facilities in hospitals, child guidance clinics, rehabilitation workshops, special 'Saturday morning' centres and home teaching schemes" (Coolahan, p. 188). Children do not necessarily remain in one type of arrangement and may transfer to special classes or ordinary classes as they make educational progress. The situation on June 30 1982 is summarised in Table 83.

Apart from mental and physical handicap some children suffer due to economic and social deprivation. A first stage in coping with this problem was the launching of the Rutland Street Pre-School Project jointly sponsored by the Department of Education and by the Van Leer Foundation in 1969. Following the report of the Commission on Itinerants in 1970 special schools were launched for their children only where integration in ordinary schools would create major problems. Preference was for special classes attached to ordinary National

Table 83: *Special Schools for the Handicapped, 30 June 1983*

Type of Handicapped	Schools	Teachers	Pupils
Mental	65	500	5,889
Impaired Hearing	5	140	722
Blind and Partially Sighted	2	16	144
Physical	18	71	749
Emotional Disturbed	15	63	490
Other special schools	15	74	601
Total	120	864	8,595

Source: Dept. of Education, Statistical Report.

Schools. In August 1985 there were 4 special schools for travellers currently operating and 100 special classes. It is Department policy to establish special classes for travellers where it has been considered there is a need and progress towards integration into the ordinary class stream is carefully monitored. The Department also grant-aids part-time tuition fees and transport costs, where necessary, for pre-schools for travellers. Such pre-schools are initially set up by local voluntary bodies who then make application to the Department for the grant. A total of 27 pre-schools for travellers are currently grant-aided by the Department. It is expected that approximately 10 to 15 further pre-schools will commence operating in the school year 1985/86. The Department also pays grants towards the cost of the services of the national co-ordinator for the education of the travelling people.

Apart from these special interventions ordinary schools with a high incidence of children with learning difficulties were assigned remedial teachers extra to the normal quota. Statistics on these arrangements are not published separately even though in 1980 about 16,000 such pupils were catered for by such teachers. In November 1984 the Dail was informed that 767 remedial posts had been sanctioned with 197 of them on a shared basis between two or more schools, 1,014 schools were involved in all. In April 1985 there were 797 posts in 1,051 schools. This was a substantial increase on the 88 males and 319 females reported earlier in the Dail for March 1979.

Capitation Schools and Religious Teachers

In an earlier section we noted the arrangement by which some national schools run by religious orders were paid on a capitation basis as far as the religious staff were concerned. Table 81 documented the slow transfer of convents from this system towards one where all staff received personal salaries. All Christian Brothers monastery schools were on a capitation basis but only two

Table 84: *Teachers in capitation schools, supernumeraries and religious in all schools 1950–1983*

| Year | Teachers in Capitation Schools | | | | | Supernumeraries | | Numbers of Religious in Classification | |
	Lay Assistants		Religious	Per cent Total	All Teachers	Total	(Trained)	Schools	Total
1950	835		2,165	3,000	23.3	n.a.		n.a.	n.a.
1951	807		2,168	2,975	23.3	n.a.		n.a.	n.a.
1952	867		2,196	3,063	23.8	n.a.		n.a.	n.a.
1953	872		2,249	3,121	24.0	n.a.		n.a.	n.a.
1954	881		2,303	3,184	24.2	663	(196)	n.a.	n.a.
1955	936		2,260	3,196	24.2	670	(170)	n.a.	n.a.
1956	988		2,248	3,236	24.4	581	(172)	n.a.	n.a.
1957	1,032		2,287	3,319	24.8	569	(174)	n.a.	n.a.
1958	1,091		2,265	3,356	24.8	564	(211)	n.a.	n.a.
1959	1,235	(69)†	2,276	3,511	25.5	480	(136)	n.a.	n.a.
1960	1,289	(74)†	2,221	3,510	25.3	546	(187)	n.a.	n.a.
1961	1,313	(83)†	2,254	3,567	25.4	498	(159)	n.a.	n.a.
1962	1,394	(139)†	2,285	3,679	26.1	461	(134)	n.a.	n.a.
1963	1,417	(213)†	2,245	3,662	25.8	404	(129)	n.a.	n.a.
1964	1,490		2,246	3,736	26.1	436	(136)	n.a.	n.a.
1965	n.a.		2,203	n.a.	n.a.	374		n.a.	n.a.
1966	1,606		2,148	3,754	25.7	369	(123)	n.a.	3,023
1967	1,725		2,059	3,784	25.8	317	(108)	n.a.	2,937
1968	1,785		2,011	3,796	25.7	301	(120)	n.a.	2,920
1969	1,712		1,654	3,366	22.8	225		1,154	2,808
1970	1,581		1,361	2,942	19.8	184		1,490	2,851
1971	1,432		1,017	2,449	16.2	147		1,615	2,632
1972	1,163		866	2,029	13.1	110		1,713	2,579
1973	1,064		773	1,837	11.4	89		1,790	2,563
1974	826		525	1,351	8.2	49		1,879	2,404
1975	767		402	1,169	7.0	35		1,929	2,331
1976	694		264	958	5.6	19		1,949	2,213
1977	190		64	254	1.5	3		2,130	2,194
1978	n.a.		n.a.	19[a]	0.1	4		n.a.	2,089
1979	n.a.		n.a.	19[a]	0.1	2		n.a.	2,023
1980	n.a.		n.a.	18[a]	0.1	—		n.a.	1,910
1981	n.a.		n.a.	15[a]	0.1	—		n.a.	1,861
1982	n.a.		n.a.	n.a.	n.a.	—		1,785	1,785
1983	n.a.		n.a.	n.a.	n.a.	—		1,684	1,684

†Figures in parentheses are Temporary Additional Assistants paid by the Department and included in total.

[a] Includes temporary unqualified teachers.

Source: Department of Education Statistical Reports.

among the other orders. The speed of transfer increased from the mid-'sixties as the economics of capitation favoured classification schools. The CBS schools transferred in the late 'seventies and by 1982 capitation schools ceased to exist.

Tussing (1978) has reviewed the contribution made by religious teachers, some of whom worked for nothing either as supernumeraries or at after hours tasks. Others received salaries but ploughed them back into the school funds. The decline in vocations, Tussing predicted, would add to the costs of education. It would be useful, therefore, to have some record of the numbers of religious involved. There is no problem for religious working in capitation schools but religious working in classification schools were not identified separately until 1966. In that year both capitation and classification schools employed 3,023 religious or 21 per cent of all teachers. Tussing reckoned that this proportion held back to 1956. Table 84 records their numbers since 1966. By 1982 their share of the teaching staff had fallen to less than 9 per cent.

Pupil–Teacher Ratios (PTRs) in National Schools

The calculation of average pupil teacher ratios at primary level does not present as many pitfalls as at other levels since the length of the teacher's week coincides with that of the pupils. Even so decisions are called for, e.g., whether to use enrolment, average attendance or attendance on a specific day; whether to include pupils in secondary tops attached to national schools. What teachers to include must also be decided — walking principals (who visit classes but do not teach)?, remedial teachers?, teachers in special schools? etc.

One index that is potentially unambiguous would appear to be the schedule of appointments by which teachers are allocated. These do not appear to have been published, apart from that of 1st July 1962 reproduced in *Investment in Education*. If that schedule is any guide this source is itself fraught with difficulties. For example, the threshold at which an additional teacher may be recruited was not the same as that by which a surplus teacher in a declining school would be let go. An expanding school, for instance, could obtain an extra teacher when average enrolment reached 90 but a contracting school need not give up such a teacher until enrolment had fallen to 80. Thus two schools of 85 pupils could be entitled to different numbers of teachers. A second problem was the uneven spacing between thresholds in that year, i.e., 36, 60, 90, 140, 210, etc. where school size was increasing, 190, 125, 80, 45 and 28 where school size was declining, so that PTRs would be influenced by the size of the school and whether it was growing or reducing.

It is unfortunate that there is no officially published target for pupil-teacher ratios. The use of calculated PTRs is unsatisfactory since various people calculate the ratio on different bases. Table 78, for example, gave the result of dividing the number of teachers at the end of the school year in June into the average number of pupils on the roll. Sheehan (1981) preferred to divide these teachers into a calculated enrolment for February 1 so that the reduction in ratios in his tables is less striking. Table 78 notes that end of year enrolments are typically several thousands higher than average enrolments so that estimates on this basis would differ once again. Finally, a reply to a Dail Question (5/2/85) calculated PTRs over a period which were typically 0.5 lower than those given in Table 78. The pupils were enumerated at the beginning of the year and teachers taken to include temporary and unqualified staff.

Obviously average PTRs need careful interpretation in general. In any particular case the actual PTR within a school itself can vary in keeping with general trends in the economic environment, falling births, new suburbs, etc., though often attempts are made to iron out disparities by reallocating marginal pupils. Just as the within-school rates can vary, between-school variation occurs, as was instanced in the case of small schools in Mayo.

Another index of teacher inputs is class size. Coolahan noted that the target of the last two decades has been to reduce the numbers of classes under 30 and over 45. Table 85 documents the tremendous progress in this regard and even the reduction in classes over 40 in size. Since the full employment programme the proportion of pupils in classes of less than 30 has been increasing.

Table 85: *Percentage of pupils in classes of different sizes in ordinary national schools 1966/67 to 1983/84*

	Less than 15	15–29	30–39	40–44	45 and more
1966/67	1.6	24.5	40.2		33.7
1967/68	1.5	24.6	41.0		32.9
1968/69	1.5	24.7	42.9		30.9
1969/70	1.3	24.0	44.6		30.1
1970/71	1.3	23.4	46.5		28.9
1971/72	1.2	23.2	48.0		27.7
1972/73	1.1	22.4	51.6		24.9
1973/74	1.1	22.3	62.9		13.7
1974/75	0.9	21.8	41.0	25.9	10.3
1975/76	0.8	20.7	42.4	26.7	9.4
1976/77	0.7	20.1	43.8	26.8	8.6
1977/78	0.7	19.9	46.3	25.5	7.6
1978/79	0.6	20.4	53.0	22.3	3.6
1979/80	0.6	21.6	61.3	15.2	1.2
1980/81	0.6	22.5	63.7	12.2	0.9
1981/82	0.6	23.4	65.3	10.1	0.6
1982/83	0.6	25.8	65.2	8.0	0.4
1983/84	0.7	28.8	63.7	6.5	0.3

Source: Departmental Reports.

Chapter V.3

SPECIAL SCHOOLS AND RESIDENTIAL HOMES

Up to the middle of the nineteenth century the only provision for orphaned and neglected children was in the workhouses which had such an appalling mortality rate that a system of fosterage had to be instituted in 1862. Delinquents over the age of seven were imprisoned in the same primitive conditions as adults unless they were in the care of voluntary institutions conducted by religious orders or by charitable persons. Since these latter received no public moneys they were not subject to public inspection. In 1858 the Reformatory Schools Act provided for the certification of existing and new reformatories. Subject to satisfactory inspection a capitation grant was paid per child in care. This capitation system remained broadly in operation up till recent years though the underlying philosophy was modified by the more humane Children Act of 1908. The 1858 Act stimulated the introduction of reformatories and 10 were operational by 1865. The success of the Act also facilitated the introduction of industrial schools in 1869 to cater for neglected, orphaned and abandoned children. Within a year 22 were recognised and by 1875, 7,638 pupils were learning a trade in 50 schools. A quarter century later the total had risen to 8,422 pupils in 71 schools built without much official encouragement, largely by religious orders. These schools would appear to be largely different from orphanages whose activities do not appear to be recorded in general. Between 1941 and 1946 Departmental Reports indicate that national schools attached to these institutions were only partially State funded and therefore were separately identified. In April 1946 this situation was rectified and the schools treated like other national schools.

At the end of the Second World War (August 1945) there were 3 reformatories and 51 industrial schools with 273 and 6,565 children, respectively, "under detention". 224 boys were in Daingean reformatory — almost 10 times as many as in each of the girls' reformatories. The 15 boys' industrial schools were on average twice as large as the 35 for girls. One mixed school in Killarney subsequently became an all girls' school. In that year the 123 committals to reformatories were largely for criminal offences. Although 87 of the 946 commitals to industrial schools were also delinquents, the bulk of the children, 731, were destitute, uncared for or with parents in prison. Forty seven children were committed for begging, 91 for mitching and 10 for being in general refractory.

Numbers in detention were broadly on a plateau between 1941 and 1948 when a general decline reduced numbers from an original 6,615 to 1,371 in 1970, when the Kennedy Report caused the entire system to be revamped. Figure 15 graphs the fall using data set out in the Appendix in Table A2.14.

The Kennedy Report urged changed attitudes regarding children in need of care and called for improved methods of referral, reception and treatment of children in care. The first step towards implementation led to a reform of the operation of the system in which "special schools" were distinguished from "residential homes". The designation "special schools" is unfortunate since it is also the designation used for special schools of the handicapped. The new special schools initially comprised the three old reformatories plus industrial schools for senior boys — Letterfrack and Clonmel. As part of the new ethos the reformatories[33] and Letterfrack were phased out and were replaced by modern facilities at Finglas (1971), Lusk (1973) and Oberstown (1982). In 1980 all residential homes became the responsibility of the Department of Health except St. Joseph's, Clonmel.

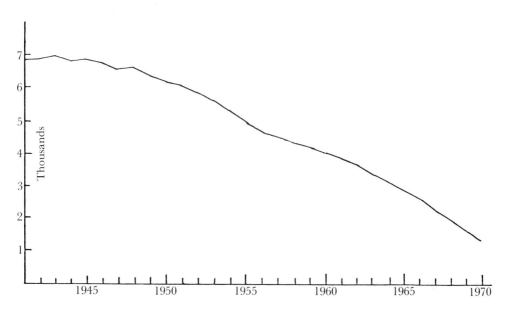

Figure 15: *Numbers of children in detention 1941 to 1970.*

[33]The girls' reformatory in Kilmacud still survives but caters little for delinquents.

The 51 industrial schools of 1945 still numbered 48 in 1963[34] but by the time of the reform had shrunk to 29. All of these, apart from the 2 senior boys' schools, became residential homes though shortly afterwards the most famous of them all, Artane, which had 300 boys in 1966/67, closed. The subsequent stability at 25 homes concealed the fact that in three areas[35] a closure was matched by a reopening in modern buildings some distance away.

Currently children can be committed to care in four ways, (a) commitments for delinquents under the Children Acts 1908 to 1957, (b) commitment on remand (c) voluntarily and (d) under Section 55 of the Health Act 1953. It would be neat if all new committals under the Children Acts (indictable offences, non-attendance at school) were assigned to special schools, as was the case with the 76 such committals in 1980/81 and all other committals were to residential homes. However, on June 30 1981 the picture was not so clearcut for the 1,030 children in care. Although 643 (62 per cent) of them were in care under the Health Acts only 572 were in residential homes. More disconcertingly for this neatness almost all the girls committed under the Children Acts and over half of the boys were in residential homes rather than in special schools. It will be noted, however, that following the recommendation of the Kennedy Report, children in residential homes go out to local schools at all three educational levels, just as ordinary children do and so cannot be deemed to be under detention in the same way as the children in the special schools for delinquents.

The Department of Education is responsible for the Children Acts whereas the Department of Health caters for children committed under the Health Acts. One statistical casualty of this divided responsibility is that the Department of Education Statistical Report did not record children in care under the Health Acts for the period 1971–1977. The incomplete series for children in care is:

	Schools	Homes		Schools	Homes
1971	225	907	1975	162	575
1972	n.a.	872	1976	157	489
1973	210	771	1977	161	423
1974	141	678			

which shows a continuation of the trend by which numbers in the former industrial schools, now residential homes, declined. New commitals also referred to the Children Acts alone.

The situation was remedied in the 1978 report as far as the population in care was concerned but not for new committals. The figures show the continued

[34]Closures were the fishery school at Baltimore (1950), Greenmount (1959). Bundoran girls' schools replaced Monaghan and Sligo in 1958.
[35]In Tipperary, Fethard replaced Dundrum, in Galway Renmore, Lenaboy and in Dublin Drumcondra replaced Whitehall.

tendency for the numbers of those committed to residential homes to fall. The Health Act component in special schools has however been rising.

| June | Special Schools | | | Residential Homes | | | |
	Committed*	Health Act	Total	Committed	Voluntary	Health Act	Total
1978	162	32	194	413	19	596	1,028
1979	171	56	227	379	12	590	981
1980	153	68	221	296	11	588	895
1981	123	71	194	253	11	572	836
1982	133	80	213	213	8	583	804
1983	142	77	219	178	1	617	796
1984	121	76	197	n.a.	n.a.	n.a.	n.a.

*Including remand.

Until 1983, when Trinity House, the new Department of Education special school at Oberstown[36] was opened, all schools were run by religious orders. For several years the special schools were financed on an audited budget basis which gave the Department greater control and access to more statistics. Residential homes were financed on a capitation basis paid by the relevant Department — Education or Health. Each child in care under the Children Act entitled the school to a grant of £68 a week which was provided jointly by the Department of Education and the local authority concerned. When overall responsibility for the homes was taken over by the Department of Health in 1984, £100 a week was paid by the Health Boards under the Health Acts and £50 a week by the local authorities under the Children Acts.

The use of the capitation system occurs in other areas of education, as we have seen. This system means that the department does not stipulate the numbers and qualifications of staff to the same degree as occurs under the audited budget system. For this reason data on staff are sparse. Before 1980 only two isolated records of staff occur for 1951 and 1956. The details are summarised in Table 86. The use of the capitation system probably led to considerable economies in staffing and perhaps encouraged the maintenance of considerable numbers in care which would be less attractive financially under the audited budget system. The use of the capitation approach raises the question whether it was adequate to cover at least half the cost of staff, which is, of course, our criterion for deeming people to be public employees.

Table 86 shows the dramatic fall in child/staff ratios though total levels of staffing were broadly similar in 1951 and 1981, i.e., 468 vs. 455. This development is presumably an expression of the changed ethos in these schools and homes. Publication of staff occupations in recent reports permits us to refine the ratio as in Table 87.

[36] In September 1984 Trinity House combined with Scoil Ard Mhuire, Lusk to become the Oberstown Youth Centre with Lusk as the open centre.

Table 86: *Employment in special schools and residential homes in selected years 1951 to 1984*

Special Schools	1951	1956	1980	1981	1982	1983	1984
Staff Full Time	26	26	138	152	157	207	216
Staff Other			13	21	12	12	30
Children	214	172	221	194	213	219	197
Child/Staff Ratio	8.2	6.6	1.6	1.3	1.4	1.1	0.8
Residential Homes							
Staff Full Time	442	352	299	303	275	281	n.a.
Staff Other			97	105	110	94	n.a.
Children	5,844	4,470	1,116	1,030	804	796	n.a.
Child/Staff Ratio	13.2	12.7	3.7	3.4	2.9	2.8	n.a.

Source: Department of Education Statistical Reports.
Note 1: Child/Staff Ratio includes full-time staff only.
Note 2: Data for 1951 and 1956 refer to reformatories and industrial schools.

Table 87: *Occupational composition of staff in special schools and residential homes June 1980 to 1984*

School type		Total	Admin clerical	Domestic mainten.	Other	Care staff	Child/care ratio
Special	1980	138+13	10+1	59+4	8[a]	69	3.2
	1981	152+21	8+2	66+3	16[a]	78	2.5
	1982	157+12	8+1	67+6	8[b]	763	2.8
	1983	207+12	10+2	81+5	19+4	97+1	2.3
	1984	216+30	10+2	77+6	24+18[c]	105+4	1.9
Residential	1980	299+97	34+10	27+53	19+26	219+8	5.0
	1981	303+105	30+11	34+50[d]	16+34[e]	223+10	4.6
	1982	275+110	32+8	28+56[f]	11+37[d]	204+9	3.9
	1983	281+94	39+10	32+40	5+39[f]	205+5	3.9

Source: Department of Education Statistical Reports.
Note 1: Child/Care Ratio refers only to full-time care staff.
Note 2: Figures give full-time + part-time. Part-time includes sessional. Sessionals included in [a]all; [b]6 full time; [c]16; [d]2; [e]1 and [f]3.
Note 3: When residential homes were transferred to the Department of Health they were added to an existing stock of 20 approved homes (e.g., orphanages) which do not appear to have been in the Health Census.

It is unfortunate that there are no full-time equivalents given of part-time and sessional staff. Table 87 shows, by comparison with the previous table, that the lower child staff ratios in special schools are partly due to greater numbers of non-care staff rather than to the differences in child-care ratios themselves. This may be due in part to the different methods of financing over the period of the tables. These figures can be compared with those for Loughan House where on January 1, 1979, 17 boys were catered for by "67 prison service staff, all of whom received a special course in child care training" (Dail Debates, 3 May 1979). During its brief existence the costs per boy must have been very high indeed compared even with special schools.

The figures cited above are from the Department of Education report. However, just before the transfer of residential homes to the Department of Health a survey was undertaken of 23 industrial schools and 12 approved homes in December 1982. Some of what are called in popular parlance "orphanages" were either such schools or homes. Some of these were funded by the Health Boards when the latter were set up. Others were financed by Church bodies, etc., and only gradually came into the public sphere in recent years. Figures for these homes are difficult to come by before they came under a budget system which began in 1975 for those already in the public domain.

The survey gave the following breakdown:

	Full time	Part time
Managers	33	1
Deputy Managers	1	—
House Parents	97	5
Asst. House Parents	105	7
Trainees	67	—
Clerical	15	19
Receptionists	3	4
Domestic	35	66
Maintenance	15	14
Gardeners	1	4
Teachers	5	23
Total	377	143

A further 8 approved homes, which made no returns, may have employed 15 house parents, 24 assistant house parents and 10 domestic staff.

These figures suggest that perhaps 151 full time and 33 part time staff were being State-funded in late 1982 in addition to those listed in Table 87.[37] In the case where Health Boards run such homes on their own initiative it is assumed that the employment is included in the Health Board totals.

---

[37] Of these about 107 full-time equivalents can be attributed to the 20 approved homes. The reason for the remaining discrepancy is not clear.

Chapter V.4

SECOND-LEVEL EDUCATION

SECONDARY TEACHERS

Secondary schools form the largest category of second-level schools, accounting for 516 out of the 847 schools aided from public funds in 1982/83. They accounted for 205,730 or 68 per cent of the 301,341 pupils enrolled in general courses in that year. Secondary schools are private[38] institutions and almost all denominational. The breakdown of ownership and management of aided schools was as follows for 1979:

Catholic religious orders	443	Protestant	23
Catholic diocesan colleges	31	Other	1
Catholic lay colleges	33	Total	531

Since secondary education was deemed a matter for private provision by the middle classes, secondary schools largely escaped the controversies of the nineteenth century. Some small funding did become available as a result of the Intermediate Education Act of 1878. However, a more direct involvement was ushered in by an Act in 1914 when a Registration Council was set up (effective from 1918) with the aim of raising and securing the status of secondary teachers. At that time only 398 of the 1,142 teachers had security of tenure and minimum salaries. The Act set out to remedy this by offering to grant-aid lay salaries, provided the school paid a minimum of £120 to men and £80 to women. At that time there were 940 full-time lay teachers and 343 part-time as against 809 full-time religious and 40 part-time. The £40,000 voted (increased to £90,000 in 1918) would not benefit almost half the staff.

It was, however, a third Act in 1921 which laid the foundation of the present system by introducing incremental salaries from 1924/25 and abolishing payment by results which had been a feature of the first Act. The initial scales were from £236 to £410 for men and £210 to £300 for women. These figures included the statutory minimum school salaries of £200 for men and £180 for women and

[38]But State-funded.

allow for the superannuation contribution of teachers. The scales operating on November 1 1946 were not much different at the bottom: £280 to £610 for men, £250 to £440 for women. These scales meant that initially the school salaries formed the larger part of the teachers' salaries but later on the incremental salaries came to dominate. However, there was an important fiction here in that the minimum school salaries were also funded by the State in an indirect manner to preserve the independence of the schools. Dale Tussing in his study of educational expenditures (page 31) commented on the complexity surrounding

> ... the extent to which finance of Secondary Schools is "public" or "private". Each teacher receives a "school salary" ... paid by the school and not the State. In addition the State directly pays recognised, qualified teachers a so-called "incremental salary". The "school salary" ... is far smaller than the so-called "incremental salary". The State has historically provided the Schools with aid in the form of grants ... from which the "school salary" is paid so both parts have a State origin. The reason for dividing the salary in this fashion and for calling the larger State share "incremental" is to support the theory that secondary teachers are private not public employees.

For the purpose of this report, secondary teachers on incremental salaries are clearly State employees since all their salaries are so funded. Where salaries are non-incremental it would appear that the teachers concerned are genuinely private sector employees.

The 1921 Act made no provision for the building or maintaining of secondary schools. The financial gymnastics necessary for initial survival impeded all schools but was particularly severe on small schools, usually located in the South West which were built and staffed by lay teachers. The absence of capital grants, thus, left an imbalance in the geographic distribution of schools which was only partly filled by the Vocational Education Committees after their establishment under the 1930 Act.

As in all education the 'sixties brought a revolution in the State's approach to education. This began modestly enough by increasing the level of local authorities' scholarships in 1961 followed by building grants in 1964. These grants were greatly improved when in 1967 the "free" secondary schooling scheme was announced. As a result over 90 per cent of schools ceased to charge fees with the Department of Education giving grants in their place, though in recent years the inadequacy of official funding has led to various fund-raising practices being condoned including voluntary donations from parents.

The 1967 innovations included free school transportation for certain pupils and also the development of secondary courses in vocational schools. Prior to this a new departure was the 1963 launching of the concept of comprehensive schools which saw the first three schools opened in areas lacking adequate post-primary facilities by 1966. The novelty here was that they were established and fully funded by the State and run by management committees; even so the schools were denominational. Perhaps because of the rather hurried and experimental nature of their launching it was decided in 1974 not to build any more than the fifteen already in existence. Preference was given to community schools which first appeared in 1973 and were joint ventures of secondary and vocational schools, if not actual amalgamations. The rationalisation and development of post-primary education has, thus, led to some decline in the number of secondary schools.

In spite of the lack of State funding for capital expenditures before 1964 the number of schools expanded rapidly in that period as did pupil numbers. Coolahan gives some benchmarks:

	Schools	Pupils
1924/25	278	22,897
1931/32	306	30,004
1941/42	362	39,537
1951/52	434	50,179
1961/62	542	80,400

Average school size was small so that in 1945/46, 243 of the 385 schools had fewer than 100 enrolled, 306 fewer than 150 while only 13 had more than 300. Figure 16 (and Table 88) documents the growth of school numbers to a peak of

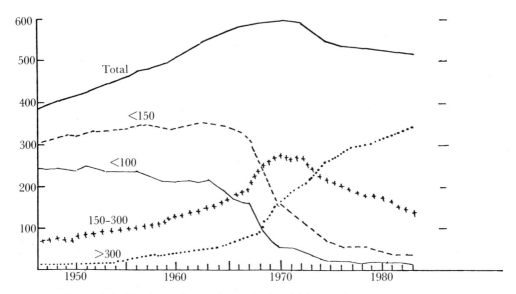

Figure 16: *Numbers of secondary schools 1946 to 1983 by size category.*

Table 88: *Number of recognised secondary schools, registered, unregistered, part time and probationary teachers 1949/50–1982/83*

Year	Number of recognised schools	New teachers registrations	Employed Teachers Registered*	Employed Teachers Unregistered	Unregistered probationers	Unregistered who were non-incremental Full-time	Unregistered who were non-incremental Part-time	Total (FTE)
1949/50	416	143	2,334	1,510	n.a.	n.a.	1,181	
1950/51	424	152	2,374	1,555	n.a.	n.a.	1,193	
1951/52	434	159	2,422	1,621	n.a.	n.a.	1,198	
1952/53	441	165	2,512	1,658	n.a.	n.a.	1,260	
1953/54	447	149	2,542	1,555	n.a.	n.a.	n.a.	
1954/55	458	168	2,612	1,805	n.a.	n.a.	n.a.	
1955/56	474	182	2,787	1,777	n.a.	n.a.	n.a.	
1956/57	480	183	2,857	1,882	n.a.	n.a.	n.a.	
1957/58	489	245	2,969	1,988	n.a.	n.a.	n.a.	
1958/59	494	265	2,983	2,049	(282)[a]	277	1,490	
1959/60	512	242	3,150	2,028	(267)	307	1,454	
1960/61	526	267	3,282	2,000	(286)	318	1,396	
1961/62	542	265	3,471	2,159	(311)	296	1,552	
1962/63	557	287	3,602	2,306	(422)	310	1,574	
1963/64	569	329	3,824	2,337	(419)	300	1,618	
1964/65	573	344	4,012	2,465	(399)	308	1,758	
1965/66	585	417	4,332	2,463	(247)	319	1,897	
1966/67	588	427	4,568	2,680	488	257	1,935	
1967/68	595	453	5,087	3,078	521	230	2,326	
1968/69	598	668	5,359	3,771	744	581	2,446	
1969/70	600	879	5,859	3,744	912	736	2,096	
1970/71	599	964	6,421	3,812	910	761	2,141	
1971/72	593	926	6,959	3,654	975	166	2,513	
1972/73	574	1,080	7,428	3,822	950	225	2,647	
1973/74	554	1,060	8,176	3,900	1,005	196	2,699	
1974/75	541	1,068	n.a.	n.a.	840	244	2,123	(757)
1975/76	538	955	n.a.	n.a.	789	239	2,143	(993)
1976/77	537	826	n.a.	n.a.	884	246	2,318	(778)
1977/78	532	864	n.a.	n.a.	906	362	2,056	(702)
1978/79	531	1,005	n.a.	n.a.	889	240	1,939	(650)
1979/80	527	856	10,690	2,843	860[b]	199	1,864	(631)
1980/81	524	664	n.a.	n.a.	899	217	1,817	(610)
1981/82	520	674	n.a.	n.a.	996	279	1,919	(625)
1982/83	516	600	n.a.	n.a.	686	192	1,865	(831)
1983/84	511	487	n.a.	n.a.	221	228	1,767	(833)

[a]Figures in parentheses are full-time unregistered University graduates who were very likely incremental probationers.

[b]Speaking in the Dail on 24 June 1980 the Minister reported 10,690 registered incremental teachers. This implies only 780 probationers on incremental salaries, also 2,843 unregistered. FTE: Full-time Equivalent of Part-time Teachers.

*1932/33 1,440 Registered; 1,235 Unregistered. 1942/43 1,927 Registered; 1,430 Unregistered.

Source: Department of Education Statistics Reports.

600 in 1969/70. It also documents the slow decline to 1962 in the number of schools which failed to reach the 100 pupil enrolment level though the number of schools with less than 150 pupils was rising. The figure also records the dramatic impact on school size of the "free" scheme in 1967. By 1972/73 school statistics were reclassified to cater for the growing number of schools with enrolment in excess of 800. Few schools now have less than 150 pupils.

The small size of the schools, plentiful religious vocations and inadequate State funding led to many unregistered teachers being employed in secondary schools. To become registered at present a teacher must possess both a University degree and a Higher Diploma in Education and also have spent a minimum of a full year's teaching at 18 hours per week. Table 88 reproduces the Department's annual record of new registrations. In the 'fifties details were also published of the total number of registered teachers, which was a greater total than the total for registered teachers currently employed, as two examples will show:

Year	Total Roll	Actually teaching	% teaching
1949/50	3,140	2,334	74
1954/55	3,930	2,615	67

Unregistered teachers were a fairly numerous group among those actually teaching. In the early 'fifties they numbered 39 per cent of all teachers and were about the same proportion at the onset of the "free secondary" education in the late 'sixties. Lack of published records prevents us knowing the extent by which they may have declined since then. They were still 32 per cent when the last figures were published in 1973/74.[39]

One important element among the unregistered teachers are those University graduates seeking to build up their year's experience prior to registration. Their numbers are given in Table 88, together with the number of those newly registered and provide an indicator of potential inflows into teaching employment. Apart from these probationers it is immediately apparent from Table 88 that the bulk of the remaining unregistered teachers are part time. Unregistered full-time non-incremental teachers are probably teachers surplus to the school's quota and who take some classes. The high numbers after the introduction of the free scheme may represent a temporary problem of adjustment.

Of more immediate interest to this subject are the teachers on incremental salaries and therefore paid directly by the State. These are recorded in Table 89 which distinguishes male and female as well as religious and lay. Incremental teachers are those which the department recognises in accordance with the quotas laid down for pupil-teacher ratios. Part-time and non-incremental teachers are additional to the schools' normal staff entitlements. The basic

[39]On the basis of a statement in the Dail on 24 June 1980 they would appear to have been 21 per cent in 1979/80.

Table 89: *Numbers of teachers and pupils in secondary schools 1949/50–1983/84*

Year	Pupils enrolled*	Total staff	"Incremental" teachers					Non-incremental	PTR
			Total	Men	Women	Religious	Lay		
1949/50	47,065	3,844	2,152	1,136	1,016	n.a.	n.a.	1,692	21.9
1950/51	48,559	3,929	2,219	1,160	1,059	n.a.	n.a.	1,710	21.9
1951/52	50,179	4,043	2,291	1,177	1,114	n.a.	n.a.	1,752	21.9
1952/53	52,151	4,170	2,359	1,213	1,146	n.a.	n.a.	1,811	22.1
1953/54	54,019	4,097	2,391	1,238	1,153	n.a.	n.a.	1,706	22.6
1954/55	56,411	4,417	2,478	1,250	1,228	n.a.	n.a.	1,939	22.8
1955/56	59,306	4,564	2,600	1,330	1,270	n.a.	n.a.	1,964	22.8
1956/57	62,429	4,739	2,701	1,383	1,318	n.a.	n.a.	2,038	23.1
1957/58	66,221	4,957	2,814	1,453	1,361	n.a.	n.a.	2,143	23.5
1958/59	69,568	5,032	2,955	1,522	1,433	n.a.	n.a.	2,077	23.5
1959/60	73,431	5,178	3,086	1,583	1,503	n.a.	n.a.	2,092	23.8
1960/61	76,843	5,282	3,234	1,660	1,574	n.a.	n.a.	2,048	23.8
1961/62	80,400	5,630	3,381	1,644	1,737	n.a.	n.a.	2,249	23.8
1962/63	84,916	5,908	3,581	1,847	1,734	n.a.	n.a.	2,327	23.7
1963/64	89,205	6,161	3,734	1,888	1,846	n.a.	n.a.	2,427	23.9
1964/65	92,989	6,477	3,992	2,024	1,968	n.a.	n.a.	2,485	23.3
1965/66	98,667	6,795	4,253	2,161	2,092	2,033	2,220	2,542	23.2
1966/67	103,558	7,248	4,461	2,245	2,216	2,035	2,426	2,787	23.2
1967/68	118,807	8,165	4,838	2,476	2,362	2,131	2,707	3,327	24.6
1968/69	133,591	9,130	6,099	n.a.	n.a.	2,278	3,821	3,031	21.9
1969/70	144,425	9,603	6,768	n.a.	n.a.	2,396	4,372	2,835	21.3
1970/71	150,642	10,233	7,272	n.a.	n.a.	2,349	4,923	2,961	20.7
1971/72	157,234	10,704	8,016	n.a.	n.a.	2,418	5,598	2,688	19.6
1972/73	162,161	11,250	8,603	n.a.	n.a.	2,495	6,108	2,647	18.8
1973/74	167,309	12,076	9,181	n.a.	n.a.	2,500	6,681	2,895	18.2
1974/75	173,188	11,798	9,431	n.a.	n.a.	2,386	7,045	2,367	18.4
1975/76	182,639	12,212	9,830	n.a.	n.a.	2,375	7,455	2,382	18.6
1976/77	189,445	12,740	10,176	n.a.	n.a.	2,337	7,839	2,564	18.6
1977/78	192,977	13,248	10,830	4,927	5,903	2,341	8,489	2,418	17.8
1978/79	196,606	13,407	11,228	5,105	6,123	2,256	8,972	2,179	17.5
1979/80	199,193	13,533	11,470	5,214	6,256	2,168	9,302	2,063	17.4
1980/81	201,093	13,774	11,740	5,304	6,436	2,106	9,634	2,034	17.1
1981/82	204,392	14,094	11,896	5,364	6,532	2,016	9,880	2,198	17.2
1982/83	206,413	14,122	12,065	5,430	6,635	1,939	10,126	2,057	17.1
1983/84	209,197	13,895	11,900	5,389	6,511	1,882	10,018	1,995	17.6

Note: PTR (Pupil Teacher Ratio) is based on incremental teachers only.

Source: Statistical Reports of Department of Education.

*Beginning of school year. Slightly lower number would apply in February.

criteria are laid down in the various schedules which also provides for principals, vice principals, guidance and remedial teachers.

Pupil-Teacher Ratios in Secondary Schools

The schedules governing PTRs in secondary school are few. Between 1963 and 1972 the arrangement was to provide a teacher for every 15 pupils with the headmaster outside the quota. For small schools, and most schools were small, this could mean very low ratios indeed, e.g., a school of 80 pupils was entitled to 7 including the headmaster. In practice the allowance was too generous and for a variety of reasons only 10 per cent of schools availed themselves of it. In April 1972 the ratio was raised to 17:1 but in August it was again raised to 20:1. By this arrangement apart from the headmaster a school of less than 35 pupils was entitled to another and from then on up an additional teacher for every twenty pupils. A guidance teacher was provided for schools of 300 or more pupils. A school of 80 was now entitled to 5 all told. Pupil-teacher ratios again tended to rise with school size — a school of 200 got 10 teachers apart from the head. This arrangement is currently in operation since Autumn 1983 with provision for a vice principal once 200 pupils have enrolled and a guidance teacher after 500 enrolments. However between August 1977 and 1983 a target of 19:1 operated whereby one teacher additional to the head operated for under 34 pupils and additional teachers were paid for every additional 18 enrolments. The guidance teacher was provided after the school reached a size of 250.

Table 89 gives the calculated PTR based on the number of teachers on incremental salaries. This method of calculation corresponds with that used to answer a Dail Question on 26 May 1982. However, Table 89 also shows that there were many teachers not on incremental salaries and many were part time. If recent relationships between part-time and whole-time posts held in earlier years then PTRs can be calculated as follows:

	Pupils	All teachers in full time equivalents	PTRs
1950	47,065	3,114	15.1
1955	56,411	3,545	15.9
1960	73,431	4,212	17.4
1970	144,425	8,251	17.5
1980	199,193	12,300	16.2
1983	205,730	12,896	16.0

It is, of course, true that these lower ratios are not the result of public funding entirely and do not reflect public policy.

In 1973 teaching hours of a full-time staff member could range from 18 to 26. An attempt by the Department to reduce the range was resisted by the teachers who sought instead a maximum of 22 hours. Such a range in teaching hours meant that in many cases pupil hours per week were greater than teacher hours. Pupil numbers need to be weighted to recognise this factor. Non-teaching posts, such as Principal, are another aspect of the equation. For these reasons the PRT needs to be treated with circumspection, quite apart from the other difficulties raised in the section on primary teachers. Some other relevant factors would be the subject taught — e.g., science might require more pupil-teacher contact — and also the aptitude of the pupils. Pupils from disadvantaged backgrounds, e.g., marital breakdown, might need more attention than others. Even when allowance is made for all these it is important not to make a fetish of lowering the PTRs. Research evidence on class size, etc., does not support the view that smaller classes on their own make a significant contribution to the quality of instruction and its absorption by the pupils.

COMPREHENSIVE AND COMMUNITY SCHOOLS

The first comprehensive school was opened in 1966 and the last in 1974. In 1973 the first Community school was opened. Thus, they are a relatively new innovation in Irish education. "They are effectively state schools which offer both 'arts' and vocational courses and they have features of both secondary and vocational schools" (Tussing, p. 29). Comprehensive schools resemble British schools of the same name except that they are specifically denominational. Since 1974 Community schools are more favoured as the school of the future. These are organised in two ways: Community Colleges run by the VECs and Community Schools which have significant representation of religious orders on the board. Some Community schools have resulted from the amalgamation of existing secondary and vocational schools.

Details of pupils and teacher employment are set out in Table 90. A curious feature of these schools is that they employ more male teachers than female though the balance is tending to be equated. They also employ increasing numbers of religious.

The PTR teacher ratios of these schools are intended to be in between those of secondary and vocational schools since they share features of both. It is not clear why the official calculations exclude the full-time equivalents of part-time teachers since such data are available. If they were included the PTR of 1981/82 would be reduced to 15:1. In interpreting these ratios the caveats referred to in the section on secondary teachers hold.

Table 90: *Numbers of teachers and pupils in Comprehensive (A) and Community (B) schools 1966/67–1983/84*

Academic Year	Number of schools		Pupils in attendance	Full-time teachers					Part-time teachers		PTR
				Total	B.Schools	Men	Women	Religious	Total	FTE	
	A	B									
1966/67	3	—	820	45		31	14	8	7		18.2
1967/68	4	—	986	60		39	21	8	8		16.4
1968/69	4	—	1,320	86		56	30	10	14		15.3
1969/70	4	—	1,473	97		63	34	10	8		15.2
1970/71	6	—	1,652	109		70	39	15	18		15.2
1971/72	9	—	2,971	182		114	68	20	31		16.3
1972/73	12	3	5,243	311	(58)	185	126	19	66		16.9
1973/74	14	12	9,964	617	(261)	372	245	56	87		16.2
1974/75	14	16	13,391	845	(443)	489	356	80	104	(36)	15.9
1975/76	14	18	15,569	976	(532)	544	432	77	103	(36)	16.0
1976/77	14	20	17,843	1,065	(607)	587	478	81	96	(34)	16.8
1977/78	15	24	20,299	1,239	(756)	685	554	94	131	(46)	16.4
1978/79	15	26	22,356	1,398	(896)	780	618	113	123	(54)	16.0
1979/80	15	30	24,612	1,545	(1041)	850	695	121	163	(80)	15.9
1980/81	15	34	26,841	1,684	(1153)	927	757	123	185	(91)	15.9
1981/82	15	38	29,568	1,856	(1318)	1,009	847	138	208	(101)	15.9
1982/83	15	41	32,207	2,021	(1480)	1,091	930	145	228	(n.a.)	15.9
1983/84	15	42	34,752	2,112	(1591)	1,131	981	148	n.a.	(n.a.)	16.5

Source: Department of Education Statistical Reports.
PTR: Pupil Teacher Ratio, mainly from Dail Debates, 26 May 1982 are based on full-time teachers only.

VOCATIONAL EDUCATION

As set out in the background section it is clear that the major breakthrough in technical education occurred at the turn of the century. Previously some schools had benefited from grants given by the Department of Science and Art in South Kensington by offering science and art subjects. These were the Metropolitan and Municipal Schools of Art, the Limerick School of Art, the Crawford and Kevin Street Technical Institutions and the Mechanics Institutes at Dublin, Cork and Clonmel, all founded at different times during the nineteenth century. Apart from these, schools preparing candidates for the British armed forces examinations gave courses in pneumatics, hydraulics, ballistics and other military sciences.

The two factors that revolutionised the situation were the establishment of the county councils in 1898 and their power to levy rates for technical education.

The second was another Act of the same year which led to the creation of the Department of Agriculture and Technical Education the following year. This new Department now took over the South Kensington schemes. As a result 65 technical schools had been set up by 1925.

The Vocational Education Act of 1930 forms the basis of the modern system. The Act replaced the Technical Instruction Committees with 38 Vocational Education Committees which were to run vocational schools, i.e., schools which combined both technical and continuation education. These schools included 10 trades preparatory schools. McElligott chartered the subsequent expansion in both schools and pupil numbers as follows:

	Schools	Pupils
1931/32	70	7,925[40]
1941/42	183	14,184
1951/52	208	21,753
1961/62	294	27,124

In his presentation of pupils he only gives the numbers engaged in full-time continuation courses of 20 hours or more per week and so differs somewhat from the data presented later. If whole-time technical courses were included 1,201 more pupils, or 4 per cent, would be added to the 1961/62 total.

One of the difficulties in drafting the 1930 Act was the fear among Church leaders that these new vocational (rather than technical) courses would lead to competition with secondary schools and the system was drafted to allay such fears. While it is interesting to note that 96 per cent of all full-time courses were other than in technical courses in 1961/62 they were none the less a dead end with no link with further education and so placated clerical opposition. The latter was further mollified by providing clerical representation on the VECs to run schools which were totally State-funded. Pupils recognised the limitations of the education provided. For example of the 2,609 scholarships awarded for second-level studies by local authorities in 1960, only 17 were taken up in VEC schools. The general shake up of second-level education in the 'sixties changed the picture dramatically.

The change in attitude towards the role of vocational schools took two forms. One was to involve the schools in secondary education. The rather abrupt decision to launch free second-level education in 1967 meant that secondary courses had to be offered in vocational schools, both to cater for increased demand and also to meet the needs where secondary schools were thin on the ground. The second approach would tend to counter this development by enhancing the status of non-academic education. To do so effectively seemed unlikely as long as

[40]McElligott gives 22,336 as the total number of pupils attending Technical Schools in 1926.

a social stigma was perceived to attach to the old "Tech". The answer chosen was to develop new forms of school which would aim at avoiding the exclusively academic orientation of secondary schools. The first stage in the process anticipated the free scheme and opted for comprehensive schools. Later community schools and colleges came to be preferred by policy makers and proved very popular with students and parents.

To open up the entire vocational approach to third-level opportunities, which had been heretofore concentrated in the nine colleges of technology, the year which saw the free scheme also saw the first of the Regional Technical Colleges open their doors. These developments were strengthened when the Dublin colleges pooled their resources to form the Dublin Institute of Technology in 1978. The work of the Vocatonal Education Committees in technical education was ably complemented by two state sponsored National Institutes of Higher Education, first at Limerick and later in Dublin. Another initiative, not under the aegis of the VECs, occurred in 1967 when AnCO assumed responsibility for industrial training from An Ceard Comhairle.

Table 91 summarises developments between 1950/51 and 1973/74 inclusive when a new format changed the basis on which pupil records were available. Earlier we noted the rise in the number of permanent schools since 1931/32 as recorded by McElligott. Table 91 also relates to permanent vocational schools. For many years the number of other venues, where instruction was given, was also recorded, e.g., 621 places in 1953/54. These locations are not to be confused with schools, not under VEC control, where instruction was financially assisted under the provisions of section 109 of the 1930 Act. These will be considered later. Numbers of permanent schools continued to rise up to the eve of the free second-level education scheme which coincided with the opening of the first of the comprehensives in 1966. When the building of comprehensives in turn gave way to the community schools, which were a joint venture between VECs and the religious orders, amalgamations and closures were frequently the order of the day. For example in 1977/78 two VEC schools with 420 pupils took this path. Even so by 1981/82 the number of schools, 263, was not very different from the level in 1973/74. The fact that there were the alternative forms of second-level education needs to be kept in mind in studying the trend in this and subsequent tables. It should also be noted that schools under the control of the VECs include not only the ordinary vocational schools but also schools of art, music and domestic science as well as day trades preparatory schools. The VECs also control nine third level colleges described in the statistics as vocational technological and the nine regional technical colleges (RTCs).

Table 91 also indicates that vocational schools traditionally employed a very large number of part-time teachers. For example, 698 full time and 598 part time taught in 98 schools in 1932. In 1950/51 full-time staff were only 10 per cent

Table 91: *Numbers of teachers and pupils in schools under the Control of the Vocational Education Committees 1950/51–1973/74*

| Academic Year | No. of schools | Teachers | | Pupils Enrolments of whom | | | |
		Full time	Part time(FTE)	Full time	technical	Part time(FSE)	Total
1950/51	198	1,125	1,021	18,042	n.a.	67,511(6,280)	85,553
1951/52	208	1,193	1,004	19,011	n.a.	68,795	87,806
1952/53	227	1,239	1,061	20,306	526	67,210	87,516
1953/54	228	1,332	1,121	20,466	534	70,500	90,966
1954/55	245	1,363	1,185	20,895	596	69,882	90,777
1955/56	252	1,427	1,192	21,336	556	73,170	94,506
1956/57	260	1,487	1,119	22,491	705	66,133	88,624
1957/58	267	1,537	1,121	23,816	855	61,928	85,744
1958/59	272	1,574	1,228	24,604	929	64,055	88,659
1959/60	279	1,606	1,446(304)	26,322	954	65,965(5,525)	92,287
1960/61	289	1,661	1,560(331)	27,150	1,060	64,927(5,378)	92,077
1961/62	294	1,750	1,641(347)	28,325	1,201	68,576(5,756)	96,901
1962/63	298	1,826	1,896(387)	29,689	1,557	71,735(5,484)	101,424
1963/64	308	1,958	1,996(427)	32,374	1,703	67,595(5,552)	99,969
1964/65	328	2,112	2,103(478)	34,756	1,670	69,567(5,915)	104,323
1965/66	342	2,340	2,287(500)	37,520	2,288	68,222(5,713)	105,742
1966/67	327	2,445	2,276(468)	40,174	2,209	60,461(5,459)	100,635
1967/68	303	2,753	2,456(582)	45,242	2,256	58,718(5,685)	103,960
1968/69	271	3,168	2,740	50,080	2,676	63,352(6,185)	113,432
1969/70	275	3,488	2,879	52,374	2,780	71,006(6,705)	123,380
1970/71	277	3,791	2,835	56,624	3,168	74,031(7,761)	130,655
1971/72	275	4,147	2,955	62,087	4,014	72,355(7,238)	134,442
1972/73	275	4,476	2,978	65,624	5,228	78,676	144,300
1973/74	267	4,675	3,010	69,399	5,585	80,281	149,680

Source: Department of Education Statistical Reports.

Number of schools includes schools of art, music and domestic science as well as day trades preparatory schools. They also include third-level technological colleges and Regional Technical Colleges.

Number of pupils is based on the number of individuals who enrolled for one or more course classified by their main course. Full time means courses of 25 to 30 hours weekly lasting the full course (40 weeks). Part time includes day release courses for apprentices, other day and evening courses.

FTE/FSE: Full-time equivalents for teachers and full-time student equivalents were calculated by reference to the teaching hours or attendance hours in each year of full-time staff and full-time students.

more numerous than part timers. This circumstance is due to the very varied nature of the instruction provided. In addition to full time continuation or technical courses of 25 to 30 hours a week, which last the full course, there were day release classes for apprentices, evening classes confined to specific pupils as well as miscellaneous day and evening courses, including adult education. No full time equivalent (FTE) figures for part timers has been published prior to 1976. However, between 1959/60 and 1967/68 teaching hours were published for both full-time and part-time staff. Teaching hours for full timers were 901 in 1959/60 and 848 in 1967/68, i.e., from 22.5 to 21 teaching hours weekly. If these are taken as the norm, part time inputs were fairly close to 0.21 FTE in each of the nine years calculated.

Students faced a great variety of course options, which included full-time day courses stressing continuation or technical instruction, day release courses for apprentices, other day courses and evening classes, some of which were confined to special groups of students. Early statistics recorded each enrolment separately so that four numbers described different aspects of the one course. For example in 1950/51 day courses lasting 20 hours or more were recorded as follows:

Total enrolments	19,377
Average enrolments	14,912
Average attendance	12,254
Individuals enroled	18,042

without any clear definition of the differences in some cases. As these figures stand, a high degree of non-attendance would appear to be suggested.

One of the purposes of vocational education would appear to be to cater for non-academic and technical instruction. Table 91 shows a small proportion of full-time students taking mainly technical courses. These have been described as those of architect, dietician, hotel cook, mechanical engineer, artist, etc., and would appear to have a large third-level component. If, however, instead we use the statistical series, published up to 1973/74, which gave total enrolments and average attendance at full-time technical courses, much higher figures are obtained. For example:

	Total Enrolment	Average Attendance
1952/53	740	564
1956/57	1,047	705
1960/61	1,476	1,134
1963/64	3,906	3,063
1966/67	4,572	3,554
1967/68	11,407	9,402
1970/71	12,015	10,166
1973/74	21,548	19,716

Given the variety of courses and their differing durations one way to calculate full-time student equivalents would be to take the attendance hours published up to 1971/72 for each type of course and divide them by attendance hours at full-time courses. The latter varied between 732 in 1960/61 and 824 in 1967/68. The results are given in Table 91 and indicate that 12 part timers were a student equivalent for seven years, after which the ratio came down to 10 to one. The difficulty with this approach is the use of attendance hours. Presumably teachers are allocated on the basis of enrolments. If attendance records for part-time and evening classes are poorer than for full-time classes this variability would play havoc with the calculation of pupil teacher ratios (PTR). Another difficulty with such calculations arises from the fact that different PTRs would be appropriate for different types of instruction. Presumably continuation classes would be less demanding than technical and second level less demanding than third level. For most of the records these different types of instruction are not clearly distinguished.

Second and Third-Level Education at VEC Schools

Several of the institutions, which the Department of Agriculture and Technical Institute inherited from the nineteenth century, have subsequently became the third-level wing of the Vocation Education Committees' activies. Currently there are nine such institutions, which we shall describe loosely as technological colleges. The six, which come from the City of Dublin VEC, have recently come together as the Dublin Institute of Technology. These are the Colleges of Catering (Cathal Brugha St.), Commerce (Rathmines), Marketing and Design (Parnell Square) and Music (Chatham Row) and the two Collegers of Technology (Bolton St. and Kevin St.). Through a partnership agreement with Trinity College, graduates of professional level courses are eligible for degrees of Dublin University. Outside Dublin are the Limerick College of Art, Commerce and Technology, the Crawford School of Art in Cork and the Killybegs Hotel (technical) college. The foundation of the Regional Technical Colleges added a further nine to this group commencing in 1968.

From 1972/73 the Department of Education has listed the number of VEC schools which provided "general courses at second level" and those which provided third-level courses. This would not appear to be a complete listing of possibilities since at least 2 (and probably 3) schools in 1981/82 provided neither. Presumably these were second-level schools of art and music. The statistics counted a school twice if it provided both. The records were as follows:

	All schools	General second level	Third level	of which RTCs	Overlap
1972/73	275	261	24	7	10
1973/74	267	254	24	7	11
1974/75	269	250	23	8	4
1975/76	267	248	23	8	4
1976/77	267	248	21	8	2
1977/78	266	247	21	9	2
1978/79	267	248	20	9	2
1979/80	267	246	20	9	-1
1980/81	262	242	19	9	-1
1981/82	263	243	18	9	-2
1982/83	265	245	18	9	-2
1983/84	268	248	18	9	-2

These figures show a general tendency for schools to specialise in either second- or third-level studies.

Table 92 shows the rising popularity of senior level continuation classes after their introduction into vocational schools in 1967 and the tendency for junior level courses to remain on a plateau over the last decade. Regional Technical Colleges' involvement with second level was there from the beginning when more second-level students enrolled than third level. This was an emergency measure to meet the temporary shortage of second-level places in some localities. By October 1979 general courses in RTCs had ceased and secretarial courses were greatly reduced. Since October 1977 a small number of second-level students have been catered for at Vocational Technological Colleges.

Similar data on teachers were only published ten years later and even then have only referred to the establishment in which the teacher has worked. This is especially unfortunate in the case of RTCs where both second- and third-level courses are taught. On the positive side, part-time teachers have been recorded in terms on full-time equivalents, based on allocations, since 1976/77. Table 93 shows the fairly rapid growth in teaching inputs in recent years.

Pupil-Teacher Ratios in VEC Schools

Any attempt to calculate PTRs in VEC schools, which wishes to avoid being misleading, runs up against an even greater number of difficulties than those commented on in relation to secondary schools. Part of these difficulties relate to the length of the student's week compared to that of teachers. In general it would appear that 24 hours is deemed a full-time job and 800 hours annually the full-time equivalent for part time teaching, though actual full-time teachers may teach more. Full-time students have been traditionally defined as engaged in courses for "25 to 30 hours a week lasting the full session" (of 35 weeks) though

Table 92: *Second and third level students in VEC schools and colleges, 1965 to 1983*

	Second level								Third level	
	Vocational schools					Regional Technical Colleges				
	Continuation								Regional Technical Colleges	Vocational Technological
Date	Total	Junior	Senior	Technical	Other	Total	Technical	Other		
1965 Feb.	30,576	29,613	—	963	—	—	—	—	—	852
1966 Feb.	33,353	32,461	—	892	—	—	—	—	—	1,007
1967 Feb.	36,740	35,796	—	944	—	—	—	—	—	1,067
1968 Feb.	41,170	37,601	2,294	1,275	—	—	—	—	—	1,202
1969 Feb.	43,595	42,361		1,234	—	—	—	—	—	1,449
1970 Feb.	45,671	44,306		1,365	—	—	—	—	—	1,704
1971 Feb.	50,345	49,897		448	—	278	n.a.	n.a.	194	2,128
1972 Feb.	54,162	53,744		418	—	529	n.a.	n.a.	590	2,447
1973 Feb.	57,892	48,222	4,991	461	4,218	560	75	485	1,214	2,707
1974 Feb.	59,034	48,927	5,757	353	3,997	526	160	366	1,600	2,907
1974 Oct.	63,850	50,577	7,756	340	5,177	482	119	363	2,694	2,561
1975 Oct.	66,852	50,558	10,112	447	5,735	863	318	545	3,234	3,097
1976 Oct.	68,572	50,319	11,232	775	6,246	832	279	553	3,523	3,313
1977 Oct.	68,498	49,301	10,693	559	7,945*	739	280	459	3,753	3,309(133)
1978 Oct.	68,120	48,424	10,853	450	8,393	716	202	514	4,274	3,337(631)
1979 Oct.	67,149	47,532	11,139	406	8,072	502	270	232†	4,945	3,937(111)
1980 Oct.	68,811	47,925	11,681	819	8,386	472	383	89	5,965	4,945(192)
1981 Oct.	72,197	48,880	13,264	516	9,537	324	194	130	7,119	5,384(340)
1982 Oct.	74,810	49,625	14,807	570	9,808	238	189	49	8,493	5,921(438)
1983 Oct.	76,916	50,253	15,956	514	10,193	418	366	52	9,107	6,459(113)

Source: Department of Education Statistical Reports.

Note: Figures in parentheses are second-level students not included in VT total. Higher Technician courses in Bolton Street were deemed second level before 1971 but reclassified as third level from 1971 on. A small number of third-level students in Vocational Schools are also omitted.

*Before 1977 Secretarial only: From 1977 on, also pre-employment courses.

†No general courses from this on, only secretarial.

Table 93: *Teachers and pupils in schools and colleges under VEC control 1974/75–1983/84*

	Teachers in						Students		
	Vocational Schools		RTCs		Technology Colleges				
	FT	FTE	FT	FTE	FT	FTE	Full time	Part time	Total
1974/75	4,069	n.a.	543	n.a.	488	n.a.	69,587	77,281	146,868
1975/76	4,279	n.a.	647	n.a.	516	n.a.	74,046	91,752	165,798
1976/77	4,324	467	674	63	534	141	76,240	108,171	184,411
1977/78	4,463	645	710	83	550	181	76,557	108,099	184,656
1978/79	4,580	638	810	56	691	162	77,106	112,508	189,614
1979/80	4,633	678	887	73	642	336	76,674	115,149	191,823
1980/81	4,790	602	1,026	65	659	402	80,411	127,033	207,444
1981/82	4,868	775	970	206	719	396	85,364	137,092	222,456*
1982/83	4,912	781	1,058	74	775	188	89,900	125,125	215,025
1983/84	4,922	532	1,077	80	838	160	93,175	n.a.	n.a.

Source: Department of Education Statistical Reports.
Note: Allocations for 1983/84 and 1984/85 in Vocational Schools were 5,612 and 5,697 FTEs. Estimates for actual employment at third level in August 1984 (i.e., end 1983/84) are 2,111 of which 241 were FTE.
*Data for Rathmines College of Commerce were not furnished.

recent reports offer no definition. Part of the difficulties lies in the heterogeneity of students at both second- and third-levels and the absence of any statistics by which to relate particular teachers to particular students. Are any adult education classes taken by full-time teachers or apprenticeship courses by part-time teachers etc? Although teachers are classified by the type of institution in which they teach, pupils other than full time, are not classified on an institutional basis but by the type of course they attended. Full-time equivalents are available for teachers but not for students. It is regrettable that teaching and attendance hours are no longer published.

One way to tackle the problem would be to examine the schedule for teacher allocation as was done for secondary teachers. However, in the case of third-level institutions allocations are negotiated rather than based on rigid formulae. In the case of second-level teachers' schedules existed until recently when a system of allocations according to bands was introduced. Thus in July 1972 a ratio of 17.5:1 was selected for Junior, Senior and Secretarial courses, exclusive of the principal and vice-principal. Guidance teachers were available for schools with 300 or more students. Special allocation arrangements were made for woodwork, metalwork and building construction classes. The following year the threshold for a guidance teacher was reduced to 250 students. Eight hundred hours of apprenticeship or adult education justified the employment of a full-time teaching equivalent. In August 1977 the ratio was reduced to 16.5 and provisions were made for remedial teachers. In the latter case the full employment programme made 200 remedial teachers available subsequently and these were allocated to second-level institutions on the basis of recommendations for the Department's psychologist. In 1981 the ratio was applied to newly established pre-employment classes. In 1983/84 the thresholds for vice-principals and guidance teachers became 250 and 500, respectively, and a band from 17 to 19 was applied to the bigger schools and community colleges.

Departmental calculations of PTRs for second-level students are based on full-time teachers and full-time students. Data were given in the Dail on 26 May 1982:

1972/73	15.9	1978/79	14.9
1973/74	15.6	1979/80	14.5
1974/75	15.7	1980/81	14.4
1975/76	15.6	1981/82	14.8
1976/77	15.9	1982/83	15.2
1977/78	15.3		

Financial difficulties seem to have put the ratio back towards its 1977 level.

Regional technical colleges teach both second- and third-level students. If full-time teachers were divided among the full-time students, ratios were obtained varying between 5.8 and 6.5 for academic years since 1974/75. To correct this finding the Department of Education calculated the equivalent whole-time numbers of technical students (EWTS) and technical teachers (EWTT) for three years, reckoning apprentice figures by dividing block release populations by three and day release students by five. Other part-time pupils were also converted to EWTS. The results were:

	EWT Students	*EWT Teachers*	*PTR*
1977/78	6,700	789.52	8.48
1978/79	7,415	854.09	8.68
1979/80	7,809	948.91	8.22

Similar calculations were not available for the Technological Colleges. The division of full-time staff into full-time students gave results rather similar to those obtained for RTCs though in recent years a divergence occurred. In 1981/82 the PTR was 8.0. The colleges, however, in that year had part-time inputs 55 per cent again of the full-time staff. It is, therefore, difficult to escape the conclusion that in third-level VEC Colleges PTRs were considerably more favourable than in their equivalent courses at Universities, etc. Even so, total costs per pupil at £1,470 in 1981 were considerably below University levels — £1,881 to 2,089 — possibly because of the much lower levels of ancillary staffing.

Career Guidance and Remedial Teachers

At the time in 1972 when it was decided to increase the PTR of secondary schools from 15:1 to 20:1 allocations were made for career guidance teachers to mitigate in part the change. These were additional to the normal quotas and are included in the teacher counts at the different second-level schools. In 1981/82 secondary schools had 363 such posts filled, VECs 102,[41] Community schools 30 and Comprehensives 14. The previous year 174 schools were without such teachers. As part of the full employment programme 200 *ex quota* posts of remedial teachers were offered to second-level schools and allocated on the basis of the Departmental assessment of priority needs. At first level these teachers were already referred to in the section on special education.

OTHER SECOND-LEVEL SCHOOLS

These schools belong to two categories — those aided by the Department of Education and those aided by other departments. In 1982/83 five schools belonged to the former category as far as Departmental statisics were concerned. One of these was the sole surviving preparatory college run by the Church of Ireland — Colaiste Moibhi. As this college shares staff with that Church's training college it will be treated with the training colleges below. The departmental statistics also distinguish two VEC colleges — The Irish-Swiss Institute of Horology at Blanchardstown, Co. Dublin, which is a joint venture of the VECs with the Swiss watch industry — the latter contributing 4/17 of the costs. This Institute receives a separate allocation in the department vote. The other college is the Dun Laoghaire College of Art and Design. It would appear that staff in both these colleges have already been included in the VEC returns.

While the departmental statistics name two other colleges, the departmental section dealing with the matter lists five. These are colleges funded under Section 109 of the Vocational Education Act of 1930. Four colleges are funded in relation to courses in home economics and one in relation to a secretarial course. These two sets of colleges are separately identified in the departmental votes. The departmental statistics identifies two:—

St. Joseph's Residential College of Home Economics, Carrick-on-Suir and

St. Anne's Residential College of Home Economics, Sion Hill, Blackrock, Co. Dublin.

[41]124 posts were allocated.

The other three are presumably excluded as being already counted in the departmental statitics.[42] They were:—

St. Angela's College of Home Economics, Sligo

and

St. Mary's College of Home Economics, Dunmanway

and in the other case:—

Alexandra College of Secretarial Training.

The method of financing these colleges is complex, based on pupil hours in each roll book corrected for typical weeks. Home Economics' grants were 37.5p per pupil hour with the probability of a 10 per cent supplement for special merit. Alexandra received 24p per hour without a special merit supplement.

In 1983/84 grants were paid in respect of courses given by 45 teachers in the Home Economics Colleges[43] and 13 teachers in Alexandra. This would be £1,825 and £1,223 per teacher, respectively. If these are converted to hours at £8.30 per hour (which is below the minimum paid to a regular second-level teacher and very much below the average) we get 220 and 147 hours, respectively. Eight hundred hours represents a full-time equivalent so that we get 12 and 2 FTEs on the basis of the above calculations. In June 1984 two of the schools closed, i.e., St. Anne's, Sion Hill and St. Angela's, Sligo involving 22 teachers averaging £1,263 or 152 hours (0.19 FTE). This was equivalent to a reducation of 4 teachers.

Schools aided by the Department of Defence are the Army Apprenticeship School of Naas and the Air Corps school at Baldonnel. Apart from military and civilian instructors, already included with the Civil Service, both schools are staffed by teachers seconded from the VECs. These 16 teachers are already enumerated under the VEC section.

The remaining twenty schools in 1982/83 were all funded by the Department of Agriculture. Five of them were administered directly by the Department viz. Mellowes College, Athenry, Ballyhaise, Clonakilty, Kildalton Agricultural and Horticultural College, Piltown, Co. Kilkenny, all of which were transferred to a State-sponsored body ACOT. The fifth was the Botanic Gardens School which did not transfer. Previously this group also included the Munster Institute, now part of University College, Cork, and formerly part of the 1838 national school system. These five schools can be disregarded since their staff were included with the Civil Service or more recently with a semi-State body.

---

[42]Until recently Beaufort College, Rathfarnham, attracted 36 students for its demonstrators' courses recognised by the Department of Education. It is closed for some years and no information was available on how it should be treated within the perspectives of this study.

[43]In a recent year the actual employment was given as 13 full-time and 33 part-time.

There were seven private agricultural colleges located at Mount Bellew, Pallaskenry, Warrenstown, Monaghan, Multyfarnham, Gurteen and Rockwell. Training in Horticulture is provided by the College of Horticulture, Warrenstown and at the Irish Countrywomen's Association College in Termonfeckin. Up to June 1984 there were residential colleges of rural home economics (RHE) and a residential school of domestic science (Dunmanway) offering courses in poultry keeping, dairying and farm home management at Ardagh, Claremorris, Ballinafad, Navan, Portumna and Ramsgrange funded by the Department of Agriculture, to which County Committees of Agriculture also provided scholarships. In 1982 the RHE college at Navan closed and the remainder in 1984.

Employment data are sparse. The figures in Table 94 refer to those staff whose salaries are recouped by ACOT, or earlier by the Department of Agriculture.

Table 94: *Staff at second-level schools funded by the Department of Agriculture 1973–1984*

	Private Agriculture and Horticultural College		College of Rural Home Economics	
	Teachers	Others	Teachers	Others
1973	54	37	24	
1978 (June)	52	48	25	2
1981 (Jan.)	56	76	24	11
1981 (Sept.)*	57	78	25	11
1982 (Jan.)	57	76	24	11
1983 (Jan.)	61	82	18	9
1984 (Jan.)	61	82	17	9

*Part-time teachers were reported: 1 (Agriculture+Horticulture) and 5 (RHE).

NON-ACADEMIC EMPLOYMENT AT FIRST- AND SECOND-LEVELS

Very little information exists on the non-academic side of employment in first- and second-levels. One important source is the periodic Census of Population but here it is impossible to know to what extent the employees involved can be regarded as being in the public sector. They could belong to the small number of non-grant-aided national schools and would therefore be private workers. They might work for grant-aided national schools but their remuneration be a charge on the parish rather than on central funds. In that case their employment would be a spin-off of State employment but not directly Government-financed jobs. The situation is more complex in the secondary sector because of the greater numbers of secondary schools which did not opt to join the "free scheme" and which are therefore partially financed by fees. Some schools have a boarding section. In the secondary scheme as a whole very few attend schools which are totally non-aided in contrast to the situation at primary level. Employees in fee-paying grant-aided secondary schools may or may not be State employees or rather State financed. In any event their jobs are at least a spin-off of Government financing.

Table 95 summarises the data in the Censuses of Population for primary and secondary schools. Non-academics are clearly more significant in terms of total employment in secondary schools, being 15 per cent of the total in 1981. It is unfortunate that we cannot discover how many of these are State funded.

Table 95: *Occupations of persons engaged in primary and secondary education as recorded in the Census of Population of 1966, 1971 and 1981*

Occupation	Primary			Secondary		
	1966	1971	1981	1966	1971	1981
Gardener	21	45	—	58	110	105
Maintenance, etc.	29	32	35	82	156	204
Clerks and Typists	28	39	190	36	107	581
Housekeepers, Cooks, Maids, etc.	156	219	156	667	821	1,048
Cleaners, Caretakers, etc.	147	149	444	121	182	627
Nurses and Professional, etc.	13	6	99	31	41	139
Sub-total	394	490	924	995	1,417	2,704
Teachers and Religious	16,644	17,358	20,048	6,326	9,304	15,562

Note: In 1981 Primary includes Special Schools for delinquents and Residential Homes but excludes Special Schools for the Handicapped. Secondary includes comprehensive (and presumably community schools).

The Census earlier included religious with teachers. It does not distinguish active teachers. Thus the Census figures for primary teachers and religious were about 2,000 higher in 1966 and 1971 compared with teachers recorded by the Department of Education. In1981, however, the figures were much closer — a gap of 700 approximately. In secondary education similar observations held but without the narrowing in 1981. The disparities were greater where only teachers on incremental salaries were considered, i.e., 15,562 versus 11,740.

Bus Drivers, Caretakers, Secretarial and Child-Care Assistants

The rationalisation programme, which closed many small schools, was accompanied by the bussing of the remoter students to larger centres. This development gave rise to a considerable number of jobs as part-time bus drivers, some of which were undertaken by contractors, others by part-time employees. The employment creation involved does not appear to have been recorded.

The full employment programme of 1977/78 introduced some new types of State-financed jobs. Under one innovation, reflected in Table 95, primary and secondary schools employing 25 or more teachers could get a grant for a clerical assistant. This stipulation was later changed to 18 teachers in a single school (or 23 teachers where two schools (e.g., primary and secondary) were combined). The stipulation for a caretaker was 16 teachers (or 20 for a combined school.) These grants have been affected by the retrenchment. Thus, posts vacated will not be filled in the future. The evolution of numbers over time was:

	Caretakers	*Clerical Assistants*
End 1979	192	354
End 1980	289	472
End 1981	314	530
End 1982	336	600
End 1983	334	574
End 1984	317	555
May 1985	313	552

In addition to these, the full employment programme provided for child-care assistants in special schools for the handicapped. Since the end of 1982, 85 were employed. Numbers have been rising since the initial staff of 74 at end 1979 but fluctuated somewhat. These posts are not affected by retrenchment.

A small number is also employed under the Youth Encounter Projects launched as pilot schemes in 1977. These 4 day-centres seek to cater for juvenile delinquents, actual and potential. The full-time staff consist of 3 teachers (one being director) a welfare officer and a community worker. Only the last named have not been enumerated in other sections, e.g., as teachers. The centre also employs 4 women as bean-a-tí, 2 cleaners and some part-time teachers not else-where enumerated. The value of these pilot schemes is currently being assessed with aid from the Van Leer Foundation.

Non-Academic Employment by the VECs

The trends in non-academic employment by the VECs, as revealed by the Census of Population, are less useful since the 1981 Census redefines the category to relate only to second-level vocational education and includes private schools of domestic economy. The figures were:

	1966	1971	1981
Total employment	3,257	4,904	7,124
of which clergy and teachers	2,586	4,071	5,630
Balance	671	833	1,494
Breakdown of balance			
Other professionals,* etc.	35 ⎱ 172	36 ⎱ 228	118 ⎱ 692
Clerks and Typists	137 ⎰	192 ⎰	534 ⎰
Repairers, etc.	85 ⎱ 499	88 ⎱ 605	192 ⎱ 802
Cleaners, maids, caretakers	414 ⎰	517 ⎰	610 ⎰

*Includes "others".

It is difficult to relate the teachers numbers to those produced by the Department of Education since many of the part-time staff might return themselves as teachers under the self declaration nature of the Census. Data on non-academics are available to some extent from other sources for other years and permit a tentative link with the Census material. For this purpose we shall assume that "other professionals" plus "clerks and typists" can be equated with "administrative" while "repairers" plus "cleaners, maids and caretakers" would constitute the maintenance group. If this is so we get the series presented in Table 96. It will be noted that the revised category for 1981 in the Census of Population is too low since it only relates to second-level schools. This can be compared with a Departmental estimate that employment in second-level schools at the end of 1982 was composed of 600 administrative and 1,061 maintenance; that is to say, a total of 1,661 some twenty months after the Census recorded 1,494. A year later the figures were 600 and 1,054, respectively. In March 1984 the total was 1,697.

Table 96: *Non-academic employment by VECs (tentative estimates) 1966–1984*

Date	Administrative	Maintenance	Total
April 1966	172	499	671
April 1971	228	605	833
June 1974	321	n.a.	n.a.
June 1975	357	n.a.	n.a.
June 1976	417	n.a.	n.a.
June 1978	712	1,599	2,311
April 1981*	(692)	(802)	(1,494)
Dec. 1981	839	1,821	2,660
Dec. 1982	846	1,882	2,728
Dec. 1983	796	1,917	2,713

Source: 1966, 1971 and 1981 Census of Population; otherwise, Departmental Records.
*Second level only.

The balance of the end year employment related to staff in RTCs and technological colleges. These third-level employees were classified as:

	1982	1983	1984
Administrative/clerical incl. library staff	256	250	244
Technical staff	254	258 ⎫	(200 part
Maintenance staff	569	561[44] ⎬ 830	time)

The figures for the previous year, i.e., end 1981 identified the RTCs separately so the subsets are not comparable. The figures were:

	Administrative (including librarians)	Maintenance	Total
RTCs	136	463	599
Others	703	1,358	2,061
	839	1,821	2,660

Again a breakdown of the administrative group for January 1981 showed it to be made up of 38 Chief Education Officers, 24 Library Assistants, Education Officers, etc., 207 Clerical Assistants, 358 Clerical Officers and 206 other Administrative and Executive staff.

These employment levels can be related to academic/non-academic ratios in the Universities. The latter had a ratio of 1 : 1.91 in December 1980. For third-level VEC institutions the ratio was 1 : 0.63, less than a third. At second level the VEC ratio of 1 : 0.35 was more than double the level of the very few grant-aided non-teaching posts in secondary schools. As noted already the low ratio at third level may compensate for the VECs high PTR at that level when compared with the Universities.

[44]Of these 219 were part time (mostly cleaners) approximately 200 in 1984.

Chapter V.5

THIRD LEVEL

TRADITIONAL UNIVERSITIES[45]

Introduction

This report is only concerned with third-level education which is pre-dominantly state funded. Accordingly it does not consider the most venerable educational body in the country — the Honorary Society of King's Inns — nor the many professional bodies set up in the nineteenth century which offer profes-sional qualifications without recourse to public funding.

The older of the two universities, Dublin University, which still has only one constituent college, Trinity (TCD), was funded by a grant of confiscated clan territory so that it is a moot point whether it is to be deemed public *ab initio*. The fall in the value of rental income caused the college to seek State aid after World War I. While the inoperative Government of Ireland Act 1920 proposed to pay an annual grant of £30,000, the impecunious Free State Government could only afford £3,000 which was later increased by an additional £2,250 for the medical school. The breakthrough in State funding occurred in 1947 when State support began to be broadly on a par with that enjoyed by the colleges of the National University which, however, did not have income from rents. McElligott (p. 168) documents the change, reproduced in Table 97.

It was only in the academic year 1964/65 when the rapidly growing State grants reached £468,000 that TCD could first be stated to belong unequivocally to the public domain with 52.8 per cent of its current income from State sources.

One factor which inhibited the growth of student members in TCD was the nineteenth century conflict over the recognition of a Catholic University in Dublin which was more or less resolved in 1908. As one of the moves in this con-troversy TCD removed the last vestige of religious tests in 1873 but, since recognition of the Catholic University in Dublin was still withheld, the Catholic

---

[45]For convenience in presentation the modern National Institutes of Higher Education in Dublin and Limerick are discussed under "Technological Universities", etc.

Table 97: *State grants* paid to Universities 1932–1962*

	TCD	UCC	UCD	UCG
	£	£	£	£
1932/33	3,000	41,000	82,000	29,500
1942/43	5,250	40,000	85,000	30,380
1952/53	100,250	100,500	233,224	73,600
1962/63 (a)	225,250	209,000	518,550	161,380
(b)	50,000	—	424,000	32,000

*McElligott excluded Agricultural grants, also grants paid to NUI Maynooth and College of Surgeons.
Note: (a) Normal Grant. (b) Special capital grants, i.e., TCD for repair of buildings; UCD for science block; UCG for accommodation.

hierarchy banned Catholics from attendance. This ban was enforced with varying vigour for a century and was only rescinded in 1970 when the prospects of a merger of TCD and UCD seemed imminent. As a result the Commission on Higher Education noted that 39 per cent of the student body were British as late as 1958.

The origins of the National University go back to 1845, since the establishment of Maynooth fifty years earlier did not lead to a viable university for lay Catholics. In that year two events occurred. One was an attempt by Peel to weaken the agitation for Home Rule by offering wealthier Catholics a Queen's University with colleges at Belfast, Cork and Galway. These were secular colleges since Parliament was unwilling to subsidise Catholic education so soon after Catholic Emancipation. As such they incurred a Catholic boycott. The second event was the founding, by Robert Kane on behalf of the Royal Dublin Society, of a Museum of Irish Industry which, as the College of Science, became part of UCD in 1926.

Public subscription enabled Newman to launch the Catholic University in 1854 but failure to get recognition for any faculty, other than medicine, caused it to limp along though it upgraded some secondary schools and comprised a number of colleges. It was a financial relief when the University Education Act of 1879 gave it a number of fellowships in a new Royal University under its new name of University College, Dublin. The Royal University replaced the Queen's University and had five colleges (Magee had been founded in 1865 by citizens of Derry). Royal University was purely an examining body to which any student could apply wherever he was educated. It is therefore interesting to note that in 1901 only 500 of the 1,779 successful candidates attended any university college.

In 1908 the Irish Universities Act abolished the Royal University and created

two universities out of its constituent colleges — The Queen's University Belfast
and the National University of Ireland (NUI) with constituent colleges at Cork,
Dublin and Galway. In 1910 Maynooth joined NUI as a recognised college and
in 1921 the partition of Ireland put Queen's outside the jurisdiction of the Free
State.

The ferment in education in the early 'sixties produced two major and
influential studies: *Investment in Education* 1966 and the *Reports of the Commission on
Higher Education* 1967. These launched a debate on university reorganisation, of
which the abortive merger proposals were one manifestation. In 1968 a Higher
Education Authority (HEA) was set up as an *ad hoc* body which was made
permanent by an 1971 Act operational from May 1972. Henceforth all State
funding of universities has been channelled through the HEA which has, in
addition, a number of "designated institutions" of third-level status associated
with it. The designations under the Act were:

March 1973 —	Royal College of Surgeons in Ireland and the College of Pharmacy
December 1976 —	The National Council for Educational Awards (NCEA), The National Institutes for Higher Education Limerick (NIHE,L) and Dublin (NIHE,D) and the National College of Art and Design (NCAD)
October 1979 —	The Royal Irish Academy (RIA)
December 1979 —	The Thomond College of Education

None of these designated institutions will be considered in this section, which
concentrates on the traditional universities, including Maynooth which opened
its doors to lay students in 1966. The omission of the Royal College of Surgeons
in Ireland is in recognition of the fact that its annual grant of £18,000 (in recent
years) is relatively so small that its staff cannot be deemed to belong to the public
domain. The National Council for Education Awards is part of the binary
system of Irish higher education in that it promotes technical, industrial,
scientific, technological and commercial education and education in art and
design outside the traditional universities, i.e., in third-level VEC institutions
and in NIHEs. It is best studied in the planned report on State-sponsored bodies,
a consideration which also holds for the HEA itself. The other bodies will be
examined in a later section.

Apart from their constituent colleges the two universities have what are
known as recognised colleges. National University of Ireland has six, which are
linked to NUI via their local University College. Of these the longest-standing is
Maynooth. The Royal College of Surgeons in Ireland joined in 1977. The other
four are colleges of education, formerly called teacher training colleges, all of

which relate to primary teaching. The four include the largest of these colleges: St. Patrick's, Drumcondra, Carysfort College, Blackrock and Mary Immaculate, Limerick who were "recognised" colleges of NUI since 1974 and prepare students for the B.Ed. degree. St. Angela's College of Education for Home Economics, Sligo, was recognised in 1978 and confers a B.Ed (Home Economics) for second-level teaching, through UCG. Dublin University has four "associated" colleges of education. Three relate to primary teaching *viz:* the Church of Ireland College of Education, Rathmines; St. Mary's (Christian Brothers) Marino and Froebel College, Sion Hill. The fourth, St.Catherines's, Sion Hill, trains second-level teachers for the degree of B.Ed. (Home Economics). Employment in these colleges will be considered in a separate section.

The Constituent Colleges Before the HEA Re-organisation

No continuous series of employment figures for the universities exists. The material in this study is, therefore, of interest as the only attempt to provide a comprehensive view of the development of employment at third level over time. The Central Statistics Office developed a detailed reporting system and published a wealth of detailed information for the National University of Ireland and its three constituent colleges plus Trinity College, Dublin, in two of *University Statistics,* one for 1938–39 and 1948–49 to 1952 and the second for 1953 alone. Complete records were collected up to and including the academic year 1968/69 and further publications prepared. The Central Statistics Office provided access to this unpublished material from which the figures in Table 98 and Appendix Table A2.16 have been extracted.

The trebling in full-time student numbers over three decades was not quite matched by the rise in full-time academic staff so that pupil-teacher ratios remained high. The Commission on Higher Education contrasted the Irish ratio of almost 18:1 with 9:1 in Northern Ireland and 7:1 in Britain in 1964/65. Unfortunately such a ratio is only a partial indicator and a more meaningful one would need to estimate full-time equivalents for both part-time students and part-time staff including staff paid on a fee basis. On an individual college basis the Commission calculated ratios of 14.1; 17.6; 21.3 and 24.1, respectively, for TCD, UCD, UCC and UCG. Some figures for 1968/69 and 1969/70 set out in Appendix Table A2.16 show how meaningless such an exercise can be. For example, UCC employed twice as many part-time staff as full time in 1968/69 while TCD employed more than four times as many full-time staff as part time. On the other hand UCC had virtually no fee paid staff but TCD employed almost three times as many in this category as it did of part timers. It was perhaps due to such vagaries as these that the Commission found the full time ratios improved in TCD from 17.1 in 1938/39 to 14.1 in 1964/65 whereas they disimproved drastically in UCG from 15.8 to 24.1.

Table 98: *Staff and students at Universities 1938/39 to 1969/70*

| | STAFF | | | | | RATIOS | | | STUDENTS | | | | |
| | Academic | | | Non-Academic | Total | Students | | Non-Acad | Full time Students | Part time Students | Sub-total | Other | Total |
	Full time	Part time	Fee-basis			Acad.+	Non-Acad.	Acad.*					
1938/39	294	138	18	303	753	17.5	17.0	1.03	5,141	265	5,406	70	5,465
1948/49	348	168	69	420	1,005	19.8	16.4	1.21	6,895	593	7,488	189	7,677
1949/50	363	192	76	436	1,067	19.4	16.2	1.20	7,048	627	7,675	389	8,064
1950/51	366	198	74	454	1,092	18.9	15.2	1.24	6,910	646	7,556	649	8,205
1951/52	386	199	80	519	1,184	17.6	13.1	1.34	6,794	669	7,463	791	8,254
1952/53	371	211	76	753	1,411	18.6	9.2	2.03	6,917	684	7,601	504	8,105
1953/54	374	203	73	787	1,437	18.7	8.9	2.10	7,011	718	7,729	709	8,438
1954/55	400	231	94	799	1,524	18.2	9.1	2.00	7,284	693	7,977	487	8,464
1955/56	423	254	107	812	1,596	17.2	9.0	1.92	7,278	788	8,066	571	8,637
1956/57	429	267	105	831	1,632	17.9	9.2	1.94	7,669	724	8,393	414	8,807
1957/58	447	264	70	824	1,605	17.9	9.7	1.84	8,019	763	8,782	450	9,232
1958/59	468	261	81	850	1,660	18.5	10.2	1.82	8,676	723	9,399	414	9,813
1959/60	497	285	87	918	1,787	18.4	10.0	1.85	9,155	842	9,997	754	10,751
1960/61	538	301	105	959	1,903	18.6	10.4	1.78	10,021	830	10,851	632	11,483
1961/62	567	359	362	1,000	2,288	18.2	10.3	1.76	10,297	1,498	11,795	875	12,670
1962/63	634	364	349	1,069	2,416	17.5	10.4	1.69	11,119	1,592	12,711	749	13,460
1963/64	675	375	189	1,170	2,409	17.9	10.3	1.73	12,085	1,743	13,828	1,031	14,859
1964/65	730	391	267	1,310	2,698	17.8	9.9	1.79	13,006	1,655	14,661	1,032	15,693
1965/66	756	453	263	1,445	2,917	18.7	9.8	1.91	14,147	2,044	16,191	1,332	17,523
1966/67	798	493	360	1,621*	3,272	19.4	9.5	2.03	15,448	1,767	17,215	1,592	18,807
1967/68	847	523	489	1,834*	3,693	18.7	8.6	2.16	15,838	2,272	18,110	2,290	20,400
1968/69	907	612	529	2,006*	4,054	18.6	8.4	2.21	16,908	2,968	19,876	2,608	22,484
1969/70††	992	543†	673†	2,116	4,324†	18.2	8.5	2.13	18,045	3,232	21,277	n.a.	n.a

Source: Published and unpublished data collected by the CSO.

Note: Universities refer to UCC, UCD, UCG, TCD and NUI.

†Acad. refers to full-time academics.

††For details of 1968/69 and 1969/70 staff see Appendix Table A2.16. No data for UCG.

*In these years TCD included research staff with non-academics. Recent revisions to the numbers in Arts and Science cast doubt on the accuracy of the pre-1971/72 figures for which revisions were not published. The revision for 1971/72 added 852 students and even more were added in the case of later years.

Non-academic staff grew almost sevenfold in the three decades. Although full time academic and all non-academic staff were roughly equal in numbers in 1938/39, employees on the non-academic side were more than twice as numerous at the end of the period. It seems probably that much of this non-academic employment was full time. In spite of these changes the Commission on Higher Education noted in paragraph 25.33 "Academic staff is a scarce and costly commodity. Common sense requires that the time of academic staff should be principally occupied in teaching and research. While it is right that academic staff should take part in university administration, excessive use of their time in this way should be avoided." This report, published in 1967, is clear that the members felt that even greater shedding of administrative duties by academics was desirable. This was a call for even more non-academic staff. While it is difficult to be certain, as we shall see, the ratio of teaching to non-teaching does not appear to have declined over the seventies in accordance with the Recommendation.

Sources of Data on Universities after 1970

The material in the last section was gathered and collated by the Central Statistics Office and published occasionally as "University Statistics". In 1968 the creation of the Higher Education Authority as an *ad hoc* body led to the belief that the HEA would be a more appropriate provider of university statistics and the CSO ceased its activities in this regard. As the HEA did not receive statutory status until the Higher Education Act of 1971, and only became operational in May 1972, a hiatus occurred in the statistics which was only finally made good when the HEA received a full complement of staff. Even then the new series differed in a number of ways from the old.

The HEA was set up primarily as a co-ordinating, planning and financing body, intermediate between the Minister for Education and specified third-level institutions with control over the creation of posts and promotions.[46] The first problem for this study is that the Minister for Education is not the only source of funds at third level. The Minister for Agriculture supports the Departments of Agriculture and Veterinary Medicine at University College, Dublin and that of Dairy Science at University College, Cork. He also funds the estate at Fota Island purchased by UCC. In this connection it should be noted that Trinity College, Dublin also had a faculty of Veterinary Medicine up to the mid-'seventies when it merged with that at UCD. The Dublin Dental Hospital, funded jointly by the Departments of Education and Health, is linked to TCD. The Cork Dental Hospital and School is funded jointly by UCC and by the Department of Health.

---

[46]Promotions were controlled for the duration of the embargo only.

Apart from direct funding by the Departments of Education and Agriculture a number of other university employees are supported by other means. A major group at UCD would be those employed in the diagnostic laboratories, i.e., the Virus Reference Laboratory, Seriological Testing, Pathology and the Medical Bureau of Road Safety. These staff are paid for out of fees obtained for the work of the labs. They are outside the remit of the HEA and are shown separately in the UCD Presidential Report. For the purposes of this report they present a conceptual difficulty to the extent that the fees are paid by public bodies. Are they to be treated like other private bodies that sell to the Government or are they merely a service located at the universities for convenience which otherwise would have been provided in-house by the public bodies concerned? Using the UN criterion and assuming that over half their sales are to public bodies this report has deemed them public employees. Similar difficulties are presented by research workers paid from research contracts. University College, Dublin records return them separately but we are assuming that by and large the contract itself is with a public body. The Higher Education Authority's statistics would tend to omit them. They are also omitted from the annual reports of Trinity College.

The situation is more clear cut with funded posts, e.g., where a bank or a firm funds a chair of banking or marketing. Here the source is clearly the private domain. The extent of such funding can be gauged from the fact that at the end of December 1981, 45 such posts existed in UCD. These were all full time except one academic post and were made up of 38 academic, 4 technical and 3 executive. These posts were included in the annual report of UCD. The difficulties of definition with such positions can be seen in the case of TCD where in 1973/74, for example, the costs of 3 medical appointments were covered by hospital sessions and those of another covered by private earnings surrendered. All four appeared in the TCD annual report.

A second feature of HEA statistics is the accent on established posts. The orderly funding of third-level education is based on the creation of such posts. The Authority, therefore, records the number of posts though some of these may be vacant at the time of the Census. In December 1980 the colleges of the NUI reported 142 vacancies in HEA departments, or almost 5 per cent of all posts. In 1979, 35 posts were recorded for NIHE Dublin although all of these were vacant.

Originally it has been intended to avail of the assistance of the HEA and with the active collaboration of the staff considerable time was invested in producing a consistent time series. However, the statistics, which were developed to serve the internal purposes of the HEA, were not always amenable to adaptation to the purposes of this study for the reason stated above. Accordingly preference was given to the data contained in the annual reports of the Universities, which married in well with the CSO series and so continuity was ensured. They also had the merit of recording levels at the same time each year. The HEA figures used different dates before settling on a standard December base. University records, however, are not without their problems since no standard procedures have been evolved for reporting either employment or accounts. Indeed the evolution of agreed comparable tables is an important goal of HEA records.

University Reports as a Data Source

The use of annual reports as a source of data does not solve all the difficulties of comparability. Colleges, for example, differ in the timing of their analysis. This was brought forcibly to the notice of the Government when the July 1981 embargo on recruitment was introduced and confirmed in December 1981. The new regulation required that only one in three of jobs vacated be reappointed. In July university staffing levels are at the annual trough. Old staff have left and new staff not taken up appointment. In UCD, for instance, language teachers were employed on an 8 month basis — October 1 to May 31. Records in June or September would, therefore, omit this group. For this reason recent records at UCD have favoured December 31, which ties in with the timing of general Civil Service enumerations (January 1). The other 3 colleges continue to favour the traditional September 30 timing.

A second major area, lacking uniform treatment, relates to the question of establishment levels, i.e., the total permitted staff. As we have seen, this is the statistic preferred by the HEA for its planning purposes.[47] Both TCD and UCC also favoured this return in some years though TCD has identified vacancies separately since 1982. The accent on establishment levels creates the difficulty of classifying full-time staff taken on a temporary basis pending sanction of their posts. Since they are above the quota they will not appear in HEA records but will show up in a count of actual employment. For example, in the development of NIHE Dublin after it opened its doors in 1980 it had 52 established posts filled and 12 vacancies. The fact that it also had 25 temporary fixed term posts illustrates the potential for differences between figures compiled on differing bases.

A more intractable problem dealing with published records is the differing bases for returning part-time staff in the various institutions. The accent on established posts has tended to favour recording all staff in terms of full-time equivalents. Such an approach has many attractions and is probably one of the best gauges of total inputs. Trinity College has used the FTE approach since 1976/77. This has the merit of avoiding experiences, such as that of UCG, where a decision to omit casual lecturers from the part time headcount in 1979/80 reduced it by 100 from 445. Similar calculations would show that the inputs of

---

[47]Adopting the FTE approach enabled NIHE Limerick, for example, to allocate money for sanctioned full-time posts to its departments and leave them free to fill them with either full-time employment or part-time equivalents.

part timers were highly significant in UCC and UCG in some years. In contrast in 1979/80 part-time academic staff in TCD made only one-tenth the input of full-time staff. Even if the accent is on FTE it need not exclude supplementary details of the number of jobs involved. For example, it is useful to know that the 124 FTE of part-time jobs in cleaning and catering at TCD in 1980/81 provided regular employment for 190 people. These permanent staff, whose remuneration fell below a minimum level, were returned as part time in the early seventies, much as cleaners are in the Civil Service.

Calculation of FTEs for teachers is only half the picture. It is also necessary to calculate full-time student equivalents. Very little work appears to have been published in this area. Where it has, post graduate students are typically deemed to be more than one student equivalent (e.g. 1.2 or 3.0 (Ph.D.)).

Apart from the use of FTEs there are definitional problems. For example, TCD regarded many demonstratorships as a means of funding graduate students rather than as a source of employment and omitted them. Other colleges included them as part-time staff; others again, e.g., UCD, as full-time, part-time and fee-paid staff. Some converted their input to full-time equivalents assuming a fixed ratio; others used hours worked; others favoured cash outlays which were related to a standard (differing between colleges). Apart from the problem of demonstrators it is useful to distinguish part-time posts from lecturing (or tutoring) on a fee basis. The former are part of the teaching staff of the institution as listed on the staff. Increasingly the latters' inputs have come to be recorded in cash terms alone. Another problem relates to research staff, especially if their activities are not funded by the Department of Education. They may therefore be omitted or excluded from the teaching body.

A final source of difference relates to non-academic staff. Trinity College employs staff for all the work connected with the University, apart from some connected with construction. In other campuses the catering franchise is given to a private company and the same may also apply to security. University College, Cork records the employment levels of its contract caterer but not of its cleaning contract as an annex to its staff tables. Failure to appreciate that colleges differ on this question of outside contracting can vitiate inter-University comparisons which focus on direct employment alone, although a comparison based on cash expenditures per student may pick it up. These differences can also affect comparisons of the academic:non-academic ratios between universities and colleges of technology in that, the Department of Education suggests, the VECs prefer to employ additional academic staff rather than resort to greater use of technicians and demonstrators as University Departments of Engineering and Science do.

Table 99: *Staff at Traditional Universities by College 1970/71 to 1983/84 distinguishing academic and non-academic, full time and part time*

	1970/71	1971/72	1972/73	1973/74	1974/75	1975/76	1976/77	1977/78	1978/79	1979/80	1980/81	1981/82	1982/83	1983/84
University College, Dublin														
Academic Full Time	490(a)	513(a)	513(a)	506	540	539	587	590	627	607	627	624	628	617
Academic Part Time	218	196	184	85}	90	94	74	65	49	53	59	62	58	56
Academic Demonstrators				78}	79	81	90	92	101	127	102	100	104	119
Academic Fee paid(b)	404	435	549	619	307	475	567	612	626	693	964	982	1,040	1,129
Non-Academic Full time	1,087}	1,145}	1,213}	1,126	1,088	1,048	1,090	1,145	1,145	1,121	1,126	1,129	1,092	1,076
Non-Academic Part time					52	74	78	59	60	54	51	56	60	59
Non-Academic Grant-aided/Diagnostic				133	151	151	156	151	168	171	161	165	154	154
Non-Academic Total	1,087	1,145	1,213	1,259	1,291	1,273	1,324	1,355	1,373	1,346	1,338	1,350	1,306	1,289
University College, Cork														
Academic Full time	159(a)	166	173(12)	178(17)(d)	183(23)	197(10)	204	219	244	255	265	268	271	269
Academic Part time	86	85	85(8)	91(9)(d)	85	80(15)	69	75	72	69	78	75	94	86
Academic Demonstrators	192	201	198	210	232	240	220	210	275	275	278	303	394	360
Academic Researchers	Above	10	13	15	15	23	27	30	34	36	55	54	63	74
Non-Academic Full time	283}	294}	308(13)}	343(15)(d)	372(17)	404(7)	418	422	443	473	487	497	500	500
Non-Academic Part time		3	3	4	4	5	10	13	14	18	38	34	41	41
Other Cork Dental Hospital(c)	n.a.	23	22	30	37	40	44	52	52	53	53	54	56	60
Other Catering(c)(e)	n.a.	n.a.	n.a.	48	50	50	52	55	53	54	54	51	49	49
University College, Galway														
Academic Full time	123	146	149	158	156	161	161	173	182	196	205	207	207	210
Academic Part time	21	148	25	26	29	29	28	27	30	32	31	31	31	30
Academic Part time Assistants	99		163	177	181	195	208	219	295(f)	172(293)	179	152	166	169
Academic Part time Demonstrators	106		86	86	96	96	105	110	110	141(120)	158	154	211	212
Non-Academic Full time	201	232	267	303	316	323	337	366	388	403	410	402	404	403
Non-Academic Part time			31	31	30	34	37	40	40	38	34	34	34	31

Table 99: (cont'd.)

Trinity College, Dublin (incl. Dental Hospital)														
Academic Full time (incl. vacancies)	258	275	283	321	331	342	330(g)	369	388(4)	412(i)	421	430	440	443
Academic Part time	74	84	91	101	103	140 FTE	17	21	30	41	40	41	42	44
Non-Academic Full time	743	748	651	709(h)	738	735	716	738	741	773(i)	778	799	799	794
Non-Academic Part time			135	133	126	132 FTE	126(92)	148(101)	142(97)	102	107(k)	116	119	118
National University of Ireland														
Non-Academic Full time (also 2 part time)	19	17	16	14	16	17(4)	18	17	16(4)	16(4)	16(4)	16(4)	16(4)	1
Maynooth														
Academic Full time	29	38	42(8)	47	46(4)	52(3)	52(11)	53(11)	60(12)	63(8)	67(5)	65(8)	68	73
Academic Part time	52	37	80	54	59	10+	5+	5+	13+56	10+65(m)	11+65	11		
Non-Academic Full time	58	65	68	50(n)	58	59(3)	75(4)	77(5)	81(1)	84(1)	87	87		
Non-Academic Part time	4	4	4	4	4	12	17	11	13	13	13			
Total including Dental excluding Maynooth														
Academic Full time	1,030	1,100	1,118	1,163	1,210	1,239	1,282	1,351	1,441	1,470	1,518	1,529	1,546	1,539
Non-Academic All Staff	(2,335)	2,461	2,617	2,828	2,932	2,965	2,998	3,103	3,171	3,224	3,263	3,304	3,277	3,254
Total above including Maynooth														
Academic Full time	1,059	1,138	1,160	1,210	1,256	1,291	1,334	1,404	1,501	1,533	1,585	1,594	1,614	1,612
Non-Academic All Staff	n.a.	2,519	2,682	2,900	2,986	3,027	3,061	3,166	3,258	3,318	3,355	3,401	3,377	3,354
Non-Academic of which part time	n.a.	n.a.	n.a.	218	251	223 cf TCD	215	229	231	243	255	269	264	

Figures in parentheses: vacancies not included in total.

Notes: UCD [a] contains some demonstrators; [b] includes some tutors and demonstrators; [c] Excluded from returns in Annual accounts. UCC [a] as UCD; [c] Excluded from returns in Annual accounts; [d] Total establishment divided by estimating vacancies; [e] Catering done by contractor, also cleaning, but employment by latter not published. UCG [f] Revision excludes 100 occasional lecturers and gives new distribution; unrevised (given in parentheses). TCD [g] Veterinary College transferred to UCD; [h] as [d]; [i] Language Laboratory (6) reclassified as non-academic; [k] These FTE figures plus 17 FTE of part-time non-cleaning staff gives 190 part time staff in total in 1980/81; [m] Maynooth part time in recent years includes FTE of casual staff, e.g., 65 in 1980/81; [n] Redefinition of secular/religious divide.

Dental and Pharmacy Schools

In its statistics TCD includes employment in the Dublin Dental Hospital as part of its staff. University College, Cork on the other hand, publishes the details separately for the Cork Dental Hospital as an annex to its staff tables. It is assumed that these staff are non-academic in aggregating Table 99.

Up to 1977 the Pharmaceutical Society of Ireland received State aid to run its college in association with UCD. As part of the merger talks it opted in that year to become the School of Pharmacy in Trinity College. At the time of merging 10 academics and 8 non-academics were employed full time. These were included in the 1976 total but unfortunately earlier figures are not available. The School of Pharmacy continued to teach and examine Pharmaceutical Assistants on behalf of the Society up to 1984 and the HEA showed about 50 such assistants separately in its records. These were not TCD students. In 1984 a two year course for Pharmaceutical Technicians was introduced involving the School of Pharmacy for academic subjects, AnCO for business training and commercial pharmacies for work experience. While the acquisition of the School of Pharmacy increased TCD's staff, about the same time other staff were lost when most of 31 full-time staff of the veterinary department transferred to UCD. These latter staff comprised 12 academic, 16 technical and 3 secretarial staff.

University Employment from 1970/71 Onwards

Staff numbers are presented in Table 99 based on University accounts. Student numbers are given in Table 100 derived from HEA sources. It will be observed that, unlike the previous tables, these tables include Maynooth. However here our concern in this study relates only to that part of its campus which is State aided and to the employment which that aid generated. This new State aid only dates from the admission of lay students in 1966 and its impact on staff and student level is immediately apparent from the annual Statistical Abstracts:

Academic Year	Professors	Lecturers	Students
1938/39	32	10	587
1948/49	34	5	475
1958/59	34	10	553
1966/67	37	7	577
1967/68	35	8	677
1968/69	31	31	785
1969/70	31	36	947

No figures for non-academic staff were published for this period. When the Statistical Abstract ceased to publish this series in 1976/77 Maynooth employed 31 professors (and officials?) and 52 lecturers to teach a student population that

Table 100: *Full-time and part-time students by University 1970/71–1983/84*

Year	UCD	UCC	UCG	TCD	Maynooth	Total†
			Full time			
1970/71	8,201	3,608	2,896	3,915*	711	19,363
1971/72	8,004	3,723	2,907	3,993*	852	19,479
1972/73	8,285	3,928	3,001	3,879*	944	20,093
1973/74	8,219	4,008	3,156	4,126*	965	20,474
1974/75	8,472	3,930	3,246	4,151*	972	20,771
1975/76	8,860	3,980	3,131	4,243	997	21,273
1976/77	8,926	4,098	3,408	4,569	1,063	22,064
1977/78	8,944	4,265	3,524	4,973	1,158	22,864
1978/79	8,697	4,294	3,608	5,140	1,181	22,920
1979/80	8,618	4,347	3,596	5,373	1,009	22,943
1980/81	8,311	4,602	3,669	5,684	951	23,217
1981/82	8,541	4,805	3,762	5,844	967	23,919
1982/83	8,723	4,865	3,878	6,003	1,066	24,535
1983/84	8,749	5,156	4,007	6,156	1,181	25,249
			Part time			
1970/71	1,970	260	166	554*	—	2,912
1971/72	1,649	255	124	510*	—	2,538
1972/73	1,178	231	207	675*	—	2,235
1973/74	872	222	198	635*	—	1,927
1974/75	1,249	582	234	621*	—	2,686
1975/76	979	603	208	745	3	2,476
1976/77	991	564	224	686	18	2,483
1977/78	1,028	732	192	691	8	2,651
1978/79	935	710	182	756	6	2,589
1979/80	941	702	256	821	62	2,782
1980/81	1,438	766	469	946	88	3,707
1981/82	1,186	643	479	1,013	98	3,419
1982/83	1,288	593	492	1,041	128	3,542
1983/84	1,210	696	472	1,098	191	3,667

Source: HEA's Accounts and Student Statistics. In cases of different numbers the most recently published have been accepted although in some cases the Department of Education and TCD provided further revisions.

*Apart from TCD, data include small numbers of students enrolled for more than one course and are therefore double counted. In the case of TCD multicategory students were *not* counted up to 1974/75.

†Users of the Statistical Abstracts will find two series of figures for NUI full-time students. Although a footnote explicitly excludes them the undocumented revisions include Art and Science students at Maynooth. The HEA annual accounts agreed with the original CSO series when first published but were subsequently revised to the totals above.

	CSO original	CSO revised	HEA (first figures)
1971/72	14,841	15,693	14,841
1972/73	15,299	16,243	15,299
1973/74	15,339	16,304	15,339
1974/75	15,648	16,620	15,648
1975/76	—	16,968	15,971

had grown to 1,582. As reference to Table 99 will show, this academic staff
record includes more than those teaching lay students. The former gave 52 full--
time academics only but also 58 non-academic support staff.

The growth of full-time academic employment since 1971 at 3.7 per cent was
faster than that of all non-academics, 3.1 per cent. We would need to have more
data on FTEs to say whether total academic inputs also grew faster but *a priori* it
would appear that the recommendation of the Commission on Higher Education was not heeded, i.e., that academic staff should be relieved of non-academic
duties. The rationale for this may have been that, in a situation of scarce funds,
the tendency has been to provide as many student places as possible.

The material in Tables 99 and 100 is graphed in Figure 17. University
College, Dublin, is by far the largest campus. Full-time student numbers in
1972/73 and 1980/81 were virtually the same. Staff numbers only grew between
1973/74 and 1978/79 and only then in every second year. The upsurge in TCD
student numbers, especially after 1974/75, produced a 40 per cent increase so
that TCD increased its population relative to UCD from 48 per cent to 68 per
cent over the interval. After a start, in which the increase in UCC students paral-
leled those of TCD, UCC diverged on to a slower track. Even at the beginning

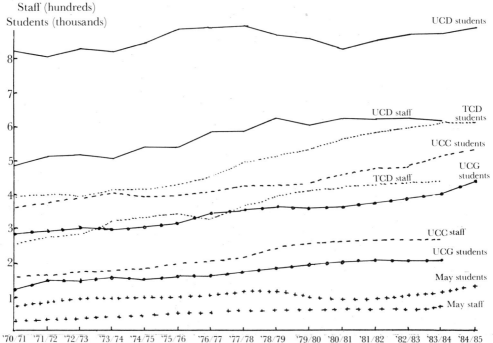

Figure 17: *Growth in student numbers and staffing at individual universities
1970/71 to 1984/85*

UCC's complement of full-time staff was much lower than TCD's but in spite of the low student rise it grew slightly faster than TCD's, perhaps by replacing part-time staff to some extent. The years of major expansion of student numbers at Galway were between 1975/76 and 1978/79 when growth rates of 4.8 per cent matched those achieved by TCD. Staffing increases were almost identical as at UCC, apart from the first year.

The interest in student numbers is to get some impression of pupil-teacher ratios. We have already seen that the only satisfactory measure is that based on full time equivalents of both staff and students. Thus the material in Table 101, based only on full time staff and students can be considerably misleading and better material is clearly urgently needed. The current PTR of 15.6, if it is any guide at all, is higher than the 12.0 target set by the HEA in its first report at a time when the British figure was 7.0 and that in Northern Ireland was 9.0.

In interpreting PTRs regard must be had to the course structure of the college. In general, the faculties funded by the Department of Agriculture tend to have low student staff ratios. Within the HEA funded faculties a great variety obtains. Medicine and Engineering, for example, have very favourable relationships compared with Arts courses, as a few instances will illustrate:

Inter–University Course	Range in Staff–Student Ratio
Education	25–32
Modern History	27
Mathematics	21–30
Accountancy	26–36
Engineering (all)	13–17
Architecture	12
Medicine/Dentistry	9–12
Veterinary	5
Agriculture	7
All Courses	14–17

The low ratios for subjects such as architecture, engineering and medicine may be dictated in part by the nature of these subjects and the number of specialisms involved, in part by the need to have qualifications accepted in the UK where, at the beginning of the 'seventies, student staff ratios were, as we have seen, much lower in general. In addition, post-graduate students need to be converted to undergraduate equivalents, e.g., doctoral students count as three undergraduates. When these latter adjustments are made the PTR figures are found to be higher.

Table 101: *Distribution of full-time students and full-time staff by colleges, 1970/71 and 1983/84, and unadjusted* student/staff ratios*

College	1970/71			1983/84		
	Student staff ratio	Share of		Student Staff ratio	Share of	
		Staff	Students		Staff	Students
		%	%		%	%
UCD	16.7	48	44	14.2	40	36
UCC	22.7	15	19	19.2	17	21
UCG	23.5	12	16	19.1	14	17
TCD	15.3	25	21	13.9	29	26
Total	18.1	100	100	15.6	100	100

*Adjustments must be made for graduate students.

Manpower Posts

A factor influencing the number of staff was the creation of what were known as manpower posts in 1979 and subsequently. These posts were created to meet predicted shortfalls in particular types of graduates, e.g., engineering, and were allocated to the various colleges. The totals were:

	1979	1980	1981	1982	1983
Academic	115	20	3	12	—
Non-Academic	85	18	2	8	3

Not all the posts created were, in fact, filled immediately. In the light of the current recession the earlier predictions of graduate shortfalls appear to have been somewhat exaggerated.

TEACHER TRAINING

The training of teachers for different levels of pupil education is carried on in different institutions. As we have seen since Independence secondary teachers needed a university degree to become registered. This was supplemented by a Higher Diploma in Education (H.Dip.) also taken at the University. Specialist vocational teachers, as we shall see, were trained at a variety of locations until many of these courses were brought together at the Thomond College of Education (TCE), which is considered in the next section. A few colleges offering specialist courses continued independently of TCE. Of these, art training is also considered in the next section. This section will consider two non-VEC schools specialising in training teachers of home economics which also escaped incorporation in TCE. These are St. Angela's, Sligo and St. Catherine's, Sion Hill, Blackrock. The former became a recognised college of the NUI in 1978 while St. Catherine's is an associated college of TCD since 1977. Both offer a Bachelor of Eduction Degree in Home Economics.

The oldest tradition in Irish teacher training is undoubtedly that of national teaching with almost one hundred and fifty years behind it, or more if Protestant teacher training is considered. However, the present system dates from 1883 when State recognition and support was reluctantly afforded to denominational teacher training for the primary level. The three major teacher training colleges became recognised colleges of the National University of Ireland in 1974. These were St. Patrick's, Drumcondra, Carysfort College, Blackrock and Mary Immaculate, Limerick. Three smaller colleges became associated colleges of TCD. One of these, the Church of Ireland Training College, Rathmines, is the descendant of the Kildare Place training school founded in 1811 and has traditionally taken lectures other than professional ones on the Trinity campus. The other two associate colleges are St. Marys (Christian Brothers) College at Marino[48] and the Froebel College at Sion Hill, Blackrock. All six colleges are now called colleges of education rather than teacher training colleges and their graduates receive the degree of Bachelor of Education (B.Ed.). Marino and the Froebel College differ from the rest in that they are not state aided on a budget basis but rather on a capitation basis. By their link with TCD the smaller colleges avail of some TCD staff on a part-time basis. Presumably these are included in the TCD returns. It will be noted that the Montessori College at Sion Hill is neither associated with a University nor grant aided. The Montessori qualification is not recognised at the primary level except in special schools for the handicapped.[49] The complex of which it formed a part at Sion Hill was remarkable since it also contained St. Catherine's, Froebel College, St. Anne's Residential School of Domestic Economy, the secondary school of Sion Hill, St. Raphael's College of Physical Education and Ling College. The last mentioned transferred to Thomond College in 1973 while St. Anne's closed in 1984.

Considerable information on the financing of primary teacher education and on pupil numbers is contained in a very thorough article by Burke and Nolan (1982) together with comparative material for other types of teacher training. Unfortunately the survey does not include details of employment in the colleges. The figures for student teachers were solicited from the colleges themselves as the authors were unhappy with the quality of the official statistics. Their table is reproduced in Table 102.

[48]For many years there was also a De la Salle training college in Waterford, founded in 1891.
[49]In 1979/80 the college employed 5 full-time and 14 part-time staff.

Table 102: *Full-time and equivalent full-time students in the Colleges of Education 1972/73 to 1980/81*

Academic year	Pre-service teacher training	Coláiste Moibhi	Special education	Remedial FTE*	Totals
1972/73	1,815	16	25	—	1,856
1973/74	2,086	16	25	12	2,139
1974/75	1,875	16	25	13	1,929
1975/76	1,724	19	25	—	1,768
1976/77	2,379	25	25	13	2,442
1977/78	2,561	24	25	—	2,878
	268†				
1978/79	2,591	26	25	13	2,655
1979/80	2,720	28	25	13	2,786
1980/81	2,801	27	25	13	2,866

Source: Burke and Nolan (1982) Table 1.
*Calculated at 50% of enrollment.
†Special Trainee Teachers.
Note: Colaise Moibhi is a preparatory college. Special and remedial courses are at Drumcondra.

A longer-term view drawn from the Statistical Reports of the Department of Education is set out in Tables 103 and 104 which show the more than five-fold rise in numbers attending colleges of education between 1949/50 and 1980/81. In 1981/82 only one student in eight was male whereas in 1964/65, the earliest year for which a sex classification was published, the ratio was three out of ten. Prior to 1963/64 only four teacher training colleges were included — Drumcondra, Carysfort, Limerick and Rathmines with supplementary detail of graduations from Marino and De La Salle, Waterford. Later all six were included. In 1968 the Froebel school of Alexandra College was included in the statistics. Froebel College, Sion Hill joined in 1976. De La Salle merged with Marino in 1972.

McElligott quotes the changes in student numbers in the four main colleges between 1926 and 1960 as:—

	1926	1960		1926	1960
Drumcondra	165	216	Carysfort	200	426
Limerick	100	260	Rathmines	135	49

As set out in the background section, six preparatory colleges were established after independence to train teachers in the use of Irish. In 1961/62 five of these had become secondary schools, leaving only the Church of Ireland Colaiste

Table 103: *Numbers in Colleges of Education (CE), Preparatory Colleges (PC) and Colleges of Home Economics (CHE) 1949/50–1970/71*

Year[a]	CE	PC	CHE	Year	CE	PC	CHE
1949/50	541	464	118	1960/61	986	521[c]	146
1950/51	633	493	136	1961/62	987	51	152
1951/52	655	498	142	1962/63	987	50	157
1952/53	681	498	137	1963/64	1,111[b]	59	167
1953/54	690	507	134	1964/65	1,131	50	166
1954/55	755	516	144	1965/66	1,177	45	171
1955/56	858	511	145	1966/67	1,182	38	172
1956/57	935	516	150	1967/68	1,185	32	170
1957/58	939	520	135	1968/69	1,161	n.a.	172
1958/59	950	521	132	1969/70	1,325	n.a.	177
1959/60	946	510	133	1970/71	1,337	n.a.	180[d]

Later figures are given in Table 104.

Source: Department of Educational Statistical Reports.

Note: [a]Timing of Census differed from year to year. [b]Up to 1962/63, 4 Colleges of Education (Drumcondra, Carysfort, Limerick and Rathmines were given with graduation details for Marino and De La Salle, Waterford. Afterwards all six were included though at one stage Froebel College replaced De La Salle. In 1968 at least, students of Froebel in Alexandra College were included. [c]Up to and including this year six preparatory colleges were enumerated. Subsequently five became secondary schools leaving only Colaiste Moibhi. [d]Statistics in Table 1 and in Vocational Section of Departmental Reports differ in the number of students. In early years some students attended Cathal Brugha Street.

Móibhí in the old category. The latter merged with the Church of Ireland Teacher Training College on the same campus.

Employment material for all these colleges has been sparse. This has been especially true where funding has been on a capitation basis. Such records, as have been collected, are presented in Table 104. Given the difficulties of measuring student numbers accurately, referred to by Burke and Nolan, it is difficult to be certain of the level of pupil-teacher ratios but a figure of about 15:1 might be a reasonable guess. If so, these levels are higher than some other third-level bodies but in line with University ratios.

Information on non-academic staff was not readily available until recently. In 1984/85, 202 full-time staff were recorded and about 32 full-time equivalents of part time in the four colleges. By colleges the figures were 98+14 (Drumcondra), 48+9 (Carysfort), 48+5 (Limerick) and 8+4 (Rathmines).[50] It has been suggested

[50]Rathmines reported 8 full-time staff in 1980/81 to 1982/83, 2 part-time in 1980/81 and 4 in the other two years.

Table 104: Academic staff and students at Colleges of Education, etc., 1971/72–1984/85

Staff at Colleges of Education paid on budget basis	1971/72	1972/73	1973/74	1974/75	1975/76	1976/77	1977/78	1978/79	1979/80	1980/81	1981/82	1982/83	1983/84	1984/85
Drumcondra	36+6	39+3	41+17	44+16*	47+15*	56+14	58+3	n.a.	60+15	65+1	65+26	63+24	64+20	64+7½††
Carysfort	26+6	38+3	38+3	41+6*	46+3*	50+3*	46+2	n.a.	50+6	61+30	64+26	63+23	61+13	60+2††
Church of Ireland	6+10	6+10	6+11	7+10*	6+18*	6+13	6+10	n.a.	9+11	9+12	9+12	9+11	10+9	10+3††
Limerick *funded by capitation*	23+4	25+7	30+6	33+6	37+7*	48+8	51+9	n.a.	51+12	60+5	60+5	60+4	60+3	57+1††
Marino**	n.a.	n.a.	n.a.	5+12	5+12	5+12	5+12	n.a.	5+12	5+12	5+12	5+12	5+12	5+12
Froebel	—	—	—	—	—	3+9	3+9	3+9	3+9	3+9	3+9	3+9	3+9	3+9
Total	91+26	108+23	115+37	130+50	141+55	168+59	169+45	n.a.	178+65	203+69	206+90	203+83	203+110	199+n.a.
Total Students	1,400	1,657	1,847	1,755	1,628	2,295	2,587	2,501	2,586	2,816†	2,689	2,511	n.a.	n.a.
Colaiste Moibhi Students	n.a.	18	16	16	20	25	24	26	28	27	25	28		
Residential Colleges of Home Economics														
Staff St. Catherine's	12+20	n.a.	n.a.	n.a.	14+21	n.a.	n.a.	n.a.	20+13	8+12	9+12	9+15	15+10	15+11
Staff St. Angela's										12+3	14+5	14+4	14+3	14+4
Students	181	177	173	156	173	175	178	177	175	183	182	209	n.a.	n.a.

Sources: HEA and Department of Education unpublished records.

*Up to 1977/78 staff in budgeted Colleges of Education included a few administrative staff paid on academic scales. Recent figures refer to academic staff only. The included non-academics were (where the figure after "+" denotes part time): 1974/75 Drumcondra (D) and Carysfort (C) 3 each Rathmines (R) 1+5 Limerick (L) 2+2; 1975/76 D 5+5, C 5+2, R+8 L 4+3; 1976/77 C4; 1977/78 C4, L5.

**Marino employed 7 non-academics between 1974/75 and 1979/80. Colaiste Moibhi staff included with Rathmines.

†Includes 100 Froebel students recorded here for the first time.

††Full time equivalents.

that in earlier years some non-academics paid on academic scales have been included with the academics. Presumably these were the higher administrative staff. In the absence of other information this study has adopted the Department's suggestion of assuming equal numbers of academics and non-academics in the years where no records of non-academics exist.

Apart from the big four, Marino has reported 7 non-academics in the latter part of the 'seventies. In the case of the colleges of home economics, statistics are more plentiful. Figures for non-academics in recent years were:—

	St. Catherine's	St. Angela's
1980/81	10+6pt.	9+4
1981/82	10+6	17+1
1982/83	11+6	20+2
1983/84	14+7	13+2
1984/85	15+8	14+3

TECHNOLOGICAL UNIVERSITIES[51] AND OTHER THIRD-LEVEL INSTITUTIONS

Coolahan, (1981), has commented (p. 136) that

> the most striking feature of third-level education has been the establishment of a binary system. This entailed the building up of the hitherto neglected non-university sector. New institutions, such as regional colleges and national institutions of higher education, have been added to the colleges of technology. This sector has its own statutory award-giving body — the National Council for Educational Awards (NCEA) — which validates courses and awards certificates, diplomas and degrees.

Some of these institutions have already been discussed as part of the remit of the Vocational Education Committees, i.e., RTCs, the Dublin Institute of Technology, etc. This section deals with some designated institutions of the HEA which are neither part of the VECs nor yet included under the traditional universities, though their teaching achievements are the equivalents of University courses.

---

[51]In a speech of October 4, 1985 the Minister for Education, Gemma Hussey, declared herself ready to set up an international assessment of the excellent work of the NIHEs with a view to establishing a technological university.

Major bodies in this area are the two National Institutes of Higher Education of Limerick and Dublin, and Thomond College of Education (TCE) which shares its campus with NIHE (L). The latter enrolled its first students in1972 and, for a brief period, came under the aegis of UCC for degree purposes following a government decision of 1974 to remove degree conferring powers from the NCEA. This decision was reversed with the change of government in 1977. The NCEA, which had operated on an *ad hoc* basis, received statutory status in 1980 on the basis of an Act of the previous year "thereby enshrining the binary system of third-level education" Coolahan (p. 251). NIHE Dublin became a designated body of the HEA in 1976 along with NIHE Limerick but only opened its doors to students in 1980.

Thomond College had to wait three years more for designation (1979). It was a reconstituted college incorporating the former National College of Physical Education at Limerick and taking over in addition responsibility for several aspects of vocational teacher training. Art and Domestic Science were excluded from this rationalisation of teacher training. Previously specialist training had been offered in widely dispersed locations. Woodwork and Building Construction were associated with Colaiste Carmain in County Wexford, Educational Woodwork at the School of Furniture in Cork, Metalwork at Ringsend and Rural Science at the Crawford Technical Institute in Cork. There were in the early to mid-'fifties other venues, e.g., Bolton Street for woodwork also Scoil Brighde in Cork, the Crawford Technical Institute for metalwork.

The growth in numbers of trainee teachers is set out in Table 105 for the old locations up to the cessation of training at the end of 1980/81. Staff at these locations have been documented in recent returns:

> 1978/79   13 full time and 39 part time
> 1979/80   10 full time and 21 part time
> 1980/81   9 full time and 16 part time

Thus the regional losses due to concentration are not large. Most of the staff concerned were included in the VEC returns.

While these courses were being wound down Thomond College was building up its staff.[52] However, as Table 106 illustrates, it was not always possible to identify it separately since TCE shared its campus with NIHE(L) and this symbiosis built up accordingly some "common" staff (e.g. chaplain, accommodation officer and library staff).

Two other designated institutions, in contrast, date from the eighteenth century. The Royal Dublin Society's "Academy for Drawing and Painting" of 1746 became the National College of Art in 1924 when it came under the aegis of

---

[52]In 1981 a one year post-graduate diploma course for teachers of business studies was launched.

Table 105: *Trainee teachers in vocational courses, 1950/51–1980/81*

	Wood	Metal	Rural		Wood	Metal	Rural	Educ.W	PE
1950/51	40	15		1966/67	69	60	21	31	—
1951/52	40	16	17	1967/68	64	56	42	31	—
1952/53	40	16	17	1968/69	44	52	20	47	—
1953/54	40	15	20	1969/70	82	56	40	47	—
1954/55	59	31	20	1970/71	65	50	59	63	—
1955/56	21	31	20	1971/72	57	45	59	63	—
1956/57	—	16	20	1972/73	72	41	41	62	—
1957/58	19	—	—	1973/74	81	70	39	78	—
1958/59	20	18	—	1974/75	76	91	58	81	279
1959/60	40	36	—	1975/76	78	101	57	72	277
1960/61	34	34	—	1976/77	64	71	55	40	249
1961/62	20	32	—	1977/78	51	71	51	20	213
1962/63	20	32	—	1978/79	51	59	50	—	176
1963/64	31	34	—	1979/80	32	39	36	—	183
1964/65	37	37	—	1980/81	24	19	20	—	
1965/66	39	48	21	1981/82	—	—	—	—	

Source: Department of Education Statistical Reports.
Wood=Woodwork also Woodwork and Construction: Metal includes Post-Primary Metalwork.
Rural=General and Rural Science. Educ. W. means Educational Woodwork.
PE=Physical Education.

the Department of Education. In 1966/67 and 1967/68 about 600 students were returned before a revision reduced numbers in one year from 612 to 148. In 1969/70, 29 students were described as trainee art teachers in the HEA Report on Teacher Education 1970. In no year were staffing levels reported. The College was reconstituted in 1971 as the National College of Art and Design and was to be governed by An Bord CNED. It became a designated institution of the HEA in December 1976.

The Royal Irish Academy was set up as a learned society in 1785 and incorporated the following year in the Royal Charter of George III. Like the ESRI it is not a State-sponsored body though it is now largely State-funded. For example, 71 per cent of its income in 1979 came by way of State grants. It became a designated institution of the HEA in October 1979.

Three other designated bodies of the HEA are not treated here for various reasons. The Royal College of Surgeons Ireland (RCSI) is not State-funded, apart from a small grant which has been static in nominal terms in recent years. Staffing at the RCSI was 117 at the end of 1976 and 120 a year later but these staff cannot be deemed in any way as public employees. The National Council

Table 106: *Staff and students at certain designated institutions of the Higher Education Authority 1971/72–1983/84*

		1971/72	1972/73	1973/74	1974/75	1975/76	1976	1977	1978	1979	1980	1981	1982	1983
		June '72	June '73	June '74	June '75		September				December			
NIHE(L)	Academic Staff	16	34	51	60	—	60	74*	78*	92(10)	112*	118*	97(10)+18	98(6)+21
	Non-academic staff	3	7	20	36	—	38	73*	77*	115(20)	133*	141*	140(8)+14	145(5)+14
	Common staff	2	14	26	33	—	33							
	Students	—	—	220	453	680	744	907	916	1,259	1,594	1,634	1,809	1,826
	Students part time	—	—	—	—	—	25	177	199	226	321	371	420	424
TCE	Academic staff		10+4	17+1	22+1	—	24+1	27+1	27+1	41(8)	55*	47(16)	65	65
	Non-academic Staff		5	12	16	—	21	21	23	37(5)	51*	49(4)	59(1)	60
	Students		—	194	279	307	249	213	167	238	316	398	543	598
NIHE(D)	Academic Staff		—	—	—	—	3*	3*	4*	3(32)	40(12)	59*	81(9)+55	89(10)+46
	Non-academic staff		—	—	—	—	—	—	—	7(22)	12(17)	63*	95(9)+2	112(14)+5
	Students		—	—	—	—	—	—	—	—	191	570	949	1,379
	Students part time		—	—	—	—	—	—	—	—	—	—	—	75
NCAD	Academic staff	n.a.	n.a.	n.a.	39	—	39+2	43*	55*	45(6)+2	45(2)+2	44(8)	48(5)	48(5)
	Non-academic staff	n.a.	n.a.	n.a.	35	—	35+9	35*	45*	46(8)+15	55(4)+15	54(3)	63(3)	63(4)
	Students		150	150	163	229	292	340	378	441	485	497	504	477
	Students part time		—	—	—	—	22	29	37	47	62	70	62	41
Total Above	Academic staff	n.a.	n.a.	n.a.	121+1	—	123+3	144+1	159+1	181(56)+2	252(14)+2	268(24)	291(24)+73	300(21)+46
	Non-academic staff	n.a.	n.a.	n.a.	150	—	160+9	162	178	205(55)+15	251(21)+15	307(7)	357(21)+16	380(23)+19
	Students		564	895	1,216	1,285	1,460	1,461	1,938	2,586	3,099	3,805	4,280	
	Students part time		—	—	—	—	47	206	236	273	383	441	482	540
RIA	Non-academic	n.a.	n.a.	n.a.	30	—	30	30	30	31(1)	33(1)	35(1)+2	38+2	38+2

Sources: HEA and direct enquiry, NIHE=National Institute of Higher Education (L) and (D) at Limerick and Dublin. TCE Thomond College of Education. NCAD=National College of Art and Design. RIA=Royal Irish Academy. Common staff are shared by NIHE(L) and TCE.

Note 1: Due to change in date of recording staff no appropriate figures are available for 1975/76.

Note 2: Figures in parentheses give vacancies not included, "*" means vacancies probably included. Figures after "+" are part time.

for Educational Awards will be treated with other State-sponsored bodies in a later study. The College of Pharmacy was designated in March 1973 but subsequently merged with TCD in1977. Although records of staffing are poor it returned 10 academics and 8 non-academics on its full-time staff in September 1976.

Two other bodies will also be excluded from the present discussion. Staff at the Military College are returned by the Department of Defence and are included already under the general Civil Service. The Central Applications Office in Galway, which allocates students to third-level institutions, claimed that it fell outside the scope of this study on the grounds that it is totally self-financing and a private company. Its monopoly role, derived from the State, would suggest that it is financed by a form of tax and so analogous to several State-sponsored bodies. In 1980 the CAO employed eight full-time staff.

The piecemeal manner by which various institutions became designated under the HEA in the 'seventies has resulted in the statistics being rather ragged, quite apart from the difficulties of HEA statistics favouring establishment levels. Where gaps occurred the lacunae were filled as far as possible by direct enquiry. The results are set out in Table 106. When PTR calculations are made on these figures a ratio of about 9:1 appears to obtain. This would be higher than those obtained in VEC third-level education. In comparisons with the universities the appropriate yardstick are those faculties which offer similar instruction, e.g., engineering, which are generally below the University average.

It will also be noted that non-academic staff tend to be fewer than comparable third-level institutions. For example, NIHE Limerick contracts out catering, cleaning and maintenance, etc. The workers involved are often quasi-permanent frequenters of the campus and clearly dependent ultimately on public funding. The NIHE (L) annual accounts give details of these staff, e.g.,

    1979:12   1980:16   1981:19   1982:19 and 1983:22

It would be useful if all such "quasi-public" employment was recorded as an appendix to the normal returns. This would facilitate comparison with other bodies, such as TCD, which employ their own staff. It would also be a useful indicator of other employment ultimately dependent on the public purse.

Chapter V.6

MISCELLANEOUS EDUCATION AND TRAINING

Adult Education Organisers

Apart from the formal institutions of education discussed already the full employment programme led to a number of innovations discussed in this final part of the education section. One of these new departures led to the selection of 50 teachers to help develop adult education. They are known as Adult Education Organisers and they are returned as if they were part of the teaching rather than of the administrative staff of the VECs.

Youth Development Officers and Core Staff in Youth Organisations

In the drive for full employment a scheme was launched which was popularly called "Heffo's Army" after the trainer of the successful Dublin football team who headed it. One proposal adopted was to fund the employment of Youth Development Officers in youth organisations. These are discussed below. However, the idea of supporting defined staff in youth organisations did not begin with the Youth Development Officer scheme. Previously youth organisations benefited from the Youth Service Grants which included a scheme which financed the remuneration of named core staff in a number of organisations on a pound for pound basis. The 59 staff involved at end 1982 were distributed as follows:

Foróige	12	National Federation of Youth Clubs	6
Catholic Boy Scouts	11	Scout Association	5
Catholic Youth Council	10	Irish Girl Guides	2
National Youth Council	7	Church of Ireland Youth Council	1
Ógra Chorcaí	5		

This financing was of specific posts. These organisations were in receipt of State support for a number of activities, e.g., programme development and in the course of such work would normally employ their own staff. For example, the Catholic Youth Council employs 47 but only 10 of these come under the named core staff scheme.

The question then arises whether to treat all or some of these staff as being in the public domain. A case for excluding the 59 core staff would be that only half their salaries are State-financed. A case for including them would be that the balance of their salaries would come from the association's kitty to which the State makes other and frequently large contributions. A similar but less compelling argument could be applied to the non-core staff. It was decided to raise the problem but not to delve in detail into all the organisations which might be financing salaries as a result of general State support. To do so would require investigating the use of State funds by such bodies as Macra na Feirme, the Irish Countrywomen's Association, the Red Cross, which, in principle, have been deemed to be outside the public domain if at least half of their funding was private. The Farm Apprenticeship Board is in a more marginal position but this will be discussed under State-sponsored and similar bodies. The whole question of state-supported voluntary bodies is complex since it involves a wide variety of departments and funding arrangements. Some others are partly funded by local authorities or State-sponsored bodies, e.g., Comhairle Le Leas Óige, Ógras. In general, staff of these bodies will not be included in this report.

The Development Officers scheme was an extension of the core staff concept. The scheme envisaged a grant of £5,000 which was deemed to be 90 per cent of the cost of the officer. This grant was to run for 4 years and the fixed contribution was reckoned to be 80 per cent, 70 per cent and 60 per cent of costs in succeeding years. It was hoped that by the end of the scheme the organisations would be able to fund the staff themselves. Recruitment, targeted at 100, proceeded gradually and covered three categories as follows:

During	Total	Youth	Sport	Community
1979	23	16	—	7
1980	52	31	6	15
1981	17	9	4	4
1982	3	1	—	2
	95	57	10	28

By 1983 those recruited during 1979 had served their four years and State funding could have been expected to end. However in January 1983 following the appointment of a Minister of State to the Department of Labour with responsibility for Youth Affairs it was decided to split up the Youth and Sport section of the Department of Education. Accordingly the 57 youth development officers were transferred to that department. Soon afterwards the grant was increased to £7,000 and the posts made permanent. In 1984 the Department of Labour, which had also taken over the core staff scheme, merged the two schemes into the Youth Service Grant Scheme.

Following the formation of the Federation of Irish Scout Associations, core staff in the scouting bodies was reduced by 6 in 1983 and additional staff given to the National Federation of Youth Clubs and Ogra Chorcai (one each) and the National Youth Council (2). Feachtas obtained one. The net effect was a total of 58. The saving of an Irish Girl Guides post permitted one for the Girls' Brigade.

As noted already youth organisations also employed non-funded staff, reckoned to be 73 in 1983. Some of these organisations had no funded core staff, i.e., Macra na Feirme (17), An Oige (8), Order of Malta Cadet Corp and Irish Methodist Youth Department (3 each), Ogras and Young Women's Christian Association (2 each), Federation of Irish Workcamp Organisations and Presbyterian Youth Council (1 each). This accounted for 37, or half the non-funded employment. Organistions with funded core staff employed the remainder. Federation of Irish Scout Associations (11), Catholic Youth Council (9), Ogra Chorcai (7), Foroige (6), Irish Girl Guides (2) and Church of Ireland Youth Council (1).

In 1984 there were 54 grant-aided staff in the Development Officers schemes and three vacancies. The major beneficiaries were the National Federation of Youth Clubs (13) the Catholic Youth Council (7) and Macra na Feirme (5). The Catholic Boy Scouts of Ireland, Ogra Chorcai and Limerick Youth Service had 3 a piece. The Scout Association of Ireland, Kerry Diocesan Youth Service, Irish Girl Guides, Foroige and Clare Regional Youth Service (2 each) and 1 each to ten other organisations — National Youth Council, Catholic Guides of Ireland, Voluntary Service International, Church of Ireland Youth Council, An Oige, Waterford Youth Committee, Junior Chamber of Ireland, Kilkenny Social Services Council, Ogras and Athlone Community Services Council.

The Department of Education retained the sport and community sections of the Development Officers scheme. In 1983 there were 9 officers in sport and only 17 in community projects. By April 1985 these were reduced to 8 and 15, respectively. Community officers were employed in four types of group — Local Welfare, Residents' Association, Disabled and Irish Language. Four types of post were filled: those of secretary, administrator, field officer and research worker.

Participants in Employment Training Programmes

Another type of state supported employment was that held by those who participated in special training schemes, often of brief duration. This brevity of work experience posed difficulties as to how to record this involvement. Annual averages would show considerable differences from numbers recorded at work at a point in time. Basing his material on averages Terry Corcoran of the Youth Employment Agency provided the data recorded in Table 107 and also the supporting commentary.

Table 107: *Average number of participants in employment/training programmes 1978 to 1984*

	Temporary Employment Schemes[1]	Work Experience Programme	AnCO Training[2]	Total
1978	1,100	200	2,900	4,200
1979	1,500	1,800	3,800	7,100
1980	1,100	2,200	3,400	6,700
1981	400	2,600	3,900	6,900
1982	1,300	4,300	6,300	11,900
1983	2,200	5,000	7,200	14,400
1984 (est)	2,300	4,000	9,100	15,400

Source: Terry Corcoran YEA.

[1] Environmental Improvement Scheme, Grant Scheme for Youth Employment.

[2] Excludes apprentices.

The temporary employment schemes were:

(a) Environmental Improvement Scheme. Beginning in 1978 the scheme financed local authorities to employ additional young people on environmental works.

(b) Grant Scheme for Youth Employment: Formerly under the Department of Education's Youth Section, like the Development Officers scheme, it was transferred to the Department of Labour. Grants were made available to youth and sport organisations to employ young people to build recreational and sporting facilities.

Work Experience Programme launched in 1973. Employers (public and private) provided up to 6 month's work experience to young people, who did not become employees. A tax free allowance (£20 up to April 1982, £30 up to early 1984 and £32.50 thereafter) was paid to the trainee.

The AnCO Training referred to here includes the Community/Youth Training Programme, introduced in 1976/77, which provided basic skills to young people in community projects usually involving the building of community amenities; it also includes participation by young people in AnCO's general training programmes.

SUMMARY

Delimiting and Classifying the Public Domain

The initial tasks facing this study were to delimit the extent of the public domain and to examine what was meant by employment. The latter examination gave rise to a number of recommendations which are outlined in the final part of this study. In pursuing the first task the public domain was seen to be wider than those areas delineated in traditional studies. Following the newly formulated international consensus the domain was decided on the basis of the nature of the function and the derivation of authority rather than on the traditional criteria of legal standing or administrative conventions. Thus all bodies, which derived on a regular basis 50 per cent or more of their income ultimately from taxation were deemed to be within the public domain. In the case of quasi-independent bodies, such as public enterprises, which are not largely state-funded, they were deemed to belong to the public domain if they satisfied the criteria of public ownership and control. *Prima facie*, these requirements are satisfied where (a) the public authorities hold the majority of the stock and (b) appoint the board. Since the area covered by these new international definitions is wider than that of the traditional branch and sector approaches of national accounts, this study uses the title 'domain' for the comprehensive category. A key concept underlying this category is the definition of the nature of government as formulated by the International Monetary Fund (see page 326).

Using these criteria, potential candidates for inclusion in the public domain were tested and classified into groups within a framework, set out in Appendix Table A1.2. Not all items in this tabulation are treated in this report since it was decided to defer reporting on the State-sponsored and allied groups until a later volume. The major groupings considered in this report are:

1. The Civil Service
2. The Oireachtas and the Judiciary
3. The Security Forces — military, police and prisons
4. Local Authorities
5. Education

1. The Civil Service

The major source of information on the Civil Service was the Civil Service Census up to 1975 when it was superseded by the computerised Staff Information System. Thanks to an unpublished memorandum of the Department of Finance Table 1 preserves the level of aggregate employment from the foundation of the State up to 1958 when a reclassification of the Census occurred. Since continuous and detailed breakdowns of the Census only survive from the late 'forties the first section, and especially Tables 2 to 4, give such information as is extant on the composition of these aggregates before January 1954.

The period 1934 to 1952 displayed a growth rate of 1.86 per cent annually, which was a higher rate than that which obtained subsequently, though in absolute terms more recent increases were much higher. Some of the existing material owes its survival to the fact that a group of civil servants, among them T. Linehan of the Central Statistics Office, were alarmed at the speed of growth in 1950 and 1951 and constituted an informal committee of enquiry, just when balance of payments difficulties in 1952 caused the levels of employment to be restricted and to decline over the 'fifties in many cases.

After this brief overview the next sections reconstruct time series for the constituent categories of the Civil Service, using every scrap of detail to ensure that the data are consistent and accurate. The results are summarised in Table 108 which distinguishes the Department of Posts and Telegraphs from other departments. It also gives information on staff outside the normal Civil Service Census since 1958. These latter can be subdivided into industrial and non-industrial staff. Some greater detail on these is provided by Table 36 and neighbouring tables as well as a set of tables in Appendix 2. It will be noted that Table 108 does not include staff outside the Census who were associated with the military nor does it include staff engaged in wireless work who later transferred to Radio Eireann. Since the table includes staff engaged in temporary schemes, as set out in Table 34 for the pre-1958 period, totals do not agree with those of Table 1 even when allowance is made for omissions.

Apart from the paucity of the early records the series was disrupted a number of times, in 1952 and 1958 by reclassifications, in 1975 by the switch over to computers and by the 1981 go-slow on recruitment. The major effect of the reclassifications was to set up a series outside the Census, first for industrial workers and then for others especially scale-paid staff in the Post Office and in Social Welfare. Table 39 documents the transition for the 1958 change. The 1975 computerisation caused teething problems so that employment levels are uncertain for much of 1976 and 1977. This makes it difficult to pinpoint the effects of the 1975–77 recruitment go-slow. The 1981 go-slow disrupted the series in the sense that an incentive to exaggerate 1981 numbers was provided by the rule under which only one in three vacancies could be filled. This compounded the uncertainty

Table 108: *Numbers of Civil Servants 1922 to 1985 distinguishing Post Office Non-Industrials but excluding wireless and civilians in defence*

	Central Civil Service	of which Part time	Posts and Telegraphs	of which Part time	Staff outside the Census[a] Central	P&T
1922	6,800	n.a.	13,500	n.a.	(b)	(b)
1932	9,082	n.a.	11,316	n.a.	(b)	(b)
1934	8,898	398	10,720	5,705	(b)	(b)
1938	10,486	n.a.	12,269	n.a.	(b)	(b)
1940	11,760	n.a.	11,285	n.a.	(b)	(b)
1950	13,566	526	14,374	5,657	6,181	1,773
1951	14,047	629	14,795	5,551	7,173	1,962
1952	15,332	607	15,175	5,483	8,841	791
1953	15,399	585	15,650	5,395	8,752	808
1954	15,015	555	15,793	5,370	8,624	886
1955	14,913	729	15,630	5,326	9,465	1,029
1956	14,872	725	15,562	5,266	9,453	953
1957	15,063	738	15,494	5,229	9,583	697
1958	14,929	734	15,166	5,215	(b)	(b)
1958*	14,481	n.a.	13,053	3,102	(b)	(b)
1959	14,551	951	13,117	3,098	8,818	2,887
1960	14,742	907	12,994	3,110	9,042	2,870
1961	14,817	904	13,264	3,093	8,717	3,076
1962	15,425	879	13,485	3,060	8,323	2,852
1963	15,751	877	13,977	3,089	9,106	3,058
1964	16,004	869	14,379	3,169	8,895	3,044
1965	16,617	860	15,058	3,107	9,073	3,165
1966	17,218	856	15,391	3,092	8,509	3,172
1967	17,520	848	15,445	3,014	7,808	3,017
1968	18,060	861	15,629	2,964	7,433	3,067
1969	18,475	839	16,031	2,866	7,132	2,966
1970	19,042	774	17,208	2,836	6,537	3,021
1971	19,948	776	18,071	2,835	6,715	3,067
1972	20,955	701	18,409	2,801	6,420	2,891
1973	22,189	664	19,151	2,746	6,027	3,071
1974	23,998	656	20,751	2,715	6,020	3,078
1975	24,906	575	22,071	2,706	6,071	2,989
1976	25,909	n.a.	22,930	n.a.	6,034	2,861
1977	26,425	n.a.	23,400	n.a.	5,825	2,892
1978	27,045	415	23,888	2,432	5,560	2,985
1979	28,225	397	24,502	2,276	6,127	3,040
1980	29,834	384	25,240	2,238	6,303	2,905
1981	31,475	276	26,692	2,048	6,622	2,950
1982	32,531	315	27,635	2,022	6,867	3,003
1983	31,980	300	27,324	1,977	7,003	2,898
1984	31,406	271	26,872	1,767	6,737	2,783
1985	30,504	251	26,282	1,372	6,333	2,653

Sources: Tables 10 to 15, 33, 34 and 36. For total see Table 114.
*Revised due to reclassification.
[a] Refers to those excluded after 1958. Prior to 1958 industrials were included in Census, see Table 1. Annual Totals do not agree with those in Table 1 since they include pieceworkers and exclude wireless and industrial workers in defence.
[b] Data on pieceworkers not available.

and probable understatement associated with the 1975 computerisation. A considerable part of the text accordingly deals with data sources and with calculations designed to overcome the consequences of these disruptions.

Efforts to correct for understatement were hampered by the fact that it is not the practice to record recruitment, though departures have been documented for decades. A major innovation of this study was to remedy this deficiency, see Table 116. A valuable by-product of the exercise was to provide the first ever estimates of departure probabilities by length of service, i.e., wastage rates. Disaggregating departures by sex revealed that women were more than twice as prone to leave as men and provided a mechanism by which understatement in the total figures could be apportioned between the Post Office and other departments. The figures in Table 108 for the years after 1975 contain this element of correction. The processes of adjustment are detailed in Tables 12 and 15. Due to this refinement, recruitment levels could also be disaggregated between the Post Office and other departments.

Having defined the flows and general levels of central departments and the Post Office, some sections were devoted to the structures making up these totals. Rapid expansion increased the youthfulness of the age structure. The high departure rates of women led to high recruitment rates so that women were more numerous than men among recent cohorts of entrants in the central Civil Service. Three-quarters of the women had less than ten years service and even among men only a quarter had served more than 18 years. Women were much less numerous in the Post Office and their duration of service even shorter. Very few women were over 35 years of age but almost half the men. In 1975 almost two out of every three women were under 21 years of age.

Taking the long-term view the proportion of women in the Civil Service doubled in the decades up to 1975 and then stabilised until the recruitment go-slow began to erode their position. In the process women took over to a large extent the grades of Clerical and Staff Officer which were very heavily male in 1932 (see Table 19) and strengthened their hold on the grade of Clerical Assistant. Their share of executive officers reflected their overall numbers. In higher posts, up to Assistant Principal Officer, their representation increased greatly though their propensity to leave the service before the age of 35 may account for them not being more numerous. Even so in 1982, 82 per cent of all women were either Clerical Officers or Assistants.

Another type of analysis concentrates on the grade structures. In the central Civil Service higher paid posts expanded more rapidly than lower. In the Post Office the share held by postmen fell. The tendency of lower paid staff to decline in numbers or grow slowly is to be found generally in the public domain where unskilled jobs, such as cleaner, roadworker, etc., have not shared in the high expansion rates of recent decades. A brief glance at the highest paid group showed a great variety of growth rates among the grades with that of Assistant Principal Officer exhibiting the most rapid increase. Growth rates of the higher paid Assistant Secretaries and the lower paid Higher Executive Officers were more modest.

Yet another structural approach focuses on departments. Over time staff have been hived off to State-sponsored bodies and departmental functions rearranged. To some extent comparisons over time can mitigate this latter problem by grouping departments. Time paths of change varied with rural departments growing in the 'sixties, law enforcement and central administration more recently. Education grew relatively slowly in spite of the explosion in pupil numbers.

Staff may also be divided into whole time and part time. Table 30 shows that the Post Office was the chief employer of part-time staff. These were mainly part-time postmen in the provincial branch. Other departments mainly employed women, frequently for office cleaning. Part-time working has declined to less than a third of its 1951 levels. Part of the reason is the substitution of contract cleaning in many of the new offices but a major factor has been the 1958 reclassification of some staff paid on a scale basis.

As Table 108 indicates, some workers have been excluded from the Census since 1958 or earlier. Separate enumerations distinguish industrials from other excluded staff. Figure 8 shows that these industrial workers are quite different from those recorded in the Census of Industrial Production. They are also somewhat different from those identified in the National Accounts and were associated predominantly with rural activities, such as forestry and drainage. Numbers have tended to decline though there has been some recovery since 1978. Non-industrial workers have been largely scale-paid Civil Servants: managers of sub-post offices and of social welfare branches. Prior to 1958, scale-paid staff were returned as part time.

Although workers paid on a fee or similar basis are not included in the data, Table 32 gives an indication of numbers involved at a time when such information was collated.

Oireachtas, Judiciary and Security Forces

Table 109 sets out the numbers for the groups in this section.

The numbers of members of the Oireachtas, or parliament, are governed by the size of the population as set out in the Constitution and subsequent legislation. The Judiciary are paid for out of special funds, set out in the Finance Accounts, and their numbers are also subject to legislation. Since 1975 provisions have been made for secretarial assistants to TDs and Seanadoiri and these provisions have become more generous with the passage of time.

The stability in the numbers of Gardai up to 1971 is well illustrated in Figure 11.

Table 109: *Employment in Oireachtas* Judiciary and Security Forces, 1950–1985*

	Oireachtas, Judiciary	Police	Defence Forces	Civilians in Defence
1950	279	7,083	8,113	1,477
1951	279	6,904	7,880	1,437
1952	279	6,724	10,004	1,531
1953	278	6,691	10,562	1,565
1954	279	6,774	10,412	2,077
1955	275	6,826	9,692	2,183
1956	275	6,800	8,735	1,993
1957	274	6,568	8,846	1,870
1958	271	6,481	8,130	1,420
1959	269	6,492	9,188	1,615
1960	268	6,580	8,965	1,623
1961	268	6,612	8,868	1,593
1962	268	6,531	8,451	1,641
1963	265	6,401	8,449	1,658
1964	262	6,452	8,221	1,674
1965	262	6,568	8,119	1,576
1966	262	6,545	8,159	1,596
1967	262	6,536	8,331	1,507
1968	262	6,546	8,312	1,518
1969	262	6,543	8,232	1,514
1970	262	6,532	8,574	1,515
1971	262	6,612	8,663	1,516
1972	262	6,961	9,050	1,538
1973	262	7,794	10,466	1,591
1974	263	7,990	10,654	1,619
1975	279	8,419	11,602	1,943
1976	279	8,449	13,653	1,964
1977	289	8,485	14,662	1,958
1978	293	9,182	14,750	1,977
1979	298	9,396	13,676	2,068
1980	317	9,693	13,372	2,125
1981	342	9,882	13,764	2,121
1982	374	9,943	15,318	2,029
1983	483	10,831	14,457	1,945
1984	484	11,232	14,125	1,861
1985	476	11,387	13,891	1,831

Sources: Tables 40, 41, 49 and A2.13.
Civilians in Defence 410 in 1932, 627 in 1939.
*Includes President.

Since then numbers have increased year by year though numbers only rose marginally between 1975 and 1977, and numbers in training in early 1982 were as low as 25 for a short while due to changes in procedures for the entrance competition. Records of inflows can be estimated from wastage figures and changes in strength since 1969 and Figure 11 shows these to have fluctuated very considerably. Women have now been integrated into most types of police work.

In the main text a brief discussion of the prison service follows the section on the police and presents some estimates of inflows and outflows of personnel as well as of staffing structures. Prisons are not included in Table 109 since they were given already as part of the central Civil Service in Table 108.

Employment in the Defence Force has followed a more erratic path than that for the police. This mainly reflects the changes in numbers of privates since NCO levels have shown a steady increase over most of the period (see Figure 10). Over time the Defence Force have tended to become more officer intensive. Privates initially enlist for a three-year term of duty. Demand tends to be greatest when job opportunities are few and and renewals of contracts least when economic conditions are generally favourable. This tends to produce some elements of a counter-cyclical pattern, though the strife in Northern Ireland has been the major factor in the expansion after 1969. Data on losses through wastage were not available to this study so that gross levels of recruitment could not be calculated except for cadets (see Table 42). Detail was available on the structure of the permanent Defence Force by corps (see Table 43). Women soldiers have remained few to date.

Employment in the Defence Forces is not generally regarded as extending to age 65 for most staff. Many military personnel retire after a fixed term of duty and follow other careers. On retirement they join the first line reserve for a number of years (see Table 44). Second line reserve are not generally paid except during attendance at annual camp. The text provides some idea of the numbers involved for some years.

Civilians with the Defence Forces are non-military personnel whose conditions of employment are governed by the 1954 Defence Acts. Levels of employment were discussed in the text under "staff not included in the Staff Information System" but are presented in Table 109 because of their association with the security forces. Staff working for the police are, however, included with industrials, etc. Details of the occupations followed are given on pages 132 and 133.

Local Authorities including Health

The summary of employment with the local authorities is set out in Table 110, which also includes details on voluntary hospitals and homes for the mentally handicapped. In the case of these private bodies it is impossible to say when their dependence on state funding reached a point which put them within the public

Table 110: *Employment in health and in local authorities 1950–1984*

| | Local Authorities | | Health Boards | Joint Board Hospitals | Voluntary Bodies | | Local Authorities | |
| | | | | | Voluntary Hospitals | Homes for the mentally handicapped | County Committee of Agriculture | |
Date†	Total	Local Administration					Instructors	Others
1950	55,751	n.a.		n.a.			212	(27)
1951	60,142	47,049		13,093			219	(28)
1952	62,486	n.a.		n.a.	Records are not available		230	(29)
1953	62,266	n.a.		n.a.	nor is it clear when		247	(32)
1954	55,739	n.a.		n.a.	more than half staff		261	(34)
1955	57,438	n.a.		n.a.	salaries were State		273	(35)
1956	56,461	n.a.		n.a.	funded for the first		287	(37)
1957	53,337	n.a.		n.a.	time.*		301	(39)
1958	47,367	30,485		16,882			313	41
1959	46,389	n.a.		n.a.			328	(42)
1960	44,056	n.a.		n.a.			352	(43)
1961	45,420	27,617		17,803			354	(43)
1962	47,658	n.a.		n.a.			355	(43)
1963	48,105	n.a.		n.a.			362	(44)
1964	47,618	n.a.		n.a.			402	(46)
1965	47,351	n.a.		n.a.			438	(48)
1966	48,341	27,824		20,517			464	50
1967	49,722	n.a.		n.a.			496	(64)
1968	52,004	28,298		23,706			502	(66)

Table 110: (cont'd.)

Year								
1969	52,527	28,082	24,445				509	(69)
1970	54,489	n.a.	n.a.				555	(89)
1971	55,746	30,526	25,220		10,672		593	105
1972	(56,114)	30,154	(25,960)		(11,466)		n.a.	110
1973	57,367	30,667	24,901	1,799	(12,086)		654	115
1974	61,033	31,993	27,286	1,754	12,913		652	120
1975	(62,665)	31,692	29,173	(1,800)	(12,992)		667	123
1976	(64,390)	32,149	(30,430)	(1,811)	(13,071)		670	(123)
1977	(65,862)	(32,353)	31,682	1,830	13,984		698	(124)
1978	(67,521)	(32,633)	33,038	(1,850)	14,672	3,560	686	125
1979	(71,937)	(33,146)	36,771	2,020	15,100	3,846	703	(126)
1980	75,100	34,834	38,058	2,208	15,381	4,061	713	127
1981	77,747	35,710	39,640	2,397	15,993	4,322		
1982	77,600(est)	35,885	39,285**	18,721**		4,611**	transferred	
1983	77,550(est)	36,261	38,860	18,640		4,579	to	
1984		35,598					ACOT	

Sources: Tables 57, 63, 69, 76. For Figures 1938–1949 see Tables 57 and 76.

†Date refers to Jan., Feb. or March, see source tables. **September.

Note: Local Administration in August 1977 and 1978 (32,658 and 32,583) converted to January equivalents by interpolation. Figures in parentheses are estimates.

*Mental and other non-local authority hospitals had the following levels of employment recorded in the Census of Population. The figures included homes for the mentally handicapped, nursing homes and hospices for the dying. 1951, 722 mental + 5,573 other; 1961, 769 + 8,691 other; 1966, 861 mental + 10,792 other; 1971, 14,145 combined.

domain. Voluntary hospitals went over to a budget-based funding system in 1973. Homes for the mentally handicapped switched over in many cases in 1975 partly because the capitation scheme had become increasingly unprofitable and partly because there was a desire to raise the quality of service in response to the 1975 Year of the Handicapped. St. Michael's House did not become part of the public domain until 1981. ¯

Prior to 1971, when the regional health boards were established, health was combined with local administration except where united health authorities had been created in the four county borough counties. The major group of workers were engaged in construction activities, mainly on roads, and salaried officials, or officers, were a small but growing fraction of local administration. In contrast employment levels of manual workers have tended to decline, a phenomenon also observed with industrial Civil Servants. The dominance of these "servants" in the total for local administration has kept aggregate growth levels down or even negative. Within the aggregate the higher paid the post the more rapid the expansion in numbers (see Table 65).

When growth in employment in local administration is studied by type of authority, the urbanised authorities were seen to have faster increases then the more rural, e.g., county boroughs grew much faster than county councils.

In 1947 the Department of Health began its existence separate from its parent Department of Local Government and Public Health. With the 1953 Health Act the increased accent on health care and the rejection of the Poor Law ethos led the public authorities increasingly into the arena of health care provision. In the urban areas, but mainly in Dublin, the absence of public hospitals caused the local authorities to involve the voluntary hospitals increasingly in their schemes. It was not possible, within the context of this study , to determine when the public authorities became the main source of voluntary hospital revenue. With the 1973 decision to fund these hospitals directly they were clearly within the public domain. However it is also clear that they were in it *de facto* under the previous more fragmented scheme. Unfortunately employment records for this earlier period are meagre, apart from the Census of Population. The recording of employment levels in homes for the mentally handicapped is still more recent.

Even the public hospital and health care employment levels are difficult to disentangle from other local authority activities prior to the setting up of regional health boards except in the United Health Authorities. The Census of Population provides some indicators and an occupational breakdown (see Table 70). The 'seventies have produced a variety of sources, not all completely consistent with each other. Of these the most important is the annual census of the Department of Health.

Education

(a) Academic staff at first and second levels

Our knowledge of state-funded teacher employment is summarised in Table 111 for primary and second-level schools. These figures exclude private primary schools and non-incremental teachers in secondary schools.

Primary schools include special schools and classes for the handicapped as well as schools assoicated with residential homes and special schools for neglected and delinquent children. Teaching staff include those engaged in the secondary tops section. Up to recently some of these schools were financed on a capitation basis (see Table 82) but these have all switched over.

The rise in teacher numbers has been accompanied by a greater predominance of women teachers, the closing of many of the smallest schools, virtual disappearance of untrained teachers, a slower rise in pupil numbers accommodated in schools of improved design and standards. The rise in the number of special schools for the handicapped has been striking. Figures on staff inflows and outflows since 1978/79 in Table 81 show considerable drops in both in each subsequent year. Although the number of religious-managed schools has remained stable in a declining population of schools, the number of religious teachers has almost halved since 1966. Since that date class size has improved dramatically with very few pupils currently in classes of 45 or more.

Numbers of secondary schools increased to a maximum of 600 in 1969/70 and since declined. In part the accent has been on larger schools, i.e., in excess of 300 and in part there has been competition from community and comprehensive schools. The big boost to teacher employment was the introduction of the "free" scheme in 1967. The decision to improve pupil-teacher ratios in 1977 has been reversed due to shortage of State finances so that current teacher numbers have stabilised at their 1981/82 level. As Table 88 indicates, secondary schools have employed unregistered teachers in addition to those on State-funded incremental scales. Even excluding these, schools have reduced pupil teacher ratio to about 17 from being over 24 when the free scheme was launched. Women teachers have become numerous than men.

Comprehensive schools anticipated the free scheme by a year. With their successors, the Community Schools, they have become a growing challenge and alternative to the traditional secondary schools and have continued to grow while the latter stabilised their employment in recent years. These schools are remarkable in that they employ more men than women teachers and also an increasing number of religious.

Schools run by the Vocational Education Committees do not fit neatly into this section since some of their schools cater for third-level students. They are also engaged in apprenticeship and day release courses as well as adult education. Table 93 gives a breakdown of teachers distinguishing second-level voca-

Table 111: *Academic staff in first- and second-level schools including all VECs*
1950–1985

Date	National	Incremental Secondary	Comp. and Community		Vocational		Agricultural Home Economics etc.
			Full time	Part time	Full time	Part time	
1950	12,870	2,152	—	—	1,179	900	n.a.
1951	12,792	2,219	—	—	1,125	1,021	n.a.
1952	12,883	2,291	—	—	1,193	1,004	n.a.
1953	13,000	2,359	—	—	1,239	1,061	n.a.
1954	13,144	2,391	—	—	1,332	1,121	n.a.
1955	13,231	2,478	—	—	1,363	1,185	n.a.
1956	13,262	2,600	—	—	1,427	1,192	n.a.
1957	13,402	2,701	—	—	1,487	1,119	n.a.
1958	13,554	2,814	—	—	1,537	1,121	n.a.
1959	13,753	2,955	—	—	1,574	1,228	n.a.
1960	13,866	3,086	—	—	1,606	1,446	n.a.
1961	14,032	3,234	—	—	1,661	1,560	n.a.
1962	14,091	3,381	—	—	1,750	1,641	n.a.
1963	14,218	3,581	—	—	1,826	1,896	n.a.
1964	14,297	3,734	—	—	1,958	1,996	n.a.
1965	14,469	3,992	—	—	2,112	2,103	n.a.
1966	14,614	4,253	—	—	2,340	2,287	n.a.
1967	14,672	4,461	45	7	2,445	2,276	n.a.
1968	14,794	4,838	60	8	2,753	2,456	n.a.
1969	14,733	6,099	86	14	3,168	2,740	n.a.
1970	14,859	6,768	97	8	3,488	2,879	n.a.
1971	15,080	7,272	109	18	3,791	2,835	((75))
1972	15,450	8,016	182	31	4,147	2,955	((77))
1973	15,612	8,603	311	66	4,476	2,978	78
1974	16,137	9,181	617	87	4,675	3,010	((78))
1975	16,718	9,431	845	(36)	5,100	n.a.	((78))
1976	17,055	9,830	976	(36)	5,442	n.a.	((77))
1977	17,273	10,176	1,065	(34)	5,532	(671)	((77))
1978	17,595	10,830	1,239	(46)	5,723	(909)	77
1979	18,387	11,228	1,398	(54)	6,081	(856)	((78))
1980	18,811	11,470	1,545	(80)	6,162	(1,087)	79
1981	19,356	11,740	1,684	(91)	6,475	(1,069)	80
1982	19,926	11,896	1,856	(101)	6,557	(1,377)	81
1983	20,381	12,065	2,021	(111e)	6,745	(1,043)	79
1984	20,732	11,892	2,108	((100))	7,723		78
1985 Jan	20,884	11,892	2,183	((100))	((7,920))		

Source: Tables 78, 89, 90, 91, 93 and 94. FTE in parentheses. Double parentheses denote a guess.

tional schools from Regional Technical Colleges and other technological colleges such as the Dublin Institute of Technology. Due to heterogeneity of courses and the fact that many teachers and pupils are part time, pupil-teacher ratios have proved extremely difficult to calculate especially since the abandonment of the publication of teaching hours.

It should be noted that career guidance teachers were introduced on an extra-quota basis in 1972 to compensate for the decision to increase the pupil numbers for secondary teacher allocations. More than 500 have been appointed and are included with other second-level teachers in their school type. Similarly 767 remedial teachers have been included with the rest of the primary teachers.

Employment in other second-level schools has been poorly documented. The major category has been the schools of agriculture and horticulture and the colleges of rural home economics funded until recently by the Department of Agriculture and subsequently by ACOT. The last colleges of rural home economics closed in 1984. Other second-level education promoted by the Department of Defence or by the Department of Education in the case of home economics and secretarial training has been on a small scale or else included in other returns.

(b) Non-academic employment at first and second levels

The scrappy nature of the records for non-academic employment is well illustrated in Table 112 which summarises available material.

Table 112: *Non-academic employment in first- and second-level education some years 1951 to 1985*

	Special Schools and Residential homes		Agricultural schools, etc.	Caretakers and clerical assistants	Child care assistants* (handicapped)	Vocational Educational
	Full time	Part time				
1951	468		n.a			n.a.
1956	378		n.a			n.a.
1966	n.a.	n.a.	n.a.			671
1971	n.a.	n.a.	30*			833
1973	n.a.	n.a.	37			n.a.
1978 (June)	400*	100*	45*	n.a.		2,311
1979	420*	105*	46*	243*	70	2,392*
1980	437	110	48*	546	74	2,477*
1981	455	126	50	761	82	2,556*
1982	432	122	87	844	85	2,660
1983	488	106	91	936	85	2,728
1984	n.a.	n.a.	91	908	85	2,713
1985	n.a.	n.a.	n.a.	872	85	n.a.

*Estimated employment.

Sources: Tables 82, 86, 94 and 96.

Special schools and residential homes for delinquents and neglected children were not included in the previous section as their staffing is not academic. Children usually go out to school in the normal way from residential homes. Figure 15 illustrates the way in which numbers of children in detention fell in the three decades up to 1970. Most of the earlier institutions have been replaced and present day funding is tending towards being on a budget basis. In 1983 Trinity House, run by the Department of Education, became the first institution not under the control of a religious order.

Caretakers, Clerical Assistants and Child Care Assistants in special schools for the handicapped are manifestations of the 1977 Full Employment Programme. Budgetary stringency since 1981 has tended to reduce the number of Caretakers and Clerical Assistants permitted and to restrict expansion of the child care programme.

The considerable non-academic employment of VEC committees is inadequately documented. Earlier figures from the Census of Population may not be comparable with returns by the VECs themselves. Figures for colleges funded by the Department of Agriculture can be expected to contract with the closing of the colleges of rural home economics.

(c) Third-level employment

Table 113 summarises the records of employment in third-level education. In the case of the Universities it is not clear if Trinity College, Dublin, had entered the public domain by the end of March 1950. It had traditionally enjoyed large investment income and rents. At that stage Maynooth clearly had not, since it only reopened its lectures to lay students in 1966.

Up to 1968, university statistics were published by the Central Statistics Office but relinquished on the establishment of the Higher Education Authority which became the conduit through which Department of Education funding found its way to many third-level institutions. Since the HEA did not have a brief for private funding or funding from other departments its statistics do not treat all university employment and in fact its planning role makes it favour establishment levels rather than posts filled. Consequently the figures in Table 113 tend to rely on the published accounts of universities which are far from being uniform. Some universities deem demonstrators as staff, others regard them as post-graduates with scholarships. Some colleges contract out services which others provide in-house. For many reasons, therefore, "Other academic" employment is a rather meaningless category. It would be preferable if fee paid, part-time and demonstrators were recorded as full-time equivalents (FTE). This is the practice of the HEA which unfortunately does not publish employment levels nor cover all employed. Because of the absence of FTEs calculation of pupil teacher ratios is hazardous, even if student numbers could be weighted for type of course, e.g., undergraduate, masters, Ph.D.

Table 113: *Employment in third-level education excluding VECs 1950 to 1985*

Year ended March	Universities Academic Full time	Other	Universities Non-Academic Full time	Other	Teacher training academic	Other third level Academic	Other
1950	363	268	436		n.a.	[a]	[b]
1951	366	272	454		n.a.	[a]	[b]
1952	386	279	519		n.a.	[a]	[b]
1953	371	287	753		n.a.	[a]	[b]
1954	374	276	787		n.a.	[a]	[b]
1955	400	325	799		n.a.	[a]	[b]
1956	423	361	812		n.a.	[a]	[b]
1957	429	372	831		n.a.	[a]	[b]
1958	447	334	824		n.a.	[a]	[b]
1959	468	342	850		n.a.	[a]	[b]
1960	497	372	918		n.a.	[a]	[b]
1961	538	406	959		n.a.	[a]	[b]
1962	567	721	1,000		n.a.	[a]	[b]
1963	634	713	1,069		n.a.	[a]	[b]
1964	675	564	1,170		n.a.	[a]	[b]
1965	730	658	1,310		n.a.	[a]	[b]
1966	756	716	1,445		n.a.	[a]	[b]
1967	798	853	1,621		n.a.	[a]	[b]
1968	847	1,012	1,834		n.a.	[a]	[b]
1969	907	1,141	2,006		n.a.	[a]	[b]
1970	992	1,216	2,116		n.a.	[a]	[b]
1971	1,059	1,252	2,385[c]		n.a.	[a]	[b]
1972	1,138	1,196	2,519		107[c]+56[c]	16*	5*
1973	1,160	1,474	2,682		124[c]+53[c]	44*+4	26*
1974	1,210	1,542	2,900		132[c]+68[c]	68*+1	58*
1975	1,256	1,276	2,768	218	143[c]+70[c]	121+1	180
1976	1,291	1,463	2,776	251	155+76	122[c]+2[c]	186[c]
1977†	1,351	1,393	2,930	131	185+74	123+3	190+9
1978	1,425	1,445	3,048	118	187+59	144+1	192
1979	1,531	1,661	3,130	128	194[c]+72[c]	159+1	208
1980	1,574	1,673	3,189	129	198+78	181+2	236+15
1981	1,625	1,980	3,219	136	223+84	252+2	284+15
1982	1,635	1,924	3,262	139	229+107	268	342+2
1983	1,656	2,161	3,227	150	226+102	291+73	395+18
1984	1,656	2,235	3,208	146	232+123	300+46	418+21
1985					241**+36		

Sources: Table 98, 99, 104

[c]=Estimate.

*Excludes National College of Art and Design and Royal Irish Academy.

**Includes full time equivalents.

†From 1977 full time university staff includes full time equivalents in TCD.

[a] Only National College of Art in existence. Employment is included with Department of Education.

[b] As [a] but also non-academic staff in the Royal Irish Academy.

Details of employment in teacher training colleges has been hard to come by for earlier years so it has been impossible to substantiate the claim of some researchers that training has been highly efficient compared with other third-level studies.

Other third-level institutions refer to those funded by the HEA. Of these two are centuries old, the Royal Irish Academy and the National College of Art and Design. The remainder are the product of the ferment of the early 'seventies which firmly established the binary system of education at third-level, i.e., the academic and the technological.

Miscellaneous

Among the miscellaneous types of employment can be listed the doctors and pharmacists whose services are purchased by the General Medical Services Payments Board and who appear to be a modern form of the old dispensary doctor system. Earnings can be high. Two doctors earned in excess of £50,000 during 1979.

Another group of State-funded employees date from the Full Employment Programme — the Youth Development Officers whose activities supplement the State-funded work of core staff in youth organisations already being financed from earlier budgets.

Finally there are the participants of employment training programme many of whom engage in actual work such as neighbourhood improvement schemes. It is difficult to know how to classify these people as few of them obtain more than a few month's training. In some ways they can be deemed to be a more sophisticated version of the old Emergency Employment Schemes.

Aggregate Employment

The data on the preceding tables are collected together in Table 114 with the exception of those series for which the records are incomplete. Table 108 is summarised into full-time staff in the SIS records and others. The others are part-time staff and staff outside the SIS, such as industrials. Non-SIS staff include large numbers of casual workers, and since it has not proved possible to get a breakdown of part-time and casual staff for all departments in every year the entire group has been included with part timers. The third column gives the totals for Table 109. A small number of civilians with the defence forces are not identified in the table but can be discovered by reference to the more disaggregated tables.

The fourth column gives all local authorities including health boards and joint board hospitals. It does not give employment in State-funded voluntary bodies, such as hospitals and homes for the mentally handicapped, since there is doubt when these became part of the public domain, and also because records

Table 114: *Employment in the main categories of the public domain 1950 to 1985 excluding incomplete series**

Early in	Civil Service inc. P&T Full time	Indust. and Part time	Oireachtas Security etc.	Local authorities inc. Health and Agriculture	Education Full time and FTE	Part time	Total with cols. 2 and 6 Excluded	Included
1950	21,757	14,137	16,952	55,990	17,000	1,168	111,699	127,004
1951	22,662	15,315	16,500	60,389	16,956	1,293	116,507	133,115
1952	24,417	15,722	18,538	62,745	17,272	1,283	122,972	139,977
1953	25,069	15,540	19,096	62,545	17,722	1,348	124,432	141,320
1954	24,883	15,435	19,542	56,034	18,028	1,397	118,487	135,319
1955	24,488	16,549	18,976	57,746	18,271	1,510	119,481	137,540
1956	24,443	16,397	17,803	56,785	18,524	1,553	117,555	135,505
1957	24,590	16,247	17,558	53,677	18,850	1,491	114,675	132,413
1958	24,146	(16,000)	16,302	47,721	19,176	1,455	107,345	(124,800)
1959	23,619	15,754	17,564	46,759	19,600	1,570	107,542	124,866
1960	23,719	15,929	17,436	44,451	19,973	1,818	105,579	123,326
1961	24,084	15,790	17,341	45,817	20,424	1,966	107,666	125,422
1962	24,971	15,114	16,891	48,056	20,789	2,362	110,707	128,183
1963	25,762	16,130	16,773	48,511	21,328	2,609	112,374	131,113
1964	26,345	15,977	16,609	48,066	21,834	2,560	112,854	131,391
1965	27,708	16,205	16,525	47,837	22,613	2,761	114,683	133,649
1966	28,661	15,629	16,562	48,855	23,408	3,003	117,486	136,118
1967	29,103	14,687	16,636	50,282	24,042	3,136	120,063	137,886
1968	29,864	14,325	16,638	52,572	25,126	3,476	124,200	142,001
1969	30,801	13,803	16,551	53,105	26,999	3,895	127,456	145,154
1970	32,640	13,168	16,883	55,133	28,320	4,103	132,976	150,247
1971	34,408	13,393	17,053	56,444	29,696	4,105	137,601	155,099
1972	35,862	12,813	17,811	(56,114)	31,473	4,182	141,260	158,255
1973	37,930	12,508	20,113	58,136	32,914	4,522	149,093	166,123
1974	41,378	12,469	20,526	61,805	34,846	4,640	158,555	175,664
1975	43,696	12,341	22,243	63,455	36,455	1,495*	165,849	179,685
1976	(45,703)	12,031	24,345	(64,390)	37,714	1,716*	172,152	185,899
1977	(46,833)	11,709	25,394	66,684	39,345	1,536	178,256	191,501
1978	48,086	11,392	26,202	68,332	41,151	1,564	183,771	196,727
1979	50,054	11,840	25,438	72,766	43,345	1,790	191,603	205,233
1980	52,452	11,830	25,507	75,940	44,955	1,819	198,854	212,503
1981	55,843	11,896	26,109	77,747	46,638	2,133	206,337	220,366
1982	57,829	12,207	27,664	(77,600)	48,149	2,065	211,242	225,514
1983	57,027	12,178	27,716	(77,550)	48,956	2,402	211,249	225,829
1984	56,240	11,558	27,702		49,130	2,448		
1985	55,163	10,609	27,585					

Note: For composition see text "Aggregate employment". Figures in parentheses contain estimates.
*See Table 115.

were not available. These bodies are treated in Table 115. In presenting the totals for local authorities it would have been useful to distinguish officers from servants since this would provide a useful parallel to the dichotomy given in the case of the Civil Service between full time and others. Almost all of the decline in local authorities can be attributed to reductions in the numbers of road workers, etc.

In the case of education two columns are given. The first gives teachers at first and second level, full-time academic and non-academic staff in universities and other HEA institutions. It also includes from Table 112 caretakers, clerical assistants and child care assistants. This column is understated slightly since it does not include staff at the Royal Irish Academy or at the National College of Art and Design for earlier years. However in the latter case staff were included with the Department of Education for years before the college was reconstituted. The part time refers to those employed part time by VECs, Comprehensive and Community schools up to 1973 or 1974. When full-time equivalents were recorded subsequently these were included with the full-time staff. Other part time relate mainly to part-time and fee paid staff at universities and other institutions included in the previous column.

Incomplete Series and State-sponsored Bodies

The figures on Table 114 are incomplete since they do not contain staff in voluntary organisations which in earlier years were not paid for on a budget basis. For some of these, i.e., voluntary hospitals, records began to be available from the early 'seventies; others were only recorded at the end of the 'seventies, e.g., special schools and residential homes, homes for the mentally handicapped. The details are given in the footnote to Table 115.

This study has not examined the employment record of State-sponsored bodies. Some tentative figures are included in Table 115 to give a comprehensive idea of the total scope of employment in the public domain. It is hoped to under-take a study of the State-sponsored bodies at a later stage so that firmer figures might be available. The "Grand Totals' given on Table 115 indicate the source of the 300,000 Civil Servants, often referred to in the Press. The table shows that some of these are casuals or part time; others are working directly with voluntary associations, often religious orders in the fields of education and health. Only about one in ten is a conventional Civil Servant.

Inflows and Outflows

Although the bulk of the report is devoted to establishing accurately the levels of employment obtaining each year, in some cases it was possible to quantify the dynamics underlying these levels. These flows have never been reported before and, in fact, some of them were only developed within the context of this study.

Table 115: *Aggregate employment in the Public Domain 1971–1983*

	Non-industrial full time	Industrial, part time and servants	Incomplete series available only since:–		State-sponsored bodies	Grand total
			1971	1978		
1971	113,519	41,580	(13,247)	833+	60,069	229,248
1972	117,908	40,347	(14,127)	n.a.	n.a.	n.a.
1973	125,519	40,604	(14,832)	n.a.	n.a.	n.a.
1974	134,106	41,558	15,728	n.a.	n.a.	n.a.
1975	141,824	37,861	(15,911)	n.a.	n.a.	n.a.
1976	147,815	38,084	(16,076)	n.a.	58,985	n.a.
1977	153,898	37,603	16,945	n.a.	60,003	n.a.
1978	159,434	37,293	17,684	6,383	61,721	282,515
1979	167,119	38,114	18,111	6,775	63,932	294,051
1980	173,088	39,415	18,463	7,097	66,795	304,858
1981	179,665	40,701	19,179	7,471	68,373	315,389
1982	184,964	40,550	19,546	7,875	68,787	321,722
1983	184,871	40,958	19,522	7,901	(68,500)	(321,752)

"Series since 1971" includes Voluntary Hospitals, GMS doctors and pharmacists (assumption 2,200 in 1971 and 2,250 in 1972) Training Colleges (total assumed twice full-time academic) 190 in 1971 Agriculture Schools.

"Series since 1978" include non-academic VEC, homes for the mentally handicapped, special schools and residential homes and residential schools of domestic economy (assumed 12).

State-sponsored bodies figures for 1977 to 1982 based on Table 40 Humphrey's 1983. Other figures are very tentative pending a more detailed study.

Note: Columns 1 and 2 differ from those in Table 114 in that "servants" of local authorities are now included with industrials, part timers, etc. Estimates are given in parentheses.

Any study of the potential for public employment needs to have these data as a point of departure. Table 116 gives the figures for Civil Servants, gardai and primary teachers.

In the text an attempt was made to measure wastage rates as a valuable tool in personnel management. While some insights were obtained and reported, an attempt to develop a wastage function from cohort records proved difficult due to imperfections in the manner in which outflows were recorded. It is hoped to overcome these problems in a separate study.

While it is interesting to have historical series of inflows and outflows as a measure of the absorption capacity of the public domain the figures indicate that when the economy is in difficulties departure rates also tend to reduce. Only two women primary teachers resigned on marriage in 1984 and both were leaving Europe. Effective manpower planning would need to know more about the mechanics of wastage and whether departure rates can be expected to resume after a lag. It would also be interesting to know the influence of the abolition of the marriage gratuity on the mobility of women.

Table 116: *Inflows and Outflows from certain categories of the public service 1950 to 1984*

	Civil service including P & T		Gardai		Primary Teachers	
	Intake	Outflow	Intake	Outflow	Intake	Outflow
1950	n.a.	n.a.	n.a.	n.a.	372	400
1951	n.a.	n.a.	n.a.	n.a.	261	384
1952	n.a.	n.a.	n.a.	n.a.	421	429
1953	n.a.	n.a.	n.a.	n.a.	485	507
1954	n.a.	n.a.	n.a.	n.a.	586	508
1955	n.a.	n.a.	n.a.	n.a.	468	503
1956	n.a.	n.a.	n.a.	n.a.	521	567
1957	n.a.	n.a.	n.a.	n.a.	668	612
1958	1,433	1,277	n.a.	n.a.	737	746
1959	1,471	1,370	n.a.	n.a.	759	593
1960	1,764	1,771	n.a.	n.a.	578	511
1961	2,283	1,396	n.a.	n.a.	624	514
1962	2,282	1,491	n.a.	n.a.	536	499
1963	2,268	1,685	n.a.	n.a.	445	418
1964	3,084	1,721	n.a.	n.a.	546	467
1965	2,730	1,777	n.a.	n.a.	670	498
1966	2,329	1,887	n.a.	n.a.	731	586
1967	2,612	1,851	n.a.	n.a.	661	603
1968	3,006	2,069	n.a.	n.a.	n.a.	n.a.
1969	4,090	2,251	253	259	n.a.	n.a.
1970	3,944	2,176	184	147	n.a.	n.a.
1971	3,863	2,409	295	137	n.a.	n.a.
1972	4,154	2,086	857	125	n.a.	n.a.
1973	6,074	2,625	537	125	n.a.	n.a.
1974	5,158	2,841	510	148	n.a.	n.a.
1975	4,143	2,281	370	104	n.a.	n.a.
1976	2,696	1,710	87	104	n.a.	n.a.
1977	2,951	1,843	537	172	n.a.	n.a.
1978	5,257	3,463	722	164	1,665*	996*
1979	5,984	3,637	309	127	1,512	982*
1980	6,904	3,811	446	133	1,264*	801*
1981	3,949	1,950	134	73	1,099*	688*
1982	1,718	2,580	986	98	1,339*	780*
1983	1,045	2,071	581	180	996	699*
1984	238+	1,140+	367	212	n.a.	n.a.

Source: Tables 6, 8, 12, 15, 51, 79, 81. See Tables 53 and 54 for prison officers.
Note: It is probable that similar data exist for the defence forces.
*Academic Year. +Civil Service only. n.a.=not available.

RECOMMENDATIONS

Employment creation is recognised as one of the most important tasks facing Irish society. Any plans to tackle this task require a clear understanding of the current situation. Timely reports are vital.

The public domain employs more people than either manufacturing or agriculture. It needs to be recognised statistically for the important segment of society that it is. No adequate and comprehensive series exist at present and this study revealed just how fragmented existing recording is, even where it does exist in reality. One important step in this direction would be to classify all employment in the Census of Population by whether it belongs to the public or private domains and to publish the results. This would not call for additional questions on the Census form but rather for different analysis. An analysis of the industrial volume of the 1971 Census indicated that of the categories separately identified 112 or 79 per cent contained some public employment.

The Census of Population takes time to process. The classification proposed in the last paragraph would act as a benchmark and as a check on other methods of data collection. More rapid methods of manpower information are required and are feasible, given the computerisation of much of the public domain. This information is required not merely for employment planning but also for financial control since expenditure on public salaries is a major element in the national budget. It is ludicrous that quarterly output and employment figures should be collected from the manufacturing branch and no up-to-date figures required from the areas under direct Government control.

The task of providing timely monthly information on employment and its associated cost levels calls for some inputs of imagination and planning but requires little expenditure. Although individual groups of departments operate their own computerised system for paying salaries all terminals are linked to the Kilmainham Central Data Processing Unit. At a very minimum each pay centre of the Unipay system should be required to furnish monthly the numbers in receipt of pay and the total sum involved. Aggregated on the computer this would provide a valuable record of how budgeted expenditure is progressing. Since other groups, such as local authorities and health boards, are also computerised it is a simple matter to link up with their output to form a more comprehensive picture. However there is no technical or cost reason why the analysis should be at this minimum level. The computer can also provide details of the structure of employment and costs by department, grade, sex and employment status (e.g., temporary, etc) as well as a statement of numbers of permanent staff being paid for the first time or for whom payments had ceased. This is already the practice with the Gardaí. The value of this work would be greatly enhanced if it formed part of an integrated approach to governmental information systems based on a building block procedure which permitted different configurations in the summing up process, i.e., for personnel management, for national accounts, etc.

In the development of a set of employment tables the first task is to define clearly the boundaries of the public domain. The criteria suggested in this study follow international practice and merit careful consideration. However, given the suggestions that a third sector might prove a feasible adjunct to employment in the more clearly public and private sectors, it is important to keep records of those whose earned income is derived in part from public sources but where the fraction is less than half, and for two reasons. One, a situation may arise in which the fraction exceeds half of a regular basis, and it would then be useful to have earlier records. This happened in the case of several voluntary organisations in the past, most notably voluntary hospitals. For a long period before their finances were put on a budget basis in 1973 these hospitals were *de facto* dependent on public funding for most of their income. Modern definitions of public employment would have classified such employment as public, irrespective of the legal form in which it was made.

Two, the very size of the public domain causes it to impinge on many in the private sector. Even if the people concerned cannot be deemed as public it is valuable to be able to estimate the numbers that could be affected by changes in policy. A clear case here would be the bovine tuberculosis eradication scheme which has been of considerable benefit to the veterinary profession. Consultants and legal agents would be other instances. The fact that such records were kept before the advent of computers means that a new series would be feasible and would not create precedents. This practice would also have the advantage of avoiding breaks in series as when cleaning services move from in-house to outside contract.

In 1975 a Staff Information System was introduced to record all full-time and part-time staff in the Central Civil Service. The success of this aid to manpower planning depended on the active co-operation of all personnel officers in the different employment centres with the team set up in the Department of the

Public Service (DPS). Failure on the part of a few could vitiate the entire exercise. Although the system works on a goodwill basis it would be preferable if a set of incentives could be devised which would ensure the timely transmission of changes and which would eliminate any advantages accruing to under- or overstatement.

A first check that the numbers being recorded are accurate would be to relate them to salary cheques issued. This would give an up-to-the-minute indicator of employment levels. As we have seen, cheques are not paid from a central source and many sections have their own computerised systems of Unipay. It would appear that the codes used for personnel in the Unipay system do not correspond with those used in the DPS Census. This prevents an electronic cross-check of the two sets of files. It is recommended that this system be remedied by including both codes on one set of files. The numbers are not large and the gains of cross referencing would help initiate an extremely valuable management tool, which is severely defective at present.

The goodwill system of collaboration can prove very frustrating to a DPS team committed to excellence in the production of the Census. It is a measure of their commitment that the system has been as good as it is. It is, therefore, regretable that a team which had done so much to iron out the difficulties of the late 'seventies should be disbanded over one weekend and replaced by others who, however diligent, were inexperienced and without the active benefit of any of the old team. That this was not an isolated phenomenon is indicated by a similar experience, scattering the statistics section of another department. The system of abrupt changes employed in the Civil Service is frequently counterproductive and not merely when it is a case of the development of statistics. In the latter case it demonstrates the lack of commitment to any system of rational management based on records.

The development of management information systems, MIS, calls for expertise and flair. It is by no means certain that the current departmental strategies are justified by which staff are allocated to the statistic sections for a period as part of their general training in the work of the department. Staff, who have no feel for figures and who accept uncritically information furnished, are unlikely to prove an asset in the development of MIS. Information must be checked and queried and continuity must be ensured. If promotion makes transfers inevitable it is vital that these occur piecemeal so that experience can be transmitted to those replacing the departing statisticians.

Staff records are not merely required for Census purposes. Data should be accurate enough to permit the development of the modern tools of personnel management. Good reliable records could be valuable aids in forecasting and in measuring the potential impact of policy change. The attempt in this study to develop wastage functions proved that the present records are gravely inadequate and no improvement has been apparent since. In some cases the embargo has reduced staff numbers and made the department concerned less willing to provide what it sees as the bureaucratic irrelevancies of the DPS. Such attitudes in turn prevent DPS from demonstrating the value of MIS.

In the case of Census taking it would be useful if some common standards were adopted. The first of these refers to the date of the Census. This should be taken on a date which is most representative of the employment situation. Failing the existence of such a date, it would be useful if an agreed date was selected. Many organisations have come to favour December 31 or the first working day in January. A difficulty arises when both these data are used simultaneously by different agencies in that the first can be given in a table as referring to, say, 1984, whereas the second would indicate 1985. Often tables do not specify which day of the year is concerned. Other censuses have favoured other dates — Health February 28, Teachers June 30, etc. Electronic records have meant that some bodies, such as the Police and the Defence Force, have accurate monthly records and can adapt themselves to any date selected. By and large December 31 would appear to have become the most popular and should be adopted universally.

A census at a point in time may give an inadequate reflection of employment. The public domain contains large numbers of workers engaged in drainage, forestry, manning tourist centres, etc., who are unlikely to be at work in mid-winter. A uniform system of these workers is required. It would be useful if records could indicate the average number alongside an appraisal of the range in numbers over the year.

In the case of part-time workers it would be useful to distinguish casual workers from permanent. For the former the calculation of full-time equivalents (FTE) is particularly important. This could also be true of permanent workers though care needs to be taken in interpreting such FTEs for the latter. If the part-time permanent worker happens to be a cleaner working, say, 20 hours a week it is unlikely that she or he could be replaced by a full-time worker doing the same task. A similar consideration would apply to guides at tourist centres working for a few months. It is quite clearly different in other cases, such as teaching. Fee-paid staff at Universities frequently could be replaced by full-time staff. It is impossible to evaluate trends in these cases if staff, other than full time, are only indicated on the basis of a head count. It is frequently valuable to know the number of heads in addition to the FTE, especially in cases like the cleaners cited above, where there is no question of introducing full-time employment.

Our appreciation of a given situation is greatly enhanced if, in addition to the classifications given above, some indication is given of temporary staff and of authorised vacancies. It has been traditional for the Estimates of the Public Service to indicate staffing levels budgeted for in the current and coming year. A major innovation in this format has been publishing of the budgeted costs alongside the previous year's provisional outturn rather than the previous year's budget. It would be very beneficial to anyone interested in public accounts if the employment figures cited could be based on the actual level of employment in the previous period, rather than the previous budgeted level. Since the Book of Estimates is one of the most up-to-date sources of information on public expenditure this format would provide a convenient means of publishing detailed employment figures.

It is one of the more bizarre aspects of public expenditure accounting that the Book of Estimates which merely refers to spending intentions is presented in fine detail whereas the Appropriation Accounts, which are the audited record of actual spending, is given in a much more summary form. If the purpose of the detail is to enable the Dail to grasp what public spending is proposed, surely it is even more relevant to record in the same detail what was spent in fact. If the purpose is to inform deputies so that they can engage in intelligent well-documented debates on public activities it is essential to provide them with this detail. In the context of a more informative layout of the Appropriation Accounts audited levels of employment would be valuable sources of incontrovertible information. Since audited levels of salary costs are already provided this extra information would not impose any serious extra burdens.

It is important to be able to gauge the numbers of staff entering and leaving in a year and to get some idea of their composition. Much of this recruitment is done through the Civil Service Commission. For a number of years now the Commission has published reports. The value of these would be greatly advanced if they gave statistics of the numbers of people from outside the public service who took up posts. Statistics of the numbers offered posts, published in recent reports, can be uninformative since these offers may not have been accepted, multiple offers may have been made to the same person or the person may have been already within the service but competing in an open examination.[53]

There are some staff who receive public pay without going through the Civil Service Commission. Presumably such employment requires authorisation before payment can be made: e.g., cleaners at Garda Barracks. It would be valuable if records of such authorisation could be furnished to the Commission to enable it to keep the public informed of this supplementary employment. Since the Commission is the recruiting agent it should also be in a good position to track numbers leaving the different departments and so evaluate the vacancies which it is its task to fill. In the past the record of departures has been carefully

[53]The Committee on Public Expenditure in its interim report on *Recruitment by the Civil Service Commission and Local Appointments Commission* noted that 75 per cent of successful candidates did not take up offers of employment. They also recommended publishing the vacancies filled in the Commission's Annual Report and also in the *Comprehensive Public Expenditure Programme.*

recorded. It is therefore all the more amazing that recruitment figures have never been compiled. Even at present records of recruitment levels, implicit in the Staff Information System, are inadequate. These changes in the reports of the Civil Service Commission would, therefore, be very valuable, especially if entries were related to the examination in question. This is the practice with published statistics on offers of appointment.

The recording of industrial workers and casual staff has been rather hit and miss in recent years. Better procedures are needed. As a first step regular full-time industrials might be given the benefit of a computerised system. Where small numbers are involved individuals might be included in the SIS as an adjunct, e.g., the four staff regularly returned by the Stationery Office. A similar extension might be applied to the scale-paid staff, such as managers of social wel-fare branches. In all cases some indication of full-time equivalents would be very valuable.

Records kept by the Gardaí are very complete as far as the Gardaí themselves are concerned. These are available monthly by rank and with details of inflows, outflows and numbers in training. This system seems to be more efficient than any in the public sector. There are also ancillary staff, outside the SIS, such as yardmen. Prior to the 1981 embargo such casuals appear not to have been recorded. It would be useful if they could be grafted in to the Gardai files in some form where they can be readily accessed.

Records of the Defence Force are also up to date. It would be useful if some indicators of inflows and outflows were attached to these, since privates normally sign on for a three-year period. Indeed, all staff are engaged for a working life that is normally shorter than for Civil Servants. This causes employment levels to be more volatile than is usual in the public domain and makes inflows and out-flow material more essential. A large number of civilians are attached to the permanent Defence Forces. Their records do not appear to be computerised in the same way as Defence Forces and might benefit from such a change.

Information on local authority employment was provided for this study by the personnel section of the Department of the Environment. Since no direct part-icipation was experienced with the compilation no recommendations suggest themselves. It will be noted, however, that until recently when the personnel section took firm measures, numbers given for years in the mid-'seventies, to take one example, were conflicting. This difficulty appears to have resolved itself. Figures for inflows and outflows were not available. This would be an area where the Local Appointment's Commission might exercise a role like that suggested for the Civil Service Commission.

The Department of Health surveys health employment annually and pub-lishes the results in the Manpower section of the Department's *Statistical Informa-tion relevant to the Health Services*. Although information is collected on homes for the mentally handicapped, industrial schools and approved homes, it is not published in this section. Such publication would be a useful addition to this detailed series. It is not clear whether information on staff turnover could be provided.

Statistical information on employment in education is fragmented and some centre for collating all the data and publishing them is needed if comprehensive statistics are desired.

The nucleus of such a system is already covered by the Department of Education's Statistical Report. This report covers teacher statistics at primary, secondary, comprehensive and community, and vocational school levels and has the advantage of reporting the full-time equivalents of vocational and other teachers. It does not cover employment in the only preparatory college nor in schools aided by other departments. It also omits any information on employment in schools which come under Section 109 of the Vocational Education Act. The largest employers among these are the schools funded by the Department of Agriculture. While the Department of Education is not responsible for these, for the convenience of all interested in education it would be useful if an arrangement could be made with the other departments so that all first- and second-level facts could be available under the one cover. In the process the small number of teachers omitted but funded by the Department of Education itself could also be included.

Education's statistics focus rightly on schools, pupils, teachers' courses and examinations. Ancillary employment is ignored. Several thousand are employed by the Vocational Education Committees and State financed. At first- and second-level a variety of State-funded posts also occur — caretakers, clerical assistants, child care assistants, bus drivers. Comprehensiveness requires that some record be kept of these employees as well.[54] Detailed staff information is provided for special schools for young offenders and for residential homes. There is a danger that this series will be disrupted following the transfer of the residential homes to the Department of Health. Perhaps the Department of Education could continue publication on behalf of the Department of Health? Alternatively the statistics should be included in Health's own statistical report.

At third level data are very scattered. Teachers and FTEs in third-level VEC schools are given in some detail in the Department of Education's statistics but no other staff are reported. Some few classes in these schools are for second-level pupils. No other third-level employment is included in the Department's Annual Report.

An obvious co-ordinator of third-level employment statistics is the Higher Education Authority which channels most State funds to third-level institutions. The HEA's annual accounts provide a wealth of information on student

[54]It would be useful to have some idea of non-funded employment as well.

numbers and courses followed but no details of staffing, though such information is collected. The Authority's own requirements tend to limit the value of its statistics since its accent is on permitted levels of establishment rather than on posts actually filled. The HEA could, however, publish separately posts filled and vacancies.It disregards non-HEA State-funded posts where the finance comes from, e.g, the Department of Agriculture. It also omits posts funded by other means, such as endowed chairs. This is, of course, a legitimate procedure for the Authority to adopt. However for the benefit of others interested in third-level education more comprehensive figures, carefully annotated, should be provided. Such figures should distinguish academic from non-academic employment and provide the full-time equivalents of part-time and fee-paid staff. The HEA has been endeavouring to introduce uniformity into University accounting and statistical procedures. In this connection it would be useful to have the employment content of services contracted out and to have a ruling on whether demonstrators are to be deemed staff or students with scholarships.

The HEA does not deal with teacher training at primary level or in home economics. Perhaps these are best left to the Department of Education's statistical report and the section in that, which gives details of trainee teachers, expanded to include both academic and non-academic staffing.

Some unpublished records of inflows and outflows of staff are available. Publication of this material would be a valuable supplement to the existing information on employment levels.

REFERENCES

BURKE, ANDREW and JOHN NOLAN, 1982. "Recent trends in the financing of Primary Teacher Education in Ireland", *Irish Journal of Education*, Vol. 16, No. 1.

COOLAHAN, JOHN, 1981. *Irish Education, history and structure*, Dublin: Institute of Public Administration.

COLLINS, JOHN, 1963. *Local Government* 2nd Edition, D. Roche, Dublin: Institute of Public Administration.

COMMISSION OF INQUIRY INTO THE CIVIL SERVICE, 1932–1935. *Volume 1 Final Report* with Appendices. Dublin: Goverment Publication (P. No. 1844).

COMMITTEE ON PUBLIC EXPENDITURE, 1984. *Recruitment by the Civil Service Commission and the Local Appointments Committee*, Interim Report, (Pl. 2036).

CONVERY, F., 1979. *Irish Forestry Policy*, Dublin: National Economic and Social Council, Paper No. 46.

DEVLIN, LIAM ST. J., 1972. *Review Body on Higher Remuneration in the Public Sector*, Dublin Government Publications — 1979. Report No. 20 Second General Review (Prl. 8148).

FINLAY, IAN, 1966. *The Civil Service, Introduction to Public Administration*, Series No. 6. Dublin: Institute of Public Administration.

HELLER, PETER S. and ALAN A. TAIT, 1984. *Government Employment and Pay: Some International Comparisons*, Washington: International Monetary Fund.

HENSEY, BRENDAN, 1979. *The Health Services of Ireland*, Dublin: Institute of Public Administration.

HUMPHREYS, PETER, 1983. *Public Service Employment: An examination of strategies in Ireland and other European Countries*. Dublin: Institute of Public Administration.

INTERNATIONAL MONETARY FUND, 1974. *A Manual of Government Finance Statistics*, Washington.

LINEHAN, THOMAS P., 1954. "The Bureaucrat Observed IV — The growth of the Civil Service", *Administration*, Vol. II, No.2.

McELLIGOTT, T.J., 1966. *Education in Ireland*, Dublin: Institute of Public Administration.

McKEEVER, JOHN, 1973. "Efficiency, Productivity and Pupil Teacher Ratios", *Oideas*, Foir.

O'BROIN, NOIRIN and GILLIAN FARREN, 1978. *The Working and Living Conditions of Civil Service Typists*, Dublin: ESRI, Paper No. 93.

ROCHE, DESMOND, 1982. *Local Government in Ireland*, Dublin: Institute of Public Administration.

ROSE, RICHARD, 1980. *Changes in Public Employment. A Multidimensional Comparative Analysis*, Glasgow: University of Strathclyde. Studies in Public Policy No. 61.

ROTTMAN, DAVID, 1984. *The Criminal Justice System: Policy and Performance*. Study No. 77. Dublin: National Economic and Social Council.

SHEEHAN, JOHN, 1981. "Education, Education Policy and Poverty" in *Poverty and Social Policy*, Lorraine Joyce and A. McCashin (eds), Dublin: Institute of Public Administration.

STATISTICAL OFFICE OF THE EUROPEAN COMMUNITIES, 1970. *General Industrial Classification of Economic Activities within the European Communities:* Luxembourg.

STATISTICAL OFFICE OF THE EUROPEAN COMMUNITIES, 1979. *European System of Integrated Economic Accounts*. 2nd Edition. Luxembourg.

TUSSING, A. DALE, 1978. *Irish Educational Expenditures – Past, Present and Future*. Dublin: ESRI, Paper No. 92.

UNITED NATIONS, 1968. *A System of National Accounts*. Studies in Methods, Series F. No. 2, Rev. 3, New York.

UNITED NATIONS, 1979. *Draft Manual on Public Sector Statistics*. ST/ESA/STAT 85/Rev 1 February, New York.

Appendix 1

DEFINITION OF THE PUBLIC DOMAIN AND CRITERIA FOR A TAXONOMY

In the main text a brief statement of the scope of the public domain was presented. This appendix seeks to elaborate on that statement by giving a survey of developing international practice in public statistics. The section is primarily concerned to establish the criteria by which a unit can be deemed to belong to the public domain. For those which so belong the subsequent stages seek to establish whether the unit should be assigned to the enterprise or general government sectors under the umbrella of the general public domain and then to allocate the unit to an appropriate group within the sectoral framework. The overall interest of the current study is on employment other than in State-sponsored bodies. Thus discussion of public expenditure or of State-sponsored bodies will be reserved to later studies. As an appendix this section presents a framework within which all public bodies are located following the criteria discussed earlier. Many of these bodies will be discussed in the study of State-sponsored bodies. Those bodies discussed in this current study with two exceptions will be seen to belong to the general government sector. The two exceptions — the Department of Posts and Telegraphs and the Forestry Division — belong to the enterprise sector but in view of their traditional inclusion in the Civil Service are treated here for convenience. In the general government section itself the focus in this study is on central and local authorities, as well as on public non-profit institutions serving households in the fields of education and of health.

I: DEFINITION OF THE PUBLIC SECTOR

The historical source of information in any country on the public sector has been the public accounts with supplementary data to be gleaned from extra budgetary funds and the published accounts of State-sponsored bodies. The treatment of various items of expenditure has generally been decided on the legal, institutional and administrative practices and conventions of the country's

316

public accounting traditions. In accounting practice four major traditions have been identified internationally, viz. those evolved from British, French, American and Latin American sources. The differences in the form which administration or accounting for a function or entity takes — be it budgetary, extra budgetary, special account, decentralised agency, etc. — have made it difficult to evaluate and compare the experience of different countries and have led in the last decade to some proposals for a common approach. In such an approach the criteria for inclusion in the public sector have been based on the nature of the function and the derivation of authority rather than the traditional criteria of legal standing or administrative conventions.

International Definitions of the Public Sector

These proposals have built on the considerable experience in international collaboration in the last three decades which culminated in standard treatment of national accounts procedures. This agreement is enshrined in the United Nations System of National Accounts (SNA) published in 1968. An earlier (1958) UN publication had examined the government sector within the national accounting framework and developed *A Manual for Economic and Functional Classification of Government Transactions* which has since been a standard feature of Irish national accounts. The integration of the economies of western Europe also provided a stimulus for international collaboration and standardisation which found its expression in the *European System of Integrated Economic Accounts* (ESA) which not only refined the SNA procedures but established a common basis for integrating the input-output models of the member states. Parallel with ESA a detailed industrial classification of economic activities was evolved for the EEC — NACE. This has been adopted currently by the Cental Statistics Office. A closer look at the approach used is instructive and helpful for our current task.

Basic Units

The development of national accounts, nationally or internationally, requires interrelated decisions about the appropriate statistical units to use and how to relate them to a suitable system of classification. Experience shows that no statistical unit can serve all the phenomena to be observed nor is any unit or system of classification capable of meeting all requirements. Since no system can avoid using more than one unit and/or one system it is not surprising that the concepts evolved in individual national practice have been far from identical. International standardisation does not escape this difficulty but rather seeks to standardise practice and conventions.

The basic ingredients are the statistical units — a set of entities defined and delineated to be identifiable and mutually exclusive. Units can be viewed in several ways. First basic data are provided by *reporting* units. In the production of market goods and services — the major concern of NACE — these units will either be "enterprises" — the smallest legally autonomous units or "local units" an enterprise's production unit situated in a geographically separate place. The data provided will relate to *inquiry units* — units for which records exist and information is sought. The ideal disaggregation focuses on *kind of activity units* (KAU) which separate out parts of local units which carry on a single activity in terms of the classification system. Once the building blocks are established *presentational* units can be developed for tabulation purposes. At this stage a characteristic feature of ESA and of national accounting systems is the use of two types of *analytic units* which permit two ways of subdividing the economy which are quite different and which serve separate analytical purposes.

Economic Activity Approach

This approach emphasises relationships of a technico-economic kind and is employed to represent flows in the processes of production and the balance between resources and the use of goods and services. It is particularly important in input-output analysis. The approach focuses on the *activity* which is characterised by an input of products, a production process and an output of products. The products (goods and services) can be specified unambiguously in terms of the nature, stage of manufacture and the production technique involved. The raw materials employed and the use to which product will be put may also be used. Examples would be plastics (raw materials), printing (process), agricultural machinery (purpose of product). The absence of a unique system of classification accounts to some extent for the observed differences between national practices.

Inquiry units are frequently engaged in mixed activities. Criteria are applied to distinguish principal, secondary and ancillary activities. The last named are (a) services, (b) found to be to some extent in every similar producing unit and (c) provided solely for the unit itself, e.g., administration, marketing, storage, repairs. Ancillary activities are excluded in identifying the principal activity (not always a simple task) and therefore determining the kind-of-activity (KAU) sub-units of the inquiry unit. This procedure outflanks the problems created by the modern tendencies towards vertical and horizontal integration of enterprises and of constant changes in integrated enterprises. The next step aggregates similar KAU — called units of homogeneous production — irrespective of the institutional framework in which they occur (see next section) into BRANCHES. These branches are the divisions normally found in Input–Output tables and can appear in varying levels of aggregation. The Irish National Income and Expenditure uses this approach in Appendix Table A.2 distinguishing agriculture, industry, communications, etc. In common Irish parlance these branches are frequently referred to as "sectors". This Irish usage can be a source of some confusion in dealing with the international terminology which reserves "sector" for aggregates of institutional units discussed in the next section.

INSTITUTIONAL APPROACH

For our purposes the economic activity approach is of lesser importance. The alternative division of the economy seeks to analyse behavioural relationships involving income, financial expenditure and financial transactions. For this task "institutional units" are delineated based on their function in the system. It is a basic assumption that differences in function produce differences in behaviour.

The key definition of an institutional unit is provided by the ESA: "In general a resident unit is said to be institutional if it keeps a complete set of accounts and enjoys autonomy of decision in respect of its principal function". These characteristics are a feature of independent legal entities and presence of this status automatically implies that an entity is an institutional unit. Where either of these characteristics is absent the entity is combined with the institutional unit into whose accounts its partial accounts are integrated or with the unit which controls it, as the case may be. By convention two classes of entity, which do not meet these conditions, are nevertheless deemed to be institutional units. These are households and "notional resident units" — parts of non-resident units operating in the country.

Institutional units, once established, can be combined into "institutional sectors" or simply "sectors" on the basis of their principal function. Usually six principal functions are identified giving rise to six major sectors.

The Enterprise Sector

The major group of interest to NACE are enterprises, which are the smallest legally autonomous units and whose principal function is the production of goods and market services. The boundaries of the enterprise sector are determined, therefore, by the market orientation of the units. Market services are all services which can be the object of market transactions and which are produced by a unit more than half of whose resources are derived from the sale of its output. The price charged may go by another name, e.g., fee, rate, toll, duty, voluntary payment or even a compulsion levy of a quasi-fiscal nature if made by enterprises to units whose principal activity is to provide services in exchange for these payments. By convention some services are always deemed market, e.g, trading, transport, finance. Non-market services include domestic service in households and collective services, i.e., those provided without charge or with a nominal charge to the community or particular groups of households. Again by convention some are always treated as non-market, general government services, religious, etc. Other services can be classified either way depending on the source of the unit's resources as specified above. Typically these services include teaching, health, cultural and recreational services.

The Non-Financial Enterprise Sector

The ESA regards financial enterprises as sufficiently different in function and resources from non-financial enterprises to warrant a subdivision of the sector along these lines. Later the IMF development of financial statistics reinforced this subdivision since the IMF was anxious to avoid the consolidation of public financial enterprises within the general public domain of general government and public enterprises. This will be examined more closely below. The exclusion of financial enterprises establishes the first major sector — the non-financial corporate and quasi-corporate sector. This sector consists of institutional units as defined which will be typically private or public companies, public corporations, co-operatives, partnerships and public enterprises where the last named are recognised by virtue of special legislation as independent legal entities. All must satisfy the criteria of accounts, autonomy and orientation. Apart from these units the sector may include "non-financial quasi-corporate enterprises" if these market-oriented entities lack independent legal status but display behaviour different from that of their owners (households, private non-profit institutions or government) but similar to corporate enterprises. Entities are assumed to display this behaviour if they meet yardsticks set by convention.

— In the case of government enterprises they must keep a complete set of accounts and sell more than half their output outside the general government sector. If not they belong to the general government sector.
— In the case of financial enterprises since they are subject to regulation.
— In the case of unincorporated sole proprietorships or partnerships the yardstick is employment at or above a minimum level, viz., agriculture 20 employees, industry 100 and services 50. If not they belong to the household sector.

This classification may seem surprising because it assigns virtually every Irish farmer and many other self-employed people to the household sector unless they are legally incorporated. It becomes less surprising when it is noted that current practice in *National Income and Expenditure* does essentially the same. Its Appendix 2 Table A.1 "Trading Profits of companies (including corporate bodies)" is given separately from household income which is shown as income from "self-employment and other trading income in Agriculture, Forestry and Fishing"; "Other trading profits, professional earnings etc."; wages, salaries and pensions and the actual and imputed rent of dwellings.

Financial Enterprises

The function of this group of enterprises as set out by the IMF in its Draft Manual on Government Finance Statistics, is to act as intermediaries in mobilising and distributing the community's savings by creating financial assets for the community to hold and by accepting financial claims upon others. This function involves the acceptance of demand, time and savings deposits or the incurrence of liabilities and acquiring of financing assets in the market. The IMF approach then subdivides the sector into four categories of institutions:

Monetary	*Non-Monetary*
1. Central Bank or monetary authorities	3. Insurance Companies and Pension Funds
2. Deposit money banks	4. Other financial institutions

The ESA prefers to create two sectors — one designated "credit institutions" has three subsectors corresponding to the IMF's monetary institutions and the non-monetary "other financial institutions". The IMF's non-monetary subsector — insurance companies and pension funds — becomes a sector on its own — Insurance enterprises. Its main function is to convert individual risks into collective risks and its main resources arise from contractual premia.

Apart from this rearrangement of subsectors the differing objectives of the ESA and IMF statistics lead to some differences in delimiting the boundaries between the financial and general government sectors. The IMF objectives lead to the exclusion from general government of certain activities which in some countries are performed by government agencies rather than by financial institutions:—

(a) The principal function of the monetary authorities subsector is to issue legal tender and by intervention to maintain the value of the national currency. In some countries by design or historical accident activities, such as the issue of coins, holding foreign exchange or transactions with the IMF, are retained within government. International Monetary Fund procedures call for their allocation for statistical purposes with monetary authorities, regardless of where the functions are performed.

(b) The ESA's "other monetary institutions" and IMF's "deposit money banks" in general correspond by including deposit banks, clearing and discount houses, credit co-operatives, some savings banks and post office giro agencies where the last names are institutional units. The approaches differ where the Treasury has demand deposit liabilities including a postal checking system. The ESA would leave these functions within the general government sector.

(c) The other financial institutions subsector includes those who accept time or savings deposits or who incur non-money liabilities or acquire financial claims on the capital and/or foreign markets. The only ESA/IMF difference here relates to time and savings deposits collected by government. Typically enterprises in this subsector include: savings banks, development banks, mortgage banks, building and loan societies, hire purchase institutions, and finance and investment companies. The IMF specifically exclude two types of potential members of this subsector and treats them as departmental enterprises (defined later):—

1. Lending bodies which derive *all* of their funds from the government and have no authority to incur liability to others — typically housing loan funds.
2. Savings bodies whose funds flow automatically to government and whose liabilities are not in the form of time or saving deposits, e.g., agencies selling government savings bonds — e.g, Prize Bonds or National Instalment Savings. Even here Post Office Savings Banks and Saving deposit functions of some Treasuries are not deemed departmental enterprises but rather part of this subsector.

Insurance Companies and Pension Funds

Both international bodies agree on the composition of this (sub)-sector. The criteria for including entities in the sector is, first, whether they are institutional units e.g., autonomous — otherwise they belong to the sector which controls them. Second, the contract must be voluntarily entered and the premium proportional to the risk insured. The operation by the State of separate funds for social security schemes accordingly does not warrant their inclusion in this sector though international usage recommends that in this circumstance they be separately indentifiable within the general government sector. The rationale for exclusion rests on such schemes involving compulsory contributions, unrelated to risk from large sectors of community. Government employees' pension funds, separately funded, are also excluded if they are required to invest all their funds with the employing government (and therefore are not autonomous).

Private Non-Profit Institutions Serving Households

The next sector discussed in the manual is the general government sector. However as the public sector is the focus of this study the remaining sectors will be discussed briefly first to allow a fuller treatment of the public sector later. The private non-private sector is composed of institutional units whose function is to produce non-market services for particular groups of households and more than half of whose resources are derived from voluntary contributions by households and/or from property income. The services of religious organisations, learned societies, trade unions and social work agencies are deemed by convention to be always non-market. Other services may be either market or non-market, their description hinging on whether over half their resources derive from market transactions. To be assigned to this sector entities producing non-market services must qualify as institutional units and must not get more than half their resources from the government. Those so financed belong to the government sector. Failure to meet the criteria for institutional units will result in the entity being assigned to the government or household sectors depending on the source of control. In practice where these institutions are not of major importance the ESA recommends their inclusion in the household sector. This recommendation differs from the Irish practice adopted in *National Income and Expenditure*, such as in Table 11, which presents the "Personal Income of Households and Private Non-Profit Institutions" because in the latter case these institutions would be assigned to general government under ESA conventions (i.e., as public non-profit institutions).

Households

This sector contains entities treated as institutional units by convention though they do not have independent legal status. The main function of households is consumption and the main sources of resources are compensation of employees, property incomes, and transfers from other sectors. The sector may also include notional resident units — foreigners in their capacity as local property owners. Apart from consumers a subset of households are household enterprises included in the sector because they do not have legal status or accounts kept independent of the household. The sector also includes such private non-profit institutions as are without independent legal status or are of only minor importance. These two additional categories have principal functions and sources of resources similar to those enterprises and private non-profit institutions which are institutional units.

Rest of the World

This sector does not have a principal function. It consists mainly of non-resident units in so far as they interact with resident institutional units. The ESA distinguishes three subsectors here: (a) the member countries of the EEC, (b) the institutions of the EEC and (c) others. This is of importance for our discussion of the public domain where the creation of the EEC has caused some government functions to be assigned to supranational authorities. Such activities come within the public domain of the countries concerned.

Table A1.1: *Principal function and source of resources of sectors*

Sector	*ESA Code*	Type of economic behaviour	
		Principal function	*Principal resources*
Non-financial corporate and quasi-corporate enterprises	S 10	Production of goods and non-financial market services	Receipts from sales of output
Credit institutions	S 40	Finance, i.e., the collection, conversion and distribution of available funds	Funds derived from liabilities incurred; interest
(a) Monetary authorities	S 41	Issue legal tender, defend currency	,,
(b) Deposit money banks	S 42	Create credit	,,
(c) Other financial enterprises	S 43	Borrow and lend resources received	Interest only
Insurance enterprises	S 50	Insurance, i.e., the conversion of individual risks into collective risks	Contractual premiums
General government	S 60	Production of non-market services for collective consumption and carrying out transactions intended to redistribute national income and wealth	Compulsory levies on units in other sectors, received directly or indirectly

Table A1.1: *(cont'd.)*

(a) Central government	S 61	Function over national territory	Compulsory levies on units in other sectors, received directly or indirectly
(b) Local government	S 62	Function over part of national territory	
(c) Social security funds	S 63	Provide social benefits	Compulsory social contributions
Private non-profit institutions	S 70	Production of non-market services for particular groups of households	Voluntary contributions made by households as consumers; income from property
Households — as consumers	S 80	Consumption	Compensation of employees, property income, transfers from other sectors
— as entrepreneurs		Production of goods and non-financial market services	receipts from sales of output
Rest of the world	S 90	This sector is not characterised by any principal function or principal resources; it groups together non-resident units in so far as they carry out transactions with resident institutional units	
(a) Members of EEC	S 91		
(b) Institutions of EEC	S 92		
(c) Others	S 93		

General Government

This sector is of major interest in the terms of this study. The ESA allocates to the sector all institutional units whose primary function is the production of non-market services intended for collective consumption or the redistribution of national income and wealth. Their principal resources are derived directly or indirectly from compulsory payments made by units belonging to other sectors. An implication of this definition is that those non-profit institutions serving households which derive more than half their resources from government (and therefore indirectly from other sectors) belong to this sector. Similarly those agencies providing market services to enterprises are in this sector since such services are deemed non-market if the agency derives more than half its resources from general government. We shall return to this topic later.

The ESA subdivides the sector in three, distinguishing (a) social security funds where they are autonomous (b) central government and (c) local government. The last named applies to those types of public administration whose competence extends to only part of the economic territory. Hence local government comprises all layers of subnational government which meet the necessary criteria of autonomy. In the Irish case the high level of control plus funding up to a level of 82 per cent of resources would suggest that a case could be made that local government in the UN definition is extremely attenuated.

Summary

Before studying the general government sector in greater depth it would be well to summarise the institutional approach now that all sectors have been treated briefly. This is done in Table A1.1 which sets out the sectors by principal function and principal resources.

THE NATURE OF GOVERNMENT

As is clear from the discussion and from Table A1.1 the delineation of the sectors is based on function and source of resources. The ESA definition of general government stresses the production of non-market services primarily for collective consumption and the transfer of income for the purposes of public policy, the cost of which is financed by compulsory levies on the other sectors. The IMF definition of the nature of government is more rigorous and intended to encompass the public domain in general. "The government of a country consists of the public authorities and their instrumentalities, established through political processes, exercising a monopoly of compulsory powers within a territorial area or its parts, motivated by considerations of public purpose in the economic, social and political spheres and engaged primarily in the provision of public services differing in character, cost elements, and source of finance from the activities of other sectors (p. 8).'' Using this touchstone the choice of which activities and institutions are to be counted as a part of government is based on their nature and whether they fall within the definition of government.

Producers of Government Services

In both definitions the principal function of government is seen as supplying certain goods and fulfilling certain public purposes not for commercial or financial reasons, or if so, not on a major basis or not primarily for a profit. The entities discharging this role form a subset of institutional units in the general government sector known collectively as ''producers of government services''.

The core group of such units are the primarily non-commercial departments and agencies producing public services. In the nineteenth century these were mainly engaged in what Rose calls the defining role of government — taxing, law and order, defence and foreign affairs. Gradually two new roles were expanded — the promotion of economic activity and the provision of social services. While the administration of these new roles was reserved to the core group aspects of the task are devolved to decentralised agencies.

In economic promotion non-profit institutions serving enterprises are a regular feature of most economies while in social policy similar bodies serving households are to be found. The decisions as to their being included in the general government sector hinges on whether their services are market or non-market. Where no convention governs the classification of the services produced, as we have seen, they are deemed non-market if over half their resources are derived directly or indirectly from compulsory levies on other sectors. This allocation was reaffirmed in the UN draft manual on public sector statistics which recommends that they be included in the public sector if more than 50 per cent of their current expenditures are financed on a continuing basis by government. In its view such support provides strong evidence that the institutions concerned are ''instrumentalities'' of government within the meaning of the IMF definition of government. In this sense they may be regarded as arms of government performing functions that the government would otherwise carry out itself. The UN experts deemed it superfluous to insist that government should also exercise formal control over them. In several countries non-profit institutions, such as hospitals, schools and universities, although mainly financed by government, are controlled by private boards. The effect of the recommendation is that such institutions will always be included in the public domain.

Although these institutions are included they are distinguished from general government primarily on the basis of financing and control. By the convention which limits the use of the term departmental enterprises, (see below), to industrial and commercial agencies these institutions are listed with producers of government services. In this study they are separately identified.

Sale of Goods and Services by Government Agencies

In the pursuit of its primary objectives set out above governments generally engage in minor subsidiary functions. Specifically public agencies may engage in producing and selling to the public the kinds of goods and services which are often produced by private business establishments, though they may set prices below production costs or pursue policy goals of producer or consumer welfare.

Some of these enterprises are excluded from the general government sector on the grounds that their principal function and principal resources cause them to be engaged in activities different in nature from the essence of government and thus to encounter production, cost and financing problems involving non-governmental considerations. Because these problems are believed to develop with units of significant size the two-fold criterion by which they are excluded from the general government sector is sale to the public on a large scale. Thus the post office is deemed a public enterprise outside the general government sector.

Departmental Enterprises

By definition an enterprise will remain within the sector if it does not meet this two-fold criterion — either because it is an "ancillary unit" selling predominantly to other units of government or where it does sell mainly to the public but these sales are relatively small scale, (meals at government restaurants). Frequently such bodies are closely integrated with the rest of a government department or agency and likely to hold only small working balances. By convention ancilliary units engaged in commercial and industrial activities — e.g., the Office of Public Works — and entities whose sales to the public are on a small scale are designated "departmental enterprises". Interdepartmental sale of services — such as auditing — does not qualify for such designation. In the discussion of financial enterprises earlier we noted the IMF recommendation by which two types of financial entities would be deemed departmental enterprises:
1. Lending bodies which derive all their funds from government;
2. Savings bodies whose funds flow automatically to government and whose liabilities are not in the form of time or saving deposits.

The IMF distinguishes three exceptions which do not qualify as treating the agencies concerned as departmental enterprises:
(a) Where the provision of the service to the public is regulatory in character — passports, licences, driving tests or court fees even though revenue collected may cover all costs. The rationale for this allocation can be traced to their compulsory nature.

(b)   Where the goods sold are incidental to the usual social or community activities e.g., art reproductions at museums.

(c)   By convention where fees or charges are made for services not considered to be industrial or commercial — tuition fees at public schools, charges at public hospitals, admission to public parks, etc.

Content of General Government Sector — Summary

As a result of our discussion we can now summarise the content of the general government sector seriatim.

1.   The primarily non-commercial functions of its parts, agencies and instrumentalities.
2.   Social security funds.
3.   Pension funds of public employees.
4.   Departmental enterprises — industrial and commercial.
5.   Departmental enterprises — financial.
6.   Non-profit institutions serving enterprises.
7.   Non-profit institutions serving households.
8.   Supranational agencies empowered to levy taxes.

These categories can be recombined on a territorial basis to identify supranational, central and local government elements as well as social security funds.

A third categorisation by kind of activity would divide producers of government services into seven sub-groups:

1.   Public administration and defence,
2.   Sanitary and similar services,
3.   Education services,
4.   Medical services,
5.   Other social and community services,
6.   Recreational and cultural services, and
7.   Others.

THE PUBLIC DOMAIN

The development of national accounting systems in the last three decades which culminated in the ESA, focused on the national utilisation of manpower, the consumption and production of goods and other measures of physical volume. In this regard its emphasis differed from the earlier analysis of government accounts which aimed at the registration and control of individual transactions to facilitate accountability. In the compilation of national accounts these basic public data were recast in a manner in which they could be combined with the data for other branches and sectors. In the process the extent of public activity tended to be lost sight of, being submerged in other material.

The introduction of national accounts coincided with and was promoted by the universal tendency for public authorities in all countries to play a much greater role in the economic and social affairs of their communities. As public expenditure tended to exceed 50 per cent of GNP policy-makers, legislators, research workers, businessmen, journalists and ordinary citizens were increasingly raising questions about the rate and growth of the public domain. In response to this growing interest and concern the UN in 1979 circulated a *Draft Manual on Public Sector Statistics* which sought to divide the sectors between the public and private domains. Unfortunately in its choice of terminology it used the word "sector" where "domain" or some synonym would have avoided confusion with the concept of sector as defined earlier. In this paper this ambiguity is averted by using "domain" though this differs from international practice.

The production of the UN draft manual was anticipated by the International Monetary Fund which produced a draft of *A Manual on Government Finance Statistics* in June 1974. As would be expected from its authorship the IMF placed more emphasis on financial transactions — taxing, borrowing, spending and lending — rather than on production and income highlighted in the UN's national accounting framework.

Apart from the differences noted already both approaches share much common ground but the differing objectives lead to a different marshalling of the data. In particular the IMF was anxious to prevent the consolidation of public financial institutions within the public domain while the UN had no such concern. Both were focused on the public domain which was defined not by reference to criteria of purpose or function, as institutional sectors are, but on the distinction between government and private ownership and/or control. This reorganisation of the data is derived from the belief that government influence and impact on the economy operates also through the enterprises it owns and controls and which it may use as instruments for the execution of significant government policies. The concept may also be useful in gauging the magnitude of the overall government "establishment" including all the operations and activities over which it exercises responsibility and close policy control. The magnitude of this sector and statistics on its operations may thus offer useful information on government leverage in the economy and how it is being utilised and affected in such areas as overall economic activity, fixed capital formation and recourse to the financial system.

The IMF prefers to measure the non-financial public domain separately from public financial institutions since the former's financial requirements and how they are met are important indicators of its overall operations and its impact on monetary developments in the economy. Such information would be lost in the consolidation proposed by the UN. Separate figures pose no difficulties for this study which is more limited in its scope than the analyses proposed by either of these international bodies.

Both international approaches build on the sectoral and sub-sectoral aggregates which were discussed earlier, but may combine them differently, as Figure A1.1 illustrates. For our purposes we only need criteria by which to distinguish public from private enterprises.

Non-Financial Public Enterprises

In the earlier discussion of departmental enterprises the criterion for treating an agency as a public enterprise was given as sales to the public on a large scale. In applying this yardstick, legal standing, incorporation, financial arrangements, etc., are not taken into consideration. Nor is the question of whether prices or charges are set profitably or below the full costs of production. Public enterprises are assumed to maintain their own working balances and business credit and to finance their capital formation out of retained depreciation, reserves or borrowing with some independence from the parent public authorities.

The IMF sees distinct advantages of consistency and international comparability in treating as public non-financial enterprises all publicly owned and/or controlled units with significant industrial or commercial sales to the public, regardless of legal or administrative status. The generally accepted yardsticks of public ownership and control are, however, more ambiguous than might appear

Figure A1.1: *Activity groups and institutional sectors involving transactors in the Public Domain*

Basic Building Blocks	Producers of Government Services	Departmental Enterprises	Public Enterprises	
			Non-Financial	Financial
Activity Groups	Producers of Government Services	Public Industries		
Institutional Sectors	General Government		Public Enterprises	
IMF Dichotomy	Non-Financial Public Domain			Financial Public Domain

Source: Adapted from Diagram B, p. 13. UN op. cit.

initially. The sources of ambiguity are two-fold. One relates to the definition of these criteria; the second to whether the enterprise should satisfy both criteria simultaneously.

For the UN the criterion of ownership presents fewer definitional problems, being stated as ownership of at least 50 per cent of the common stock. Since government control is pervasive in the economy it is less easy to determine what constitutes control. In the case of non-financial enterprises the UN hit on a definition which has regard to control of capital investment policies and of the quantities and prices of goods and services produced. For financial enterprises, discussed below, control should generally relate to the acquisition of assets and the incurrence of liabilities, and in the case of banks to interest rate policy. Control should be clearly seen as active rather than as a reserve power but need not relate to day-to-day activities. Control of the broader aspects of policy would suffice to meet the criterion.

In the compilation of the SNA the complexity of the criterion seeking to establish who controls an enterprise was recognised. Because of many forms in which government may exercise control over enterprises, it is difficult to describe the means of influencing the management of an enterprise which, in all cases, indicate who effectively controls a given enterprise. Various means may be used in order effectively to determine all the main aspects of the management (policies, administration and operations) of the unit. This may be accomplished, for example, by choosing the majority of the board of directors or the managing directors, providing the staff of the organisation, or specifying the policies and operating practices in detail.

The application of the dual criteria of ownership and control provide scope for four differing levels of demarcation. The core consists of those enterprises which are both owned and controlled. These are usually enterprises created or acquired by governments to implement their economic and social programmes. For purposes of international comparison this key group provides the irreducible minimum for inclusion and so it is the recommended UN standard.

However particular analytical purposes will call for enlarging this group and policymakers will need to exercise judgement in deciding what additional sets to include. If a maximum of coverage is required the most comprehensive definition would be to accept either ownership or control. The UN notes that national practices in general favour a more limited set based on ownership alone. The additional set would comprise those owned but not controlled which added to the core group gives the set of all enterprises in public ownership. The UN experts did not advocate this enlargement arguing that ownership without control does not permit governments to pursue special commercial policies. In other words the enterprises cannot be regarded of their nature as part of "the public authorities and their instrumentalities" within the meaning of the IMF definition quoted earlier even if they fulfil legal or administrative criteria. In some cases public ownership may have occurred in a haphazard unplanned fashion, e.g., to stave off bankruptcy or as a war time expedient. There will, therefore, be instances of analyses where it would be better to eliminate such enterprises.

An alternative enlargement, which would find greater merit with international statisticians, does not appear to be employed by any national government. This would use control rather than ownership and would include in public enterprises all those controlled by the government whether owned or not. This would mean including private utilities, transport companies and private companies being taken over under phased nationalisation programmes. This enlargement would be the appropriate one to use in measuring the extent of direct government intervention in business but is not relevant in the Irish context since no such enterprises exist.

The IMF summarises the scope for judgement succinctly.

Both majority ownership and control need not be present in all cases for classification as a public enterprise. Minority government ownership may be combined with effective control in a unit adjudged to be a public enterprise. Effective control may in other cases be too difficult to ascertain so that majority government ownership alone may be judged to indicate a public enterprise. In other instances majority ownership may be held by a public enterprise ... and the degree of effective government control may determine whether the unit should be considered a public enterprise. Though various circumstances may make unequivocal determination ... difficult, widespread government ownership is likely to obscure both the limits and meaning of public enterprise.

An observation which echoes the UN concern that government be distinguished from the "socialist sector" in collectivist economies.

Financial Institutions

The UN notes that one of the ambiguities of defining the public domain relates to the treatment of central banks. This arises in those countries where they enjoy a special legal status independent of government. The absence of government control or ownership should not, in the UN view, preclude central banks from the public domain since the long run policies of governments and central banks must be reconciled.

For other sub-sectors of the financial sector the criteria are the same as for non-financial enterprises.

Irish Criteria for State-Sponsored Bodies

In the light of the above discussion it is of interest to read the observation made by the Minister for the Public Service (Mr. R. Ryan) in reply to a Dail question.

There is no legal definition of the expressions "State-sponsored body" or "State-sponsored agency".

The list of bodies which follows has been compiled by reference to the following general criteria:
1. They are wholly or largely in the ownership of the State;
2. The directors/members are usually appointed by the Government or by individual Ministers; and
3. They have a permanent status.

This list excludes commissions, local authorities, health boards, harbour commissioners, boards of fishery conservators and *ad hoc* bodies. Certain of the bodies listed have shareholders in or control of other companies or organisations. These are not included in the list.

This list is of interest for its combination of ownership and control. At the time of compilation harbour boards were reckoned as local authorities. More recently they have been reclassified as public enterprises in line with UN recommendations. The question of ownership of subsidiaries and associates raised in the quotation is one to which we will need to return in a later study.

Since the criteria given by the Minister for Finance accord exactly with international practice in relation to ownership and control it is now possible to decide which agencies can be deemed to belong to the public domain. Their allocation within the domain, between the enterprise and general government sectors, can be made in the light of the UN and IMF criteria. Their grouping within the relevant sector also follows the logic of the above discussion. The net result is a framework for locating economic units within the public domain, as set out overleaf.

Table A.1.2: *Classification framework for institutional units in the public domain*

A   Enterprise Sector

1. Public Non-Financial Enterprises
   (a) *In Production*

Arramara	Electricity Supply Board
Bord Gais	Irish Steel
Bord na Móna	Min Fhéir Teo
Ceimici Teoranta	National Stud
Cork District Milk Board	Nitrigin Éireann Teo
Comhlucht Siúicre Éireann	Industries under the aegis of Údaras
Dublin District Milk Board	na Gaeltachta

   (b) *In Transport*

Aer Lingus/Aer Linte	Córas Iompair Éireann
Aer Rianta	Irish Shipping
B+I	Harbour Authorities

   (c) *In Commerce*

Irish National Petroleum Company	Pigs and Bacon Commission

   (d) *In Recreation*

Irish Theatre Company	Bord na gCon
National Film Studios	National Concert Hall Company
National Theatre Company	Radió Telefís Éireann
Racing Board	

2. Quasi–Public Non Financial Enterprises

Forestry Division	Department of Posts and Telegraphs*

3. Public Financial Enterprises
   (a) *Monetary Authorities*
       Central Bank
   (b) *Other Financial Institutions*

Agricultural Credit Corporation	Industrial Credit Company
Foir Teo	

   (c) *Insurance*

Irish Life Assurance Company	Voluntary Health Insurance Board

B   General Government Sector

1. Core
   (a) Gárdaí
   (b) Army including civilians
   (c) Government Departments not separately
       identified
   (d) *Other*

Uachtarán	Members of Oireachtas
Judiciary	Comptroller and Auditor General

*Now Public Enterprises: An Bord Poist, An Bord Telecom, Irish Telecommunication Investments Ltd.

Table A.1.2.: *(contd.)*

2. Departmental Enterprises

    (a) *Selling exclusively within Government sector*
    Office of Public Works   Revenue Commissioners (printing)
    Land Commissioners (land division)

    (b) *State-sponsored but selling to Government sector*
    Hospital Joint Services Board   National Building Agency

    (c) *Sales to public yield less than half the cost (Department of Agriculture)*
    Performance testing of bulls   Pig progeny testing
    Brucellosis Laboratory   Backweston Farm (cereal research)
    Veterinary Research Laboratory

3. Local Authorities

    County Councils   Joint Library Boards
    County Borough Corporations   Joint Drainage Boards
    Urban District Councils   Joint Burial Boards
    Town Commissioners

4. State-Sponsored Bodies Serving Government Functions

    Bord Pleanála   General Medical Services Payments Board
    Bord Uchtala   Law Reform Commission
    Comhairle na nOspidéal   Local Government Computer Service
    Hospitals Joint Administrative Bureau   Local Government Staff Negotiations Board
    Federated Dublin Voluntary Hospitals   Nuclear Energy Board
      Board

5. Public Non Profit Institutions Serving Enterprises

    (a) *Not State-sponsored, engaged in research*
    The Economic and Social Research Institute
    The Institute of Public Administration

    (b) *State-sponsored, engaged in research*
    Agricultural Institute   Medical Research Council
    Foras Forbartha   National Board for Science
    Institute for Industrial Research   and Technology
      and Standards   National Economic and Social
    Kilkenny Design Centre   Council

    (c) *State-sponsored, engaged in training*
    AnCO   CERT

    (d) *State-sponsored, engaged in economic promotion*
    ACOT   Devco
    Bord Iascaigh Mhara   Foyle Fisheries
    Bord na gCapall   Industrial Development Authority
    Bord Fáilte   Irish Goods Council
    Central Fisheries Board   Regional Development Organisations
    Regional Fisheries Board   Regional Tourist Organisation
    Comhairle Olla   Shannon Free Airport
    Córas Beostoic agus Feola   Development Company
    Córas Tráchtála   Údarás na Gaeltachta

Table A.1.2.: *(contd.)*

(e) *Not State-sponsored, engaged in economic promotion*
Irish Productivity Centre

6. Public Non-Profit Institutions Serving Households
  (a) *In Education*
    (i) *Schools*

National	Domestic Science
Primary schools for handicapped	Universities
Secondary	Teacher Training
Comprehensive and Community	Colleges of Advanced Technology
Vocational	Veterinary
Industrial schools and Reformatories	Agricultural

    (ii) *State-sponsored bodies*

Higher Education Authority	National Council for
National University of Ireland	Educational Awards
Bord na Gaeilge	Institiuid Teangeolaíochta

  (b) *In Health*
    (i) Hospitals etc.

Health Boards	Voluntary Hospitals

    (ii) State-sponsored bodies

Hospital Boards	Dublin Rheumatism Clinic
Blood Transfusion Service Board	Medico-Social Research Board

  (c) *Households in their role as producers (State-sponsored)*

Board for the Employment of	Council for Post-Graduate Medical
the Blind	Education and Training
National Rehabilitation Board	Dental Board
Bord Altranais	Medical Council
Bord na Radharcmhastóirí	Veterinary Council
Pharmaceutical Society of Ireland	

  (d) *Households in their role as consumers*
    (i) *State-sponsored bodies*

Agency for Personal Service	Irish Water Safety Association
Overseas	Legal Aid Board
Arts Council	National Road Safety Association
Comhairle Leabharlanna	National Social Services Council
Health Education Bureau	

    (ii) *Other bodies*

Comhairle le leas Óige	National Library
National Gallery	National Museum

C Private Bodies not in the Public Domain
(but frequently confused with State-sponsored bodies)

Bord Bainne	Hospital Trust Board
Commissioners of Irish Lights	Salmon Research Trust
National Dairy Council	

Table A2.1: *Numbers in the Civil Service in 1938 and from 1945 to 1959 distinguishing sex, established status, and industrial grade*

	Established		Unestablished		Industrial			Total	Total
	Males	Females	Males	Females	Males Estab.	Males Unest.	Females Unestab.	Non-Ind.	Indust.
1938	9,151	3,742	7,432	2,513	369	2,701	115	22,838	3,185
1945	9,346	3,883	8,791	3,730	348	4,108	127	25,750	4,583
1946	9,233	3,857	8,994	3,770	374	4,140	121	25,854	4,635
1947	Male 18,532		Female 7,766		4,773		108	26,298	4,881
1948	9,452	4,264	9,443	3,864	331	4,709	108	27,023	5,148
1949	9,777	4,627	9,655	3,861	390	5,052	123	27,920	5,565
1950	10,004	4,906	9,663	3,572	396	5,332	102	28,145	5,830
1951	10,444	5,280	9,797	3,531	380	5,760	95	29,052	6,235
1952	11,150	5,493	10,519	3,574	20	2,298	104	30,736	2,422
1953	11,596	5,702	10,479	3,524	20	2,383	124	31,301	2,527
1954	11,905	5,603	10,156	3,455	27	2,393	118	31,119	2,420
1955	12,103	5,509	9,964	3,293	2,355		159	30,869	2,514
1956	12,759	5,462	9,304	3,243	2,611		168	30,768	2,779
1957	12,845	5,477	9,260	3,313	2,440		162	30,895	2,602
1958	12,983	5,454	8,758	3,249	2,263		165	30,444	2,428
1959	12,976	5,646	7,699	1,718					

Note 1: Revision of coding in 1952 transferred 1,828 males out of the industrial grouping to unestablished status. Classification of industrials was also changed.

Note 2: Revision of classification in 1958 reduced numbers of unestablished status. Most were subsequently enumerated separately.

Source: Civil Service Census.

Table A2.2: *Central Civil Service in January 1982 classified by sex, year of recruitment and part-time employment, giving also cumulative totals by duration of employment*

	Total		Part-time included		Cumulative Total %	
	Female	Male	Female	Male	Female	Male
1981	957	692	2	1	6.6	3.9
1980	1,850	1,629	8	2	19.5	13.1
1979	1,824	1,408	10	2	32.1	21.0
1978	1,151	1,525	5	1	40.1	29.6
1977	759	579	6	4	45.3	32.9
1976	606	507	12	—	49.5	35.7
1975	881	742	28	1	55.6	39.9
1974	926	921	13	1	62.5	45.1
1973	1,186	865	26	1	70.3	50.0
1972	662	836	18	—	74.9	54.7
1971	580	584	19	1	78.9	58.0
1970	448	562	16	1	82.0	61.2
1969	309	496	11	—	84.1	64.0
1968	219	428	6	—	85.6	66.4
1967	146	348	4	1	86.6	68.3
1966	152	323	8	—	87.7	70.2
1965	145	422	5	1	88.7	72.6
1964	124	342	6	—	89.6	74.5
1963	85	306	6	—	90.2	76.2
1962	76	236	5	—	90.7	77.5
1961	71	258	3	—	91.2	79.0
1960–1956	280	909	25	14	93.1	84.1
1955–1951	203	648	8	6	94.5	87.8
1950–1946	337	1,085	8	11	96.9	93.9
1945–1941	246	601	1	5	98.6	97.3
1940–1936	126	353	—	2	99.4	99.3
1935–1931	82	123	1	—	100.0	100.0
1930–1926	nil	3	—	—	100.0	100.0
1925 and earlier	nil	1	—	—	100.0	100.0
Total	14,431	17,725	260	55		

Table A2.3: *Post Office staff serving in January 1982 classified by sex, year of recruitment and part-time employment, giving also cumulative totals by duration of employment*

Year	Total		Cumulative Total		Part-time included	
	Female	Male	Female	Male	Female	Male
1981	516	982	516	982	24	7
1980	911	1,736	1,427	2,718	86	38
1979	855	1,117	2,282	3,835	70	37
1978	674	1,001	2,956	4,836	71	35
1977	333	577	3,289	5,413	58	26
1976	248	613	3,537	6,026	47	43
1975	522	764	4,059	6,790	83	50
1974	646	1,181	4,705	7,971	79	65
1973	523	1,222	5,228	9,193	56	62
1972	252	877	5,480	10,070	20	57
1971	187	643	5,667	10,713	21	42
1970	197	735	5,864	11,448	14	57
1969	200	767	6,064	12,215	16	50
1968	129	444	6,193	12,659	5	39
1967	64	450	6,257	13,109	3	44
1966	27	453	6,284	13,562	3	46
1965	37	412	6,321	13,974	2	35
1964	46	535	6,367	14,509	4	42
1963	25	400	6,392	14,909	—	51
1962	27	408	6,419	15,317	—	41
1961	34	319	6,453	15,636	2	58
1960–1956	107	964	6,560	16,600	1	145
1955–1951	75	1,048	6,635	17,648	2	116
1950–1946	87	1,296	6,722	18,944	2	84
1945–1941	63	412	6,785	19,356	1	28
1940–1936	25	369	6,810	19,725	—	23
1935–1931	11	119	6,821	19,844	—	20
1930–1926	—	13	6,821	19,857	—	6
1925–1921	—	5	6,821	19,862	—	5
					(670)	(1,352)

Table A2.4: *Age and sex profiles of the Central Civil Service and of the Department of Posts and Telegraphs at 15 September 1982*

Age Group	Central Civil Service		Post Office	
	Male	Female	Male	Female
Under 20	502	1,113	673	292
20–24	3,481	5,442	3,978	2,478
25–29	2,919	4,049	3,528	1,936
30–34	2,373	1,109	2,314	792
35–39	1,881	434	2,168	359
40–44	1,261	304	1,623	241
45–49	1,124	289	1,587	209
50–54	1,209	400	1,412	243
55–59	1,283	443	1,167	138
60–64	1,268	386	1,113	91
Over 65	395	191	528	29
Total	17,696	14,160	20,091	6,808

Table A2.5: *Reasons for termination of Civil Service employment 1958 to 1974 (% of total during year)*

During	Retirement	Death	Marriage	Dismissal	Secondment	Other
			Percentages			
1958	23	9	26	5	1	36
1959	24	9	22	6	3	35
1960	20	7	18	4	21	30
1961	24	9	18	4	2	43
1962	27	7	20	6	1	39
1963	25	8	17	4	1	46
1964	22	8	19	5	1	46
1965	22	6	22	5	1	44
1966	21	7	21	4	1	45
1967	21	7	27	3	2	40
1968	21	6	25	3	1	44
1969	18	6	27	3	1	45
1970	13	6	27	3	1	49
1971	16	7	32	3	—	42
1972	17	7	36	4	1	34
1973	21	5	25	3	2	44
1974	18	5	17	2	3	55

Note: Row total = 100%

Table A2.6: *Male and female holders of certain posts in General Service and Finance Grades in 1932, 1972 and 1982*

	1932 (Jan.)			1972 (Jan.)			1982 (July)		
	Male	Female	Total	Male	Female	Total	Male	Female	Total
Secretaries[1]	21	—	21	88	—	88	103	2	105
Principal Officers	22	—	22	197	1	198	337	10	347
Assistant Principal Officers	30	—	30	392	18	410	609	198	807
Administrative Officers	21	3	24	77	16	93	110	48	158
Higher Executive Officers	174	2	176	668	97	765	888	472	1,360
Executive Officers[2]	421	8	429	764	530	1,294	1,264	897	2,161
Staff Officers	156	24	180	239	356	595	381	599	980
Clerical Officers	1,715	350	2,065	750	1,282	2,032	1,233	2,319	3,552
Clerical Assistants[3]	348	1,244	1,592	75 (+660)	5,661 (+631)	5,736 (7,027)	1,421	7,801	9,222

Note 1: Secretaries include Deputy, Assistant etc.

Note 2: Executive Officers may be recruited by open competition from the Leaving Certificate or by internal promotion. It can be regarded as the basic career grade.

Note 3: Clerical Assistants in 1932 include Shorthand Typists and Typists (all female); Writing Clerks (all male); Writing Assistants almost exclusively female and unestablished temporary clerks (70% male). In 1972 CAs so described are included with temporary male clerks. Code 35 gives the figures in parenthesis in the table for other clerical and writing assistants. 1982 includes programmers and key punch operators.

Table A2.7(a): *Composition of Grade Group 1. Numbers and Costs in 1938 and Numbers in 1940 distinguishing P+T from other Departments*

	1938		1940	
			Total	Excluding P+T
	No.	£	No.	No.
Chairman of Boards of Commission, Heads of Dept. of State	15	22,567	14	13
Commissioners and Heads of subordinate offices	24	29,360	23	23
Heads of Division and Branch (Asst. Sec., Director, Chief Clerk and Superintending Officers)	79	76,429	95	92
Principals	40	39,879	48	44
Accountants (incl. Accountant General, Asst. and Deputy)	34	29,012	35	29
Assistant Principal	57	44,068	61	55
Staff posts exceed £500 maximum	4	3,174	4	4
Junior Administrative (incl. Cadets External Affairs)	41	17,058	43	43
Higher Executive Officers	196	122,970	219	193
Junior Executive Officers	626	203,039	616	586
Revenue Commissioners				
Tax Inspectors; Chief, Senior and Higher Grade	27	24,487	27	24
Tax Inspectors; Ordinary and Asst.	58	22,360	58	58
Customs and Excise; Chief and Superintending Inspectors, Higher Collector Controlling grade and surveyor	61	51,425	61	61
Controlling Officers	431	181,256	428	420
Investigation Inspectors, Surveyor and Officers (Social Welfare?)	178	53,756	178	178
1st Class Officers Industry and Commerce	7	5,339	7	7
2nd Class Officers Industry and Commerce	23	13,701	21	21
P & T; Comptrollers (including Deputy and Asst.)	5	3,854	6	0
P & T; Superintendents (including Chief and Asst.)	43	17,682	44	0
Postmasters I and II	3	2,006	3	0
Postmasters III and IV	77	27,942	85	0
Other Grades	141	107,488	140	129
	2,170	1,098,852	2,216	1,991

Table A2.7(b): *Numbers and costs in 1952 including and excluding the Department of Posts and Telegraphs*

	Excluding P + T	Including Posts and Telegraphs	
		Nos.	Costs £
Heads of Departments of State	15	16	39,131
Commissioners, Deputy and Assistant Secretaries	70	72	162,447
Principal Officers and analogous, Accountants and Deputies on scales to maxima £1,465–£1,630*	126	135	220,265
Assistant Principals and analogous on scales to maxima £965–£1,300*	246	263	322,696
Administrative Officer and Third Secretary	62	63	44,051
Higher Executive Officer	368	402	368,571
Executive Officer	604	641	328,063
All Tax Officers including Assistant	108	108	111,246
All Customs and Excise Officers	456	456	436,317
All Social Welfare Officers	248	248	177,506
All P+T staff separately identified in 1938	0	138	93,931
Others	121	142	133,532
	2,424	2,684	2,437,756

*To aid interpretation the maxima refer to:

£965	Assistant Principal Scale 2 Unmarried	£1,465	Principal Officer Unmarried
£1,300	Assistant Principal Scale 1 Married	£1,630	Principal Officer Married

Table A2.7c(i): *Numbers and costs in 1961, 1970 and 1975*

	Numbers			Cost		
	1961	*1970*	*1975*	*1961*	*1970*	*1975*
Heads of Departments of State	⎰18	17	18	57,459	93,900	173,021
Chairmen of Boards of Commission	⎱	3	3		12,085	20,179
Deputy Secretaries	⎰22*	5	9	83,000	24,540	77,496
Asst. Secretaries not GS	⎱	4	6		21,350	50,965
Asst. Secretaries GS	42	56	67	104,938	245,104	487,410
Deputy Asst. Sec. at GS/AS scale	—	4	12	—	16,716	86,632
Other Asst. Secretaries	—	1	1	—	3,779	6,264
Commissioners etc. paid above GS/AS	—	20	22	—	119,753	249,249
Analogous to GS/AS	15	20	24	48,182	135,112	274,373
Principal officers finance	24	⎰27	46	53,905	100,411	301,196
Analogous		⎱12	10		44,996	64,675
Principal officers general	94	152	210	189,389	525,393	1,258,861
Analogous	20	23	36	47,383	112,931	261,138
Asst. Principals finance	81	⎰60	117	139,973	177,842	584,215
Analogous		⎱21	37		61,968	157,984
Asst. Principals general	172	294	443	274,792	801,361	2,100,788
Analogous	45	78	112	75,621	285,058	688,223
Second & Third Secretaries	27	33	61	44,759	103,512	278,490
Administrative Officer	20	70	85	16,567	101,925	258,682
Higher Executive Officer Max £2,385	426	680	989	525,605	1,441,022	3,804,918
Higher Executive Officer Max £2,215	26	—	1	31,476	—	3,656
Higher Executive Officer Max £2,030	48	14	3	52,477	26,758	11,487
Executive Officers formerly S.O.	127	119	96	128,755	213,776	310,190
Executive Officers formerly other	628	998	1,543	458,441	1,288,845	3,975,030
Other Higher grades	1,022	236	360	1,163,584	656,831	1,631,575
All other grades	782	782	951		1,413,530	3,304,104
Total	2,857	3,729	5,262	3,496,306	8,028,498	20,420,901

Interpretation GS/AS = General Service/Asst. Secretary. *Includes analogous.

Table A2.7c(ii): *Numbers in 1961, 1970 and 1975 distinguishing the Department of Posts and Telegraphs*

	Post Office			Other		
	1961	1970	1975	1961	1970	1975
Heads/Depts of State	1	1	1	17	16	17
Chairmen/Commissioners	—	—	—		3	3
Deputy Secretary	—	—	—	22*	5	9
Asst. Secretaries not GS	—	—	—		4	6
Asst. Secretaries GS	2	3	3	40	53	64
Deputy Asst. Sec. on GS/AS scale	—	—	—		4	12
Other Asst. Secretaries	—	—	—	—	1	1
Commissioners etc. paid above GS/AS	—	—	—	—	20	22
Analogous to GS/AS	—	—	—	15	20	24
Principal finance	3	1	1	21	26	45
Analogous		1	1		11	9
Principal/GS	5	7	8	89	145	202
Analogous	—	—	—	20	23	36
APO Finance	3	—	—	78	60	117
Analogous		2	3		19	34
APO/GS	11	16	23	161	278	420
Analogous	8	11	12	37	67	100
Second and Third Secretary	—	—	—	27	33	61
Administrative Officer	—	3	6	20	67	79
HEO Max £2385	32	48	76	394	632	913
HEO Max £2215	4	—	—	22	—	1
HEO Max £2030	6	—	—	42	14	3
EO formerly SO	19	22	11	108	97	85
Other Executive Officers	34	48	104	594	950	1,439
Other Higher grades	156	31	86		205	274
All other grades		158	137	866	624	814
Total	284	352	472	2,573	3,377	4,790

*Includes analogous.

Table A2.8: *Table amalgamating the 167 grades associated with the Administrative and Executive Group I in the computerised SIS so that they correspond with those previously employed in the CSC*

| | Maximum Salary £ | Numbers in | | | |
		Actual Grade	Equivalent Grades	Analogous Grades	Total
1 Grades above Secretary	28,499	4	—	—	4
2 Secretary and 2nd Secretary	25,610	22	10	—	32
3 Deputy Secretary	22,721	12	14	—	26
4 Assistant Secretary	19,832	94	16	26	36
5 Principal Officer Finance Scale	16,943	61	8	13	82
6 Principal Officer General Scale	15,788	278	130	(12)	480
7 Assistant Principal Finance Scale	13,708	131	10	11	152
8 Assistant Principal General Scale	12,437	662	231	7+16	916
9 Miscellaneous (P & T, Prisons)	11,104	—	—	53	53
10 Higher Executive Officer	10,414	1,310	10	371*(+1)	1,692
11 Administrative Officer	10,414	151	54	—	205
12 Higher Officer of Tax	9,735	321	—	57	378
13 Transition (P & T)	9,692	—	—	73	73
14 Placement Officer (Labour)	9,113	104	—	—	104
15 Executive Officer	8,649	2,147	128	580**	2,855
16 Officer of Customs and Excise	7,975	307	—	14+	321
17 Others	—	72	—	—	72
Total	—	5,676	611	1,234	7,521

*Inspector of Tax (Max £10,452). For further details see notes on Appendix A2.8, Row 10 below.
**Higher Tax Officers.   †Tax Assistants at Max. of Scale.

NOTES FOR TABLE A2.8

Row 1. Grades above Secretary — Secretary Department of Finance Max £28,499 — Secretaries of Departments of Public Service and An Taoiseach, Chairman of Revenue Commissioners Max £27,344.

Row 2. Equivalent grades to Secretary: Clerk of Dail; 2 Revenue Commissioners; Chairman, Office of Public Works; 2 Ambassadors I; 2 Parliamentary Draftsmen. First Legal Assistant Attorney General's Office. Chairman of Labour Court.

Row 3. Equivalents of Deputy Secretary: Director Central Statistics Office; 6 Ambassadors II; 5 Land Commissioners, Superintending Inspector of Taxes (Planning); Master Central Office of Courts.

Row 4. Equivalents of Assistant Secretary: 2 Directors of Audit, 2 Deputy Chairmen Labour Court; Accountant General Revenue Commissioners; 2 Assistant Secretaries Office of Public Works; Controller Stationery Office; 1 Registrar Supreme and High Courts; Registrar of Titles and Deeds (Registrar of Wards of Court); 2 Superintendents of Customs and Excise; 2 Superintending Inspectors of Taxes; Director of Conciliation Labour Court.

Analogous to Assistant Secretary: *Salary fixed at Maximum:* 2 Appeals Commissioners of Revenue, 2 Taxing Masters in Courts *Longer scale same maximum* 21 Envoys Extraordinary and Ministers Plenipotentiary, 1 Higher Collector Customs and Excise.

Row 5.   Equivalents of Principal Officer on Finance Scale: 2 Probate Officers, Official Assignee in Bankruptcy, Registrar I in Central Office (all Courts); Finance Officer, Defence; Comptroller of Patents, Industry and Commerce; Clerk Assistant of Dail; Clerk of Senate.

Analogous to Principal Officer Finance: Shorter scale same maximum 11 Principal Inspectors of Taxes; Accountant, P & T; Deputy Director Central Statistics Office.

Row 6.   Equivalent of Principal Officer General Service Scale: 63 Senior Inspectors of Taxes; 20 Inspectors and 2 Collectors of Customs and Excise; 30 Counsellors Foreign Affairs; 3 Deputy Directors of Audit; 4 Registrars II Central Office (Courts); Assistant Registrar Wards of Court; Assistant Probate Officer; Assistant Examiner I (Courts); Accountant (Courts); Manager Land Registry; Business Analyst (P & T); Director National Gallery; Chairperson Employment Equality Agency.

Analogous Grades: Fixed point salaries Head of Government Information Office (£13,000); Film Censor (£14,024); 6 Members, Labour Court (£15,184); *grade on scales in P & T:* Chief Inspector of Services £11,918–£14,516 also 3 Data Processing Managers (£12,748–£15,574).

Row 7.   Assistant Principal Finance Scale *Equivalents*: 7 Registrars III Central Office Courts; Senior Assistant Registrar of Deeds; Registrar Land Commission; Exchange Manager Central Telegraph Office.

Analogous: Longer scale same maximum: 5 Principal Clerks Oireachtas; 2 Examiners of Title Land Commission; Assistant Manager, Land Registry; Secretary Charitable Bequests and Donations *Different Scale* (£12,158–£13,161) 2 Governors Mountjoy and Portlaoise.

Row 8.   Assistant Principal General Services Equivalents: 78 First Secretaries Foreign Affairs; 127 Inspectors (Higher Grade) Revenue; 2 Information Officers in Finance; 8 Director and Information Officers National Manpower Service; 4 Assistant Controllers of Stores (P & T); *In Courts* 4 Assistant Registrars II, Chief Clerk, Chief Examiner District Court Assistant Probate Officer II, and 2 Assistant Examiners; Chief Clerk Land Commission, 2 Assistant Finance Officers, Defence.

Analogous: longer scale same maximum. Information Officers P & T (2) and Industry and Commerce (1); Coordination of Education Prisons; County Development Secretary: Deputy Keeper Public Records Office, *short scale same maximum:* Junior Assistant Registrar of Deeds.

Analogous: Assistant Director National Gallery (£10,595–£12,062); *In P & T* 5 Assistant Controllers Dublin Area (£10,981–£12,666) 2 Telephones Chief Traffic Superintendents (£10,981–£12,344); 2 Head Postmasters (£11,482–£12,329) 6 Prison Governors (£10,270–£12,158).

Row 9.   Miscellaneous: *Prisons* 4 Deputy Governors (£10,280–£11,037); *Post Office:* Telephone Chief Contracts Manager (£8,672–£11,104) 13 Headpostmasters (£9,545–£11,050); Deputy Chief Investigations Officer (£9,984–£11,074); on scale (£8,870–£10,324) 19 Telephone Traffic Superintendents I and 9 Telephone Contracts Managers I; 4 Senior Investigations Officers (£9,746–£10,638); *On scale* (£9,401–£10,698): Telephone Senior Traffic Superintendent and Controller Central Telegraph Office.

Row 10.   Higher Executive Officer Equivalents: Captain of the Guard Oireachtas, 5 Press Officers (Taoiseach), 3 Industrial Relations Liaison Officers and 1 Equality Officer (Labour).

Analogous 371 Inspectors of Taxes (£5,927–£10,452): Principal Welfare Officer (Justice) (£8,208–£10,413 with allowance).

Row 11. Administrative Officer Equivalent: 54 Third Secretaries Foreign Affairs.

Row 12. Higher Officers of Tax Analogous. All with same max. £9,735: *starting at* £7,975 — 5 Examiners District Court, 2 Chief Superintendents of Stamping (Revenue); *Starting at:* £8,888 13 Telephone Senior Traffic Superintendents; *Starting at* £7,673, 31 Telephone Traffic Superintendents II and 6 Investigations Officers (P & T).

Row 13. Transition: (P & T) scale (£8,607–£9,692): 16 Superintendents I Metropolitan and Provincial Offices; (£7,281–£9,204): 40 Telephone Contracts Managers II; (£7,565–£8,888): 17 Head Postmasters V.

Row 15. Executive Officer Equivalents: 125 Indoor Officers (Revenue); 2 Junior Clerks (Oireachtas), Registrar National Gallery.
Row 17. Others: 50 Local Agents (scale paid); 7 Fishery Officers (£6,511–£8,034); 13 Estate Officers (£4,812–£7,800); Fishery Manager (£3,977–£4,454).

Table A2.9: *Numbers of industrial civil servants 1959–1984 (including casual and seasonal workers and civilians in Defence)*

January 1st	Industrials other than Casual and Seasonal*		Casual and Seasonal		Office of Public Works		Total Nos.
	Nos.	*Cost*	*Nos.*	*Cost*	*Nos.*	*Cost* £	
1959	7,206	2,362,559	3,110	895,018			10,316
1960	7,313	2,477,647	3,109	922,186			10,332
1961	7,162	2,760,916	2,948	902,536			10,110
1962	7,134	2,917,137	2,630	927,712		Casuals	9,764
1963	7,245	3,233,468	3,401	1,315,706		and others	10,646
1964	7,075	3,252,754	3,394	1,373,510		separately	10,469
1965	7,402	3,860,009	3,145	1,486,654		identified	10,547
1966	7,273	3,888,208	2,722	1,232,295		included	9,995
1967	6,711	3,888,442	2,419	1,166,763		in other	9,330
1968	6,440	4,022,432	2,390	1,276,821		columns	8,830
1969	5,605*	3,805,809*	711	397,835	2,164	1,540,000	8,480
1970	5,105	3,728,350	870	595,909	1,926	1,714,470	7,901
1971	5,019	4,520,727	730	527,487	2,339	2,551,900	8,088
1972	4,747	5,180,000	756	658,685	2,263	2,619,300	7,764
1973	4,674	5,710,036	641	575,508	2,108	2,959,400	7,423
1974	4,604	6,456,356	568	559,026	2,231	3,285,500	7,403
1975	4,924	7,967,158	554	666,587	2,318	3,860,680	7,796
1976	4,808	9,984,328	565	847,147	2,375	5,532,506	7,748
1977	na	na	na	na	na	na	na
1978	4,836	11,756,914	467	1,484,593	2,400	7,167,950	7,703
1979	5,285	15,166,619	534	1,731,590	2,384	na	8,203
1980	5,273	20,754,185	572	2,207,607	na	na	8,414
1981	5,063	21,379,066	539	2,742,349	3,109	1,508,813	8,711
1982	4,634		532		2,812		7,978

*Includes 230 staff earning £58,301 who were transferred to a semi-state body, Aer Rianta, in subsequent years.

Note: Due to revisions made by the author to the official returns, the totals given here do not correspond exactly with those obtained by adding the civilians in defence in Table A2.13 to total industrials as set out in Table A2.12. The discrepancies are not large up to 1976. From 1978 onwards the estimates for the Office of Public Works differ. There may also be some other changes arising from computerisation but a more likely cause is probably the omission of some Post Office employment from the above returns. This omission is rectified in Table A2.11.

Appendix A2.10: *Industrial workers in the Agricultural Group distinguishing Forestry, Land Commission and Department of Agriculture employees by whole-time and part-time employment 1959 to 1985*

Jan 1	Forestry					Land Commission					Agriculture					Total				
	Full time	+	Casual	=	Total	F/T	+	Casual	=	Total	F/T	+	Casual	=	Total	F/T	+	Casual	=	Total
1959	4,440	+	218	=	4,658	47	+	1,006	=	1,053	298	+	569	=	867	4,785	+	1,793	=	6,578
1960	4,601	+	174	=	4,775	9	+	1,055	=	1,064	276	+	343	=	619	4,886	+	1,572	=	6,458
1961	4,568	+	137	=	4,705	9	+	986	=	995	175	+	212	=	387	4,752	+	1,335	=	6,087
1962	4,508	+	239	=	4,747	9	+	915	=	924	201	+	161	=	362	4,718	+	1,315	=	6,033
1963	4,644	+	136	=	4,780	9	+	1,074	=	1,083	150	+	180	=	330	4,803	+	1,390	=	6,193
1964	4,423	+	262	=	4,685	7	+	861	=	868	147	+	191	=	338	4,577	+	1,314	=	5,891
1965	4,716	+	87	=	4,803	9	+	822	=	831	191	+	137	=	328	4,916	+	1,046	=	5,962
1966	4,537	+	197	=	4,734	9	+	761	=	770	208	+	142	=	350	4,754	+	1,100	=	5,854
1967	4,061	+	200	=	4,261	10	+	554	=	564	207	+	155	=	362	4,278	+	909	=	5,207
1968	3,741	+	189	=	3,930	8	+	483	=	491	203	+	152	=	355	3,952	+	824	=	4,776
1969	3,657	+	64	=	3,721	5	+	432	=	437	183	+	165	=	348	3,845	+	661	=	4,506
1970	3,371	+	163	=	3,534	8	+	479	=	487	187	+	187	=	374	3,566	+	829	=	4,395
1971	3,261	+	130	=	3,391	8	+	344	=	352	187	+	220	=	407	3,456	+	694	=	4,150
1972	2,962	+	218	=	3,180	7	+	286	=	293	200	+	229	=	429	3,169	+	733	=	3,902
1973	2,840	+	106	=	2,946	7	+	274	=	281	211	+	240	=	451	3,058	+	620	=	3,678
1974	2,751	+	60	=	2,811	7	+	234	=	241	242	+	248	=	490	3,000	+	542	=	3,542
1975	2,677	+	73	=	2,750	6	+	226	=	232	296	+	231	=	527	2,979	+	530	=	3,509
1976	2,585	+	65	=	2,650	6	+	233	=	239	264	+	237	=	501	2,855	+	535	=	3,390
1977	2,560	+	70	=	2,630	(6)	+	(221)	=	227	(267)	+	(225)	=	492	(2,833)	+	(516)	=	3,349
1978	2,520	+	0	=	2,520	6	+	147	=	153	270	+	116	=	386	2,796	+	263	=	3,059
1979	2,650	+	177	=	2,827	(6)	+	149	=	155	311	+	116	=	427	(2,967)	+	(442)	=	3,409
1980	2,740	+	129	=	2,869	(5)	+	131	=	136	339	+	23	=	362	(3,084)	+	(283)	=	3,367
1981	2,758	+	109	=	2,867	(4)	+	126	=	130	156	+	—	=	156	(2,918)	+	(235)	=	3,153
1982	2,680	+	176	=	2,856	3	+	253	=	256	157	+	167	=	324	2,840	+	596	=	3,436
1983	2,541	+	163	=	2,704	3	+	580	=	583	143	+	130	=	273	2,687	+	873	=	3,560
1984	2,500	+	160(e)	=	2,660	3	+	599	=	602	134	+	109	=	243	2,637	+	868	=	3,505
1985	2,422	+	90	=	2,512	3	+	533	=	536	124	+	30	=	154	2,549	+	653	=	3,202

Figures in parentheses represent estimates.

Appendix Table A2.11: *Employment in the Department of Posts and Telegraphs not recorded in the Staff Information System (SIS) 1959 to 1984 distinguishing industrials, non industrials, whole-time and part-time employees*

Date	Part-time Sub Post Offices	Casuals					Full-time Engineering Dept.	Stores F/T	Engineering			All Non-SIS
		F/T	+	P/T	=	Total			F/T	+	P/T	
1959	2,158		+		=	401	82	124*	5	+	117	2,887
1960	2,162	183	+	188	=	371	114	133*	5	+	85	2,870
1961	2,164	227	+	205	=	432	200	123*	7	+	150	3,276
1962	2,170	135	+	90	=	225	225	128	8	+	96	2,852
1963	2,176	232	+	201	=	433	157	137	5	+	150	3,058
1964	2,176	220	+	199	=	419	169	156	7	+	117	3,044
1965	2,173	222	+	219	=	441	261	161	6	+	123	3,165
1966	2,157	199	+	216	=	415	368	164	5	+	63	3,172
1967	2,127	205	+	240	=	445	238	161	8	+	38	3,017
1968	2,120	229	+	257	=	486	252	158	10	+	41	3,067
1969	2,106	215	+	259	=	474	199	140	10	+	37	2,966
1970	2,104	174	+	297	=	471	268	136	12	+	30	3,021
1971	2,096	232	+	310	=	542	232	154	17	+	26	3,067
1972	2,097	169	+	309	=	478	141	142	20	+	13	2,891
1973	2,105	168	+	323	=	491	305	132	24	+	14	3,071
1974	2,090	162	+	298	=	460	349	136	28	+	15	3,078
1975	2,073	164	+	240	=	404	328	134	34	+	16	2,989
1976	2,080	147	+	218	=	365	237	137	30	+	12	2,861
1977	2,084	148	+	191	=	339	290	136	28	+	15	2,892
1978	2,086	154	+	172	=	326	394	135	19	+	25	2,985
1979	2,073	170	+	201	=	371	406	152	38	+	—	3,040
1980	2,075	88	+	201	=	289	339	150	38	+	14	2,905
1981	2,074	181	+	165	=	346	300	152	58	+	20	2,950
1982	(2,075)	182	+	168	=	350	340	152	61	+	25	3,003
1983	(2,077)		+		=	(300)	280	150	61	+	30	2,898
1984	(2,077)		+		=	(250)	216	(146)	61	+	33	2,783
1985	2,078		+		=	(200)	137	140	60	+	38	2,653

*Industrials in Stores 1959, 1960 and 1961 include 4, 4 & 3 full-time workers elsewhere in Post Office, 1959 + 1960 also include 1 full-time worker in wireless.

Appendix Table A2.12: *Industrial workers (apart from those in Agriculture, Civilians in Defence and in the Post Office) by major departments of employment 1959 to 1984.*

	Office of Public Works			Justice	Revenue Comm.	Stat. Office	Museum & Educ.	Transport	Defence	Other	All Industrial except Defence
	F/T +	P/T =	Total								
1959	576 +	1,135 =	1,711	3 + 1	33	4	5	207	8	50 + 8	8,854
1960	591 +	1,326 =	1,917	4 + 2	31	4	5	196	8	9	8,857
1961	607 +	1,423 =	2,030	4	33	4	5	204	8	9 + 2	8,666
1962	619 +	1,209 =	1,828	(3)	33	3	6	140	8	9 + 2	8,297
1963	625 +	1,831 =	2,456	(3)	32	3	6	154	8	9 + 2	9,158
1964	641 +	1,932 =	2,573	(3)	34	3	6	160	8	4 + 3	8,965
1965	654 +	1,959 =	2,613	(3)	37	4	6	212	8	4 + 3	9,142
1966	674 +	1,541 =	2,215	11	34	4	6	191	8	4 + 2	8,561
1967	667 +	1,462 =	2,129	12	34	4	4	199	9	3 + 2	7,790
1968	701 +	1,517 =	2,218	13	33	4	5	227	9	4 + 2	7,500
1969			2,164	15	32	4	(5)	229	9	4 + 3	7,148
1970			1,926	15	36	4	6	3*	9	3 + 3	6,578
1971			2,339	16	38	2	6	2 + 1	9	4 + 2	6,766
1972			2,263	16	36	3	6	2 + 1	8	6 + 2	6,420
1973			2,108	(15)	37	3	6	3 + 1	8		6,029
1974			2,231	(15)	(38)	3	7	9	8	+ 4	6,036
1975			2,318	16	(39)	3	7	9	8	+ (4)	6,097
1976			2,375	23 + 1	(41)	4	8	10	7	+ 4	6,042
1977			2,163	18	43	4	8	8	7	3 + (4)	5,786
1978			2,210	(16)	42 + 16	4	8	9	(7)	10 + 4	5,566
1979			2,384	25	40 + 3	4	10	9	(7)		6,081
1980			2,569	23	42 + 16	4	10	10	(7)	1 + 7	6,258
1981	2,753 +	356 =	3,109	28	43 + 18	4	14	10	18		6,627
1982	2,658 +	154 =	2,812	24 + 2	43 + 15	4	8	9	7	1 + 1	6,600
1983	2,627 +	(154) =	2,781	23 + 6	44 + 19	4	9	9	(7)	1 + 1	6,705
1984	2,515 +	(154) =	2,669	21 + 6	16 + 19	4	9	9 + 1	(7)	1	6,507
1985	2,301 +	(154) =	2,455	21 + 6	17 + 12	4	8	9	(7)	1	5,980

Note 1: "Other" 1959 49 + 5, Gaeltacht 1960–3(5), 1959–1972 Dundrum Mental Hospital, 1974–1981 Fisheries and Industry and Commerce, 1981 Taoiseach (3). Figures for 'Museum' up to 1975 at which point Department of Education secondary level takes over. Perhaps they are the same people?

Note II: Office of Public Works figures above were specially compiled for this study for 1977 to 1981. The special figure for 1981, 2,613, is not given above. Alternate figures for 1977 and 1978 are 2,835 and 2,750 (est.) which include approximately 350 gauge readers and caretakers. A third figure for 1981 of 2,755 appears to be 3,109 less these gauge readers.

Appendix Table A2.13: *Department distribution of staff (apart from the Post Office) not included in the Staff Information System but including civilians employed by the Department of Defence, 1959 59 1985*

Jan 1	Defence Industrial Civilians	Other Non SIS	Social Welfare or Labour	Education	Agric.	Ind. and Comm.	Other	Non-industrial Non SIS† Total	Part time
1959	1,406 + 56	136 + 17	109	31	—		70	3,004	n.a.
1960	1,441 + 32	133 + 17	14 + 103	28 + 6	188* +		69	3,205	2,477
1961	1,406 + 38	132 + 17	12 + 108	24 + 1	45 + 24		117	3,276	2,515
1962	1,462 + 24	138 + 17	9 + 109	5 + 1	31 + 3		100	3,033	2,400
1963	1,463 + 28	150 + 17	9 + 101	10 + 2	49 + 3		69	3,176	n.a.
1964	1,479 + 28	149 + 18	10 + 104	7 + 6	19 +		64	3,141	2,503
1965	1,394 + 14	148 + 20	12 + 100	12 + 1	38 + 36		22	3,264	2,553
1966	1,418 + 16	139 + 23	8 + 100	4 + 6	6 + 34		22	3,282	2,504
1967	1,332 + 8	144 + 23	(9 + 102)	9 + 10	3 + 1		91	3,202	2,502
1968	1,334 + 6	164 + 24	(10 + 104)	10 +	5 +		13	3,188	2,507
1969	1,317 + 10	163 + 24	11 + 107	6 + 3	22 +		12	3,127	n.a.
1970	1,315 + 8	168 + 24	6 + 100	13 +	5 +		13	3,172	2,529
1971	1,315 + 7	169 + 25	7 + 97	6 + 4	8 +		24	3,210	2,536
1972	1,337 + 7	169 + 25	11 + 100	12 + 1	13 +	8	30	3,085	2,531
1973	1,391 + 6	169 + 25	7 + 97	4 + 4	15 +	17	24	3,263	2,552
1974	1,411 + 7	175 + 26	9 + 99	9 +	14 +	25	7	3,263	2,506
1975	1,734 + 7	176 + 26	12 + 95	9 +	11 +	28	3	3,165	2,437
1976	1,741 + 13	185 + 25	9 + 97	7 +	+ 23	32	3	3,063	2,443
1977	1,640 + 10	287 + 21	10 + 100	15 +	(16) +	33 + 2	42	3,239	n.a.
1978	1,677 + 6	272 + 22	6 + 100	17 +	9 +	33 +	8	3,273	n.a.
1979	1,763 + 7	273 + 25	10 + 102	8 + 12	24 +	39 +	41	3,384	n.a.
1980	1,788 + 10	301 + 26	13 + 104	21 +	0 +	+36	32 + 41	3,277	n.a.
1981	1,776 + 10	290 + 27	13 + 105	0 +	0 +	0	27 + 80	3,262	n.a.
1982	1,710 + 17	289 + 13	19 + 109	73 +	0 +	+11	173 + 120	3,572	n.a.
1983	(1,670) + (17)	(247) + (11)	16 + 111	65 + 1	0 +	+21	222 + 103	3,454	n.a.
1984	1,508 + 138	205 + 10	14 + 110	9 + 58	0 +	0	227 + 52	3,228	n.a.
1985	1,184 + 178	452 + 10	16 + 106	8 + 57	0 +	0	284 + 136	3,468	n.a.

†Total of this row excluding defence industrial plus plus P & T non-SIS from Table A2.11. (a) *Note:* 1960–64 Revenue Commissioner (c. 60), 1961/2 Justice (c. 30) 1967 Prison (72) 1977 Transport (26) 1979 onwards Valuation and Ordnance (5 to 19), Environment (18 to 35), OPW (45–49) in 1981/82. The large recent increase in 'Other' was due to the gardai returning numbers of cleaners, yardmen, etc. employed casually at barracks, etc. There was also an increase in guides at national monuments employed seasonally by the Office of Public Works.

Appendix Table A2.14: *Pre-1958 data on some major groups included in the non-industrial non-SIS category after 1958*

| | Scale paid managers of: | | | | | | Non Ind. | Civilians | of which |
| | Sub-post offices | | | Branch Office | | Social Welfare | Casual | in | industrial |
	Men	Women	Total	Men	Women	Total	P+T	Defence	na
1932	860	1,164	2,024	74	6	80	n.a.	410	n.a.
1938	761	1,204	1,965	n.a.	n.a.	n.a.	n.a.	n.a.	n.a.
1940	755	1,214	1,969	n.a.	n.a.	n.a.	n.a.	627*	n.a.
1945	745	1,246	1,991	n.a.	n.a.	n.a.	n.a.	n.a.	n.a.
1946	755	1,248	2,003	n.a.	n.a.	n.a.	n.a.	n.a.	n.a.
1948	753	1,255	2,008	n.a.	n.a.	n.a.	n.a.	n.a.	n.a.
1949	767	1,271	2,038	n.a.	n.a.	n.a.	n.a.	1,642	1,126
1950	762	1,273	2,035	67	17	84	n.a.	(1,477)**	1,076
1951	775	1,301	2,076	63	17	80	661	(1,437)**	1,073
1952	778	1,305	2,083	63	17	80	535	1,531	1,080
1953	790	1,296	2,086	65	16	81	540	1,565	1,123
1954	795	1,302	2,097	63	19	82	516	2,077	1,172
1955	803	1,305	2,108	62	21	83	584	2,183	1,232
1956	806	1,304	2,110	61	21	82	449	1,993	1,471
1957	806	1,307	2,113	59	24	83	396	1,870	1,415
1958	na	na	2,109	na	na	80	418†	1,420	1,258

*1939. †Including 120 part time. **Source: Civil Service Census.

Source: "Civilians in Defence" up to 1957 was a Department of Defence Memorandum 14/5/57

Note: Defence industrials were not included in the post-1958 category.

Appendix Table A2.15: *Number of children in reformatories and industrial schools 1941–1972*

| Y/E | Reformatories | | Industrial Schools | | | Both |
July 31	Total Number	Committed in Year	Schools	Number of Children	Committed in Year	Total
1941	248	100	51	6,593	1,066	6,841
1942	262	105	51	6,627	1,004	6,689
1943	280	154	51	6,699	1,032	6,979
1944	288	121	51	6,525	941	6,813
1945	273	123	51	6,565	1,061	6,838
1946	237	108	51	6,510	946	6,747
1947	209	88	51	6,346	883	6,555
1948	248	144	51	6,367	991	6,615
1949	245	92	51	6,126	779	6,371
1950	210	97	51	5,984	833	6,194
1951	214	104	50	5,844	789	6,058
1952	198	82	50	5,679	732	5,877
1953	175	82	50	5,448	626	5,623
1954	173	89	50	5,128	551	5,301
1955	157	66	50	4,833	553	4,990
1956	172	93	50	4,470	596	4,642
1957	208	110	50	4,308	578	4,516
1958	192	105	49	4,135	592	4,327
1959	218*	125	48	4,043*	623	4,261
1960	225*	128	48	3,786*	608	4,011
1961	205	131	48	3,686	671	3,891
1962	177	103	48	3,517	647	3,694
1963	154	84	48	3,240	611	3,394
1964	175	110	43	2,969	446	3,144
1965	138	85	43	2,708	439	2,846
1966	145	89	41	2,456	407	2,601
1967	132	104	36	2,120	275	2,252
1968	151	120	33	1,831	211	1,982
1969	117	103	33	1,513	162	1,630
1970	100	136	29	1,271	154	1,371
	Special Schools			Residential Homes		
1971	255		27	907	(241)**	1,162
1972	241		26	872	(219)**	1,113

Source: Dept. of Education Statistical Reports.

Note: Committals exclude transfers and recommittals. *Revised; **Includes special schools.

Appendix Table A2.16: *Staff at individual Universities 1968/9 and 1969/70 distinguishing full time, partt ime, fee paid and non-academic.*

	Full Time	Part Time	Fee Paid	Non-Academic
1968/9				
UCD	440	209	371	872
UCC	126	244	10	264
UCG	101	105	—	102
TCD	240	54	148	747
NUI	—	—	—	21
Total	907	612	529	2,006
1969/70				
UCD	473	203	497	937
UCC	140	270	21	281
UCG	123	n.a.	n.a.	(152 est.)
TCD	256	70	155	725
NUI	—	—	—	21
Total	992	543 + n.a.	673 + n.a.	2,116

Source: Unpublished CSO records.

INDEX

(p. refers to page, T. to Table, F. to Figure and A. to Appendix Table)

Books:

Economic Growth in Ireland: The Experience Since 1947

Kieran A. Kennedy and Brendan Dowling

Irish Economic Policy: A Review of Major Issues

Staff Members of ESRI (eds. B. R. Dowling and J. Durkan)

The Irish Economy and Society in the 1980s (Papers presented at ESRI Twenty-first Anniversary Conference)

Staff Members of ESRI

The Economic and Social State of The Nation

J. F. Meenan, M. P. Fogarty, J. Kavanagh and L. Ryan

The Irish Economy: Policy and Performance 1972-1981

P. Bacon, J. Durkan and J. O'Leary

Employment and Unemployment Policy for Ireland

Staff Members of ESRI (eds., Denis Conniffe and Kieran A. Kennedy)

Public Social Expenditure – Value for Money? (Papers presented at a Conference, 20 November 1984)

Policy Research Series:

1. *Regional Policy and the Full-Employment Target* M. Ross and B. Walsh
2. *Energy Demand in Ireland, Projections and Policy Issues* S. Scott
3. *Some Issues in the Methodology of Attitude Research* E. E. Davis *et al.*
4. *Land Drainage Policy in Ireland* Richard Bruton and Frank J. Convery
5. *Recent Trends in Youth Unemployment* J. J. Sexton

Broadsheet Series:

1. *Dental Services in Ireland* P. R. Kaim-Caudle
2. *We Can Stop Rising Prices* M. P. Fogarty
3. *Pharmaceutical Services in Ireland* P. R. Kaim-Caudle
   assisted by Annette O'Toole and Kathleen O'Donoghue
4. *Ophthalmic Services in Ireland* P. R. Kaim-Caudle
   assisted by Kathleen O'Donoghue and Annette O'Toole
5. *Irish Pensions Schemes, 1969* P. R. Kaim-Caudle and J. G. Byrne
   assisted by Annette O'Toole
6. *The Social Science Percentage Nuisance* R. C. Geary
7. *Poverty in Ireland: Research Priorities* Brendan M. Walsh
8. *Irish Entrepreneurs Speak for Themselves* M. P. Fogarty
9. *Marital Desertion in Dublin: An Exploratory Study* Kathleen O'Higgins
10. *Equalization of Opportunity in Ireland: Statistical Aspects*
    R. C. Geary and F. S. Ó Muircheartaigh
11. *Public Social Expenditure in Ireland* Finola Kennedy
12. *Problems in Economic Planning and Policy Formation in Ireland, 1958–1974*
    Desmond Norton
13. *Crisis in the Cattle Industry* R. O'Connor and P. Keogh
14. *A Study of Schemes for the Relief of Unemployment in Ireland*
    R. C. Geary and M. Dempsey
    with Appendix E. Costa
15. *Dublin Simon Community, 1971-1976: An Exploration* Ian Hart
16. *Aspects of the Swedish Economy and their Relevance to Ireland*
    Robert O'Connor, Eoin O'Malley and Anthony Foley

17. *The Irish Housing System: A Critical Overview*
T. J. Baker and L. M. O'Brien
18. *The Irish Itinerants: Some Demographic, Economic and Educational Aspects*
M. Dempsey and R. C. Geary
19. *A Study of Industrial Workers' Co-operatives*
Robert O'Connor and Philip Kelly
20. *Drinking in Ireland: A Review of Trends in Alcohol Consumption, Alcohol Related Problems and Policies towards Alcohol*   Brendan M. Walsh
21. *A Review of the Common Agricultural Policy and the Implications of Modified Systems for Ireland*   R. O'Connor, C. Guiomard and J. Devereux
22. *Policy Aspects of Land-Use Planning in Ireland*
Frank J. Convery and A. Allan Schmid
23. *Issues in Adoption in Ireland*   Harold J. Abramson

Geary Lecture Series:
1. *A Simple Approach to Macro-economic Dynamics* (1967)   R. G. D. Allen
2. *Computers, Statistics and Planning-Systems or Chaos?* (1968)   F. G. Foster
3. *The Dual Career Family* (1970)   Rhona and Robert Rapoport
4. *The Psychosonomics of Rising Prices* (1971)   H. A. Turner
5. *An Interdisciplinary Approach to the Measurement of Utility or Welfare* (1972)
J. Tinbergen
6. *Econometric Forecasting from Lagged Relationships* (1973)   M. G. Kendall
7. *Towards a New Objectivity* (1974)   Alvin W. Gouldner
8. *Structural Analysis in Sociology* (1975)   Robert K. Merton
9. *British Economic Growth 1951-1973: Success or Failure?* (1976)
R. C. O. Matthews
10. *Official Statisticians and Econometricians in the Present Day World* (1977)
E. Malinvaud
11. *Political and Institutional Economics* (1978)   Gunnar Myrdal
12. *The Dilemmas of a Socialist Economy: The Hungarian Experience* (1979)
János Kornai
13. *The Story of a Social Experiment and Some Reflections* (1980)
Robert M. Solow
14. *Modernisation and Religion* (1981)   P. L. Berger
15. *Poor, Relatively Speaking* (1983)   Amartya K. Sen
16. *Towards More Rational Decisions on Criminals* (1984)   Daniel Glaser

General Research Series:
1. *The Ownership of Personal Property in Ireland*   Edward Nevin
2. *Short-Term Economic Forecasting and its Application in Ireland*   Alfred Kuehn
3. *The Irish Tariff and The E.E.C.: A Factual Survey*   Edward Nevin
4. *Demand Relationships for Ireland*   C. E. V. Leser
5. *Local Government Finance in Ireland: A Preliminary Survey*   David Walker
6. *Prospects of the Irish Economy in 1962*   Alfred Kuehn
7. *The Irish Woollen and Worsted Industry, 1946-59: A Study in Statistical Method*
R. C. Geary
8. *The Allocation of Public Funds for Social Development*   David Walker
9. *The Irish Price Level: A Comparative Study*   Edward Nevin